AF594402

Kathleen Ryan

Kathleen Ryan
Daisy Chain

Karma

Bob Nickas

Sculpture in the Vernacular-Fantastical Field

"I'll tell you about it because I am here and you are distant."
—Richard Brautigan, *In Watermelon Sugar*, 1964

Still life from the golden age of Dutch and Flemish painting—seventeenth-century *vanitas*, Minimalism and the reductive, the Baroque and ornate proliferation, ceramics, mineralogy, earthworks and entropy, composition and decomposition, Cézanne and Manzoni, art forms in nature, Pop, kitsch, totems and mythology, the psychedelic and the sublime, actuality and artifice, inner and outer space. The list goes on. How, we ask, do the coordinates in this improbable cosmology intersect? Across a great distance of time and mind, is unexpected overlay to be found, can parallels, if at times imperceptibly wavering, be drawn? All may be brought to bear upon the sculptural work of Kathleen Ryan, the result of her curiosity, observation, and inquiries over the past fifteen or so years. Plato defined science as "nothing but perception." In art, this activity and its echo—the stone that breaks a surface of water, a pattern radiating outward to fade across its surface, still once more—pass from the artist to the viewer and then back into the world. Art, Ryan reminds us, is about looking, looking takes time, and in time we may consider and question what it is that we've seen, whether puzzled or dazzled, at times pleasurably suspended somewhere in between.

How did she get here? How does anyone get anywhere? Some of us follow a path that's circuitously purposeful, with no particular plan, although in looking back we see that every step taken was necessary, made sense as it led to the next. Ours is the movement of bipeds, from the ground up, as it were, since we all first had to crawl. A sidewinder fascinates us with its lateral looping motion, a beautiful line in slow motion, from which the term *serpentine*. Birds will circle their nest, while avians on a perch, the body at rest, can be seen as a still life—with occasional flutter. We recall them from backyards and the sky, in pictures and from that movie, kept in a cage. The birds in numerous works of Ryan's are parrots, perched, about to fly? As humans will do, they navigate by memory. Unlike many who came of age post-'80s, Ryan wanted to make art but felt that to be an artist was "an unrealistic dream."[1] An art major in college, she took ceramics classes, enjoyed working clay by hand, the tactility of it, and minored in anthropology/archaeology. The pairing is not unrelated. Clay, after all, comes from the earth, and often the evidence of prior civilizations unearthed is in the form of pottery fragments: the jigsaw puzzle of time. Her minor may have figured in her installation *Packrat Habitat* (2006), for which she "collected branches and made a two-chambered tunnel-like structure that you could climb through. One room was like a crystal cave with giant oversize pink quartz crystals ... cast out of pink bubble-gum-scented wax and they glowed like the inside of a geode in a natural history museum."[2] Situated outdoors amid trees and brush, the work merged with its natural environment, as seen in its daylight documentation. Photographed at night, it glowed internally. That Ryan has also referred to it as a "roadside attraction" points to her sense of humor in relation to what is commonly referred to as "old weird America," whose artifacts are of more recent vintage, from before decades came to an end—the antiquity of our own time, "relics" of postwar leisurely pursuits. If archaeology is the recovery and study of material evidence from past human life and culture, from history and prehistory, Ryan's sifting and excavation in the present has aimed toward transformation and distillation. What she once thought an unrealistic dream, to be an artist—and she had not been in

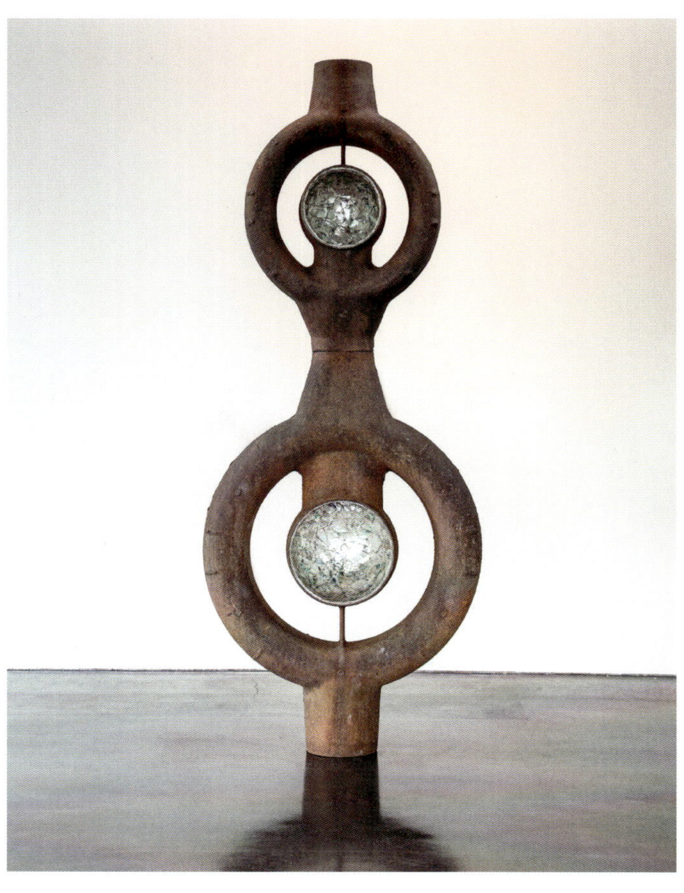

Kathleen Ryan
Mother of Pearl, 2019
Iron, abalone shell
93½ × 39 × 15 inches
236.2 × 99.1 × 38.1 cm

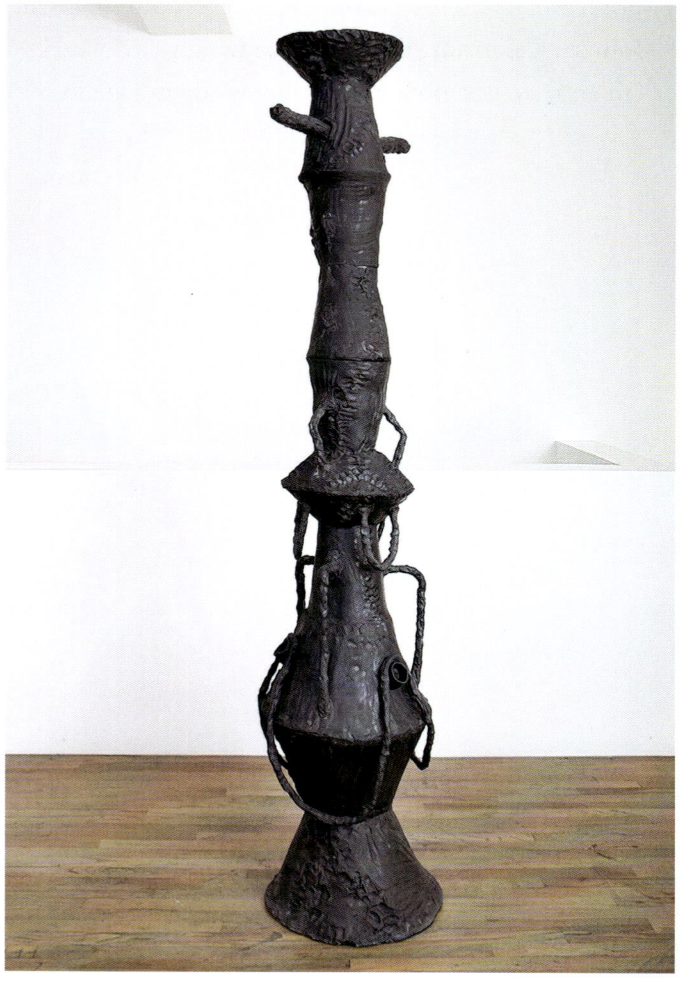

Katheen Ryan
Endless Hookah Totem, 2013
Stoneware
84 × 26 × 21 inches
213 × 66 × 53 cm

a rush to get there—would eventually be realized by way of a dreamlike realism, a heightening of the familiar toward unexpected, wilder realms—an observation of and a reimagining of the world in all its otherness. Four years would pass after graduation with art-related experience, but no art-making, before Ryan went on to UCLA, pursuing ceramics in more exploratory ways.

Still Life

Ryan is first and foremost a sculptor. Her primary interests reside in material, form, chromatics, scale, levity and density, weight in parallel to the illusion of weightlessness, the movement of line, an object's skin, its coating and outer shell, suspense and a suspension of disbelief, an occupation of space. Her subjects at times refer outside of themselves by way of their inner life. Even when recognizable, vernacular objects, things we know from the everyday but realized well past human scale, will leave us to wonder: Who left this behind? A wandering, careless giant? (Humans are relatively small in relation to the world we inhabit, and those beyond; recorded human life can't compare to geologic time and the age of the universe.) Ryan is attuned, as a given space will allow, to the rooms in which her works are shown, to near and far, drawing us toward them. Her objects invite us to probe internal and external surfaces, what we might call a topography tactile to the eye. (The human eye, used consciously, is our own magnifying glass.) Ryan's works can be seen as image-objects. While abstracted from the everyday—elements having a dual identity, bowling balls that register as pearls from a distance, fishing rods as gently bent cherry stems, and as themselves in proximity—they are representational; with an oversize beaded necklace, doubly so. Ryan pays particular attention to composition and luminosity, concerns, at least until the Light and Space artists of the '60s in her native Southern California, that are more readily associated with painting from centuries past; we regard them now as if preserved in amber. Ryan's works of the past few years that have rightly attracted considerable attention present fruit in various states of decomposition, all realized at greatly larger than life-size—grapes, cherries, lemons, peaches, watermelons, and, most recently, a pumpkin carved as a jack-o'-lantern, its lid adjacent, just taken off, or about to be replaced. These "decomposing" objects suggest that one of her subjects, one that goes back to her earliest work, is time.

Five glazed ceramic columns, *The Rise and Fall* (2014), which appeared to be part of the architecture of the exhibition they were made for, might also allude to the rise and fall of civilization. A sense of mortality—everything created may not last but will outlast its maker—is integral to art and culture's equation. Since the '60s, with sculpture especially, as well as for ephemeral expression, musical composition, performance, and dance, artists have referred to their works as "pieces," but pieces are all we have ever had. Fragile, crumbling, dusted, as they fall in slowly through our fingers, as anyone cleaning out a garage, an attic, or that most archeological of suburban sites, the basement, will attest. Ryan's *Endless Hookah Totem* (2013), made of stoneware, appropriately, may for some recall a Brancusi column, one alluding to the sky above as well as to the ground below. A companion of a sort, though it did not appear for another half-dozen years, is *Mother of Pearl* (2019), equally totemic, two round forms within a vertical structure suggesting a figure: the top, its head, with a Cyclopic eye; the bottom, its belly, a symbol of fertility.

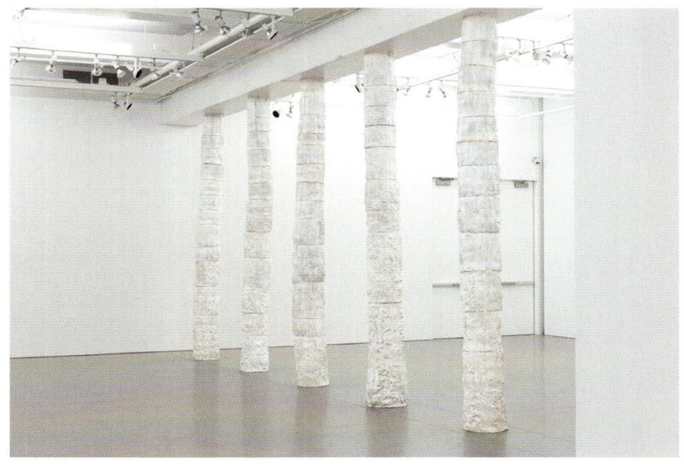

Kathleen Ryan
The Rise and Fall, 2014
Glazed ceramic
144 × 18 × 18 inches
365 × 45 × 45 cm

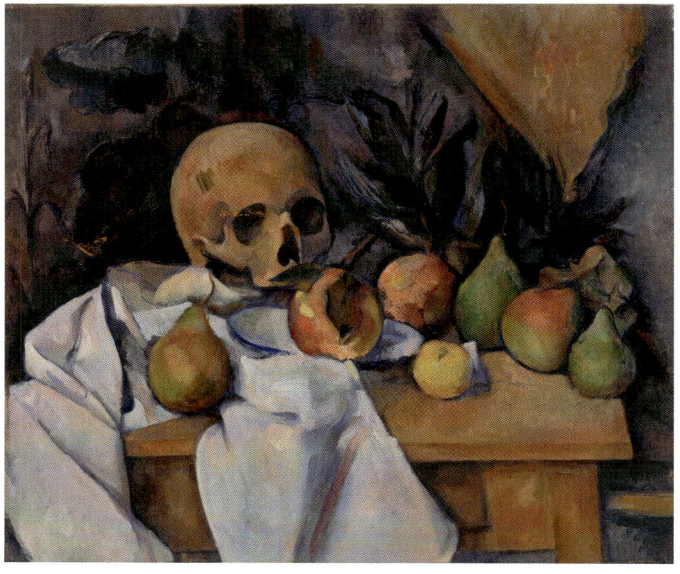

Paul Cézanne
Still Life with Skull
(Nature morte au crâne), 1890–93
Oil on canvas
25¾ × 21⅜ inches
65.4 × 54.3 cm
The Barnes Foundation Collection
Image © 2022 Barnes Foundation

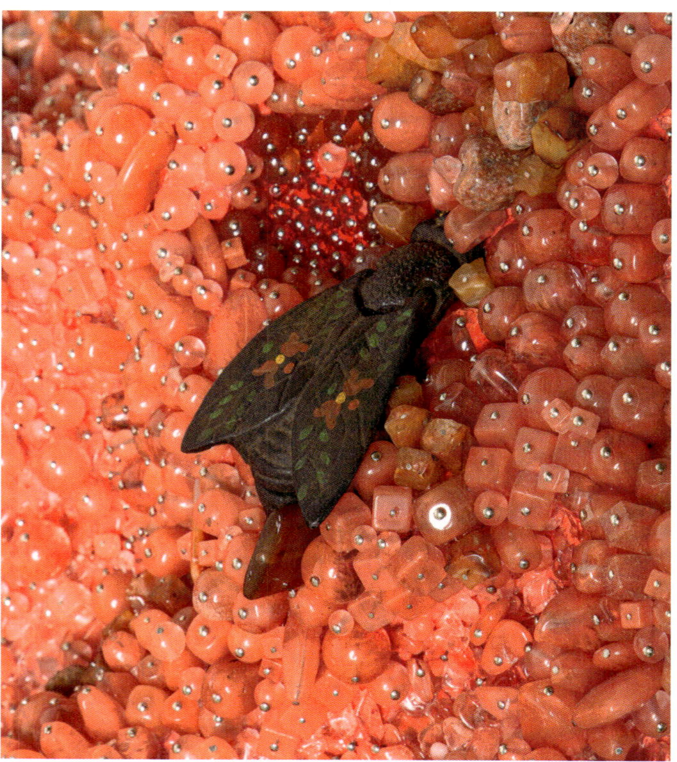

Bad Melon (Big Chunk), 2020 (detail)
Cherry quartz, agate, smoky quartz, amazonite, jasper, aventurine, rhodonite, rhodochrosite, labradorite, quartz, Botswana agate, carnelian, glass, cast iron and brass flies, steel and stainless steel pins, polystyrene, and aluminum Airstream
38 × 49 × 62 inches
96.5 × 124.5 × 157.5 cm

Ryan's fruit works, as noted, have been compared to vanitas, still lifes from seventeenth-century Dutch and Flemish painting, images that represent the fleeting pleasures in life, and of earthly existence itself, symbols of disintegration and death, reminders of our inevitable fate. Art not only as a foreshadowing, but with a moral conveyed. Vanitas, from the Latin *vanus*: vain, void, empty. A painting that sets jewels and a crown alongside a skull makes—the phrasing here too tempting to avoid—no bones about the transience of material wealth, power, and the law. Ryan's works are not moralistic in this way, and as she has remarked, she "didn't set out to depict decay." The temporal element made her rendering more layered, gave the objects an inner chemical life. The small cast-iron and brass flies added to some of the watermelon chunks? Surely they were drawn to the fermentation of the fruit, to its sugars. As Robert Smithson once memorably mused, "Why should flies be without art?"[3] As to sculpture: "The stillness round my form / Was like the stillness in the air."[4]

The aspect of painting and time suggests, if indirectly, an artist who followed the Dutch masters, who obsessively engaged the practice of painting, still life notably: Paul Cézanne. In his 1890–93 *Still Life with Skull*, ripe apples, green pears, and a lemon share the small stage of a cloth-draped table with a human cranium, its hollowed-out eyes triangulating with an apple on a plate. As if just plucked from a tree in the artist's garden, the stem and two dark leaves remain. The form of the nearest leaf is in close correspondence with that of the skull's gaping nasal cavity: in stilled life we see there is no sweet scent to be inhaled, and that it had only been sensed intermittently by the painter. Cézanne gave three or four years to this canvas, as for many others. The skull, in its elemental state, would remain unchanged. The pieces of fruit the artist carefully arranged, especially working in the warmer months in the South of France, most certainly went bad, and many times over in the long course of his labors, in various seasons and locales, Cézanne an often itinerant artist.[5] Not widely known, and to be measured against our appreciation of his realism and direct rendering, is the fact that Cézanne sometimes employed artificial fruit, objects that would retain their robust color and full form, would reveal no outward signs—no blemishes, no withering—of eventual decay, no matter how many months or years he toiled toward completion. Grapes in a Cézanne are never reduced to raisins.

In one of Ryan's most stunning sculptures, *Bad Grapes* (2020), the fruit has collapsed in on itself, its violets, blues, blacks, and greens, the fruit's bruising and desiccation, realized with clusters of two dozen different types of stone, among them clusters of amethyst, amazonite, garnet, turquoise, obsidian. The visual thrill of this piece, which beckons and rewards close inspection, belies the very idea of disintegration. The way it reflects light, in particular off the silvery tips of the pins that hold the stones in place, breathes life itself. The wistfully titled *Pleasures Known* (a play on those *Unknown?*, mysterious, yet to come), and for the artist alluding to American nostalgia and promise past, is a tour de force. Created the year prior, a graceful arrangement of fruit is topped with a bunch of similarly desiccated grapes, set upon an old cart. Were it not for the rubber tires placing it within the vicinity of our time, the cart might have been encountered in one of Breughel's rustic scenes, left behind, evidence of the absent villagers, now depleted in their revelry. The wonder of Ryan's art, as with Breughel's, is in the details, the pleasure one takes in those that emerge and multiply after the initial instant hit. Viewers will discover more on second take: *Had it been there all along? Bad Lemon (Sea Witch)* (2020), for example, a "moldy" halved lemon, returns us ever so

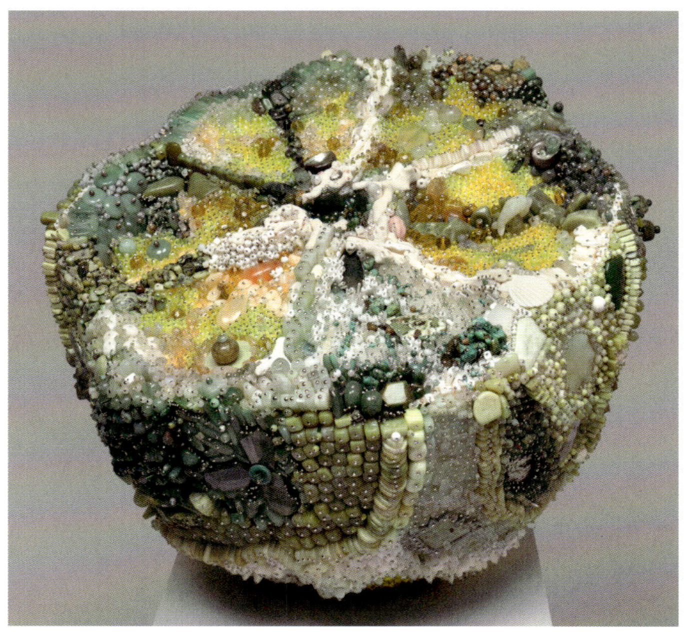

Kathleen Ryan
Bad Lemon (Sea Witch), 2020
Aventurine, serpentine, prehnite, chrysoprase, rhyolite, agate, moss agate, jasper, peridot, moonstone, magnesite, lilac stone, turquoise, citrine, calcite, feldspar, ruby in zoisite, labradorite, Swarovski crystal, quartz, mother of pearl, freshwater pearls, glass, and steel pins on coated polystyrene
16½ × 18 × 20 inches
41.9 × 45.7 × 50.8 cm

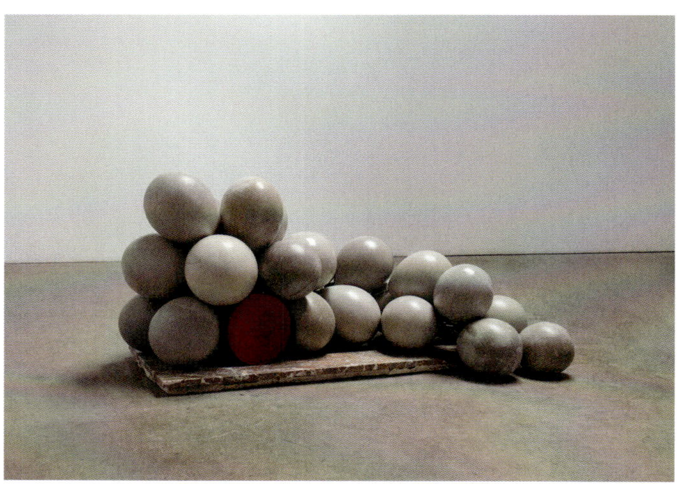

Kathleen Ryan
Reclining at the Hearth, 2016
Concrete, stainless steel, painted steel trash can, and antique marble hearth
25 × 58 × 35 inches
63.5 × 147 × 89 cm

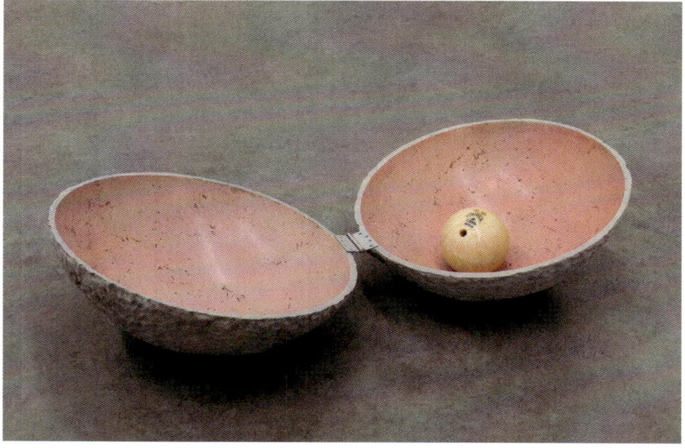

Kathleen Ryan
Caprice, 2016 (detail)
Concrete, steel, and bowling ball
17 × 66 × 33 inches
43.1 × 167.6 × 83.8 cm

subtly to the Cézanne. Amid a proliferation of stones, beads, and shells, including aventurine, moss agate, citrine, mother-of-pearl, and freshwater pearls, are tiny bone-white skulls, carved from magnesite beads; a small sly wink slipped in for those who would closely explore the object's encrusted, seductive surface. In doing so, the supposed gnarliness of rot is nowhere apparent. Beauty reigns supreme. (As for despised mold, the agent of disintegration, we acknowledge that from mold came lifesaving penicillin, a modern miracle.) Interestingly, for Ryan there is a reversal in her choice of what to employ in representing the coexistence and contrast of a fruit's ripeness and decay. She uses "glass and plastic beads for the fresh parts and … natural materials for the rotten parts."[6] We are left to ask, will picture-perfect food in the future be grown or engineered to look pleasing to the eye but nearly devoid of taste?

Stilled Life

While parallels can be drawn between Ryan's image-objects and painting, as attuned as she is to chromatic composition—referring as she does to her palette of bead colors, and below, unseen, rough underpainting as she plans out the surface of beads and semiprecious stones, modulating contrast from one area to another, luminosity and shadow—the terrain she explores is decidedly sculpture. The fruit she initially cast were grapes, having been struck by their form, physicality, and relation to the body in a painting of a bacchante she saw at the Getty museum: a woman clutches the source of her inebriation, a bunch of grapes, amplified, made corporeal, by her half-exposed breasts. Ryan would later describe her as squeezing, rather than holding, the grapes, imagining the juice within about to burst forth. What she felt almost palpably was a pressure, which she recalled as bulbous, between them. She wondered, "How do I get that feeling of pressure that has to do with sex and that tension on the skin? How do I do that in a sculpture?"[7] Over a period of four years, between 2015 and 2018, she went on to create numerous *Bacchante* works, enlarging the grapes as spheres of concrete, mostly gray and white, unnatural, monotone, ghost grapes with the feel of solid balloons. They are heavy, though not at first glance, some draped from atop tall pedestals. A number that are horizontally oriented suggest a figurative reading that returns us to the woman in the painting, drunken, now recumbent; Ryan has subtitled them *Reclining Nude* (2015) and *Reclining at the Hearth* (2016). The spheres of the grapes led to, even as she may have already had them in mind, a number of works with bowling balls, weighty objects also suggestive of the body, held in the palm of the hand, with prominent finger holes. She presents them such that their heft appears to possess buoyancy. The earliest of them, *Caprice* (2016), sets a Caprice bowling ball inside what looks to be a fully opened shell: the ball as a precious pearl found there. (In terms of the artist's sensibility and humor, a caprice, it should be noted, is a sudden and unaccountable change of mood or behavior, a whim, and, as Ryan is surely aware, a classic American sedan, introduced in 1965 and sleekly sculptural in its own right.) A related work, *Barbed Wire* (2017), is a sinuous line of black balls, appearing to be an enlarged strand of black beads about to come loose and roll away, or a snake slithering across the floor. Ryan had previously made large snake "rings" and "bracelets" in concrete and rebar, and *Roadside Eyeglasses* (2014), a pair of mangled frames (inadvertently stepped on?) realized with thin copper pipe. With these works, as with *Rise and Fall* (2017), which appears both to emerge from and disappear into the floor, we grasp her sculptor's mind for delineation by way of Paul Klee's oft-quoted definition: "a drawing is a line going for a walk." That same year, Ryan conceived *Pearls*, another oversize "necklace" meant to be installed as if draped

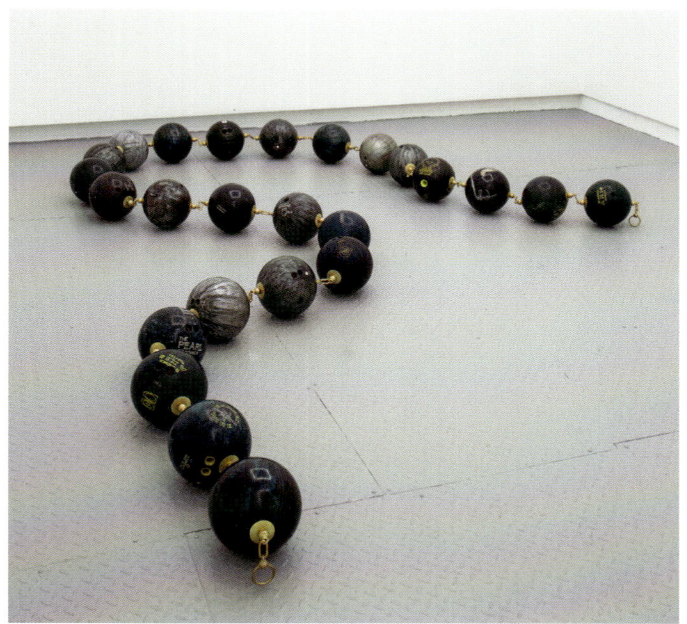

Kathleen Ryan
Barbed Wire, 2019
Bowling balls, brass lamp hardware
8½ × 8½ × 310 inches
21.5 × 21.5 × 787.5 cm
Installed dimensions variable

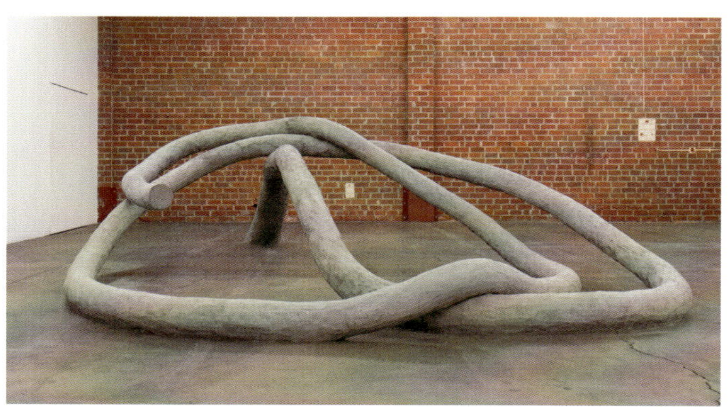

Kathleen Ryan
Rise and Fall, 2017
Stucco, chicken wire
56½ × 246 × 167 inches
143.5 × 624.8 × 424.2 cm

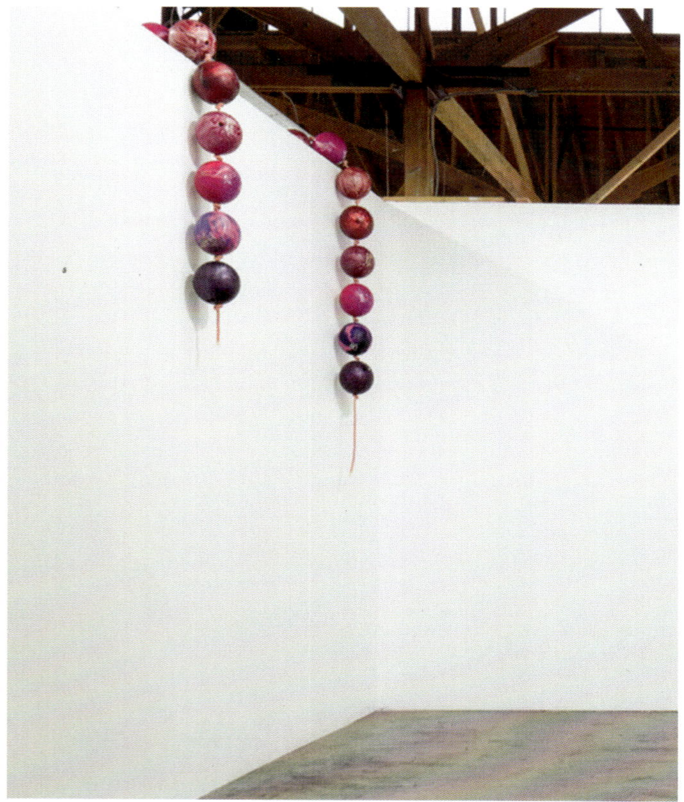

Kathleen Ryan
Pearls, 2017 (back view)
Bowling balls, rope
Installation format variable
35 bowling balls
8½ inches each in diameter
21.6 cm each in diameter

over the top of a gallery wall. With its reveal in the room behind, the rest of the object seen on the wall's opposite side—the way it would be on the back of a neck—Ryan made an otherwise discrete piece site-specific, moving the viewer back and forth to appreciate its precarious balance, in an exhibition she titled *Weightless Again*.

The aspect of time in Ryan's work, in the shadow of vanitas and its symbolic reminders of mortality, along with her attraction to rounded and ovoid sculptural forms—grapes/balloons and bowling balls, evoking both fragility and solidity—bring to mind an unlikely figure: Piero Manzoni. In 1960, with a series of works he titled *Fiato d'artista* (Artist's Breath), Manzoni expanded our notion of what else sculpture could be, precisely by means of an act of expansion, the use of his own lungs, his life's breath, to inflate a balloon to its full form. The balloons were tied off with a length of braided twine and held by two lead seals, each affixed to a small wood base bearing a metal plate with the artist's name and the title. To encounter them in a museum today is to see the base, the plate, the seals (ultimately ineffective over the long term), and the slightly frayed rope, at the end of which is a flattened, seemingly melted blob of rubber—a deflated state the artist knew the balloon was destined for just as surely as himself.[8] And the shriveled condition of Ryan's *Bad Grapes*? They have looked exactly like this since the day they were completed in the artist's studio. As for her balloon-grapes, they will forever retain solid form, in counterbalance to, more than a half century later, the near-immaterial gesture of the Italian provocateur.

Concurrent with the *Bacchante* and her sculptures with bowling balls, Ryan introduced the figure of a tropical bird, the aforementioned parrots, making their appearance in 2015 and pursued over the course of four years. The earliest of these works are both simple and poetic (in *Hollow Song*, a pair of vibrant lime-green birds perch on a magenta acoustic guitar hung face to the wall), and complex (an untitled sculpture with the subtitle *Chandelier* has a small flock of birds atop an elaborate skeletal light fixture—an inverted cage, their revenge?—that has come to rest on the floor, the birds serving as feathered illumination). Although closer to three-dimensional silhouettes of birds than to lifelike re-creations, the birds yet suggest a potential for flight, space outside of the gallery, freedom rather than captivity. After producing a number of pieces with, usually, a handful of birds, as few as one or two on a narrow perch, and always less than ten, Ryan created sculptures occupied by small flocks, having as many as three dozen, as *Parasol* (2017) does. She followed this with a pair of gently imposing works, *Frequency* and *Satellite in Repose* (both 2018). While *Frequency* appears to be a beach umbrella for which the parrots, some 150 of them, serve as delirious fringe, the title pushes our reading in another direction, beyond leisure and into the realm of communication. Parrots, natural mimics, can learn to repeat what we say to them, even if most don't grasp the meaning of the words. The parrot is still an amplifier, and in a way notably distinct from other vocalizing animals. In titling the floor-bound work *Satellite in Repose*, Ryan takes our reading further, turning the birds into the receivers, carriers, and conveyors of signals, while the structure of the technology, a bare-bones satellite dish, is seemingly in collapse. And if there's a last message sent? Nature, in the end, wins out?

Receiver, which dates from the same year, shifts this line of inquiry in a wholly optimistic direction. Taking clearly the form of a medium-size, wall-mounted satellite dish, its concave face is tiled with

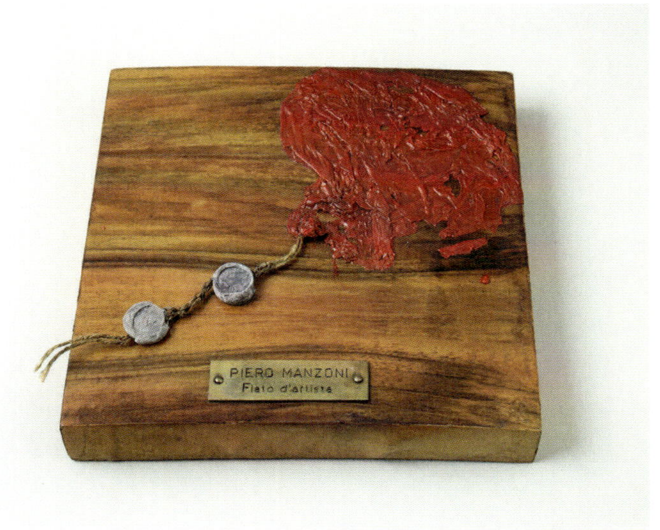

Piero Manzoni
Fiato d'artista (Artist's Breath), 1960
Balloon, rope, lead seals, and
bronze plaque on wooden base
$1\frac{3}{8} \times 7 \times 7\frac{1}{4}$ inches
$3.5 \times 17.8 \times 18.4$ cm

Collection of the Tate
Photo: © DACS 2020

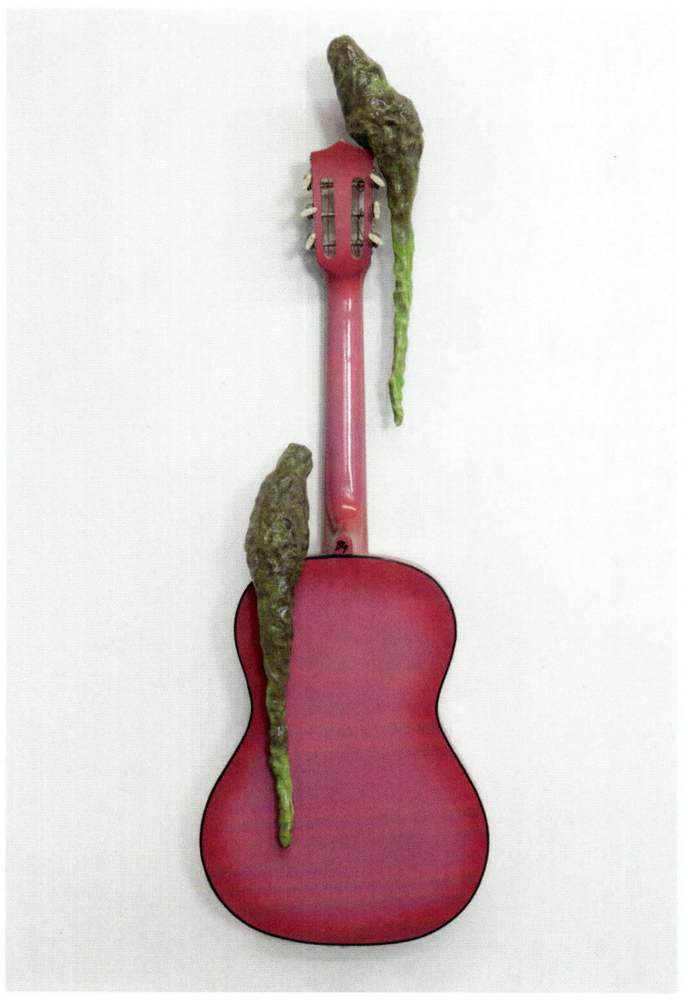

Kathleen Ryan
Hollow Song, 2015
Glazed ceramic, painted guitar
$37 \times 13\frac{1}{2} \times 5\frac{1}{2}$ inches
$94 \times 34.5 \times 14$ cm

abalone, the shell of sea snails, its inner layer comprised of nacre, commonly known as mother-of-pearl. Prized for its iridescence, abalone diffracts light, with coloration that wavers as our eyes pass across its surface, a temporal, visually animate experience. In an essay on the intersection of fractal aesthetics, diffractive patterns, pleasure, and beauty, "Why Our Wandering Brains Are Wired to Love Art and Nature," Thomas Nail, a professor of philosophy at the University of Denver, relates how

> scientists have come to believe that so-called background noise in the brain may be more crucial to consciousness than previously thought. Recent research found that these fluctuations make up 95% of brain activity; conscious thoughts account for merely 5%. Cognitive fluctuations are like the dark matter or "junk" DNA of the brain, in that they make up the most significant part of what's happening but remain mysterious.[9]

Certain visual stimuli attract this fluctuating brain activity, elicit and accelerate perceptual response: the eye as it roves. In being open to these signals, willing to wander, viewers may come to understand: we are the receiver. The patterns we encounter in Ryan's shimmering kaleidoscopic surfaces—in particular the highly articulated skins that cover objects magnified from nature, with sections of squared pieces that read as tesserae, a mosaic fragment, possibly, or as bleached crystals like those built up on boulders spiraling above the waterline on the Great Salt Lake—enliven the act of looking, magnified at every turn.

Distilled Life

Ryan's major work of 2020, the half dozen watermelon pieces collectively known as *Bad Melon*, have as their rinds sections of an Airstream trailer dissected by the artist. Although we expect a rind to be green rather than silver and shiny, Ryan wanted the metallic hull to be left in its original state, carefully cutting parts so as to leave in numerous details: reflectors, taillights, a section of window frame, protruding electrical wires, an antenna, a partial logo: AIR, with the R only a trace of itself, so the logo reads as AI—artificial intelligence? The Airstream, evoking American postwar leisure and the open road in the '50s, that time of invasion fantasy, its gleaming streamlined form sailing by on the highway, this must have evoked the sensation of an earthbound UFO. Of course, Ryan's objects are fantastical but not unidentified, and, in this case, can be imagined as at one time flying. These sculptures extend a suggestive sci-fi narrative: strewn as so much juicy wreckage across the gallery floor, the scattered pieces, when seen together, might be described as the melon that fell to earth, shattered on impact. In cutting up the Airstream trailer, using everted pieces to hold the watermelon, wedges and chunks of fruit, large and small, some moldy, others yet tempting, its red flesh now visible, she has opened both the structure and her subject inside out. Cruising in an Airstream, bowling, fishing—pleasures known from days gone by.

One of Ryan's newest works, *Daisy Chain* (2021), seems an outlier when we consider her art thus far, yet this view would be based entirely on those works that have been presented in exhibitions. A visit to her studio reveals, as she admits, a predilection for collecting "fake flowers and fruit … the cheapest mass-produced plastic kinds," which she finds "interesting in the way the parts are

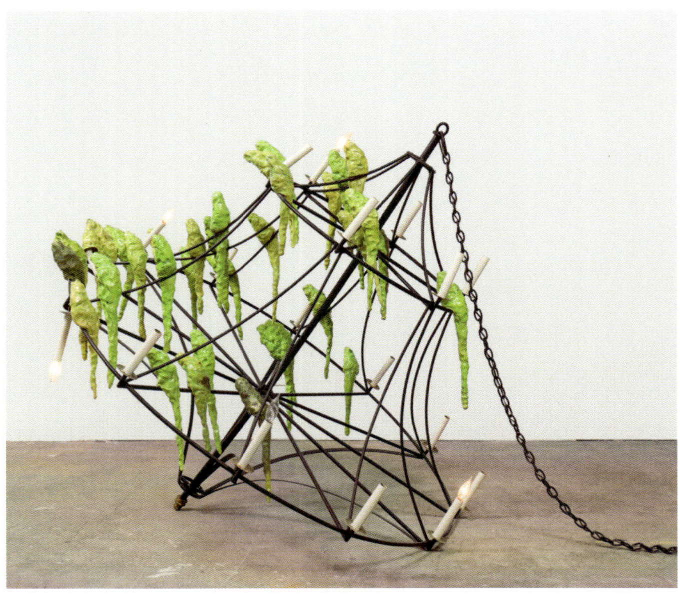

Kathleen Ryan
(Untitled) Chandelier, 2015
Glazed ceramic, painted steel, lamp wiring, and hardware
55 × 60 × 67 inches
139 × 152 × 170 cm

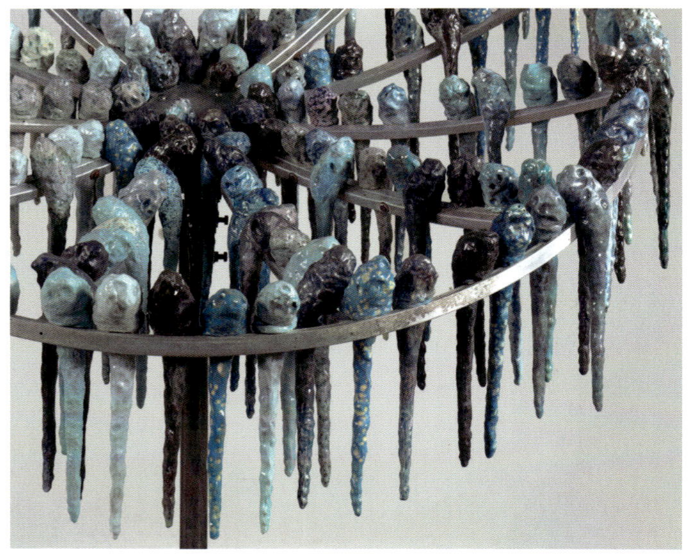

Kathleen Ryan
Frequency, 2018
Glazed ceramic, aluminum satellite dish, and steel
108 × 75 × 60 inches
274.5 × 190.5 × 152.5 cm

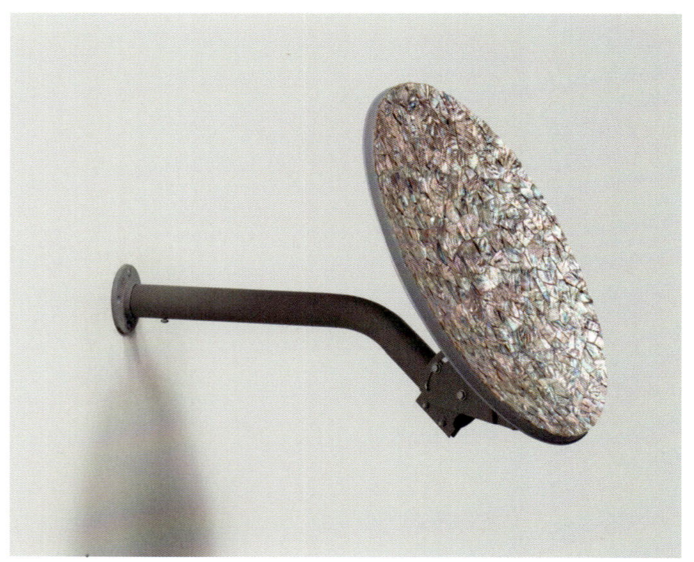

Kathleen Ryan
Receiver, 2018
Steel, abalone shell
18 × 21 × 26 3/8 inches
46 × 53 × 67 cm

stylized and mechanized to be molded and then popped together."[10] Overall, the appearance is wreathlike, a form she has previously explored, here not a little sad and droopy, as well as scaled up, as is her preference. While it reads as "springtime," especially given its debut at an East Coast gallery over May and June, with its plastic shine and sag it could be any time of year, anywhere, part of a display at a suburban garden center near winter's end. For all its flowery presence, this isn't nature, a fact the scale greatly amplifies. Ryan collected the various elements because they reminded her of a flower. Lengths of green hose became the stems; the bumblebee-yellow drain covers seen as pollen caps; green shovel scoops form the leaves. In its circularity, hence the title, the hose/stems suggest a watering system, a flower that can water itself. Not such an outlier after all. In Ryan's body of work, it finds correspondence with *Bad Grapes*, whose life-giving stems were created with copper tubing and fittings—plumbing, in effect. The disparate elements in *Daisy Chain* were "never intended to go together in the real world, but together in the sculpture … they suggest a flow. The important part for me is how they fit together and," as she allows without any trace of superiority or malice, "that everything is plastic."[11] Sculpture, we are reminded, was once commonly referred to as the plastic arts because certain materials, clay being exemplary, were malleable. But, for Ryan, everything is capable of being shaped, formed, or altered—from pewter, concrete, and copper pipe to cast iron, terra-cotta, and two tons of granite, even the aluminum shell of an Airstream trailer.

Ryan's ultimate probe into inner space, as of this writing at least, appeared in the form of a giant jack-o'-lantern she humorously personified as *Jackie* (2021), the artist still occupied with the idea: *What lies within?* Many of us will recall this object from childhood, from Halloween and trick-or-treating, a holiday perhaps the most magical, fantastic, scary time of youth. Pumpkins would be carved, often with a simple face, two holes for eyes, a triangular opening for the nose, and a wide, nearly toothless, grinning mouth. Traditionally, jack-o'-lanterns have candles placed inside, illuminating at night their mischievous leering. (How near in its elemental features to a skull, an object closely associated with the spookiness of Halloween.) With *Jackie*, a luminosity that seems almost to pass through the solid structure, radiating from within, as if its skin was translucent, is the result of intricate bead and stonework, magnified by thousands of reflective, silvery pins holding them in place. This astounding object's interior features an electric, plugged-in carpet of rose and smoky quartz, red aventurine, Ching Hai jade, carnelian, and lapis lazuli, among nearly twenty different stones. There are many geodes embedded, prominently in the eye sockets and the gaping mouth, and spread inside, turning the hollowed-out pumpkin into a geode-desic dome/cave. Those who find significance in the power of crystals and gems, who study magic in relation to mineralogy, will wonder if Ryan is attuned to the stones' esoteric properties, chooses and employs them to specific ends. Their very profusion signals that the stones have not been singled out for a particular purpose, but are deployed for their material qualities, their vibrant color and translucency, and how they can be orchestrated, to use a gem-energy term, for greater vibration. In Ryan's studio, a room is set aside solely for the stones, for storing and sorting them, and she does sense the energy when she's in there, readily admitting that it feels good. Although used primarily for esthetic/compositional ends, with *Jackie* we can imagine the work's power as a reversal related directly to one of the stones employed, amethyst. From the Greek, the word is a merging of "not" and "to intoxicate," the material's properties believed to ward off drunkenness. *Jackie*, like the bacchante that Ryan was drawn to so many years ago, offers no such protection.

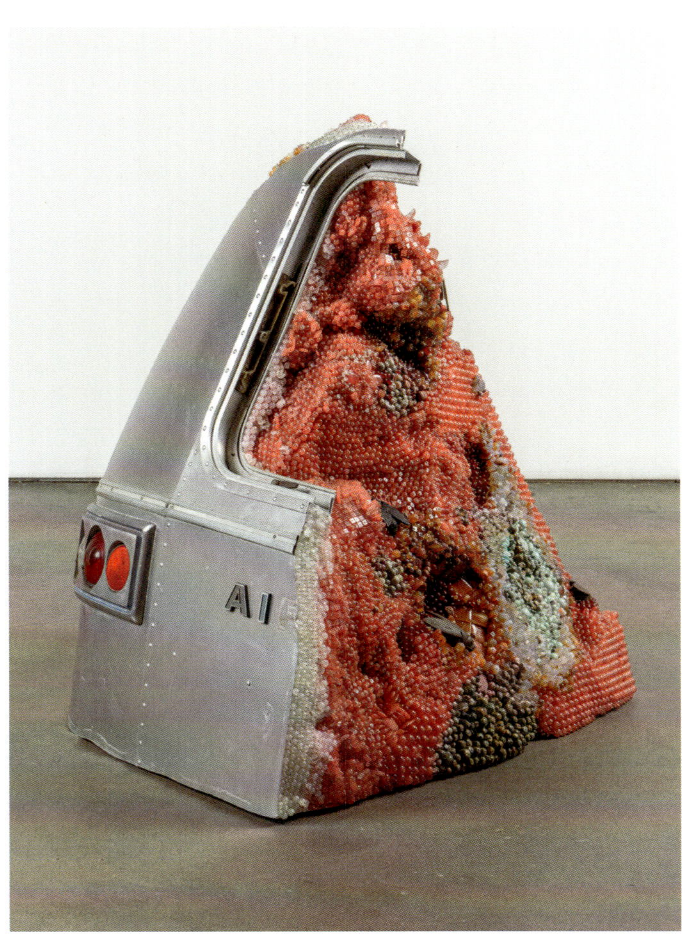

Kathleen Ryan
Bad Melon (Wedge), 2020
Cherry quartz, rose quartz, agate, amazonite, jasper, aventurine, rhodonite, rhodochrosite, labradorite, smoky quartz, quartz, Botswana agate, carnelian, horn, citrine, glass, cast iron and brass flies, steel and stainless steel pins, polystyrene, and aluminum Airstream
63 × 23 × 21 inches
160 × 58.5 × 53.5 cm

Viewers willingly abandon themselves to its joyous seduction. We know that the chemical reaction that is fermentation, which, in *Bad Fruit*, can be imagined as visible due to the presence of flies attracted to the watermelon's nectar, results in alcohol. In the process of distillation, the alcohol is separated and removed. But distillation also refers to essential meaning. Art's essence? Once it was beauty, now even more admired when redefined, where we hadn't noticed it before. And even then, is art only skin deep? The works of Kathleen Ryan often induce a state of heightened sensation; art, with all the otherness of the world intact, arrayed before the magnifying glass of our own eyes, distilled to an essential reaction—no less than pure visual pleasure.

A general note on scale, from small to large, and back again, scale being important to this artist. It was Alex Hay who said, after being asked why he scaled up the objects he painted, that he thought about how, when you hold something in your hand, close to your eye, it actually looks larger than it is. Rather than actual scale, it appears as an enlargement in proximity. (We know that actual scale, with distance, is variable. The Washington Monument, for example, from the far end of the Mall, is only about as large as your raised index finger. But with nearness?) This is why I think fondly of Alex Hay as a proverbial brother from another planet. And that reminded me of what the *Apollo 11* astronaut Michael Collins, recently departed, said when he recalled going to the moon in 1969. On seeing Earth from space he observed, as if writing a perfect poem: "Tiny, very shiny, blue and white, bright, beautiful, serene." In one of his many obituaries, it was poignantly noted, "Later in life he would sometimes look up at the moon and say, 'Oh my god, I've been there. Kind of takes me by surprise despite all these years.'" And thus the epigram for this essay from Brautigan, written five years prior to NASA's mission to the moon.

1 Kathleen Ryan, quoted in "Ali Subotnick in conversation with Kathleen Ryan," in *Kathleen Ryan: Bad Fruit* (New York: Karma, 2020), 7.
2 Ibid., 10.
3 Robert Smithson, "Incidents of Mirror-Travel in the Yucatan," *Artforum 8*, no. 1 (September 1969): 34, available at https://www.artforum.com/print/196907/incidents-of-mirror-travel-in-the-yucatan-36477.
4 Emily Dickinson, "I heard a Fly buzz – when I died –," written in 1862, published in *Poems by Emily Dickinson*, third series (Boston, MA: Roberts Brothers,1896), 72, ten years after her passing, her third posthumous collection.
5 Cézanne in these years moved between North and South, from Paris to Aix, back and forth, as well as working in the forest at Fontainebleau, painting indoors and out.
6 Ryan, quoted in Subotnick, 19.
7 Ibid., 15. Ryan would present the ultimate expression of pressure—without compression—with the sculpture *Between Two Bodies* (2017). In this work, two blocks of granite, each weighing a ton, one hovering over the other, are separated by three oranges between and somehow not crushed by them, as we would expect, whether actual oranges or Ryan's made of glazed ceramic. The blocks of granite were "mounts for machinery from Northrop Grumman" (Subotnick, 12), the aerospace behemoth, and today one of the world's largest manufacturers of weapons, who also produced the *Apollo 11* Lunar Module, which landed on the moon in 1969. The oranges not only represent nature, life, and good health, but are associated with the artist's home state, California, and also with Florida, where *Apollo 11* was launched.
8 Manzoni, who had connected the fragility and transience of life with his art, would unexpectedly die less than three years later, age twenty-nine, from a heart attack in his studio. At the same time as he produced iterations of *Fiato d'artista*, he made many works for which he left his inked thumbprint on an egg, all titled *Uova con impronta*, 1960. The shells of some today, unsurprisingly, are cracked.
9 Thomas Nail, "Why our 'wandering brains' are wired to love art and nature," Salon.com, June 15, 2021, https://www.salon.com/2021/06/15/why-our-wandering-brains-are-wired-to-love-art-and-nature/. Worth noting in relation is the myth that we only use about 10 percent of our brains. There is no evidence in neuroscience, not even the flimsiest, to support what has become a common misapprehension.
10 Kathleen Ryan, email message to author, June 18, 2021.
11 Ibid.

Shannon Mattern

Fresh Decay

To find the freshest fruit, we typically attend to color, texture, and density. We look for lemons with smooth, bright, evenly hued skin and firm, hefty bodies. We look for grapes that are firm, plump, and securely attached to the stem. Cherries should be a deep, saturated, glossy red; their stems, green. A fresh pumpkin, orange and hard-shelled, should sound hollow when we knock on it. Fresh fruits often epitomize their chromatic namesakes. Their outside touch hints at their interior structure and texture. Yet there's an affective dimension to ripeness and freshness, too. As artist Kathleen Ryan has described, ripeness is also about pressure—simultaneously concrete, elastic, and erotic.

In her *Bacchante (Tall White)* (2016), Ryan evoked pressure with balloons and polished concrete—juicy, bowling ball–sized orbs bunched together with stems composed of metal chain. By making utilitarian materials "sexy and lush," Ryan juxtaposed buoyancy and weight, ripeness and inertness, organicism and industrialism. In her summer 2021 exhibition at Karma gallery in New York, Ryan extends this exploration through new floral forms: cherries, lemons, pumpkins, and daisies that express their "lushness" not through erotic pressure, but through decay—and that, for those attuned to more pervasive forces of social and climatic disintegration, might reveal how ripeness and freshness are products of industrial apparatae and vast extractive infrastructures.

Upon entering the gallery, we first encounter *Daisy Chain* (2021), a garland bearing all the chromatic indicators of peak freshness: snowy white petals, sunny yellow disc florets, and verdant stems. Yet this chain, like Ryan's grapes, is composed of industrial materials: petals made of vinyl, sepals fashioned from green funnels, leaves contrived from green garden spades, yellow drain head florets, and interspliced stems of green irrigation hose—all components of industrialized agriculture's *manufacturing* of freshness. An earlier piece, *Bad Grapes* (2020), used copper pipes as stems and branches.

"Far from a natural state," freshness, geographer Susanne Freidberg argues, depends on "a host of carefully coordinated technologies, from antifungal sprays to bottle caps to climate-controlled semi trucks."[1] We could add to this list patented, genetically engineered seeds, refrigerated warehouses, irradiation, shrink wrap, and food safety laws—along with irrigation hoses and sprinkler heads.[2] Ryan's colossal floral assemblage, sure to win any 4-H prize for "biggest daisy," hangs from three metal ceiling hooks, reminding us that agribusiness's genetic modification and selective breeding also prioritize size: bigger farms, bigger plants and animals, bigger yields, bigger profits. These expansive tendencies cultivate chickens too big to stand on their own two legs, apples that sacrifice taste for girth, and exploitative labor practices. Poorly paid, precarious migrant laborers must move quickly to push fresh produce to market—markets those same laborers typically can't afford. As Freidberg acknowledges, "the qualities that make freshness seem natural have also traditionally made it a marker of wealth and social status."[3]

Ryan's plastic garland, propagated polymerically for perpetual verdure, might direct our attention toward the artificial apparatae and infrastructures scaffolding our organic aspirations toward freshness and abundance. Immediately behind the garland sits a massive steel basket, originally manufactured to transport large tanks of liquid, like pesticides—another emblem of industrialized farming—but which here holds jumbo cherries the size of basketballs. Ryan's *Bad Cherries* (2021)

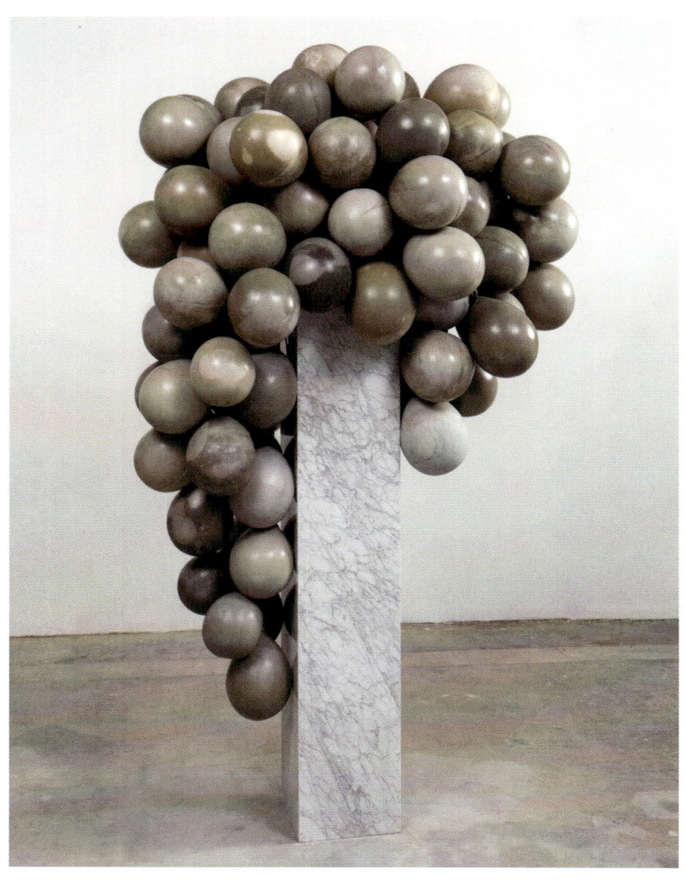

Kathleen Ryan
Bacchante (Tall White), 2016
Concrete, marble, and stainless steel
94½ × 55 × 42 inches
238 × 139 × 106 cm

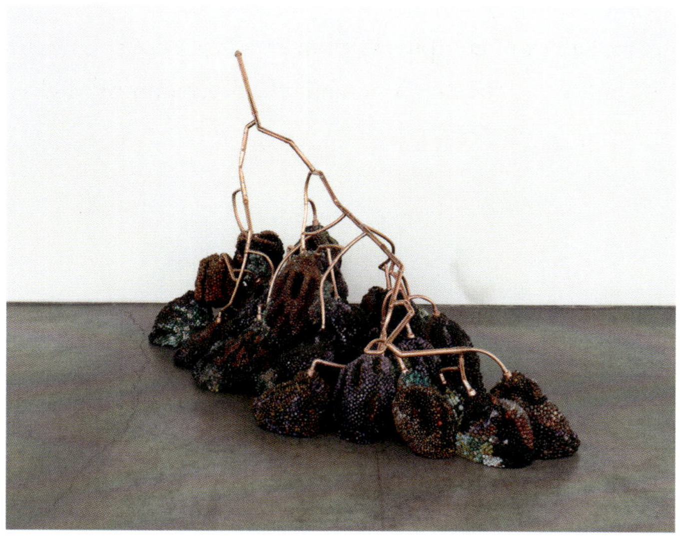

Kathleen Ryan
Bad Grapes, 2020
Amethyst, aventurine, agate, garnet, pyrite, ruby in zoisite, tektite, tigereye, turquoise, serpentine, obsidian, blackstone, Indian unakite, labradorite, Sierra agate, red agate, black agate, serpentine, quartz, marble, amazonite, rhyolite, calcite, dalmation jasper, glass, steel and stainless steel pins, copper tube and copper fittings, and polystyrene
59½ × 90 × 54 inches
151 × 228.5 × 137 cm

are firm and glossy, as ripe cherries ostensibly should be, but here that shine isn't an index of freshness. These fruits, carved from polystyrene, are "bedazzled" with gems and minerals: red aventurine, jasper, rhodolite, and carnelian create a gradation of reds; while amazonite, aventurine, fluorite, turquoise, malachite, angelite, labradorite, freshwater pearl, quartz, and rainbow moonstone evoke an iridescent blue-green-white mold; and dark agate and garnet signal rot. The fruits' stems are composed of fishing rods weighted with lead sinkers, creating another kind of material tension: unlike the ripe, erotic pressure building up inside the grape skin, the tension here is that of gravity pulling these languishing bodies toward the ground.

Walking into the back gallery, we then encounter a rotting pumpkin, *Jackie* (2021)—a sad post-Halloween jack-o'-lantern almost the size of Cinderella's pumpkin coach (some of Ryan's earlier works also referenced technologies of mobility; *Bad Melon*, 2020, was constructed inside chunks of an Airstream trailer). Visible steel nails affix orange acrylic beads to the pumpkin's warty exterior. Its carved-out top is cast off to the side. Peering into the gourd through its roughly carved facial features, or from its crown, we find a veritable Hall of Gems: radiant rocks and geodes that symbolize stale flesh, mold, and decay—from the pinks and whites of rose quartz, red aventurine, quartz, and calcite; to the golds and oranges of citrine, brecciated jasper, and carnelian; the greens of Ching Hai jade, moss agate, and malachite; the blues of azurite-malachite, lapis lazuli, and labradorite; the purple of amethyst; the blacks of smoky quartz and onyx; and the polychromatism of agate.

A few doors down 2nd Street, in Karma's other gallery, we add some additional fruits to our basket: four loose cherries and three lemons. Lemons are complex symbols: their juices are used to preserve and purify, yet to call something a "lemon" means that it's defective, disappointing. These lemons—with their flesh made from gray-yellow prehnite and yellow-green peridot, and abundant mold fashioned with Swarovski crystal and pearl—turn the defective bits into treasure.

As with many of the other fruits in Ryan's cornucopia, the more spoiled the spot, the more precious its component materials. Her work comments on the extensive physical resources and financing required to impede natural forces of decay, to counter entropy. Yet food waste—epitomized here by the tradition of carving a pumpkin only to discard it after it serves its seasonal ornamental role—remains a massive problem, and industrialized agriculture commands much of the world's water supply and generates widespread pollution.[4] The portrayal of rot also reminds us of the increasing vulnerability of our food supply to global pathogens—particularly in an age of monocultural cultivation and climate change.[5]

Yet Ryan's gems and geodes also refract our gaze, compelling us to consider the potential value of decay itself. Consider spalted wood, which features colored marbling that reveals the traces of fungus-induced decay, and is prized by woodworkers. Think, too, about fermentation, which involves the *controlled* breakdown of a substance by microorganisms, and can generate food with greater health benefits and enhanced food safety.[6] As American Studies scholar Justin Abraham Linds explains, fermentation was central to the creation of value in the Caribbean plantation system: fermentation transformed raw sugarcane into a commodity, and it allowed colonists to collect and preserve natural history specimens. "Fermentation and rot had to be mastered by

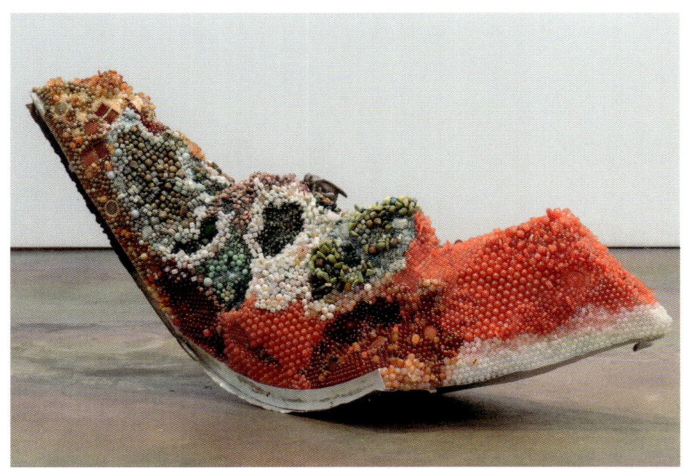

Kathleen Ryan
Bad Melon (Moldy Slice), 2020 (detail)
Cherry quartz, rose quartz, agate, amazonite, jasper, aventurine, rhodonite, rhodochrosite, labradorite, smoky quartz, quartz, Botswana agate, carnelian, horn, citrine, glass, cast iron and brass flies, steel and stainless steel pins, polystyrene, and aluminum Airstream
23 × 63 × 21 inches
58.4 × 160 × 53.3 cm

colonists desiring to produce ideal commodities, ideal nature, and ideal human bodies," Linds writes.[7] In the production of kimchi, alcohol, and sugarcane—as with the creation of Ryan's artifacts—degradation is not a product of neglect; to the contrary, fermentation and rot are meticulously plotted and executed with great knowledge and care.

Planned decay is also deployed in archivy, where cultural heritage practitioners face limits on what they can preserve, and thus must orchestrate the "graceful degradation" of particular materials.[8] Art conservators face similar challenges with works that are meant to be ephemeral: performance pieces, sculptures made of ice, audio tapes that eat themselves. Geographer Caitlin DeSilvey, echoing Freidberg, notes that "massive amounts of energy are invested to keep heritage systems"—like historic sites, landscapes, and monuments—"in a steady state so that the matter contained within them will continue to function as a cultural mnemonic device." Instead, she advocates that historic preservationists embrace the ethos of "curated decay"—letting things go, letting things change, letting things collapse, accepting that "processes of aging and decay can be additive as well as destructive," acknowledging that "what may appear as erasure on one register may be generative of new information on another."[9]

Ryan's sculptures are composed of materials—plastics and rocks—that will surely outlast any exhibition or gallery. But in using these nonperishable substances to capture the fragility of life, she prompts us to consider the resources deployed in its preservation, and to wonder if we might find beauty and humility in its cultivated decomposition.

1 Susanne Freidberg, *Fresh: A Perishable History* (Cambridge, MA: Harvard University Press, 2009), 2.
2 See Benjamin R. Cohen, *Pure Adulteration: Cheating on Nature in the Age of Manufactured Food* (Chicago: University of Chicago Press, 2019).
3 Freidberg, *Fresh*, 7.
4 Courtney Lindwall, "Industrial Agricultural Pollution 101," Natural Resources Defense Council, July 31, 2019, https://www.nrdc.org/stories/industrial-agricultural-pollution-101
5 Myles Karp, "Rotting-Fruit Art Points Up Plants in Peril," *National Geographic*, December 27, 2019, https://www.nationalgeographic.com/science/article/rotting-fruit-art-points-up-plants-in-peril.
6 Anna Kårlund et al., "Harnessing Microbes for Sustainable Development: Food Fermentation as a Tool for Improving the Nutitional Quality of Alternative Protein Sources," *Nutrients* 12, no. 4 (April 2020): https://www.ncbi.nlm.nih.gov/pmc/articles/PMC7230334/; Chrysa Voidarou et al., "Fermentative Foods: Microbiology, Biochemistry, Potential Human Health Benefits and Public Health Issues," *Foods* 10, no. 10 (December 2020): https://www.ncbi.nlm.nih.gov/pmc/articles/PMC7823516/.
7 Justin Abraham Linds, "Fermentation, Rot, and Power in the Early Modern Atlantic," *Edge Effects*, August 11, 2020, https://edgeeffects.net/fermentation-rot-and-power/.
8 Bethany Nowviskie, "Graceful Degradation," Bethany Nowviskie (website), July 10, 2009, https://nowviskie.org/2009/graceful-degradation/.
9 Caitlin DeSilvey, *Curated Decay: Heritage Beyond Saving* (Minneapolis University of Minnesota Press, 2017): 11, 13, 20.

Heather Davis

All the Wonder of Putrescence

Every November, porches, walkways, and stoops become the site of unplanned science experiments, with varying stages of rotting pumpkins unabashedly displayed. These remnants of festivities sit with increasingly lopsided grins, breaking down in unexpected ways, neglected, yet fecund, gradually merging with concrete or wood until someone remembers to put them in the compost or garbage. Sometimes they look perfectly fine from the outside, surprising someone with a wealth of new bacterial growth if they are curious enough to look inside. Encountering the giant version of this phenomenon is startling, and also rather humorous. Kathleen Ryan's *Jackie* (2021) depicts a perfectly happy nearly-eight-foot-wide jack-o'-lantern, with its lid resting to one side. It seems uncharacteristically fresh upon first glance, but the inside bursts with various colors and stages of rot and mold. The humor, or maybe more pointedly, the irony, is compounded by the fact that upon closer inspection the giant pumpkin, like the other oversize rotting fruit for which Ryan has become known, is entirely beaded with gems, acrylics, and glass—all long-lasting materials. Constructed in the same manner as kitsch fruit kits that were popular in postwar America, the collection of works titled *Bad Fruit* remain faithful to the crafting technique, with a basic foam armature meticulously beaded to resemble the various fruits. In these giant renditions, healthy flesh is composed of manufactured plastic and glass beads, whereas rot is depicted with semiprecious gemstones and healing crystals. Ryan explicitly makes decay itself valuable: the more advanced the state of decomposition, the more precious the stones used to depict that putrefaction. Bacteria and mold sparkle and glitter, joyously multiplying on the outsize, decadent fruit. The rot is teeming, threatening to release sticky juices, contaminating other biological matter nearby, barely containing the squishy insides. Yet the most potent reminder of rot—smell—is absent here, sanitizing and beautifying decay for artistic effect, asking the audience to look closer to the forms of purification. The hardness of what would be soft, yielding skins combining opposite potentials that playfully resound: a technique the artist has used throughout her work.

Bad Fruit—which, for this solo exhibition at Karma, includes five *Bad Cherry* sculptures and three *Bad Lemons*, in addition to the pumpkin—can be understood as a contemporary version of Dutch vanitas paintings from the early seventeenth century. Vanitas paintings are known for their display of imported and exotic fruit that often rotted during the process of painting, as a statement of luxury itself, for the fruit was indeed quite precious, gained through colonial exploitation. The decomposing fruit was often depicted with skulls and other objects as potent reminders of mortality and life's renewal. In *Bad Fruit*, the tradition is extended into three dimensions as a critical commentary on the excesses of luxury and waste. Decay is not a simple idea in this work. Putrescence evokes a world in decline, where growing inequality speaks to a profound abandonment of the earth and all its beings. The artworks evoke the relationship between colonialism and advanced capitalism, by referencing the vanitas tradition re-presented for contemporary audiences, and the supposed necessity for boundless growth despite the obvious waste and rot involved. In fact, waste and rot continue to be the engines of capital gain and exploitation. Nothing, not even waste, is simply left to decay; it is itself turned into a process of commodification within the voracious economic system we find ourselves within, and these artworks are a potent reminder of that fact. The works also cannot be read apart from the art world within which they are situated, displaying how art itself is at the center of accumulation, consumption, waste, and inequality. They seem to invite a luxuriant nihilism, reveling in the waste, excesses, and decline of our present moment.

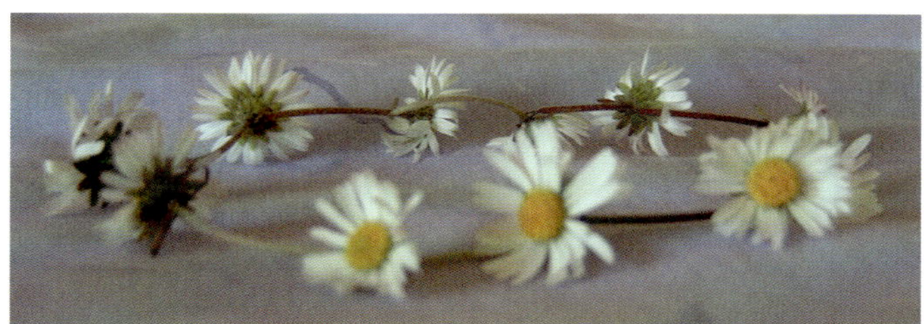

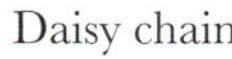

Daisy chain

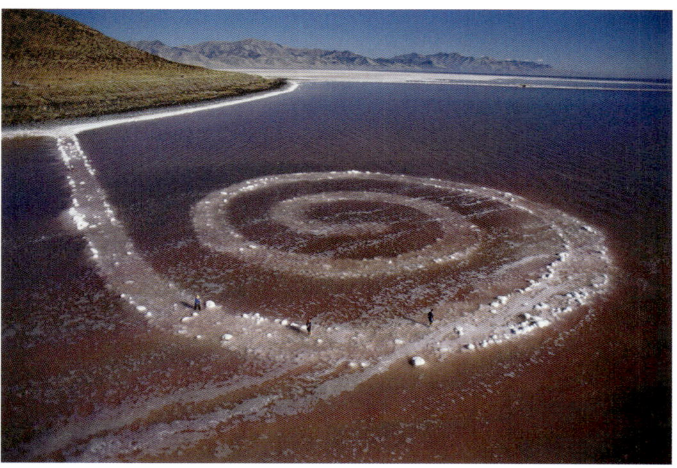

Robert Smithson
Spiral Jetty, 1970
Black rock, salt crystals, earth, and red water
18,000 × 180 inches
45,720 × 457.2 cm
Collection of Dia Art Foundation
© 2022 Holt/Smithson Foundation and Dia Art Foundation / Licensed by Artists Rights Society (ARS), NY
Photo: George Steinmetz, courtesy Dia Art Foundation, New York

And yet, beyond this pointed critique, there is also an excess that cannot be contained or corralled for economic gain. Decomposition offers the vision of another world being birthed, a putrescence that is completely alive, a multitudinous takeover of the singularity of each fruit. In particular, for this exhibition, the mold really does dominate, as the entire case of *Bad Cherries* (2021) has gone bad and the lemons look like they've been forgotten for months. The beauty of the stones, the explicit valorization of bacterial abundance, conveys a deep appreciation for the vivacity of life itself, and for the possibilities of transformation.

The sculptures also get at something important about an often unstated but deeply held belief embedded in artistic objects: the desire for them to last, untouched and untainted, forever. Museums put a huge amount of effort and energy into maintaining works in perfect condition. Everything from humidity and temperature controls, to glass cases, to the work of conservators is geared explicitly to the goal of indefinite preservation. Even works that were originally meant to transform over time, such as Robert Smithson's iconic *Spiral Jetty* (1970), are now carefully protected and preserved. Visualizing the arrest of decay and decomposition through materials, such as acrylic and stone, that are incredibly long lasting, foregrounds these conservation practices that are often taken for granted. Yet there is a productive tension here. Even though a sculpture like *Daisy Chain* (2021) that is also included in the exhibition—a giant chain made to resemble a child's wreath of flowers, constructed from gardening and industrial tools—might originally strike the viewer as freezing a moment of innocence in time indefinitely through its reliance upon various forms of plastic for its construction, the work, much like the armature used to create the giant fruit sculptures, is not as stable as might be imagined. Even the semiprecious stones, gems, and crystals may not be as permanent as received wisdom would have us think. Geology is often presumed to be fixed, and, certainly in relation to the lifespan of a ripe fruit or a human, it is. But if we take a longer view, we can see that even geology is not stable. Geology itself is neither eternal, unmoving, nor completely solid. Volcanoes and earthquakes are potent reminders of the way that the earth itself, our rocky foundation, is also in a state of flux, fluidity, and movement—that what might appear permanent and stable from our vantage point is actually constantly transforming. And so, the choice to use gems, stones, glass, and plastic beads might not only be a productive tension between stability of form and decomposition, but also shows the ways in which these two extremes themselves may not be entirely in opposition to each other, but instead dependent upon the view, or the timescale.

By using gems that some people believe can heal, and by configuring the rocks into the shape of life as abundance in decomposition, there is an implicit questioning of the boundary between life and nonlife. The rocks and gems within these works carry the most vitality, brilliance, and possibility for transmogrification, rendered as they are as tumultuous rot. They seem to challenge received notions that rocks themselves are inherently inert, inanimate, and neatly classifiable as nonlife. As Elizabeth Povinelli notes, the strict division between life and nonlife is increasingly being challenged by contemporary science that understands that all beings rely upon their environment, and cannot neatly be separated from it.[1] Although it may be difficult to discern if a rock dies, it certainly has an origin. And it is thought that, for some kinds of rock, that origin is bacterial.[2] So, Ryan's artistic rendering of bacterial flourishing in rock may not just be a particularly effective form to communicate beauty, or a productive tension by juxtaposing two

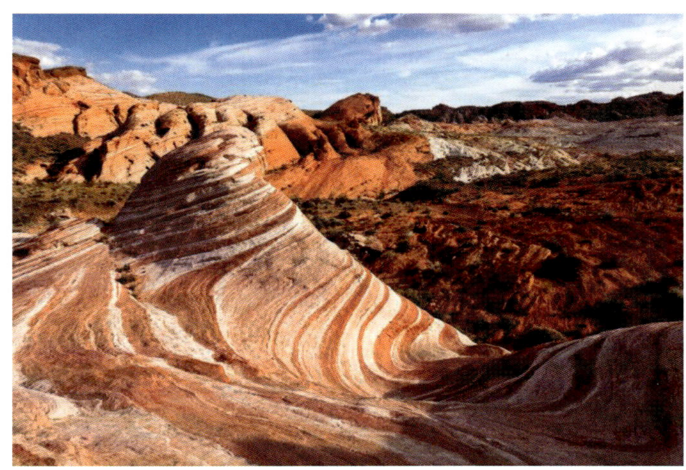

Rock formation
Valley of Fire, Nevada

opposites, but may also point to certain scientific facts. The works question this neat division between life and nonlife, suggesting an animate quality within the rocks themselves.

The exhibition portrays a deep fascination with the profundity of objects that are both decadent and mundane. And there is an obvious delight in the materials themselves, both in the intricate construction of each sculpture, and in the feeling of repulsion and attraction of rotting fruit. Basking in the sensuality of materiality, Ryan creates a world that brings more attention to matter itself, how it is tied to systems of commodification and luxury, but also how it can never be entirely captured.

1 Elizabeth Povinelli, *Geontologies: A Requiem to Late Liberalism* (Durham, NC: Duke University Press, 2016), 43.
2 Ibid.

Daisy Chain, 2021

Plastics

153 × 128 × 48 inches
388.6 × 325.1 × 121.9 cm

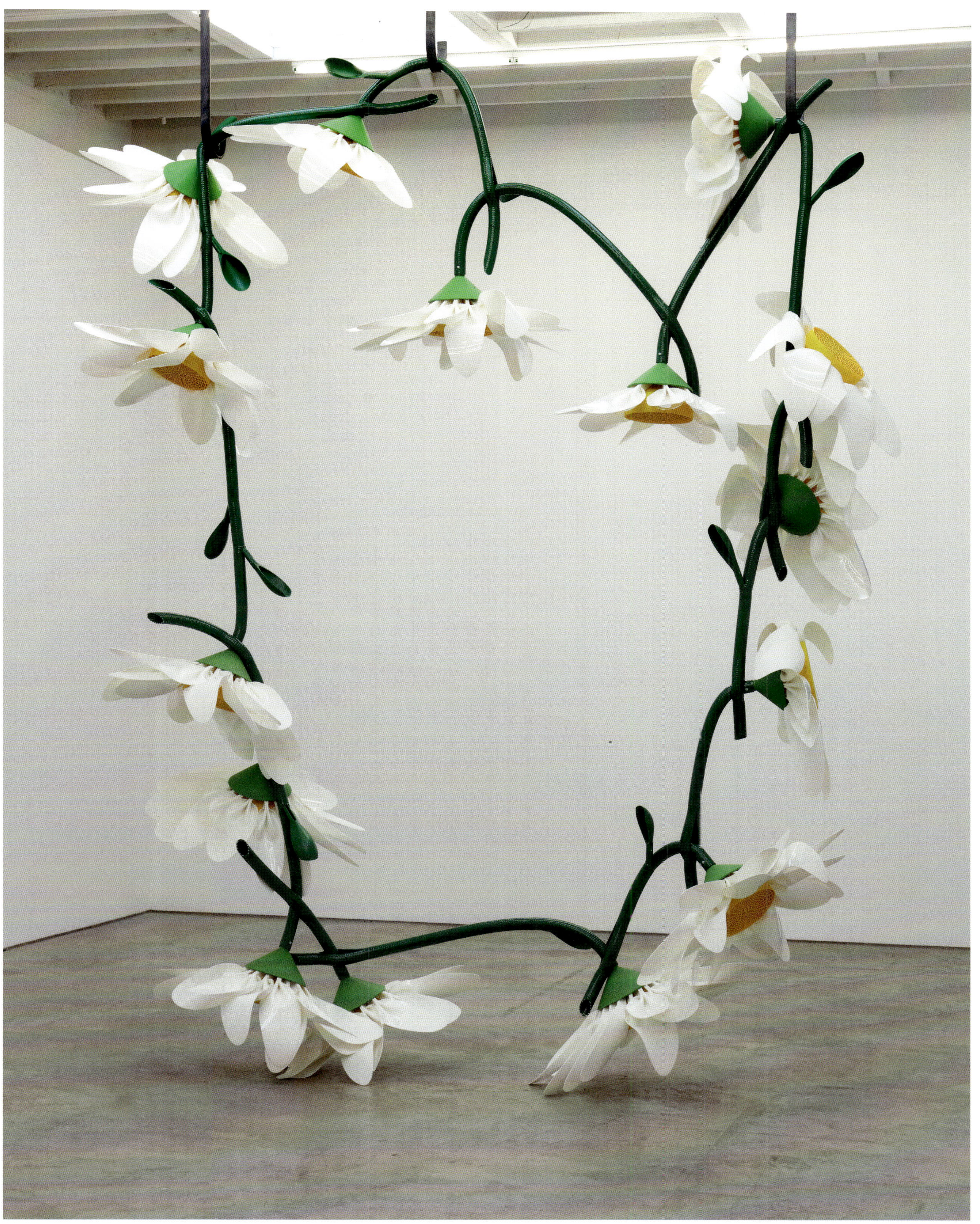

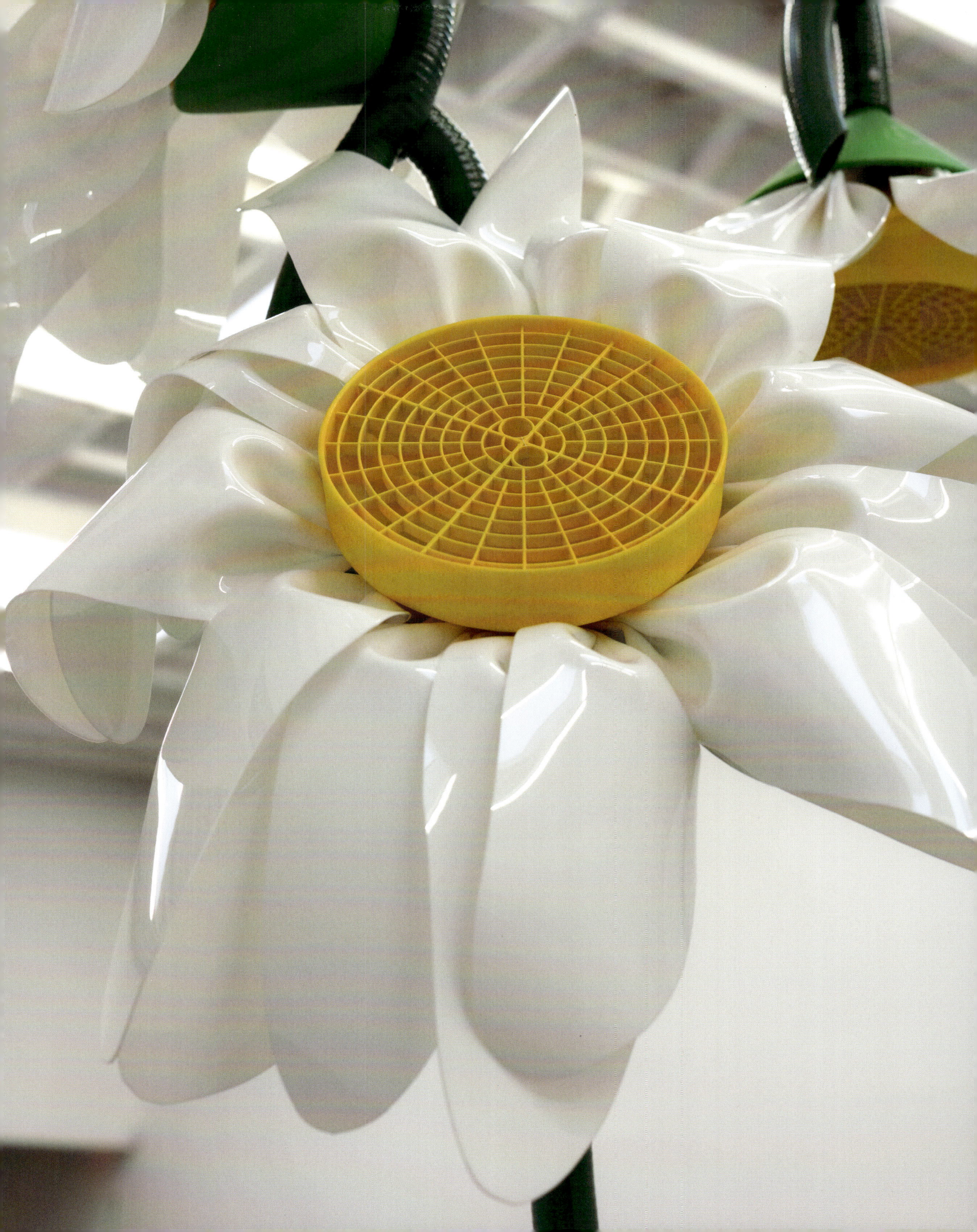

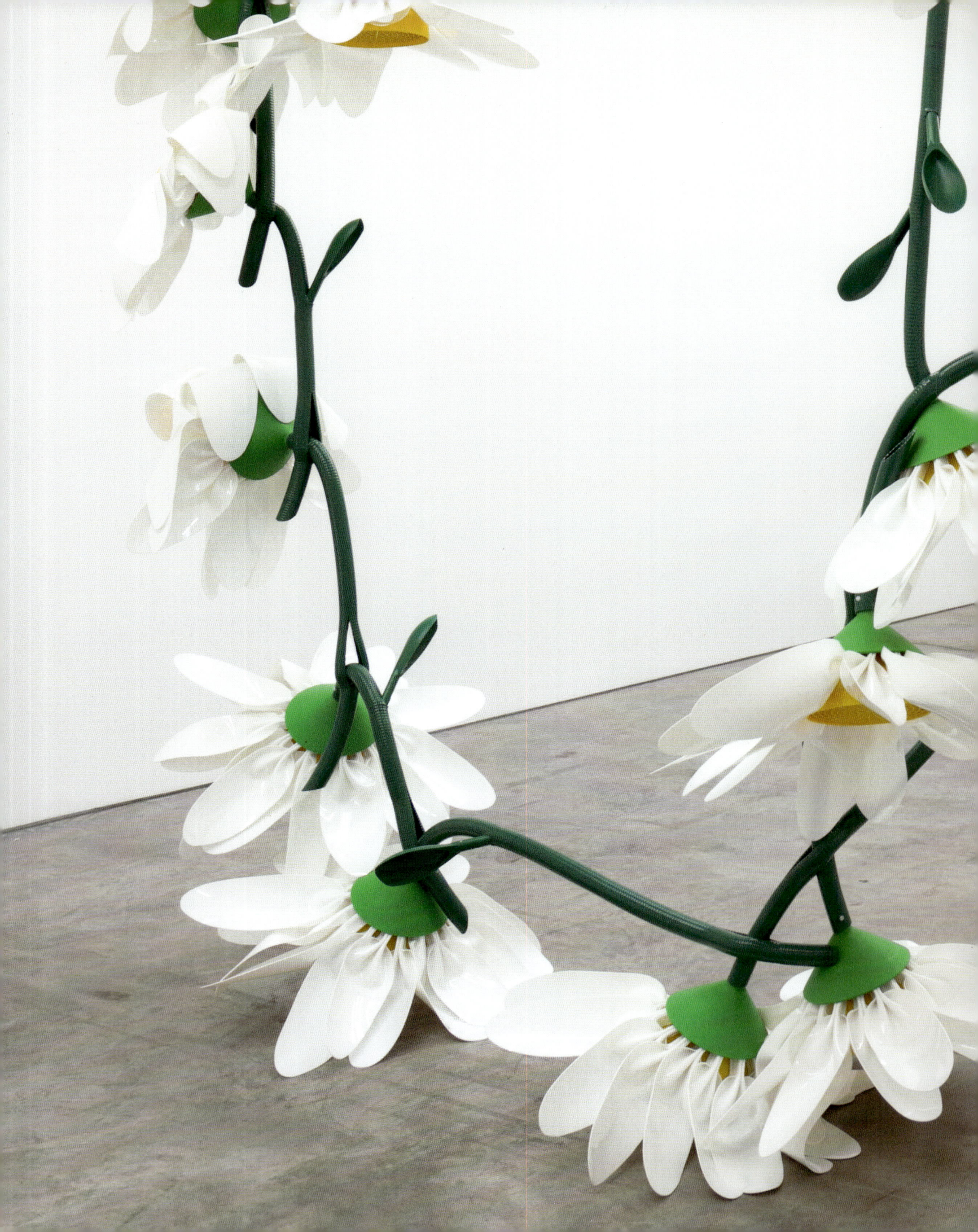

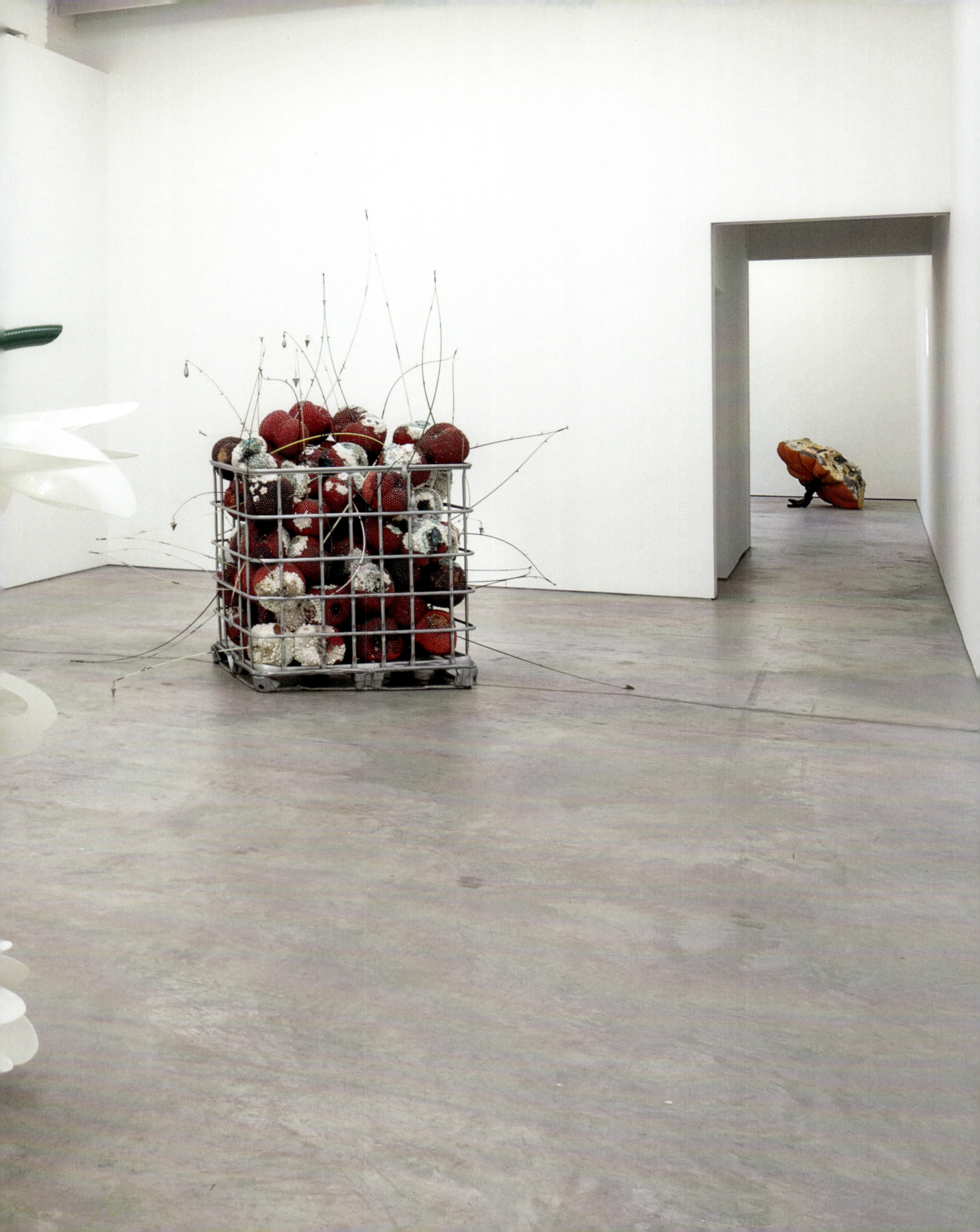

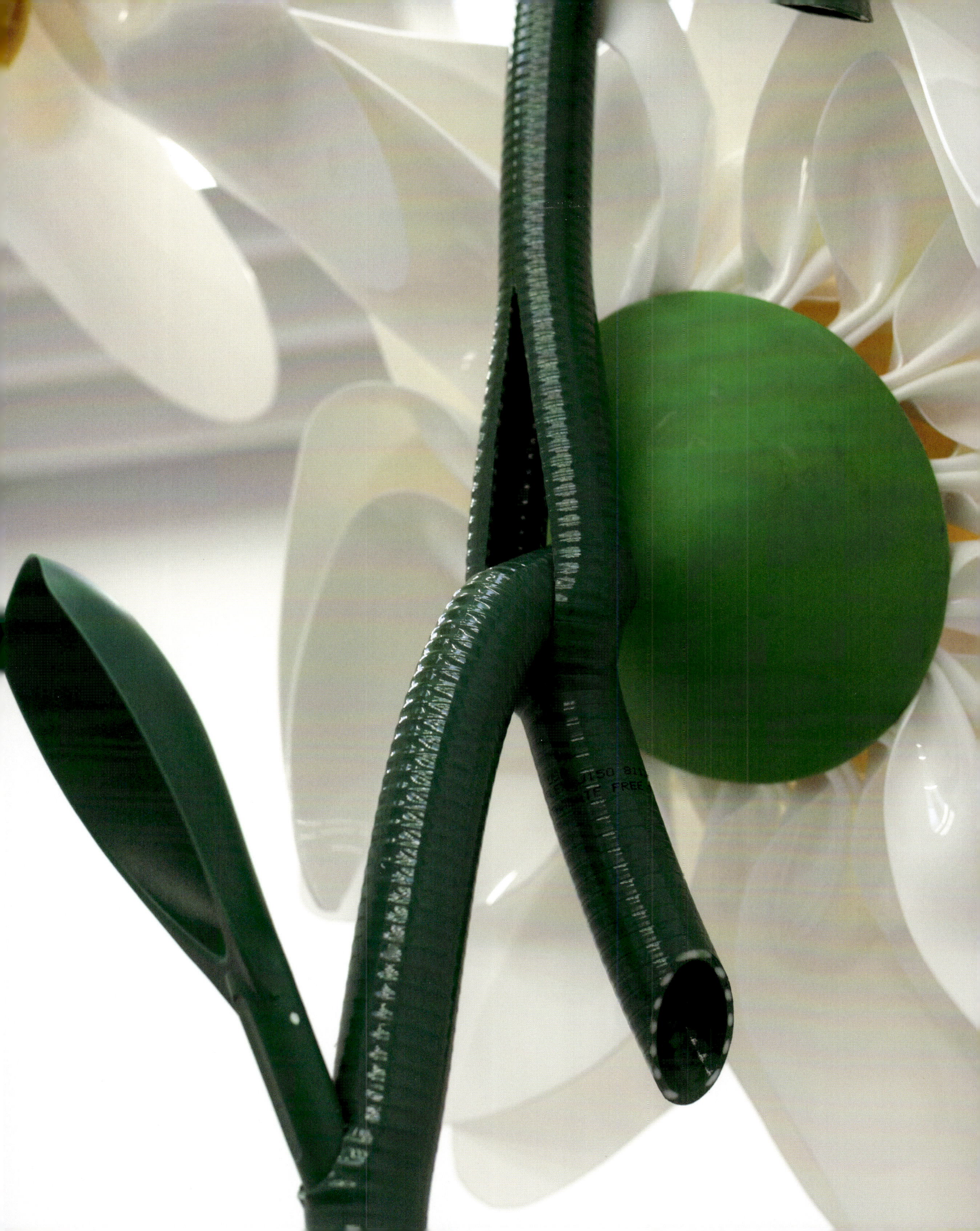

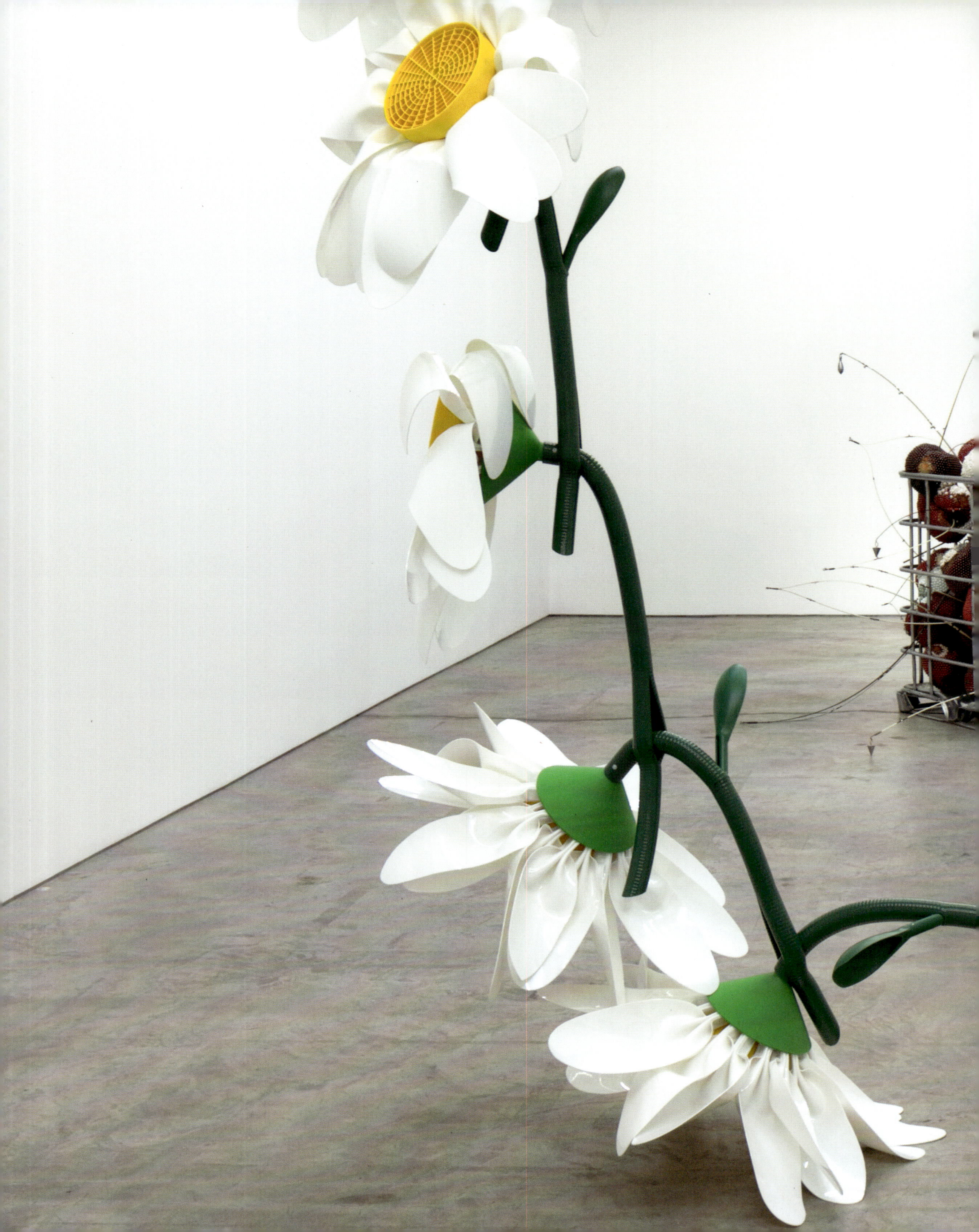

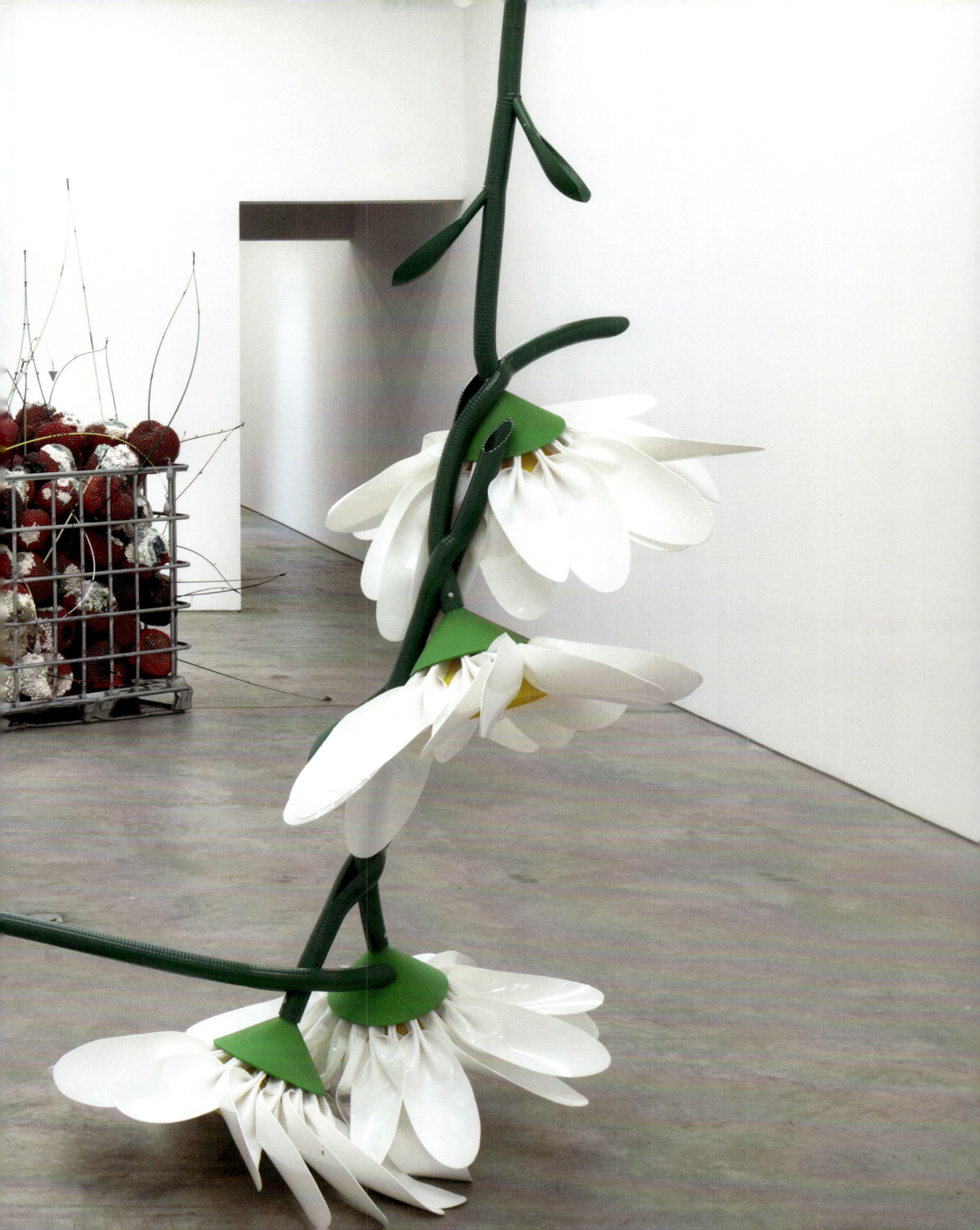

Bad Cherries, 2021

Amazonite, aventurine, fluorite, turquoise, malachite, angelite, labradorite, smoky quartz, quartz, rose quartz, citrine, magnesite, aquamarine, green line jasper, sesame jasper, pink aventurine, agate, tiger eye, garnet, carnelian, lapis lazuli, moonstone, mother of pearl, shell, freshwater pearls, wood, acrylic, glass, steel pins on coated polystyrene, fishing poles, lead sinkers, and steel pallet cage

98½ × 100 × 110½ inches
250.2 × 254 × 280.7 cm

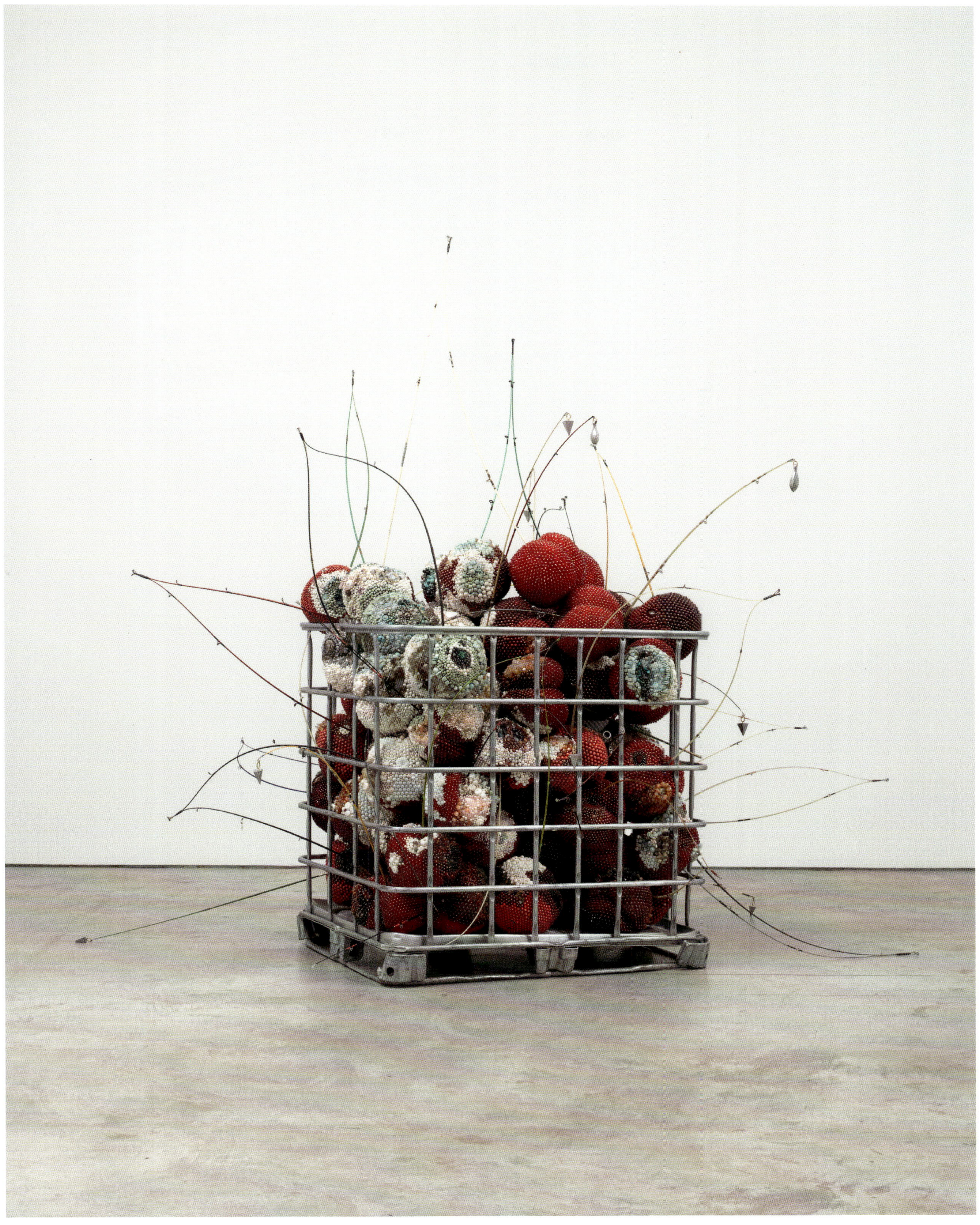

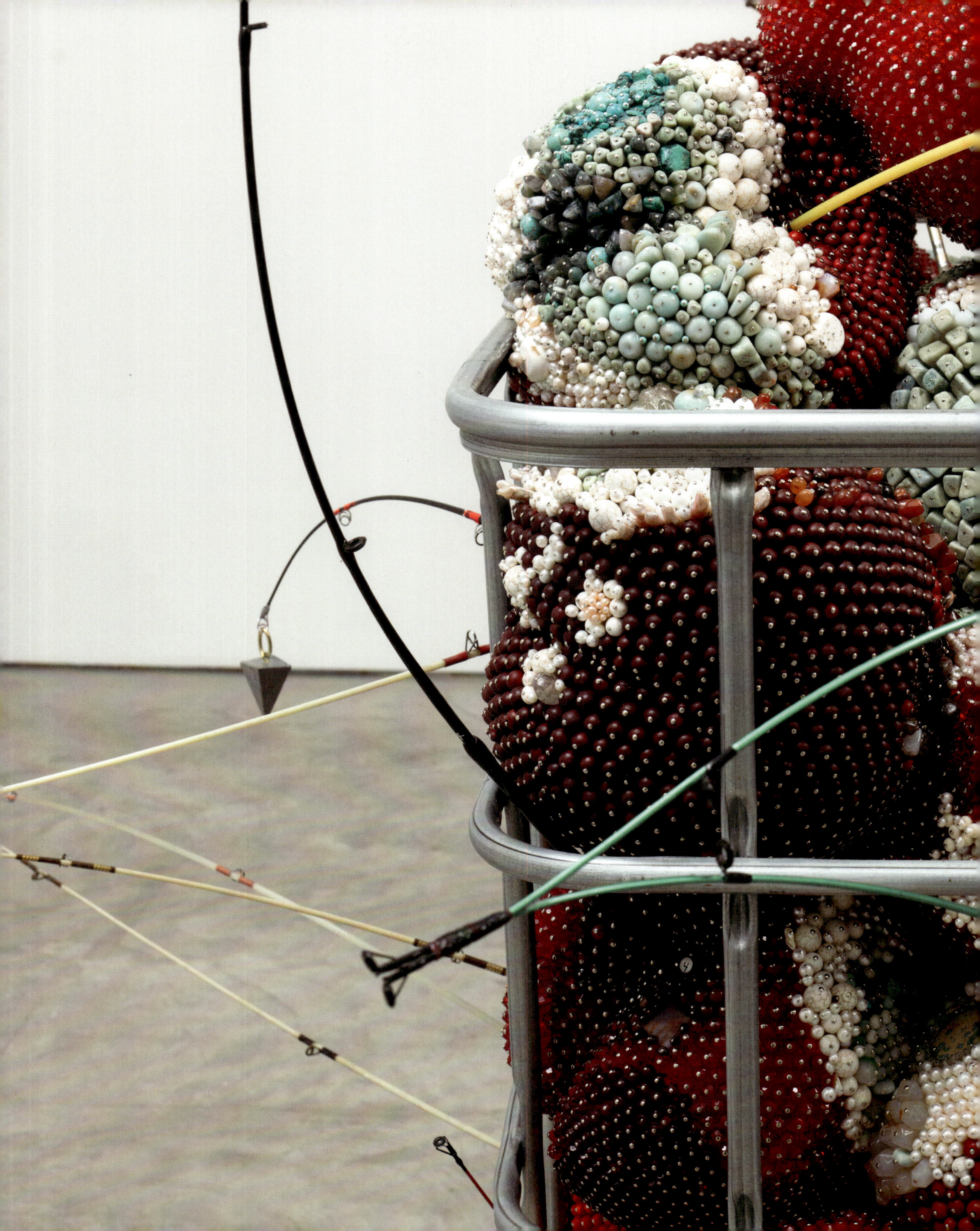

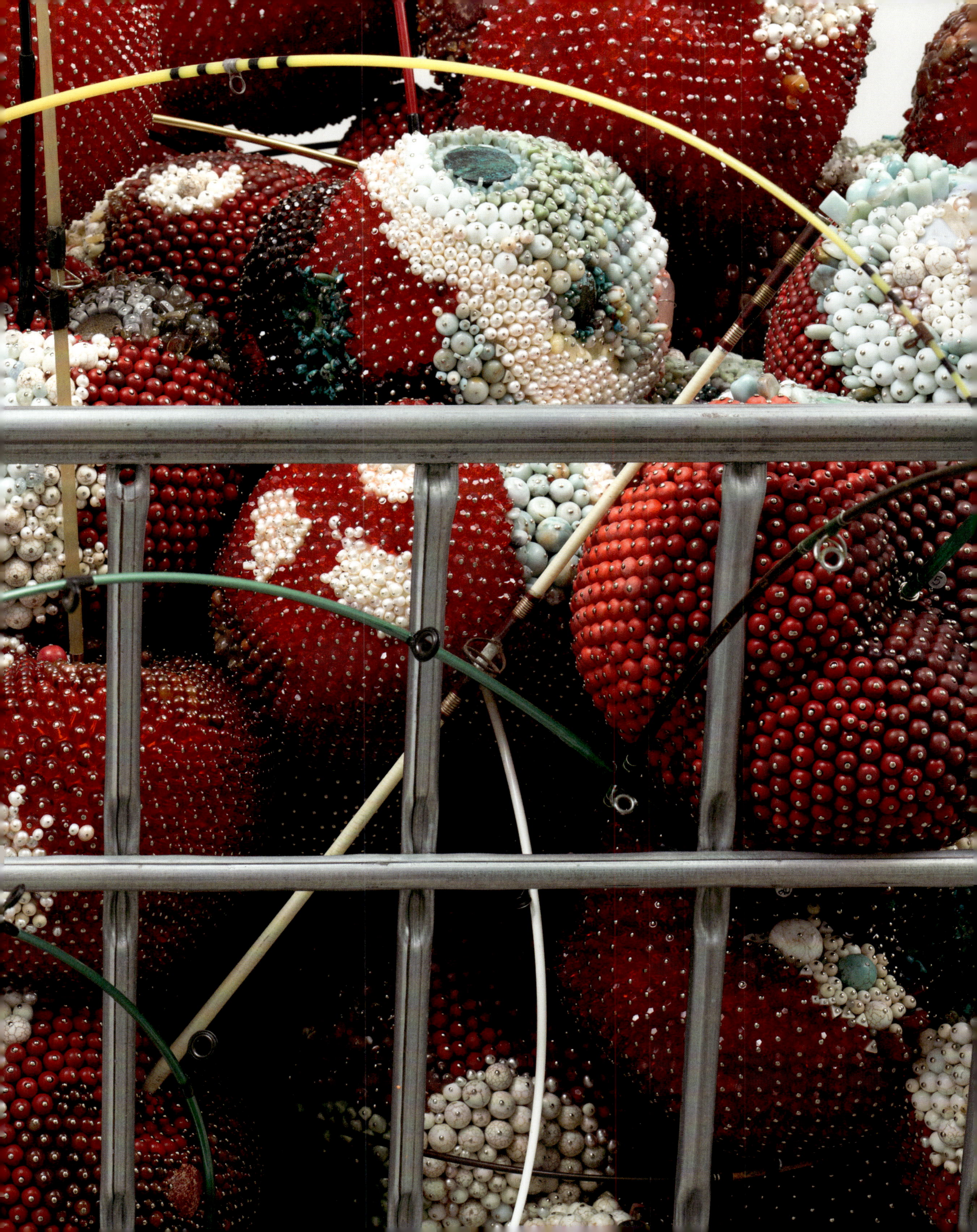

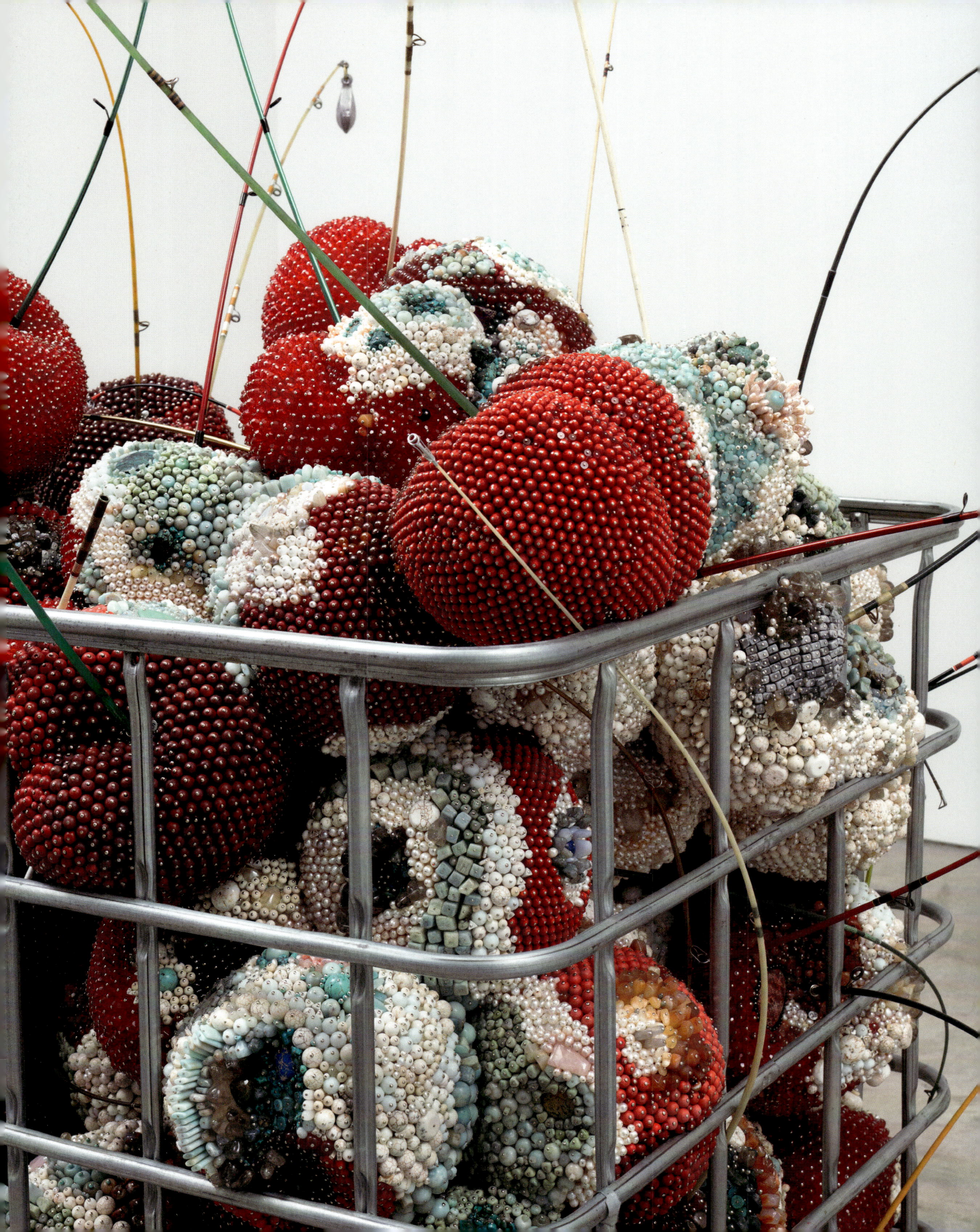

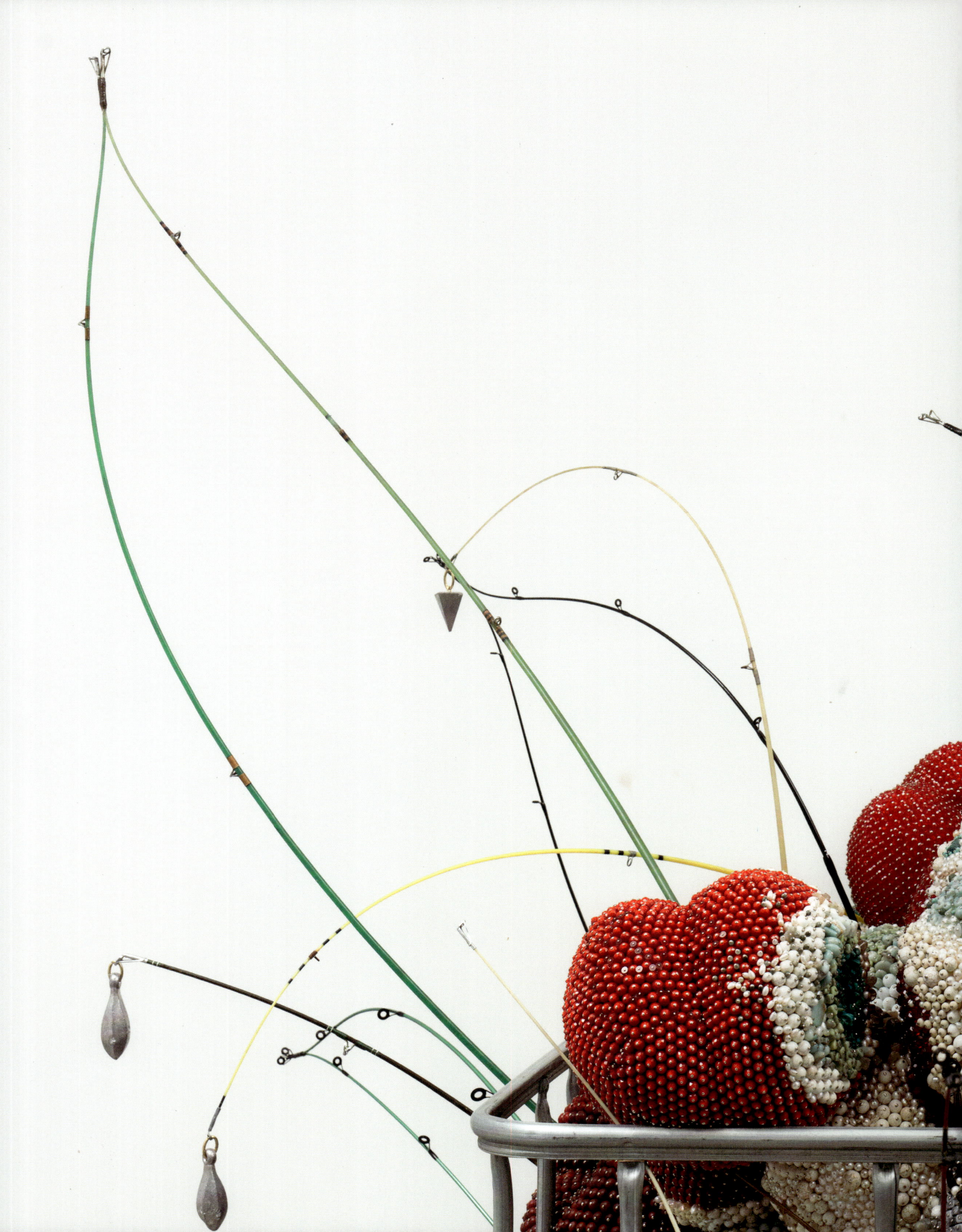

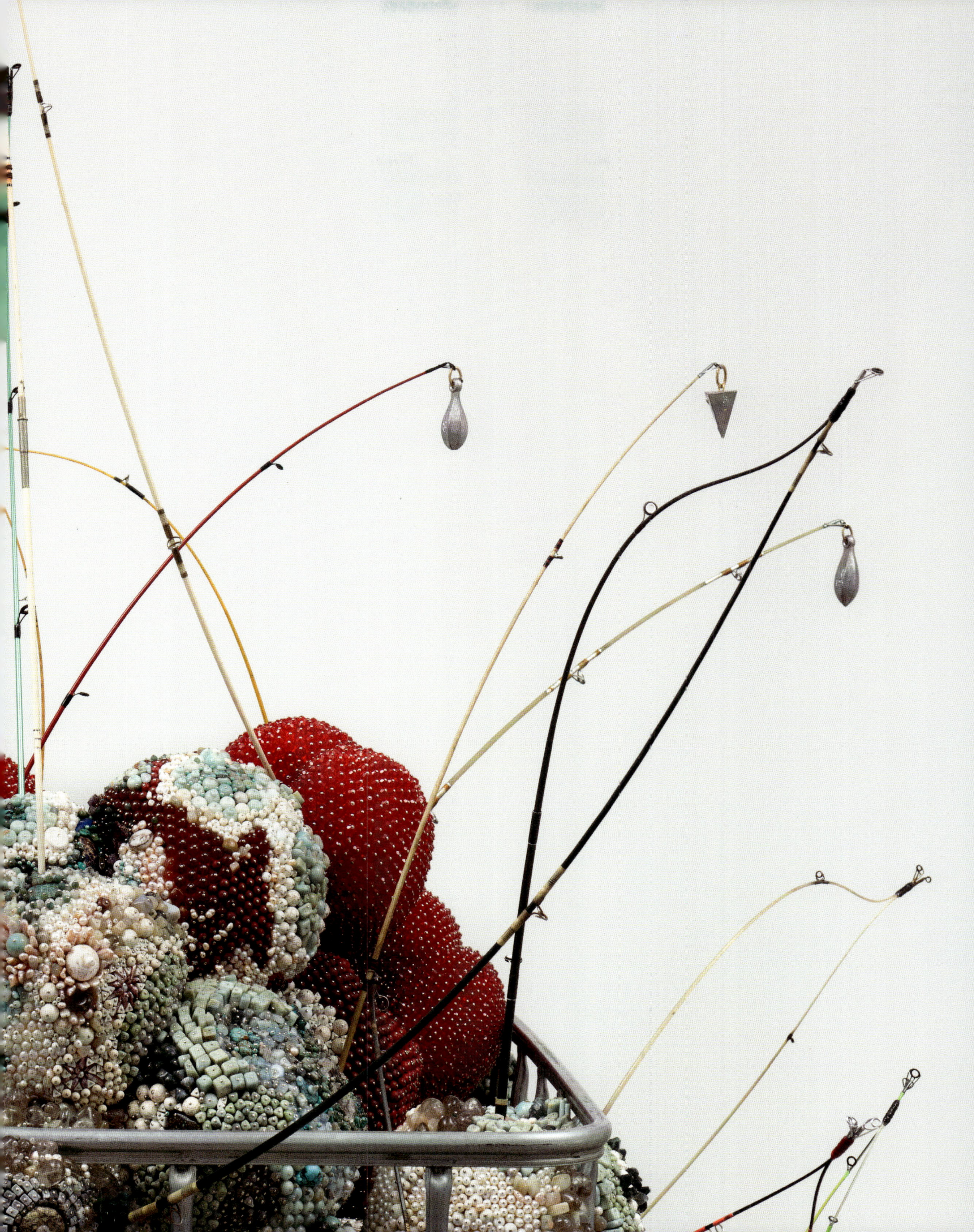

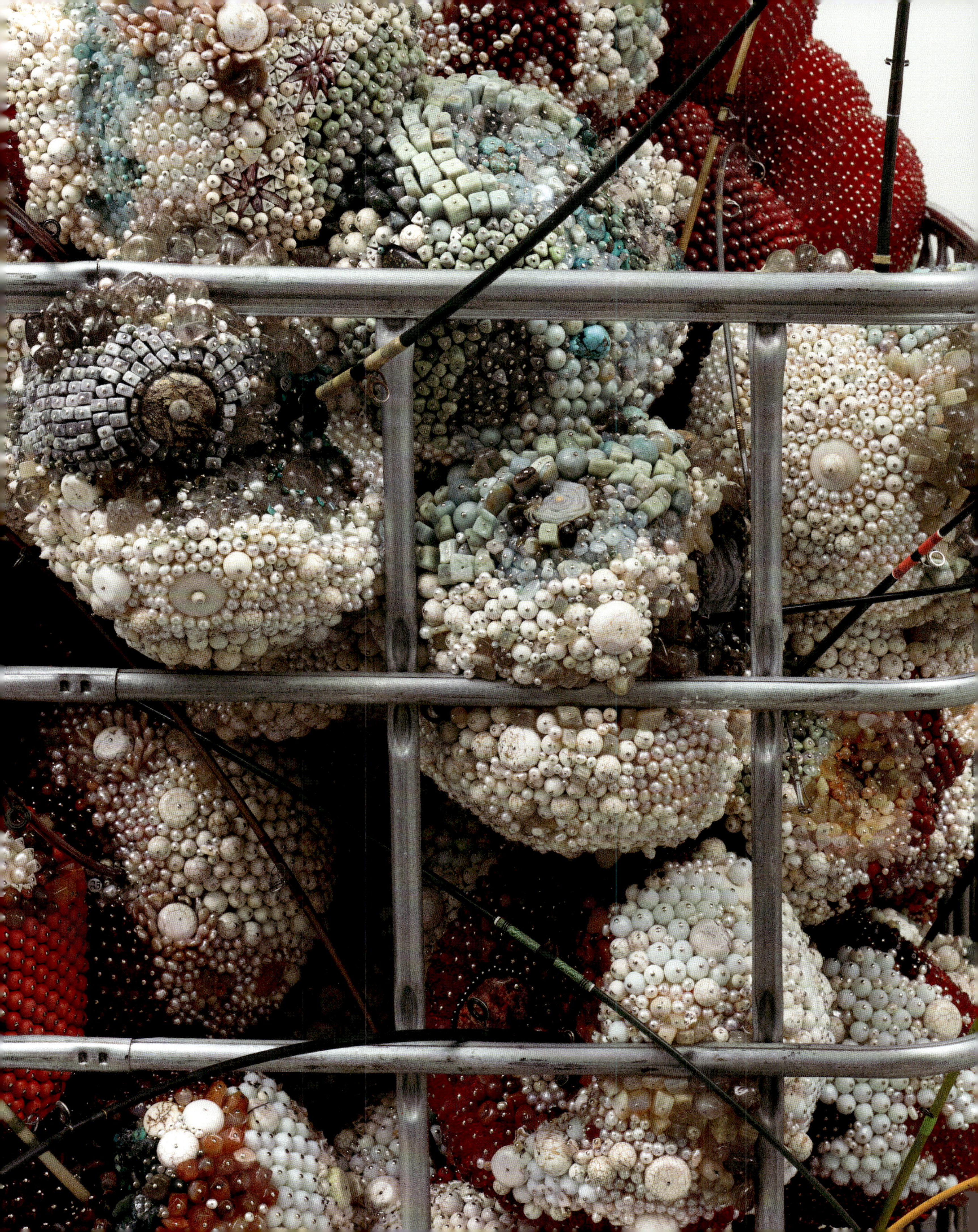

Jackie, 2021

Azurite-malachite, lapis lazuli, agate, black onyx, brecciated jasper, moss agate, malachite, calcite, labradorite, rose quartz, smoky quartz, Ching Hai jade, red aventurine, carnelian, citrine, amethyst, quartz, acrylic, polystyrene, fiberglass, nails, steel pins, and wood

66 × 90 × 86 inches
167.6 × 228.6 × 218.4 cm

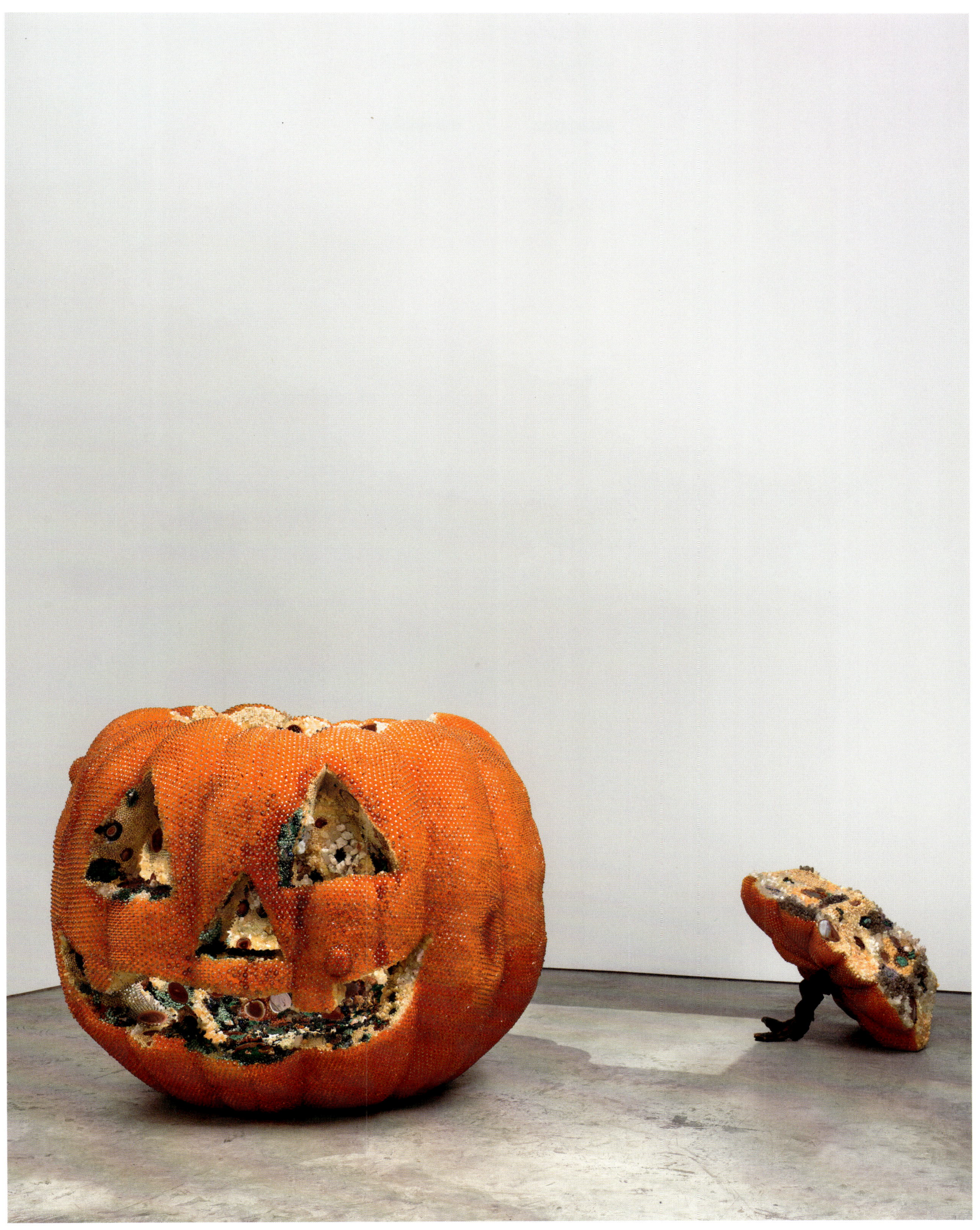

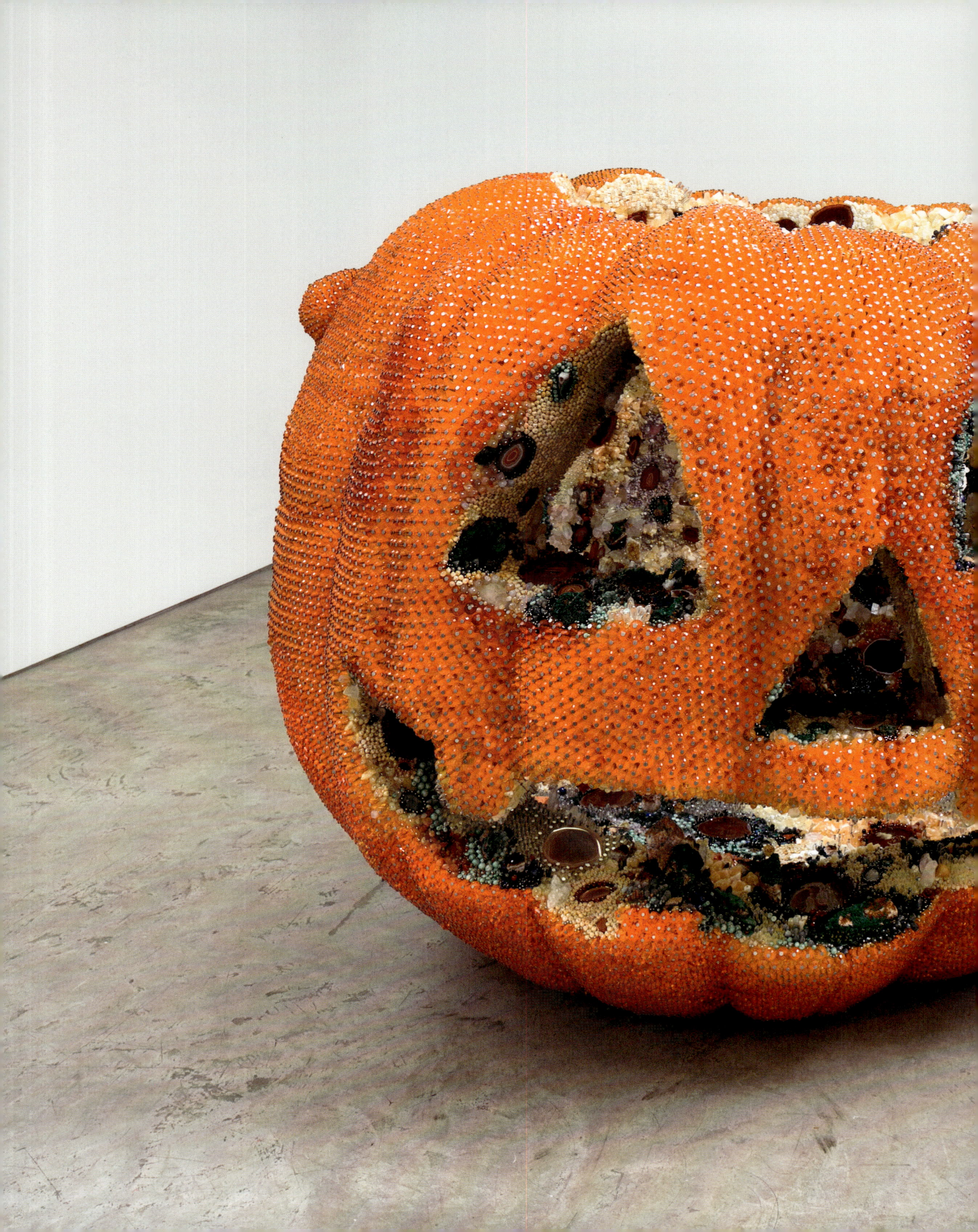

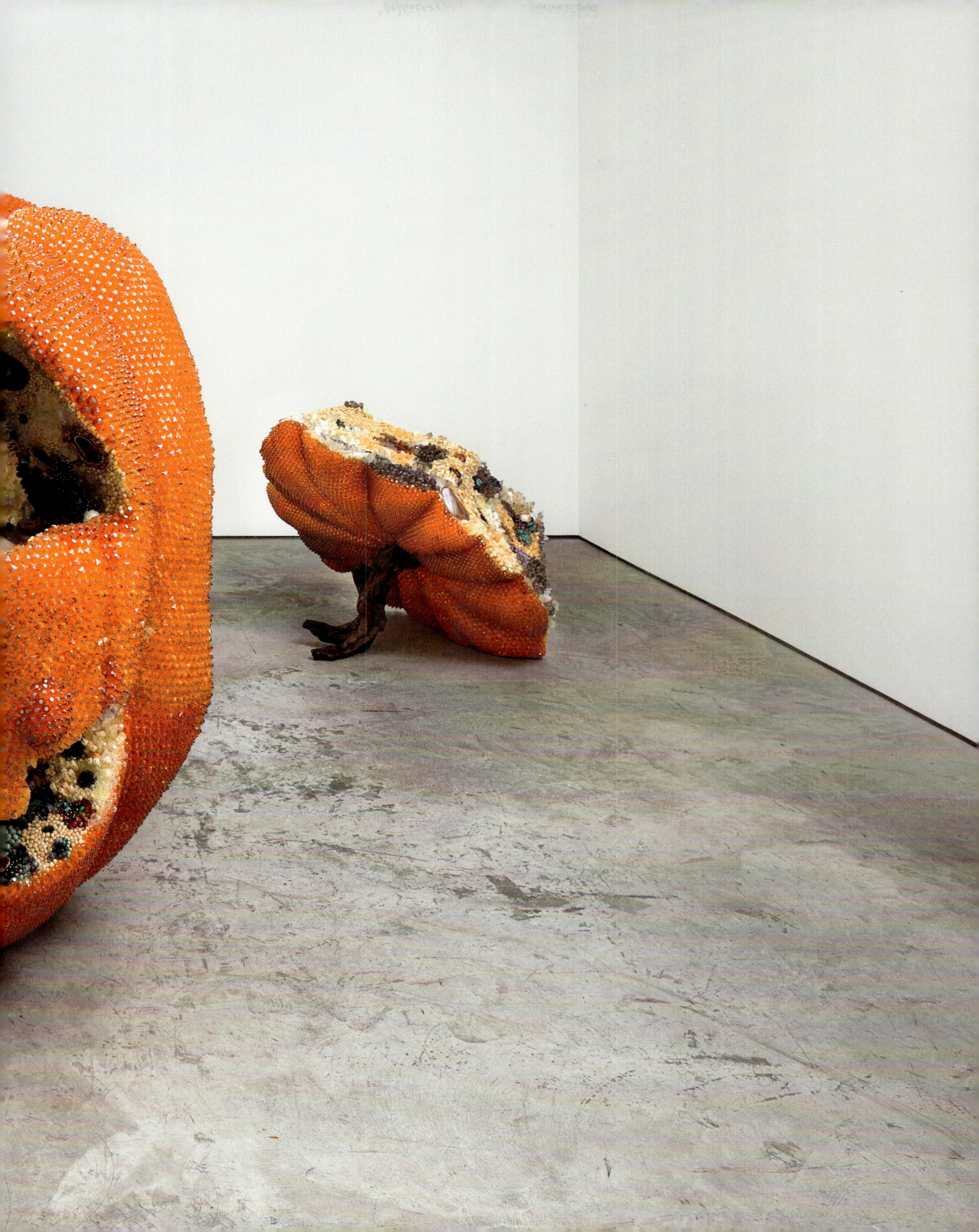

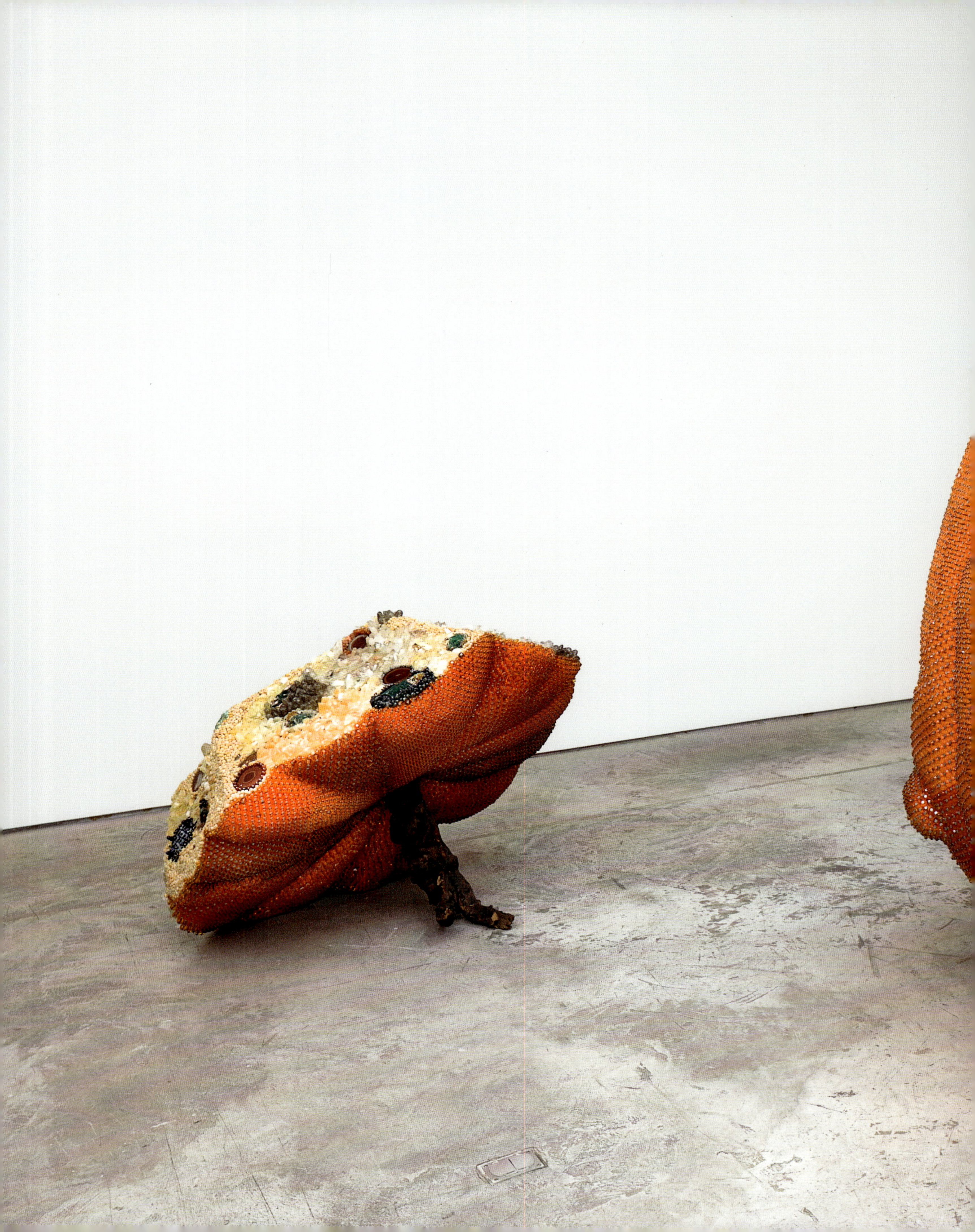

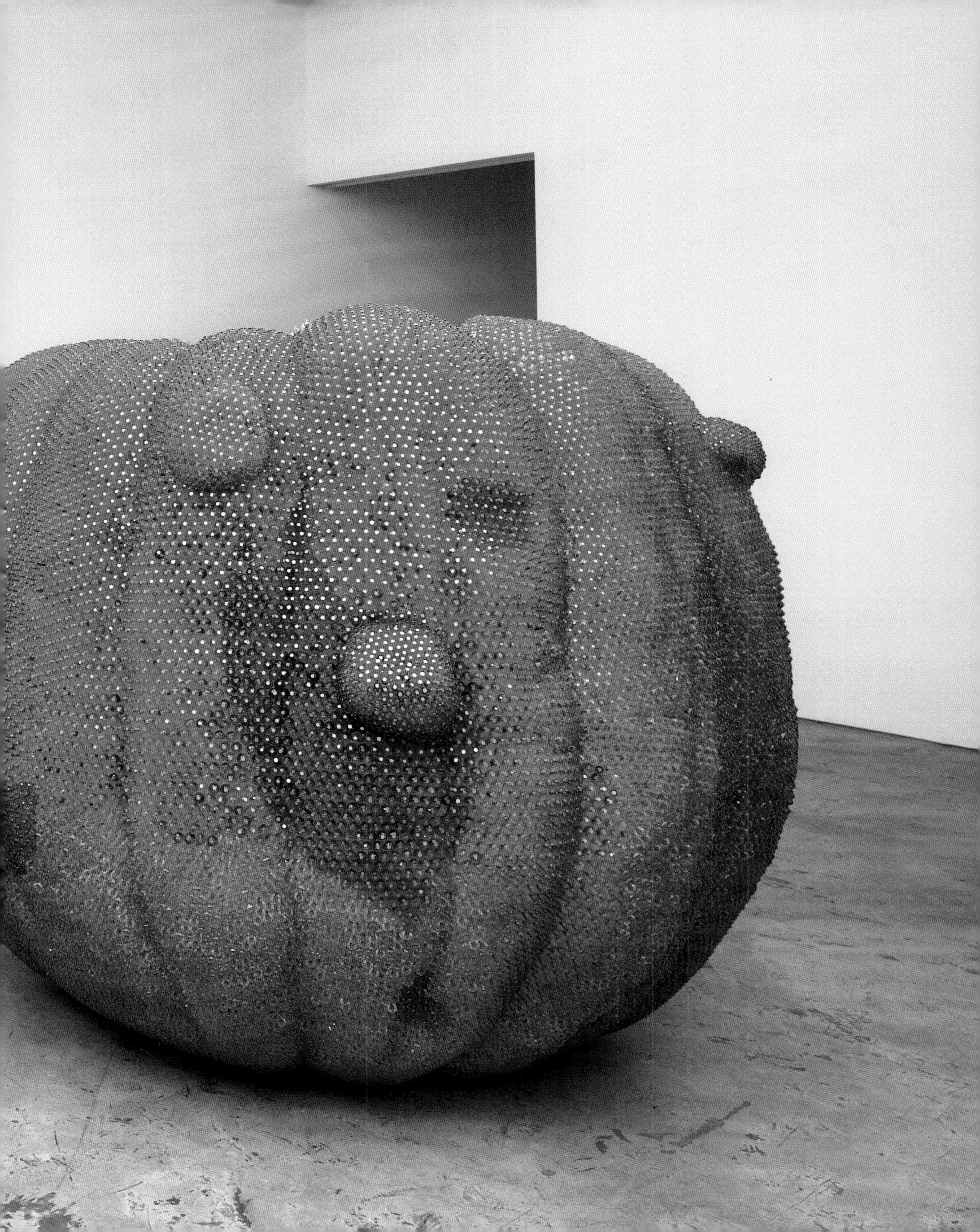

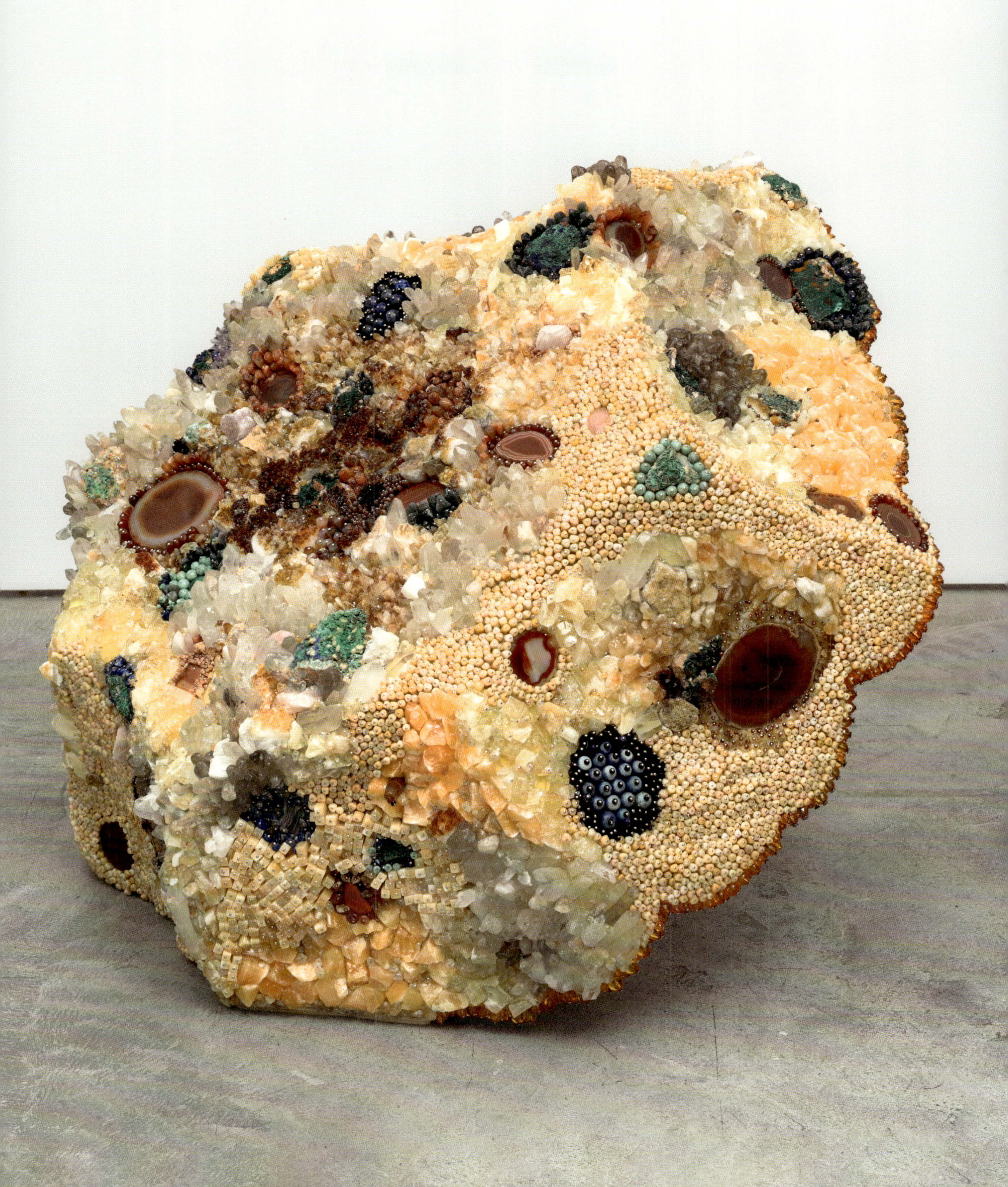

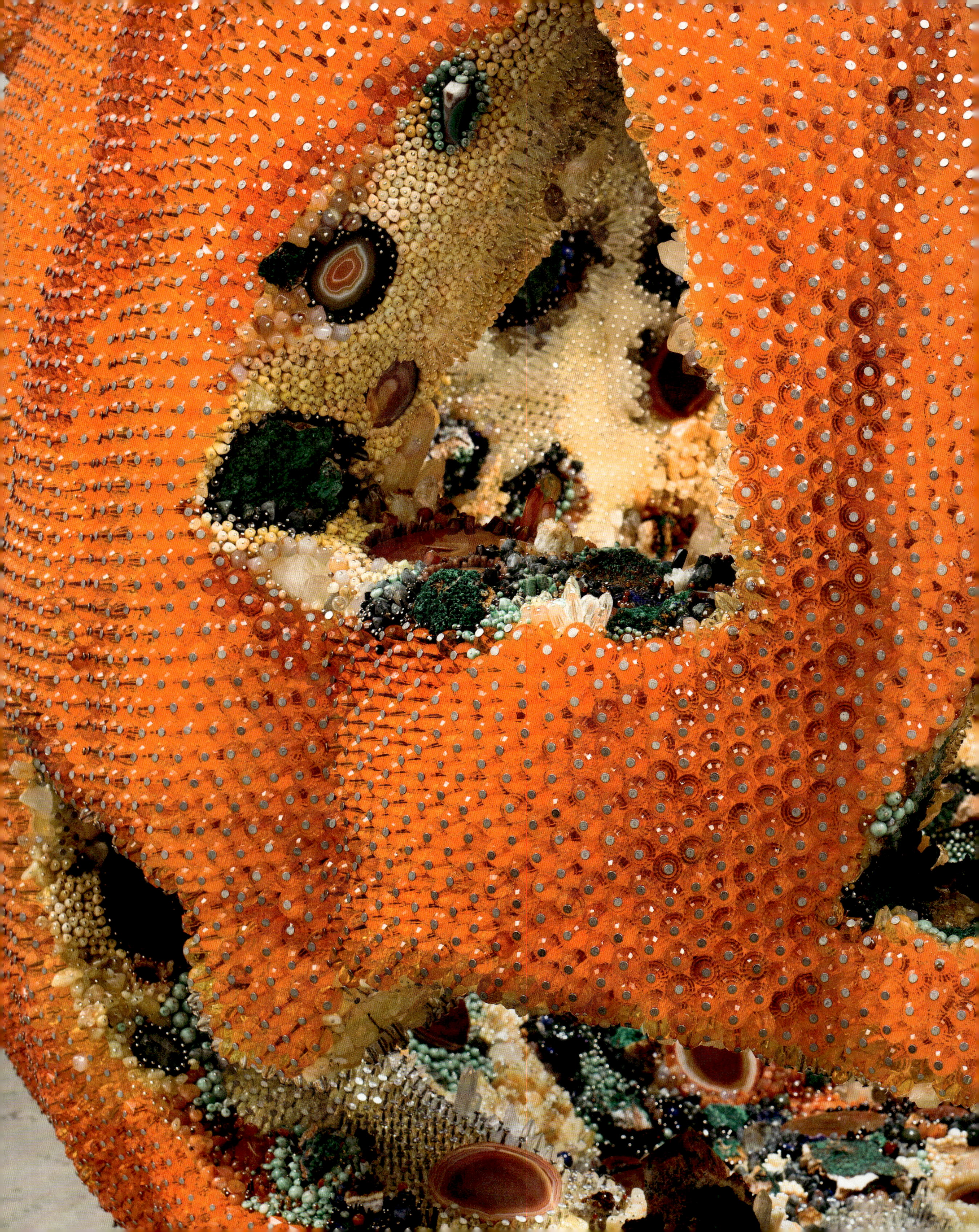

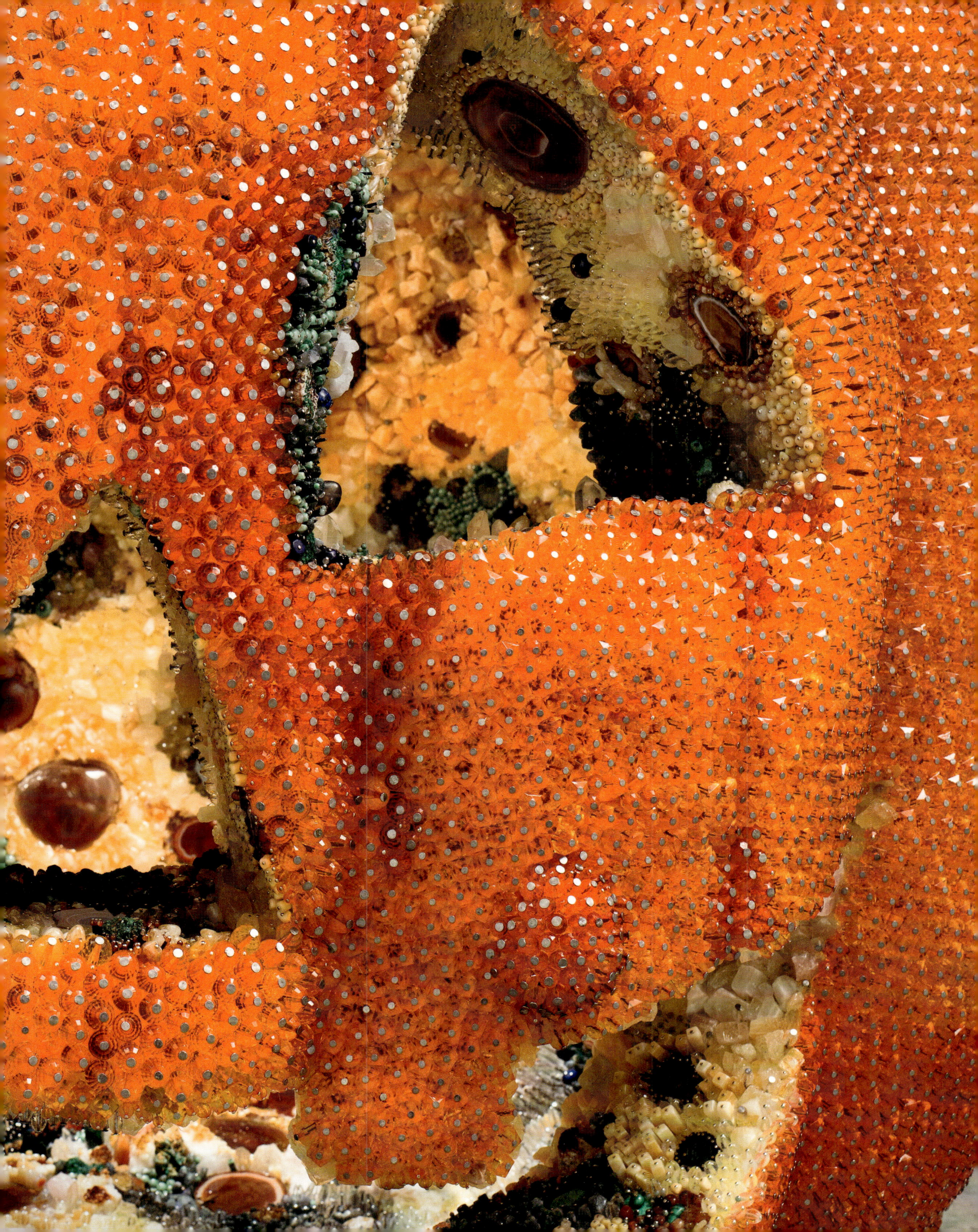

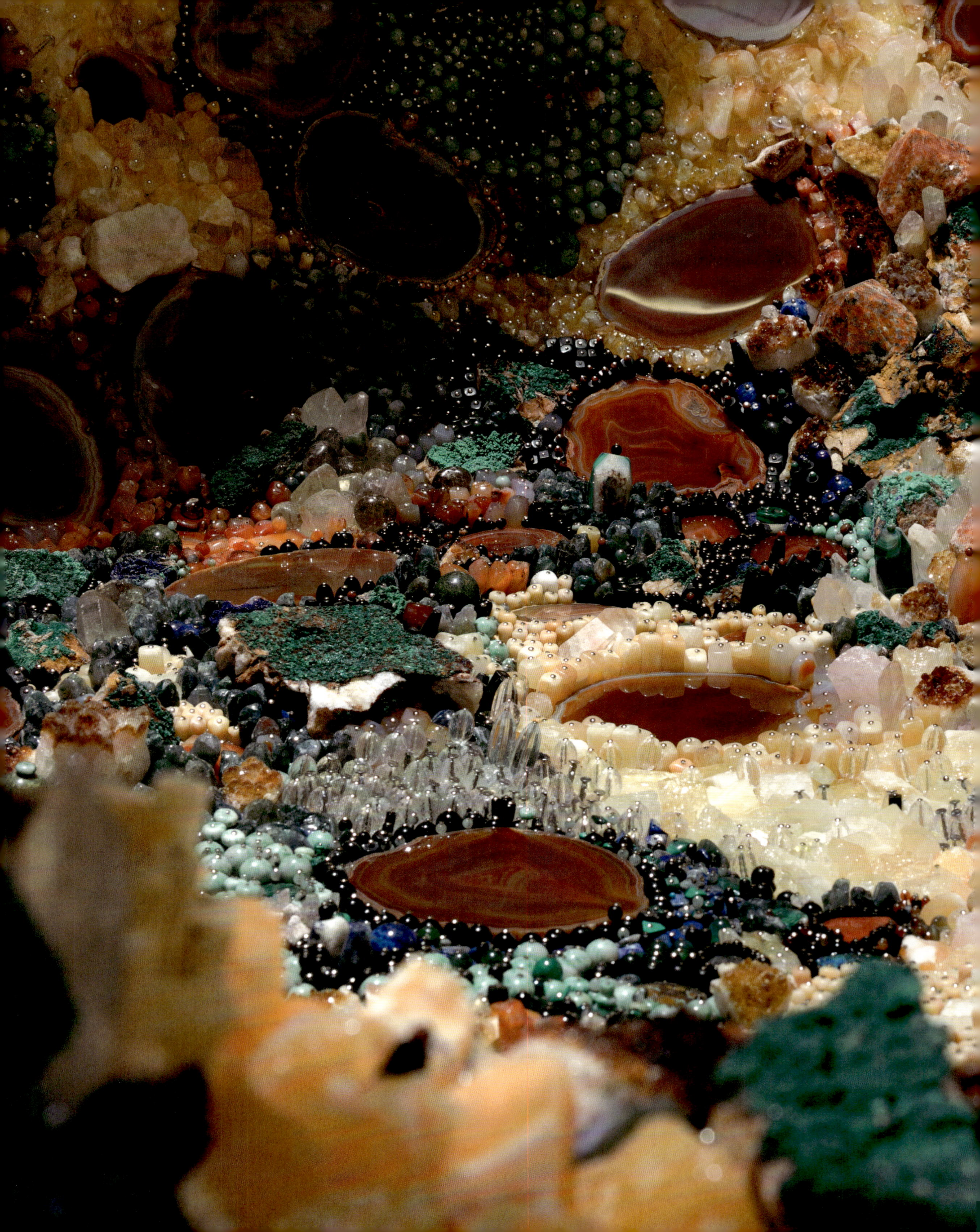

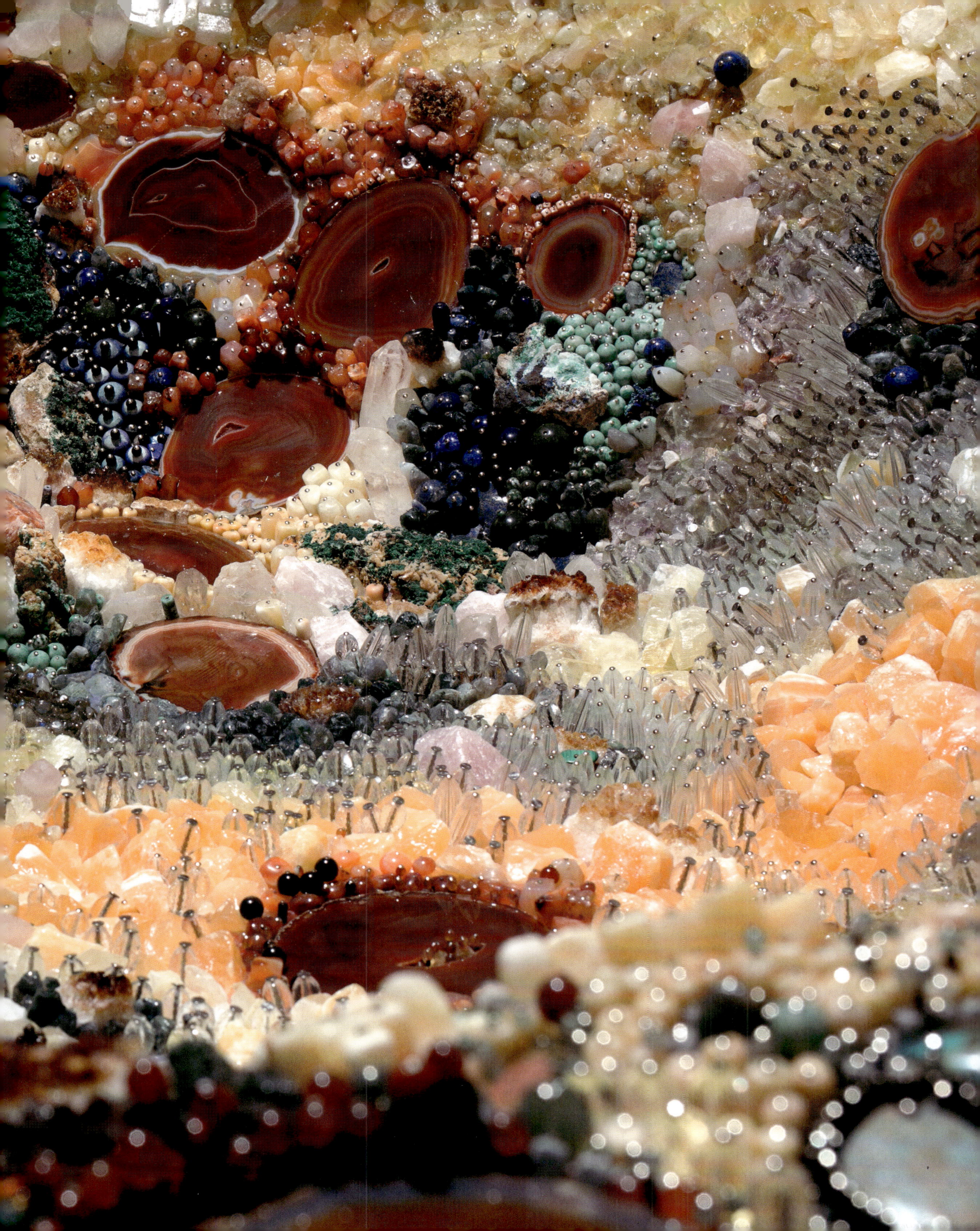

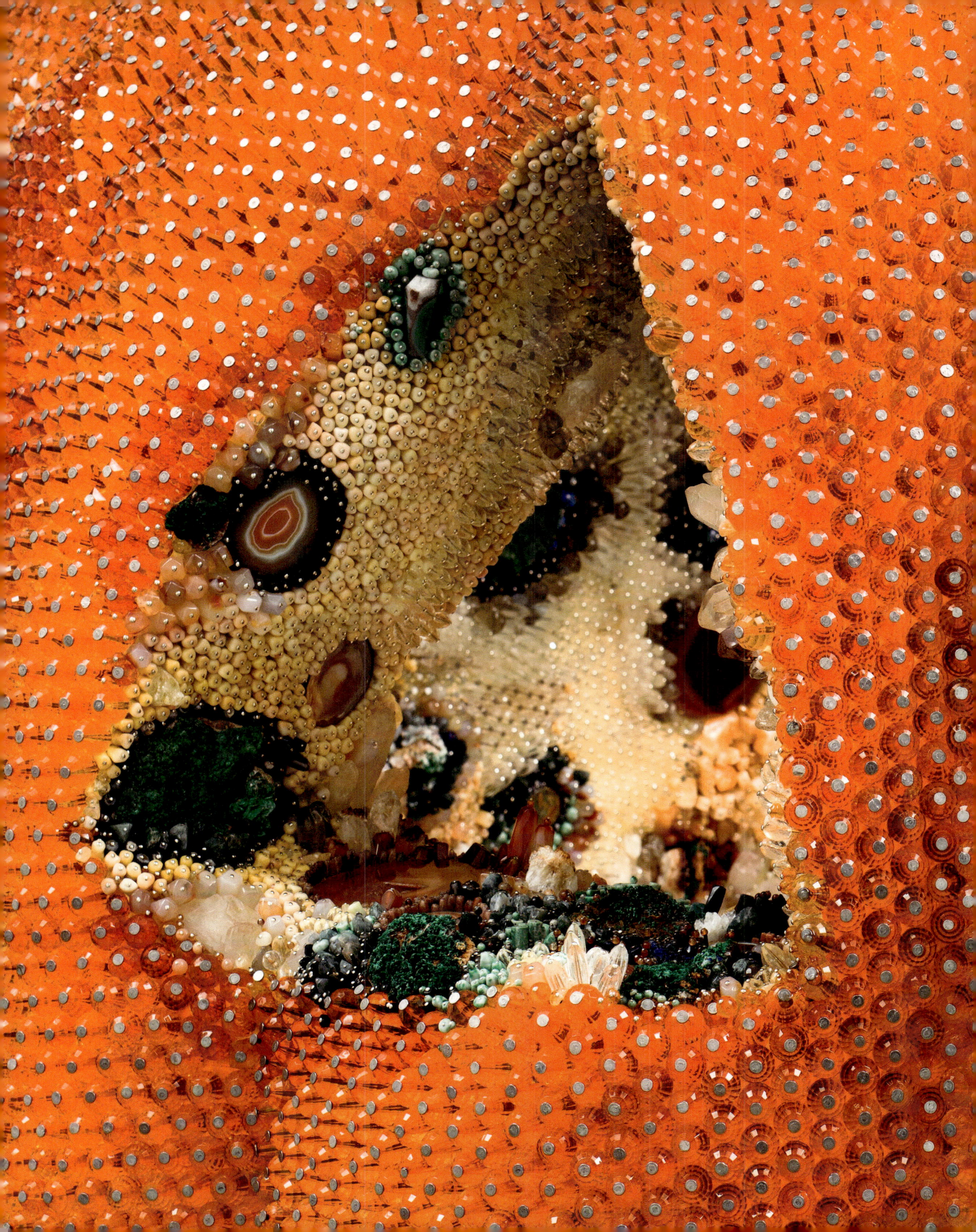

Bad Cherries (Shirley Temple), 2020

Carnelian, garnet, rhodonite, rhodochrosite, amethyst, marble, agate, moss agate, lava rock, red aventurine, flower amazonite, brecciated jasper, hessonite, pink opal, tiger eye, glass, steel pins on coated polystyrene, and fishing poles

39 × 23 × 11 inches
99.1 × 58.4 × 27.9 cm

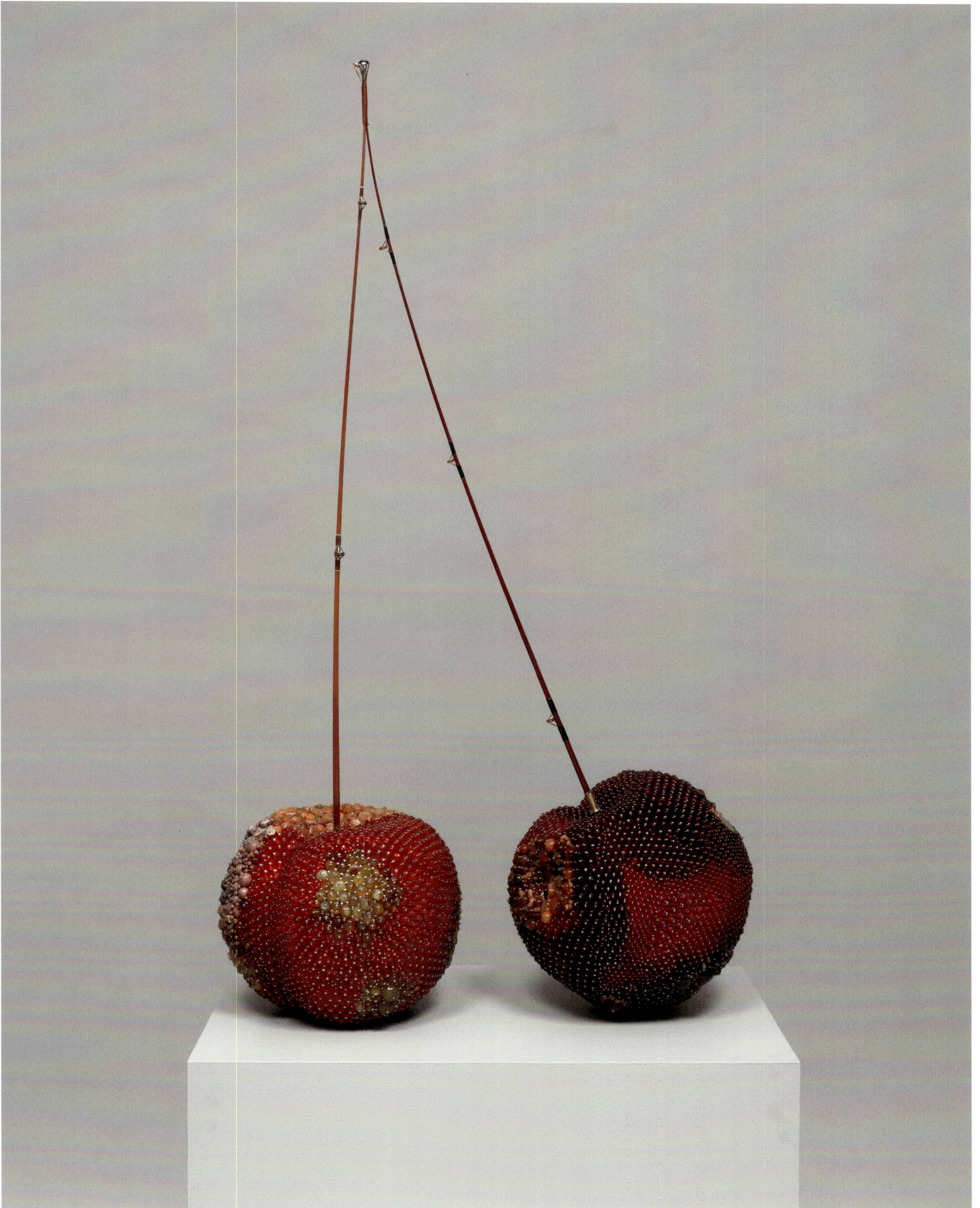

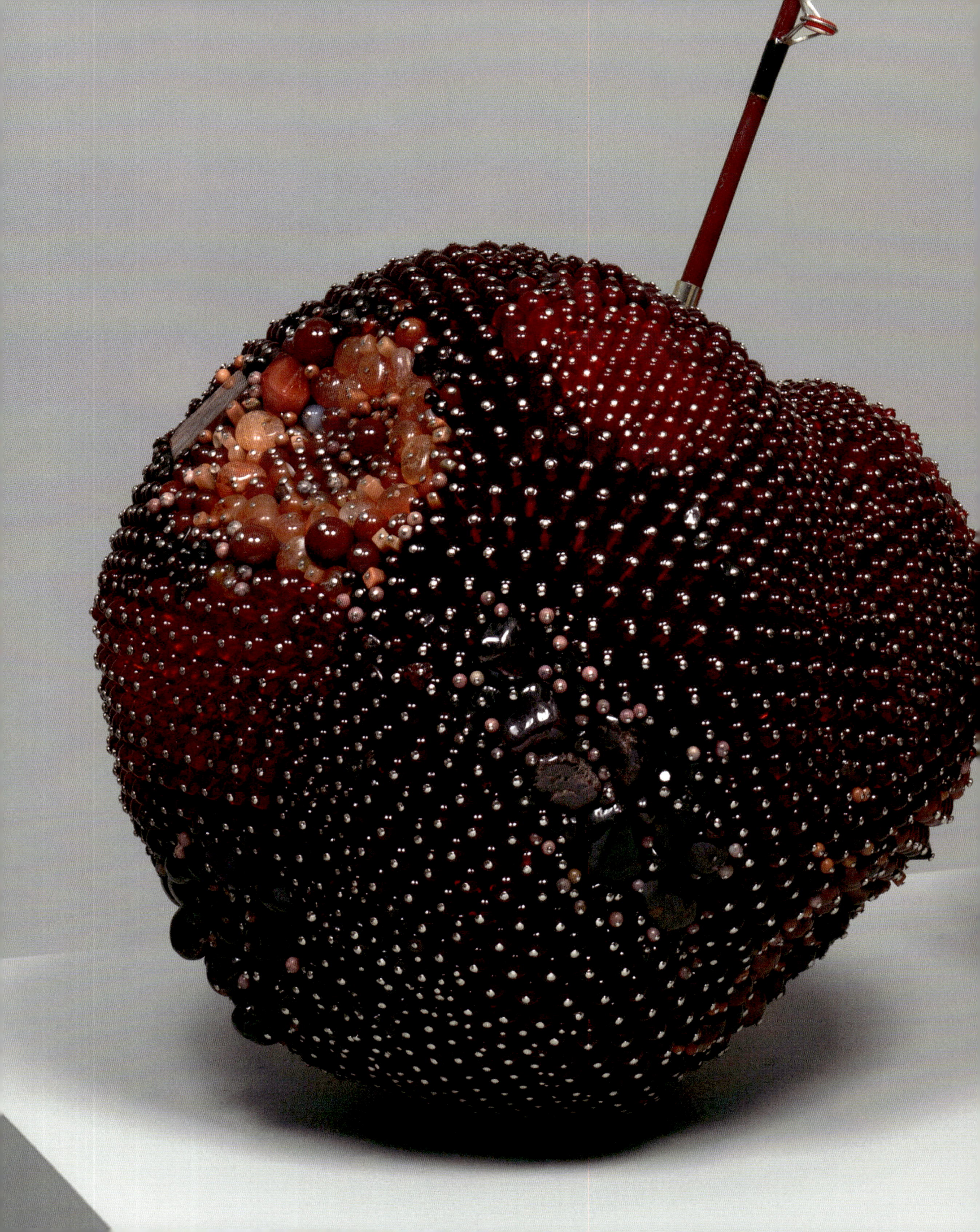

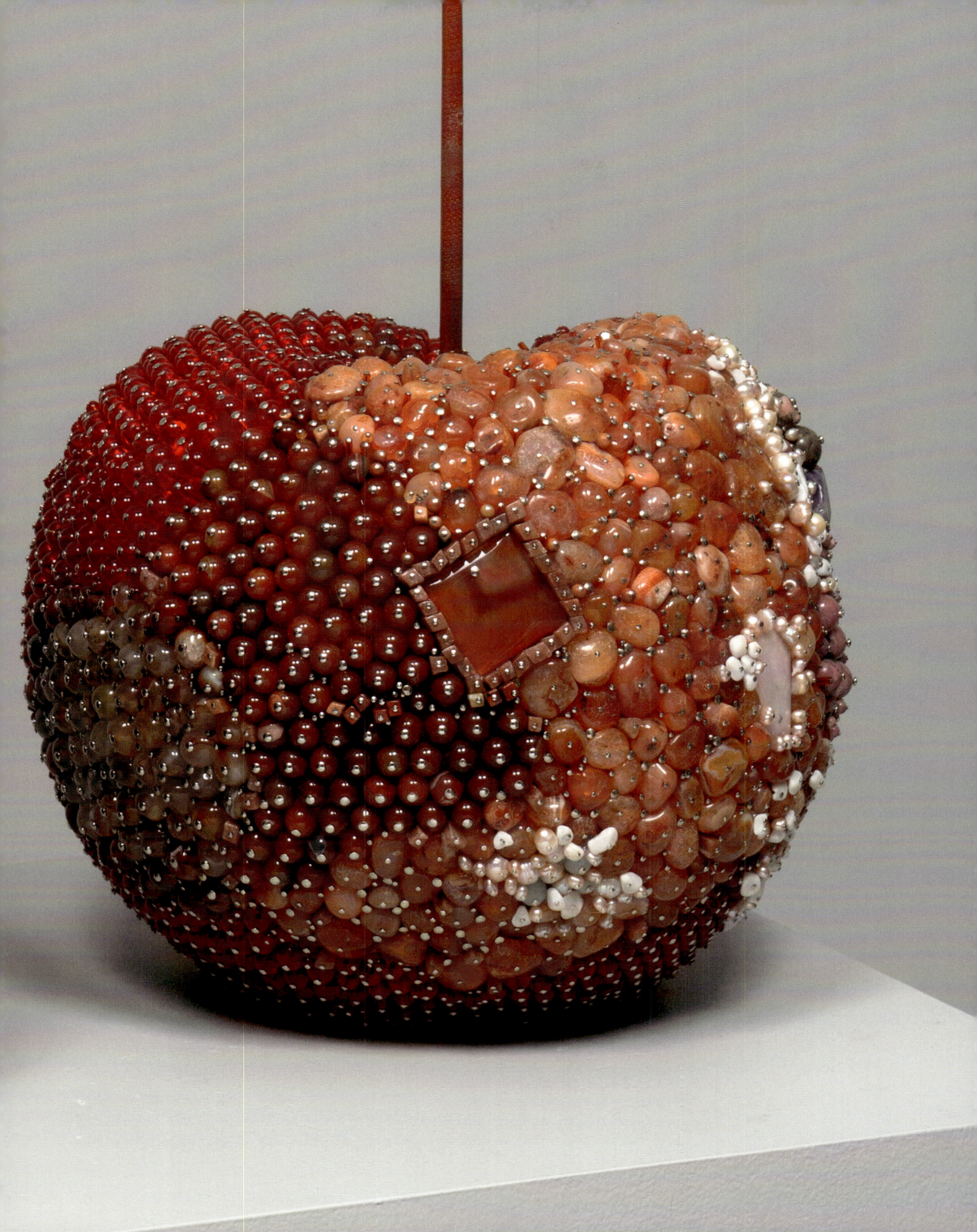

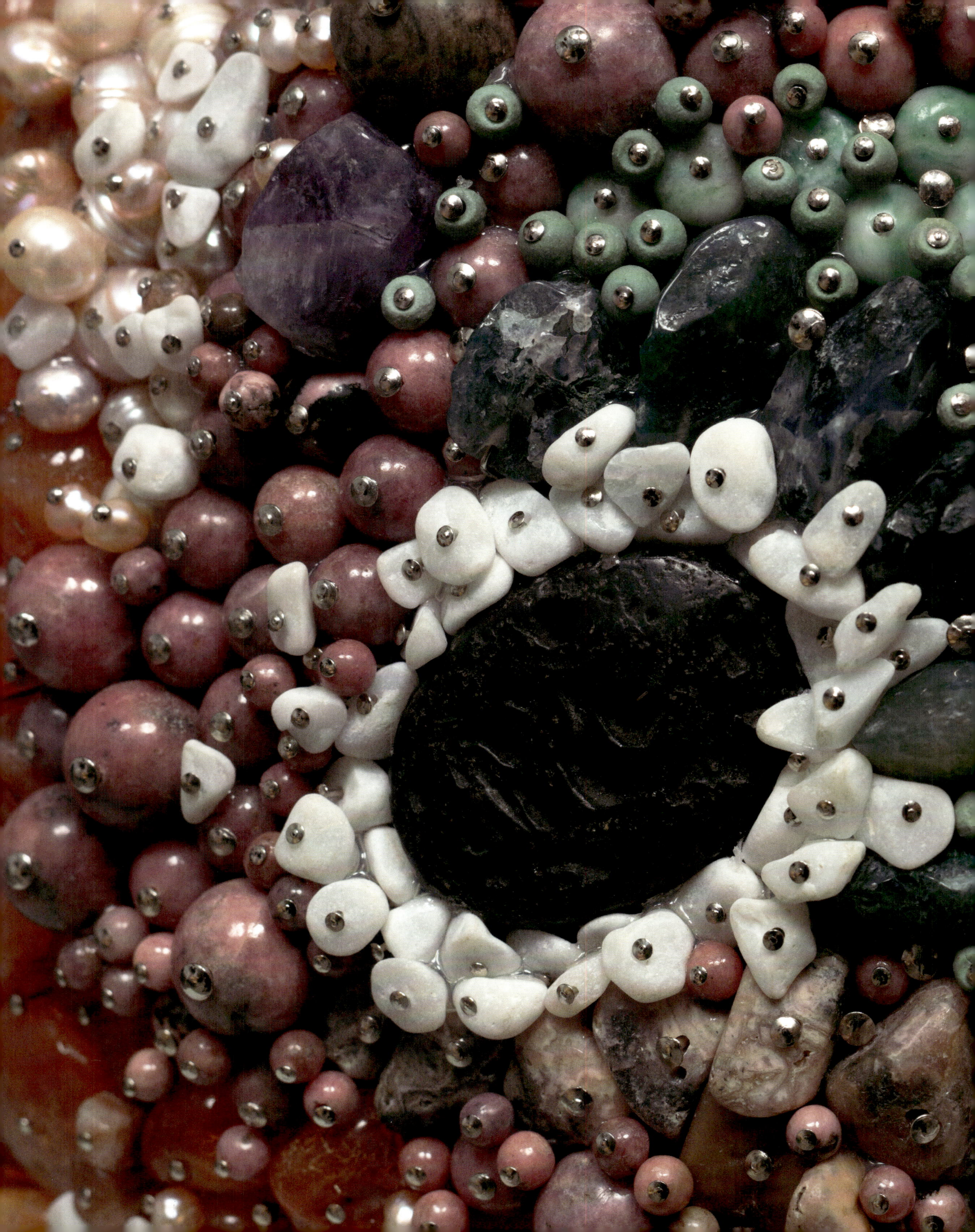

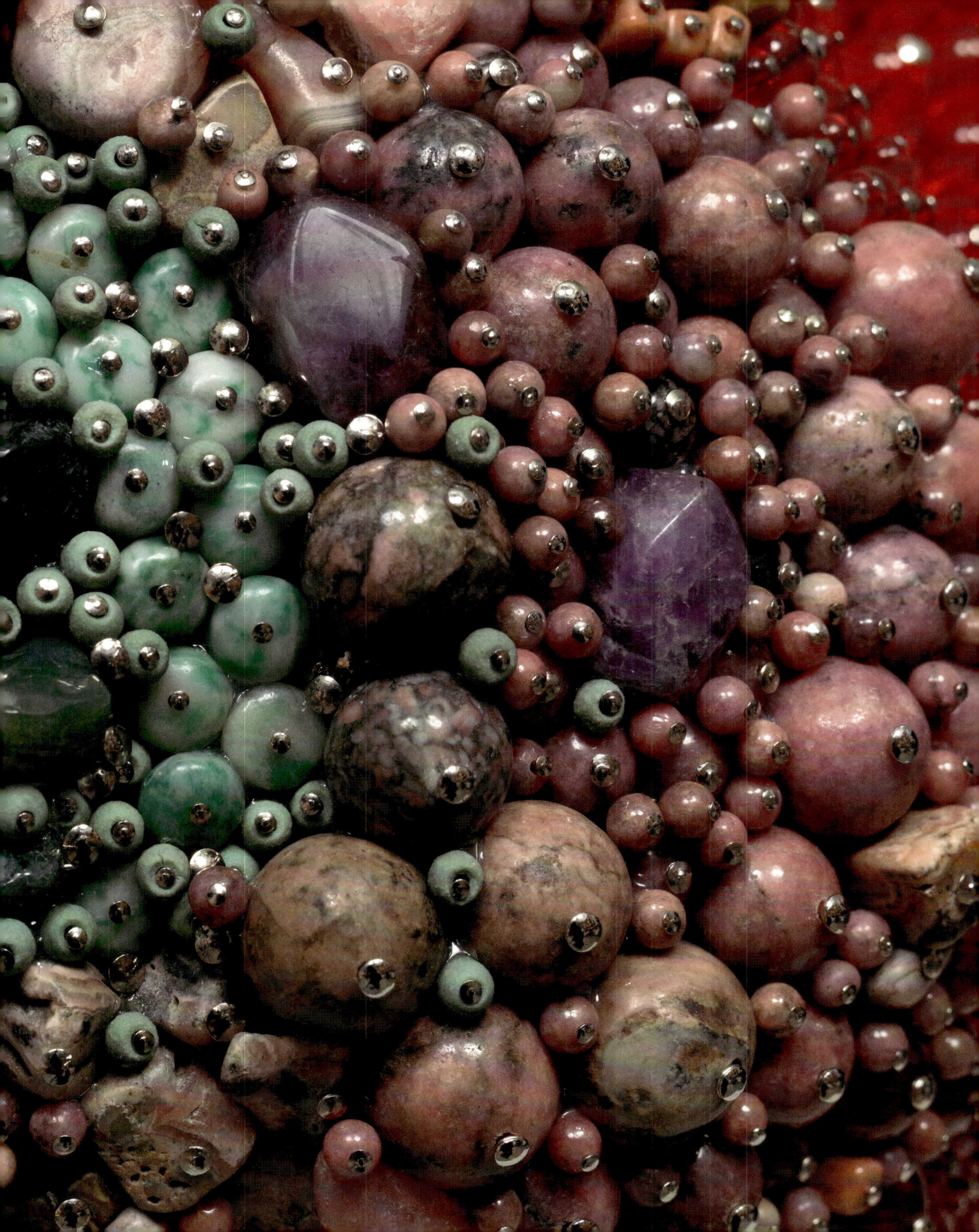

Bad Lemon (Sea Witch), 2020

Aventurine, serpentine, prehnite, chrysoprase, rhyolite, agate, moss agate, jasper, peridot, moonstone, magnesite, lilac stone, turquoise, citrine, calcite, feldspar, ruby in zoisite, labradorite, Swarovski crystal, quartz, mother of pearl, freshwater pearls, glass, and steel pins on coated polystyrene

16½ × 18 × 20 inches
41.9 × 45.7 × 50.8 cm

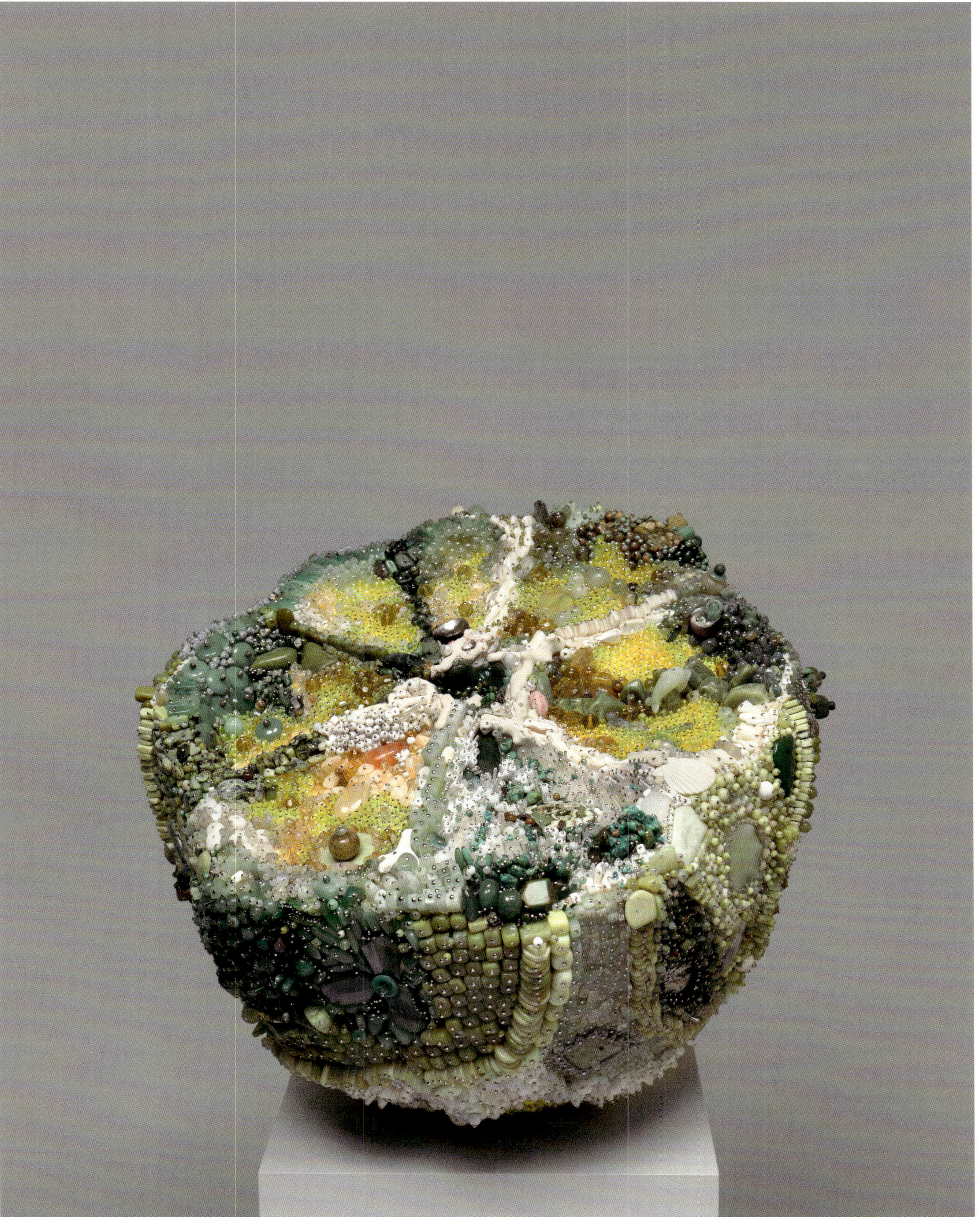

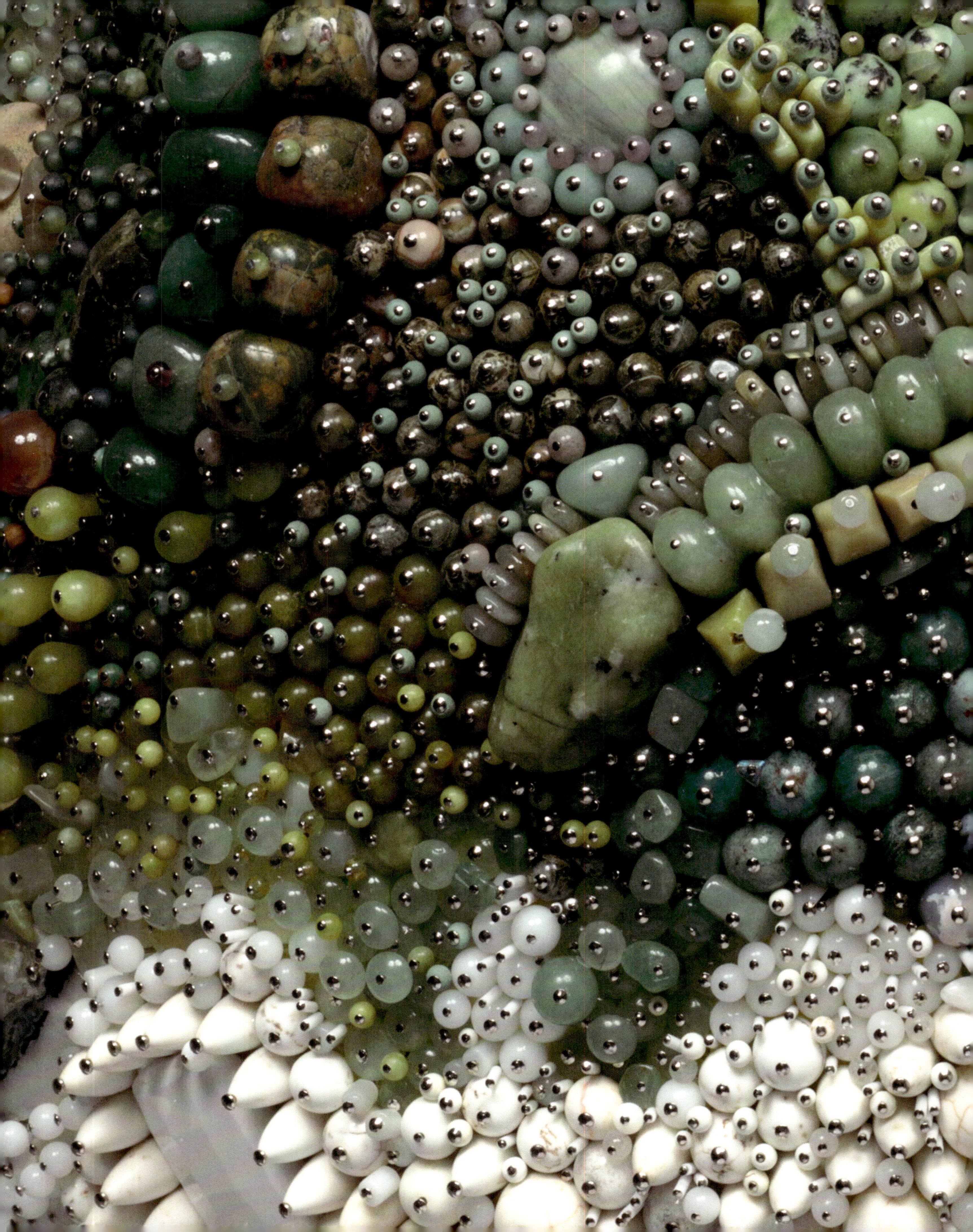

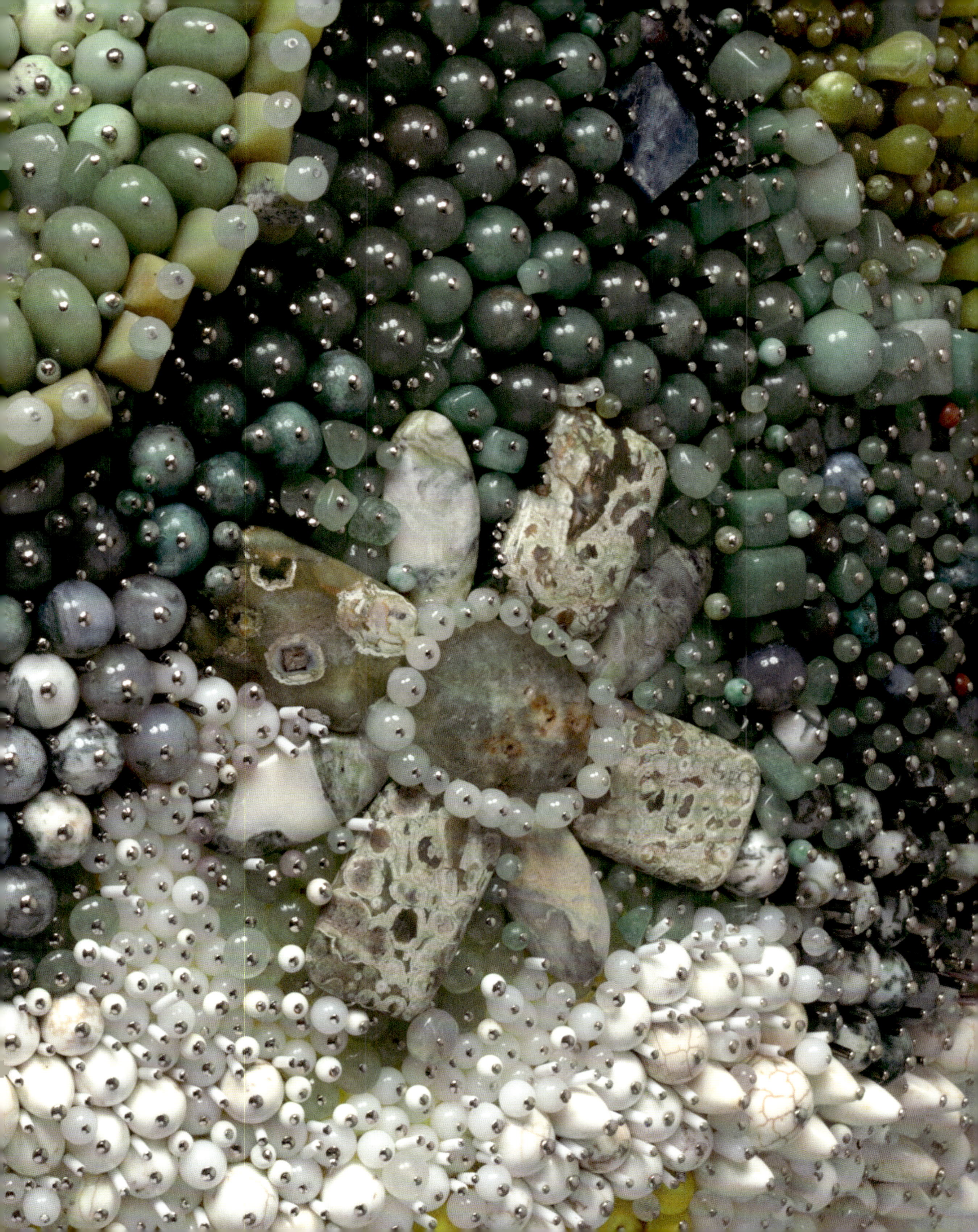

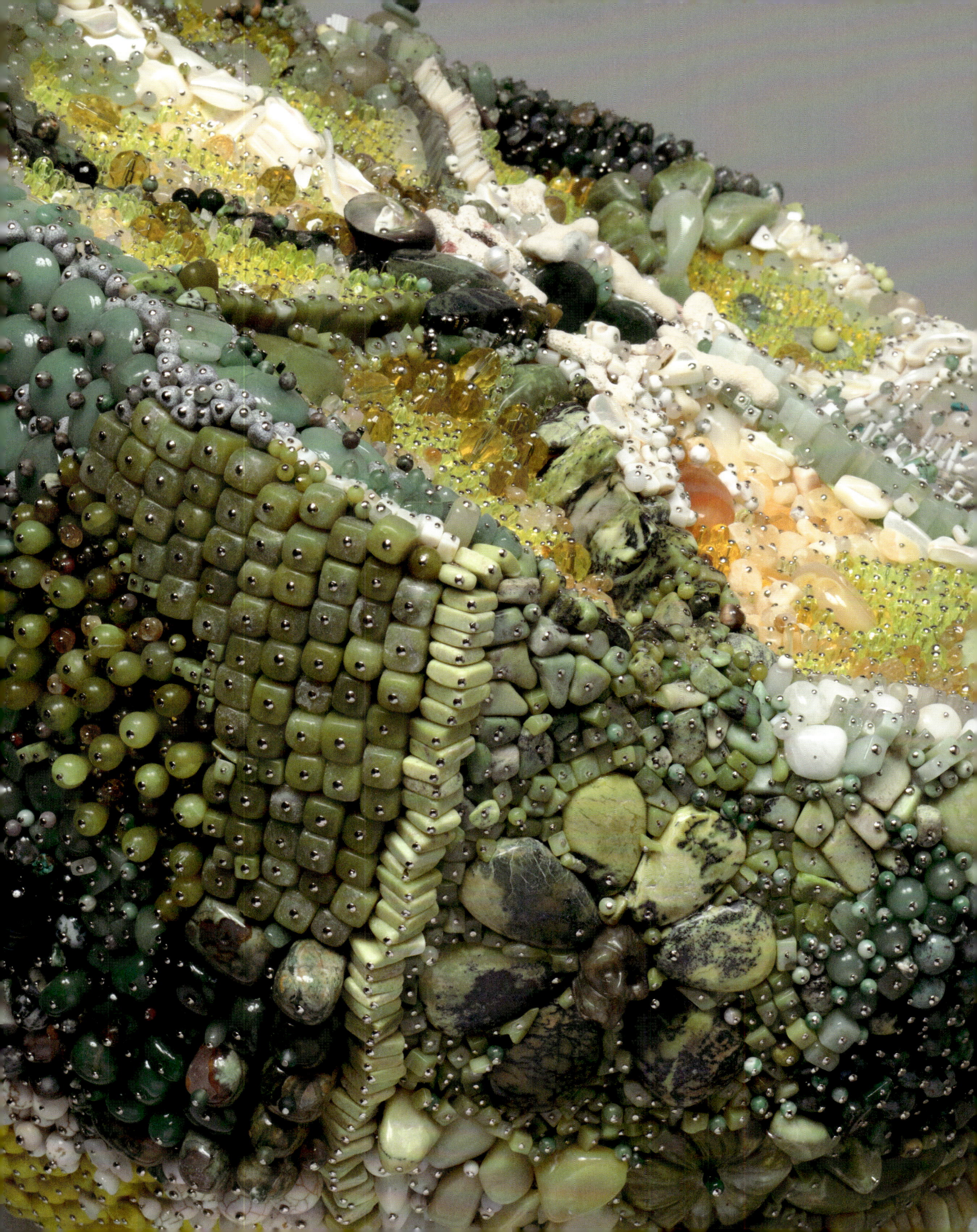

Bad Cherries (Twins), 2021

Freshwater pearl, magnesite, quartz, moonstone, agate, turquoise, lapis lazuli, amazonite, garnet, citrine, serpentine, jasper, limestone, rose quartz, unakite, rhodonite, pink opal, calcite, glass, steel pins on coated polystyrene, fishing poles, and lead sinkers

36½ × 49 × 16 inches
93 × 125 × 41 cm

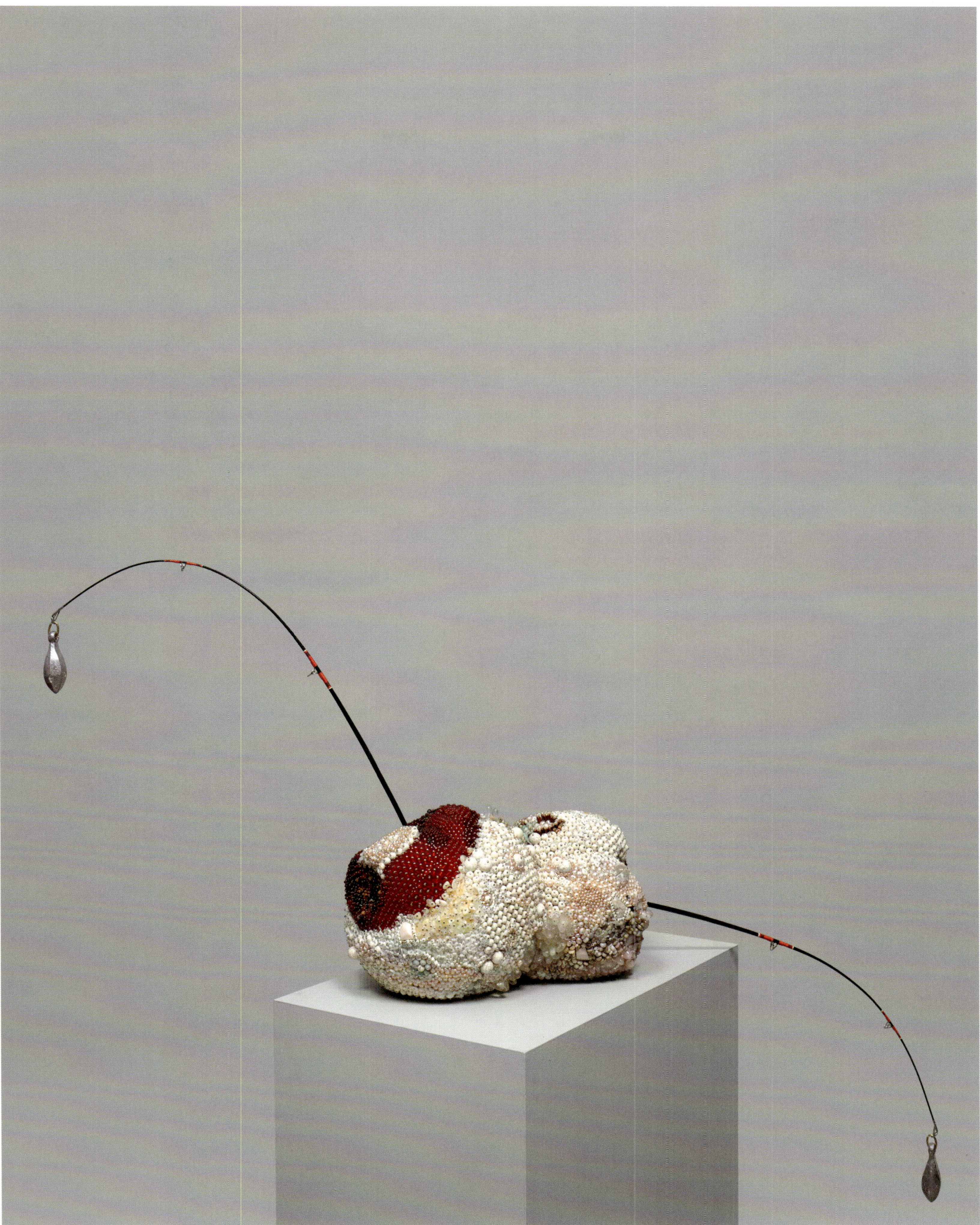

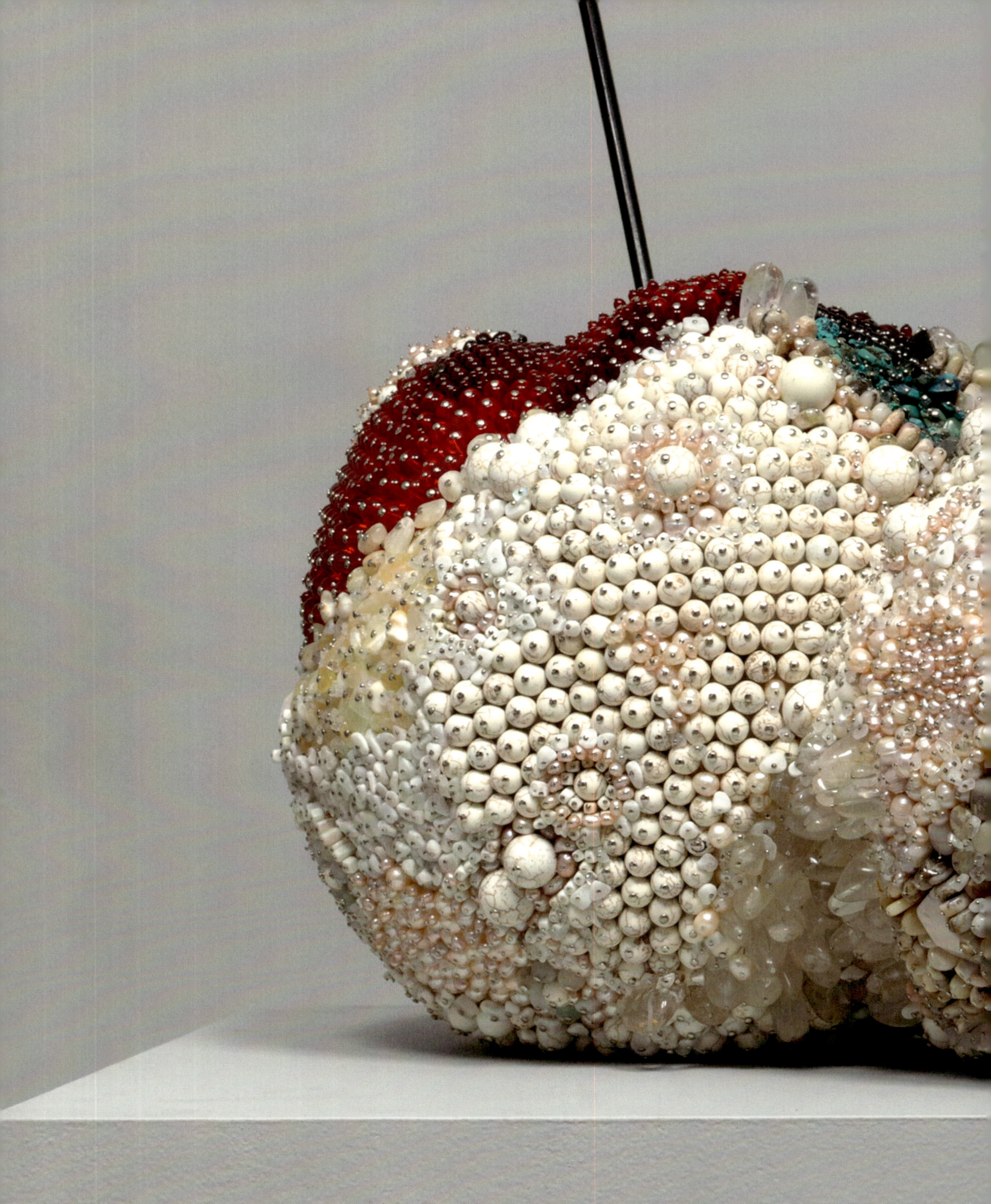

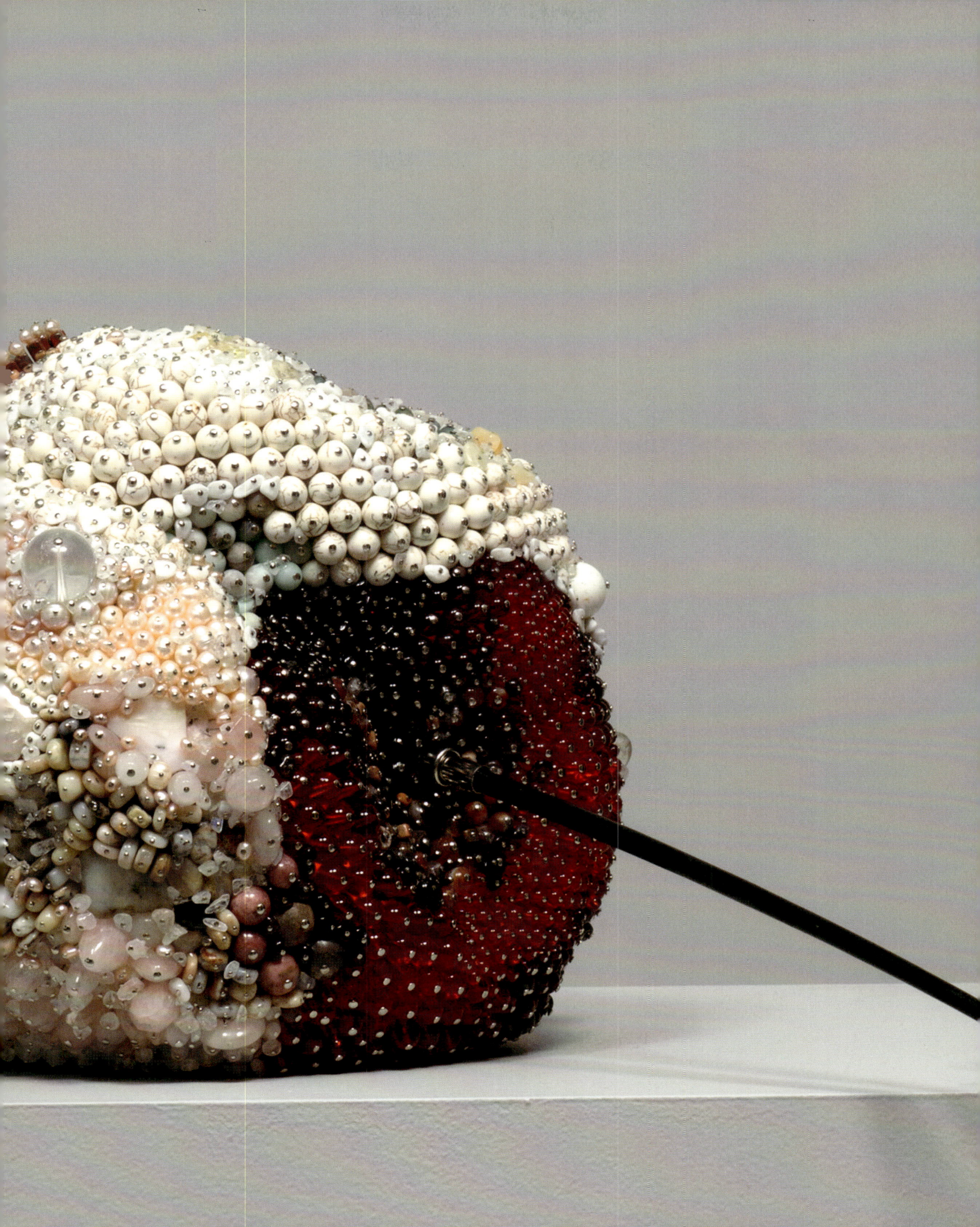

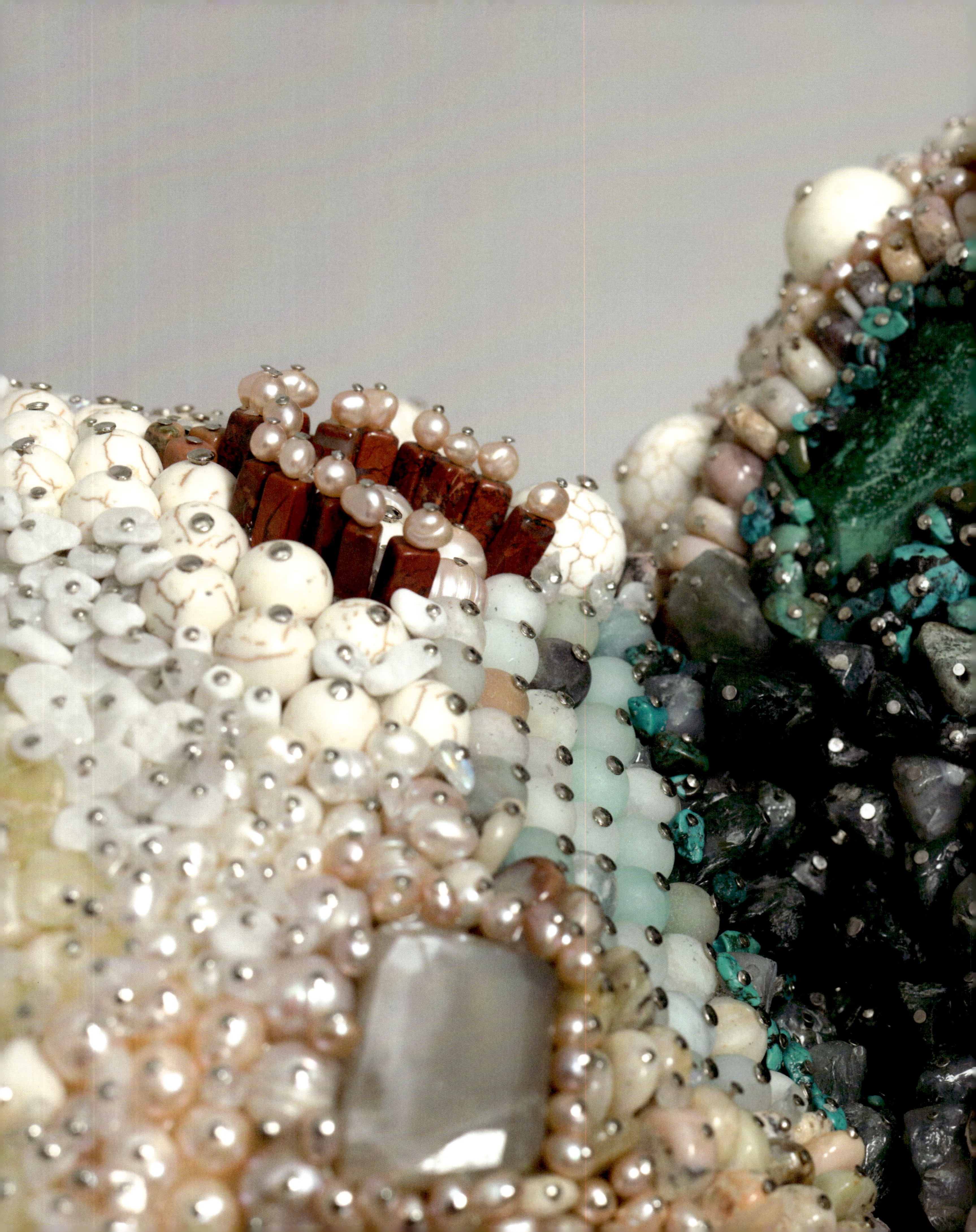

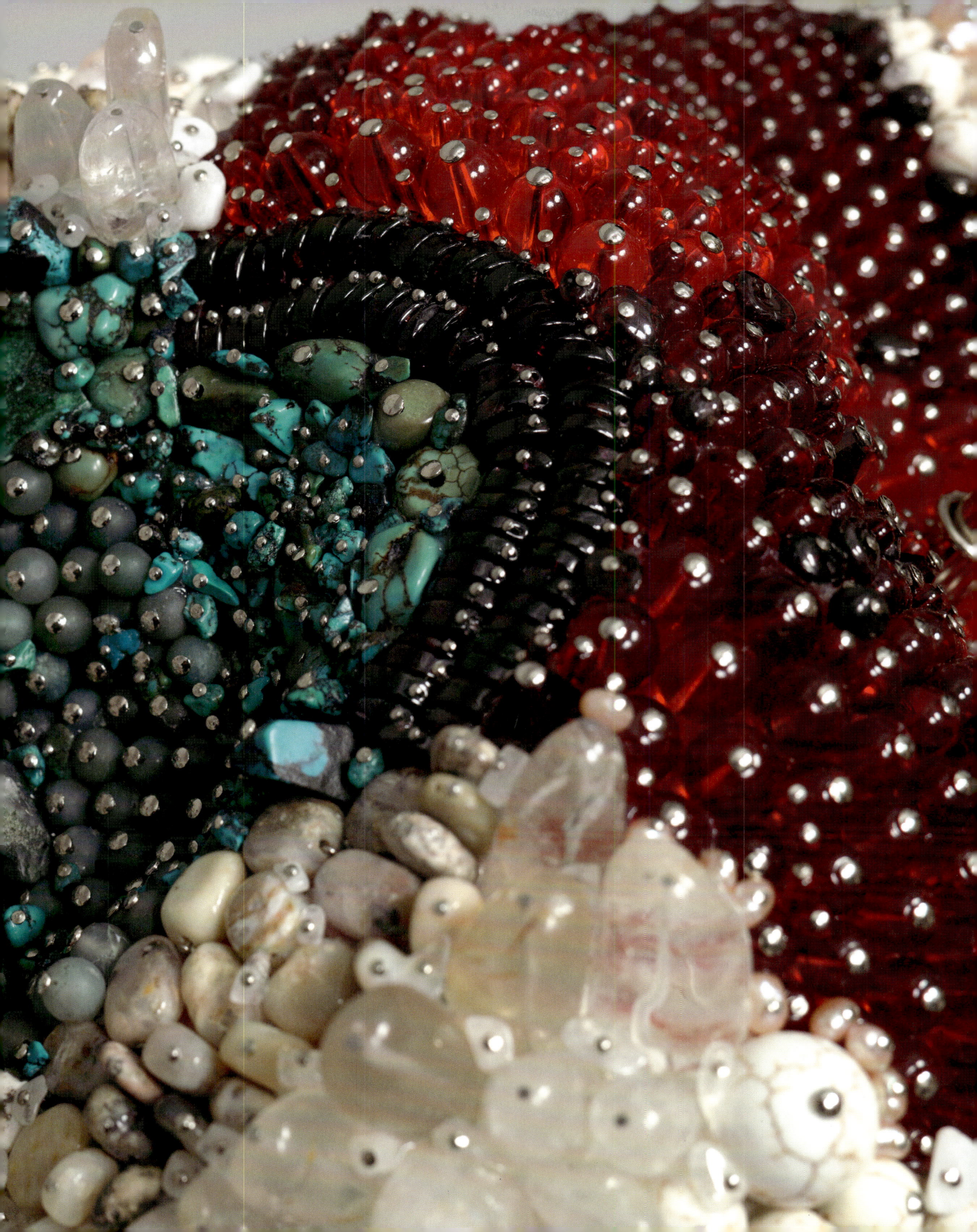

Bad Lemon (Armadillo), 2021

Tiger eye, tektite, limestone, agate, amber, lava rock, turquoise, magnesite, carnelian, serpentine, garnet, citrine, brecciated jasper, tigerskin jasper, unakite, moonstone, pyrite, mother of pearl, black turban shell, horn, acrylic, glass, and steel pins on coated polystyrene

21½ × 28 × 18 inches
55 × 71 × 46 cm

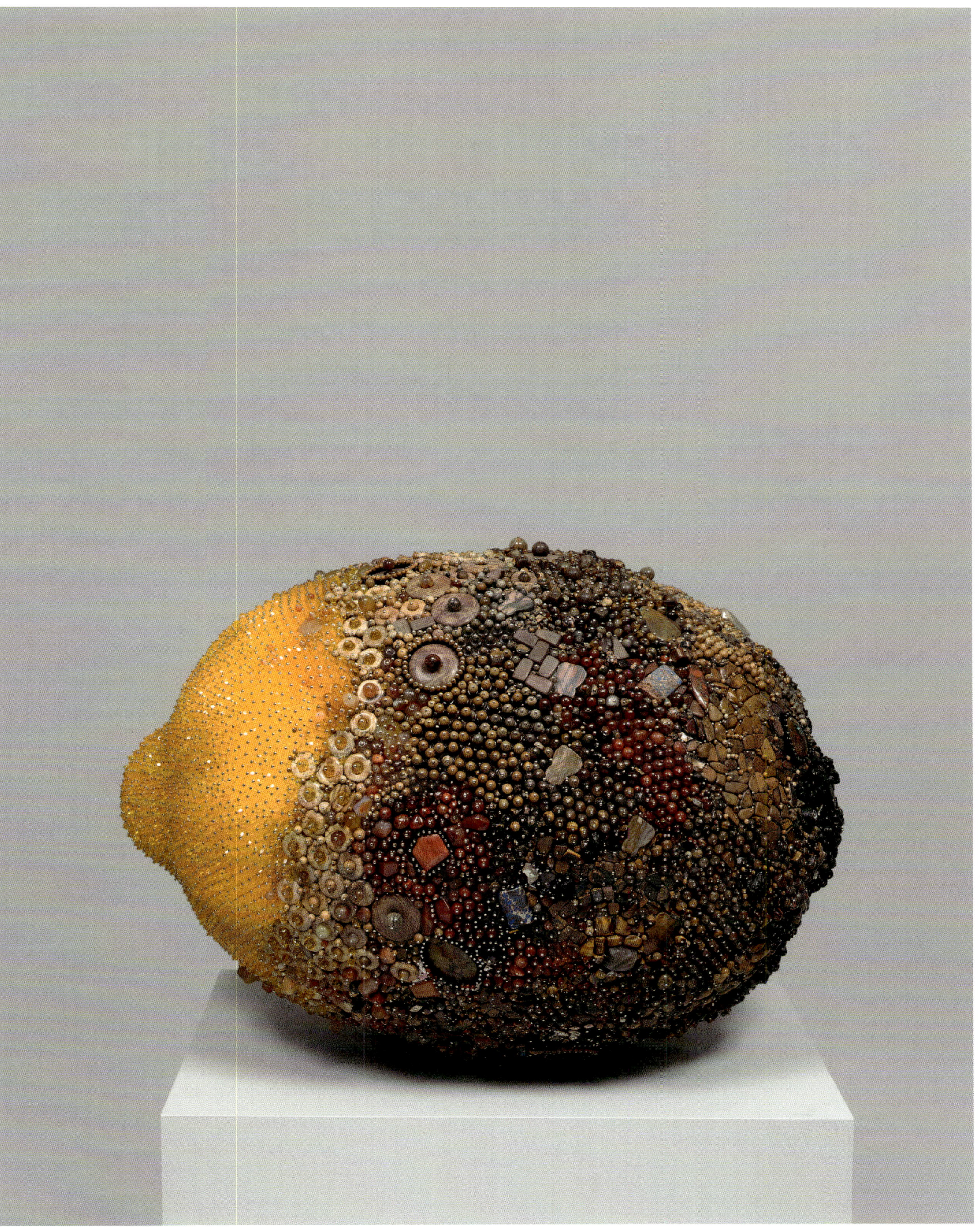

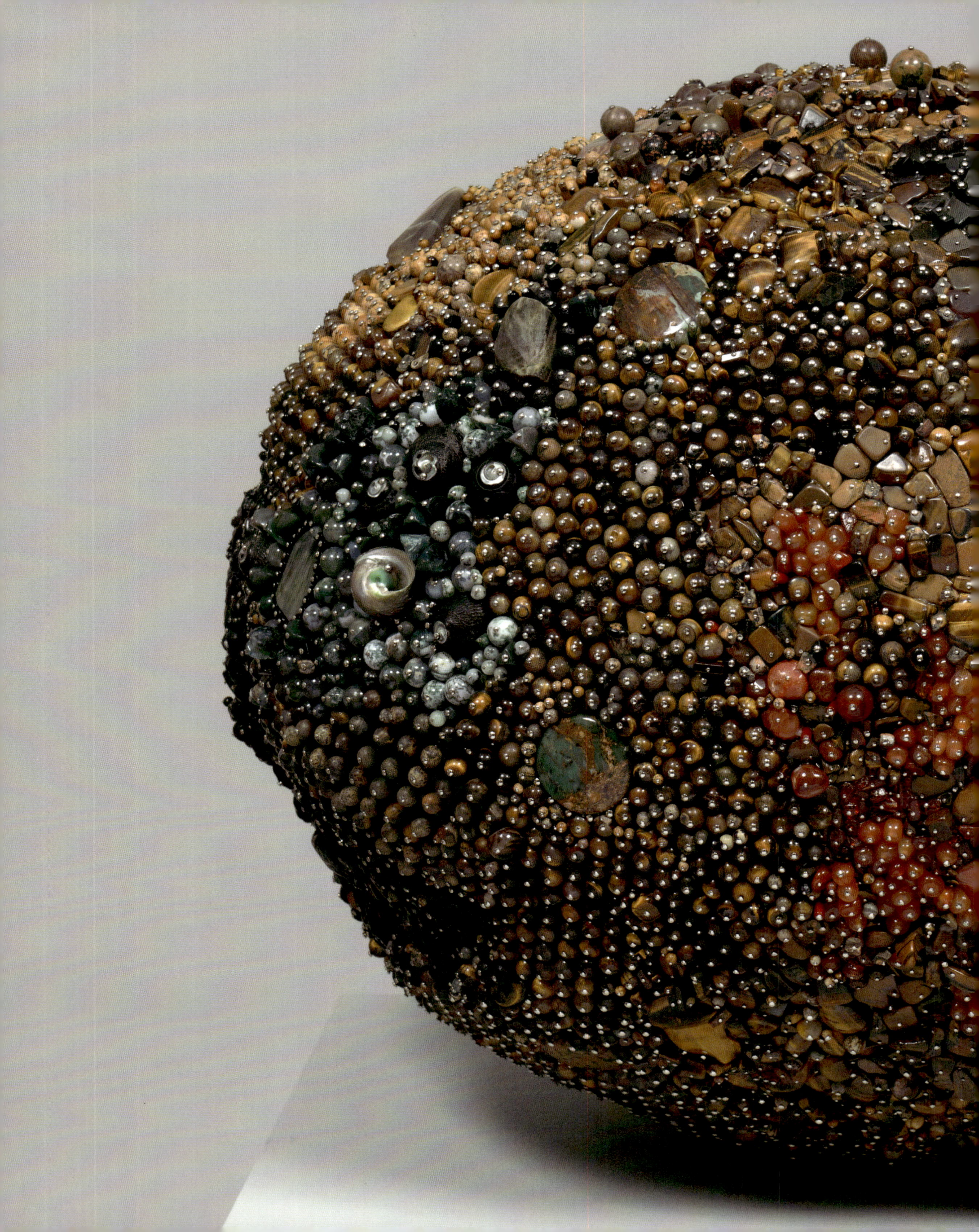

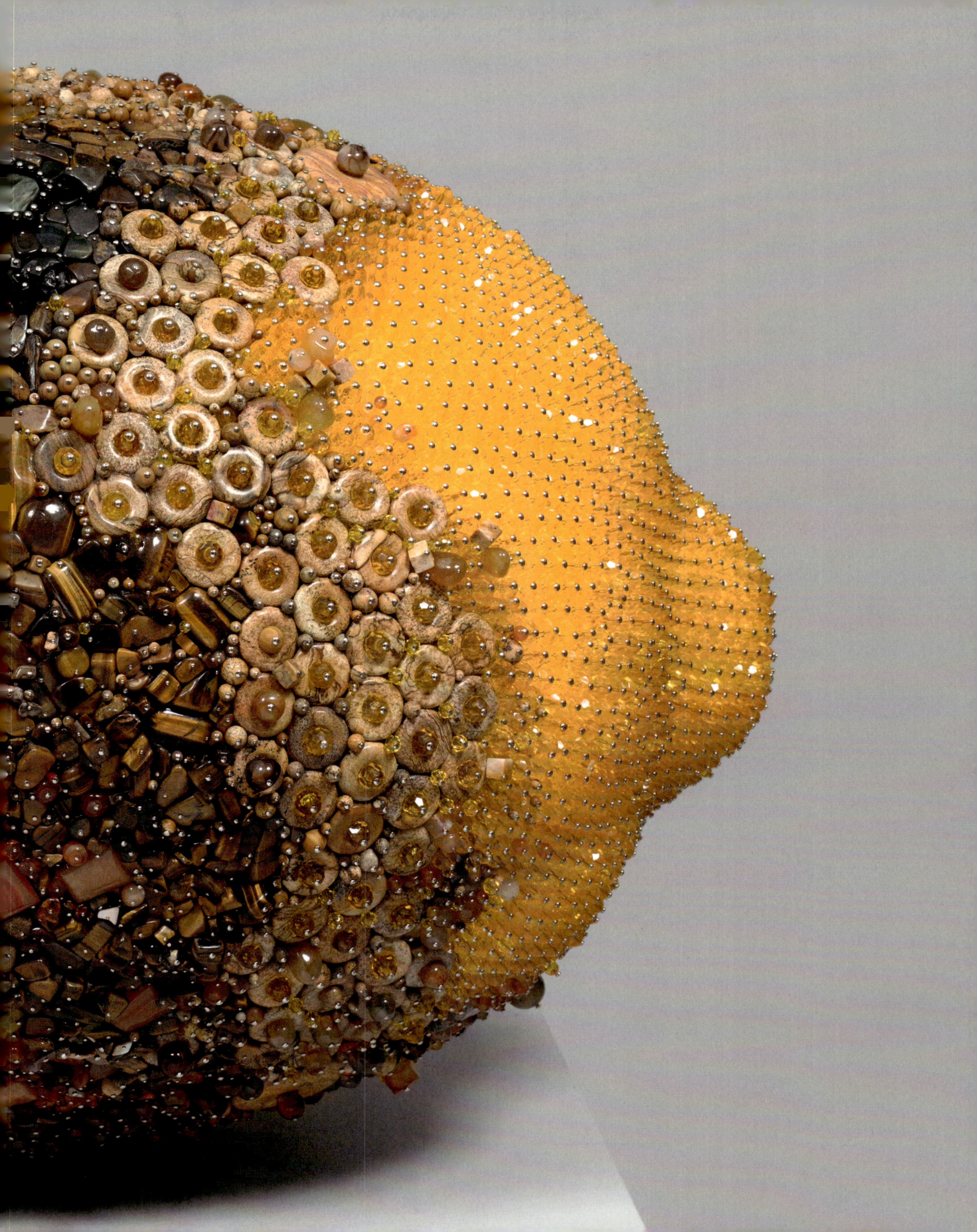

Bad Cherry (Junior), 2021

Garnet, aventurine, rhodonite, serpentine, quartz, marble, agate, pink opal, amazonite, jasper, moonstone, carnelian, smoky quartz, limestone, unakite, freshwater pearls, glass, steel pins on coated polystyrene, fishing pole, and lead sinker

32½ × 23½ × 17½ inches
82.6 × 59.7 × 44.5 cm

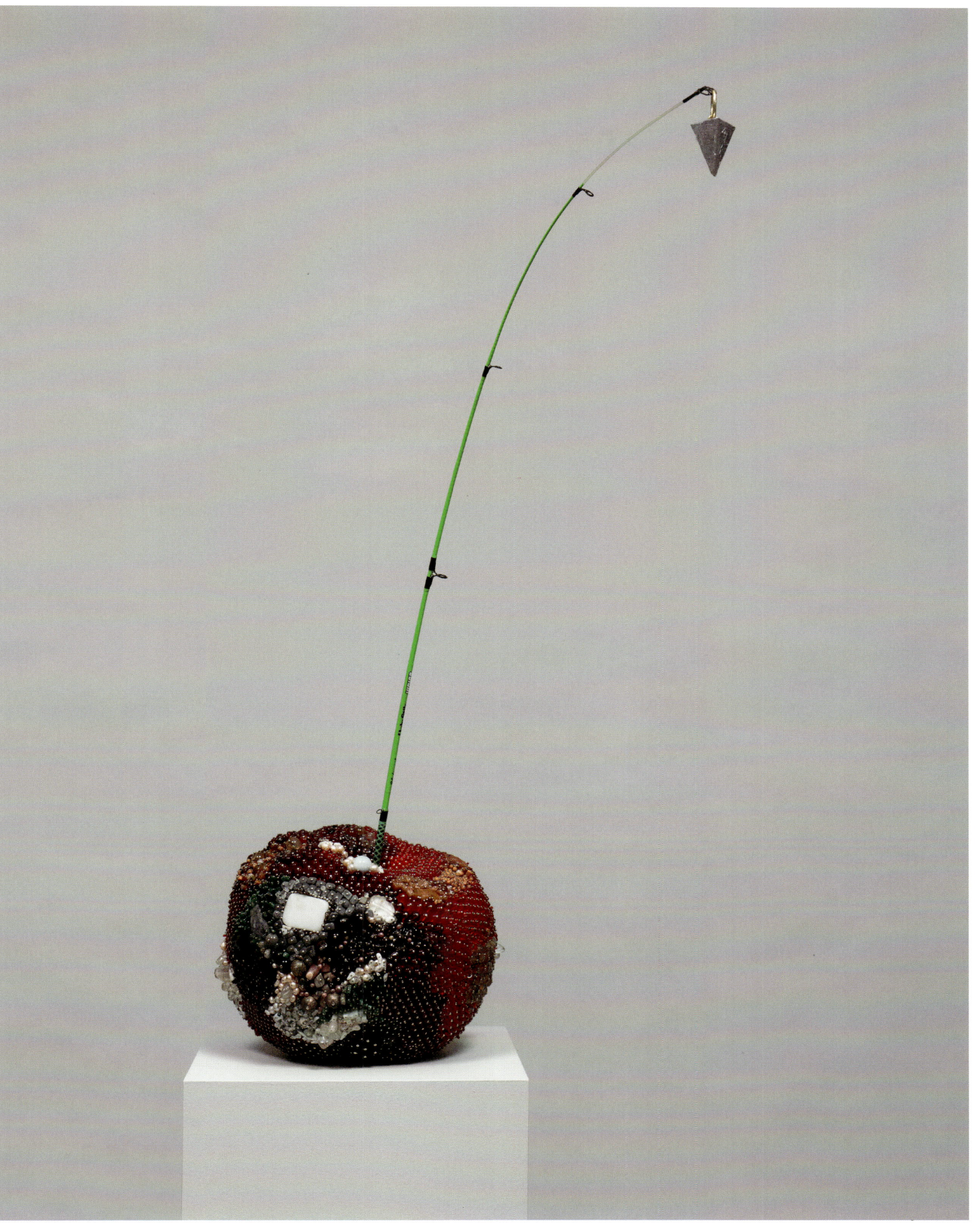

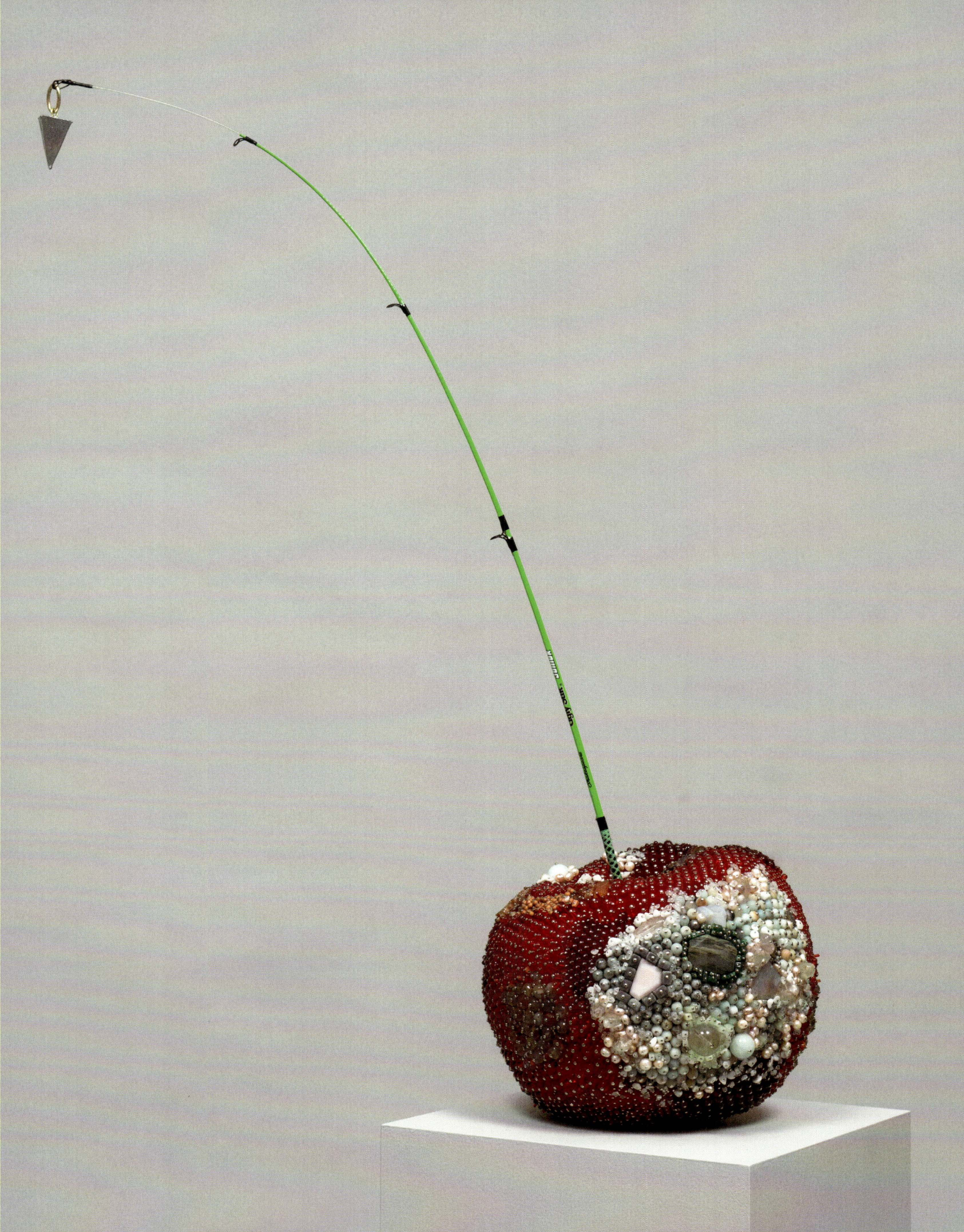

Bad Lemon (Sour Blush), 2020

Aventurine, smoky quartz, rhodonite, calcite, quartz, labradorite, green line jasper, kambaba jasper, pink opal, citrine, amethyst, rose quartz, agate, serpentine, pink lepidolite, malachite, mother of pearl, freshwater pearl, bone, glass, acrylic, and steel pins on coated polystyrene

19½ × 28 × 18½ inches
49.5 × 71.1 × 47 cm

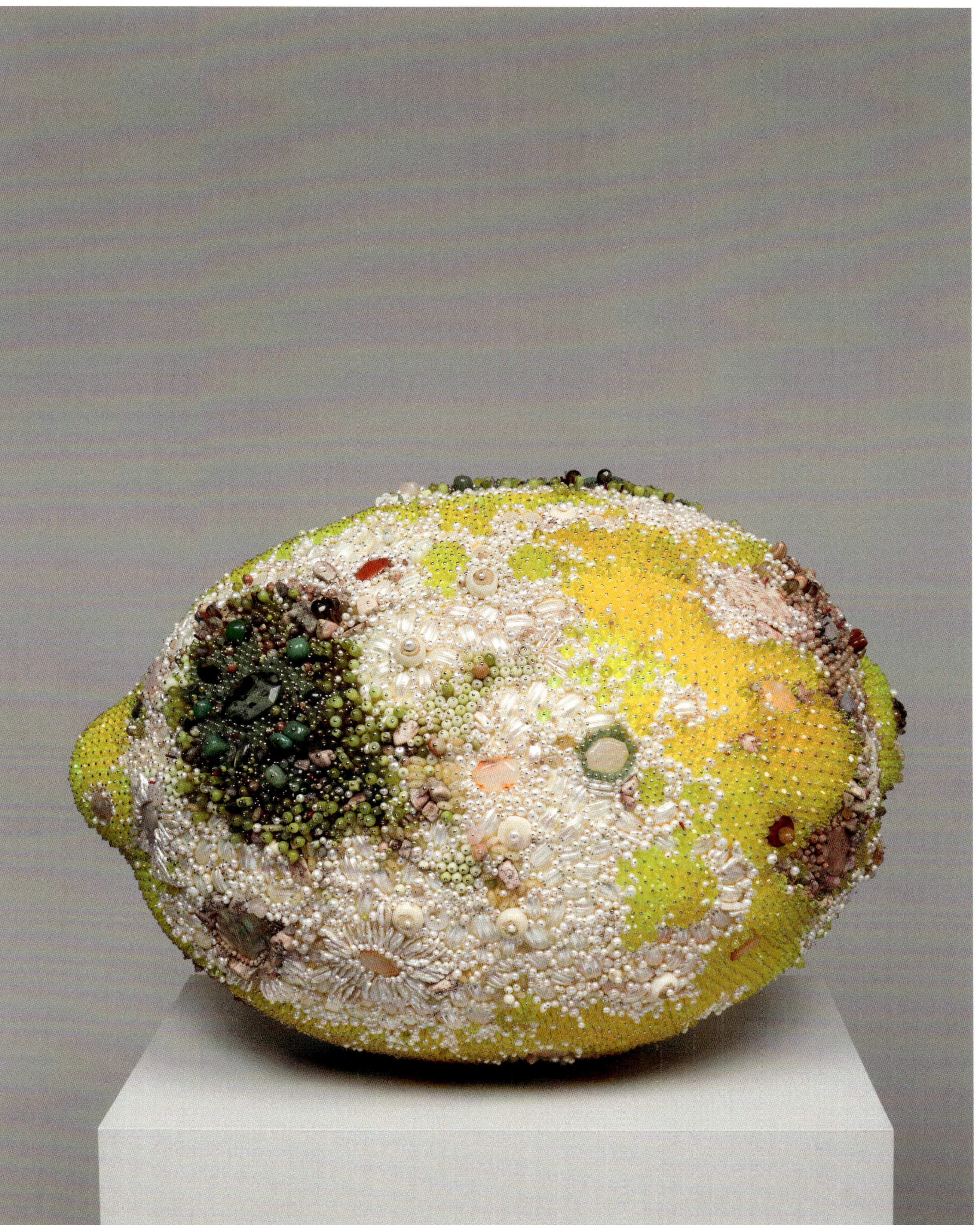

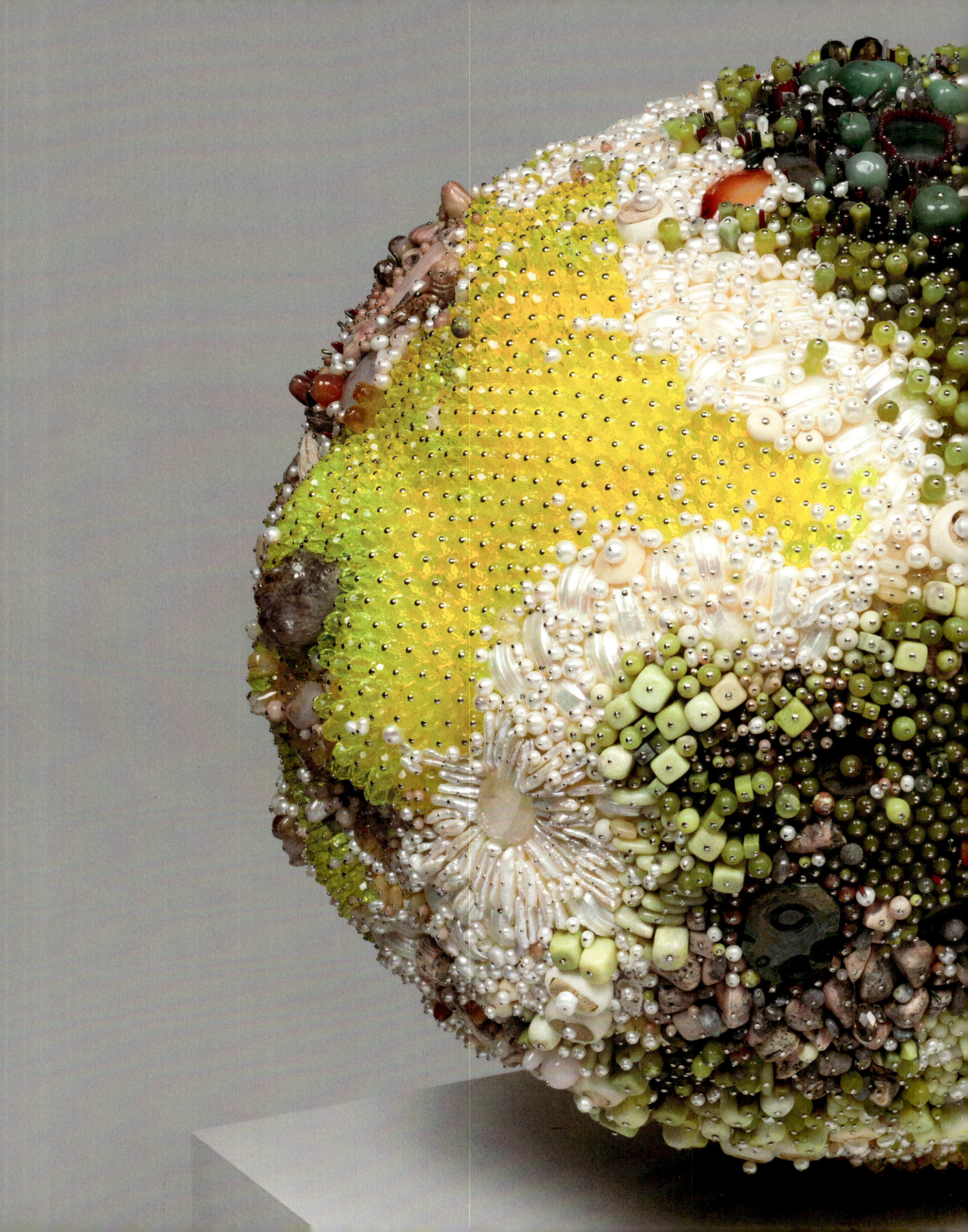

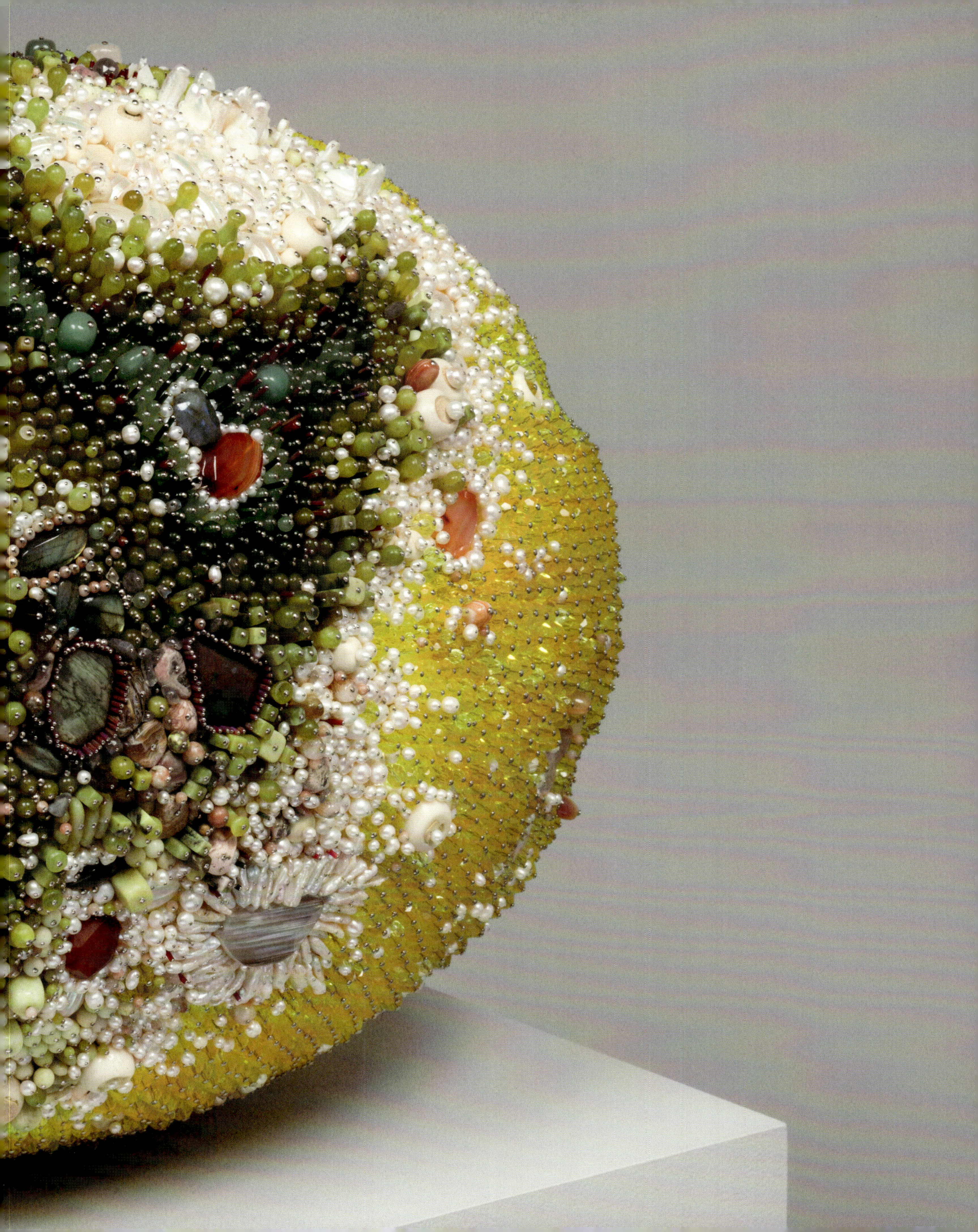

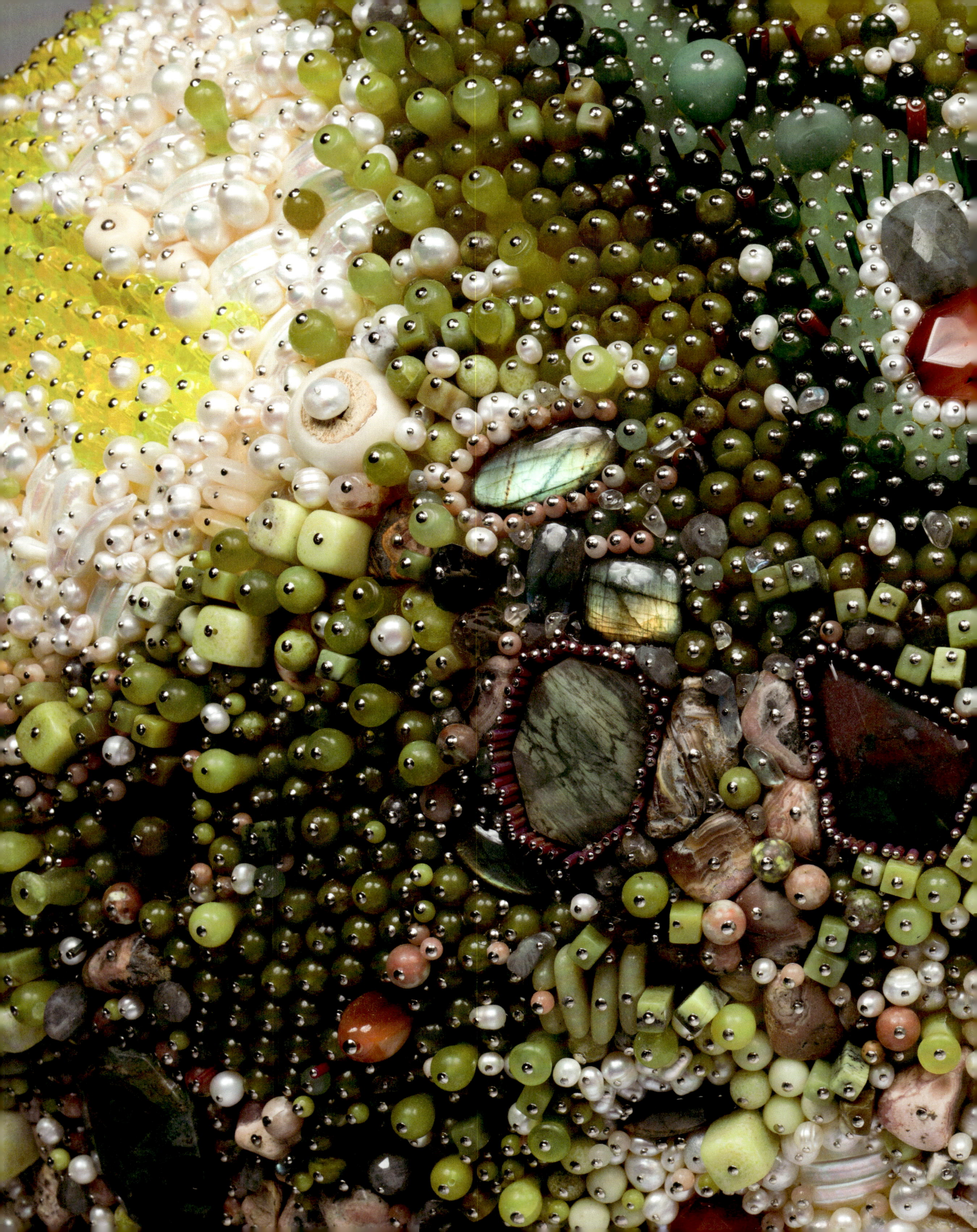

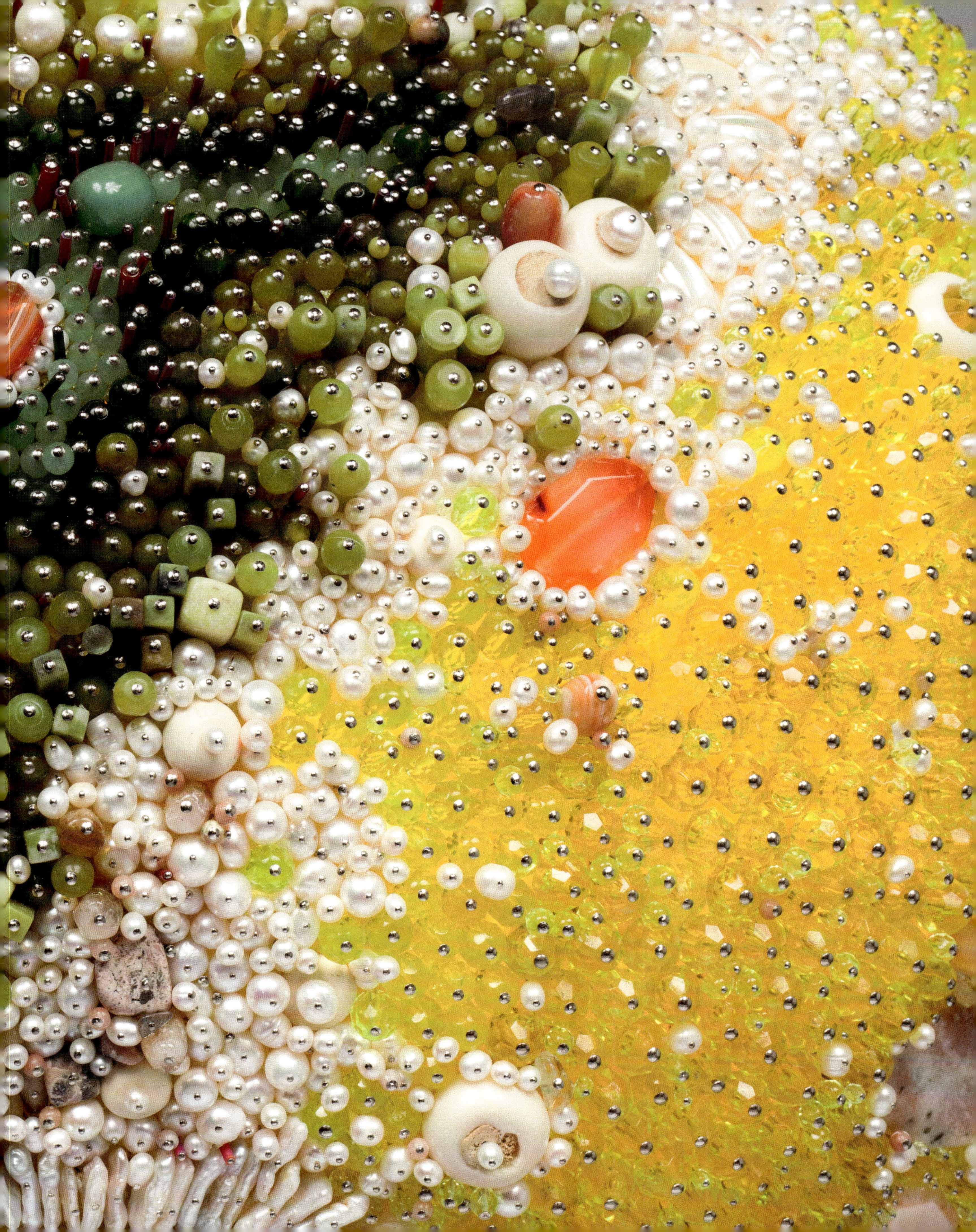

Bad Cherry (Bite), 2021

Garnet, pink opal, agate, peach moonstone, red aventurine, smoky quartz, quartz, carnelian, brecciated jasper, magnesite, glass, steel pins on coated polystyrene, fishing pole, and lead sinker

11½ × 31½ × 10 inches
29.2 × 80 × 25.4 cm

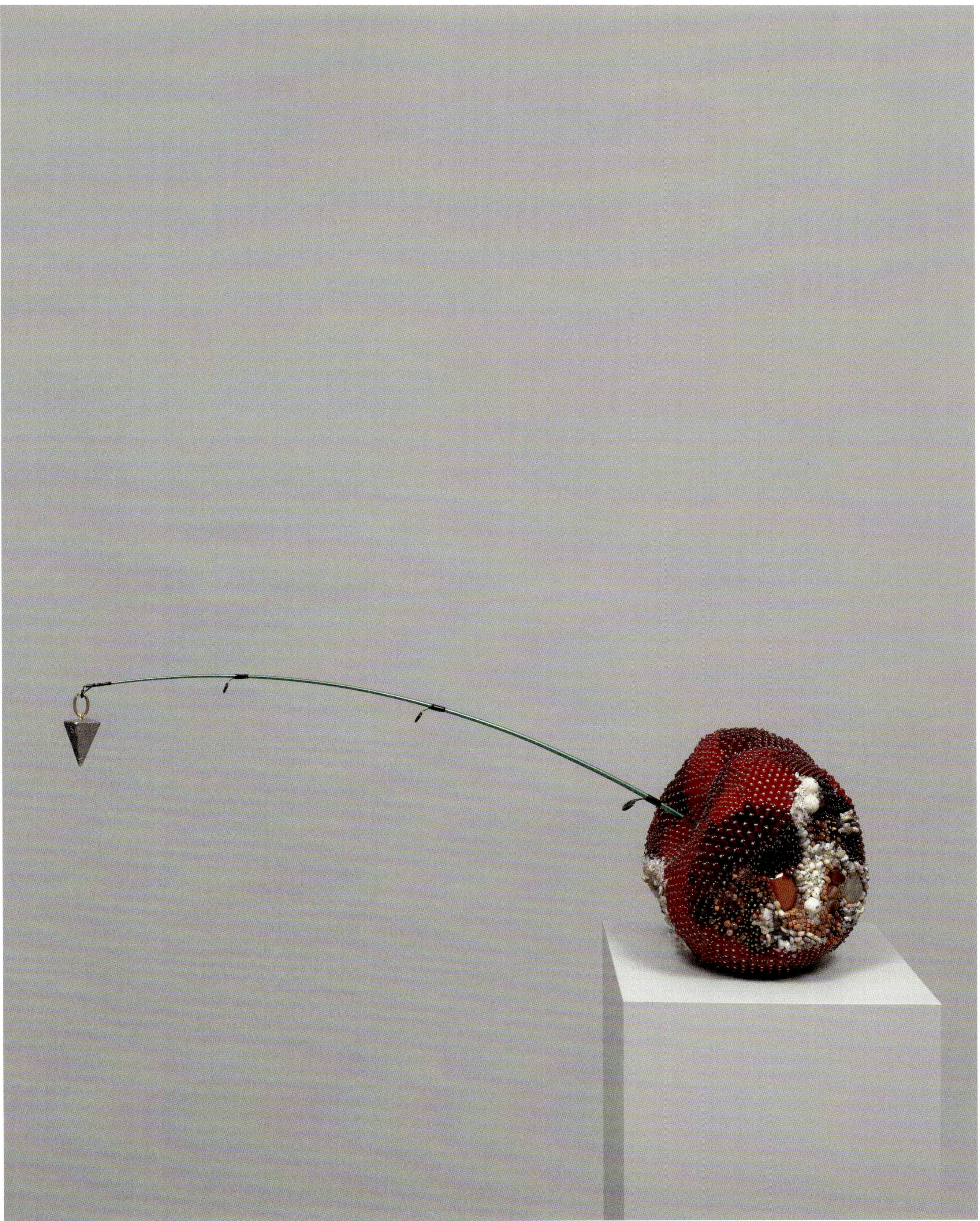

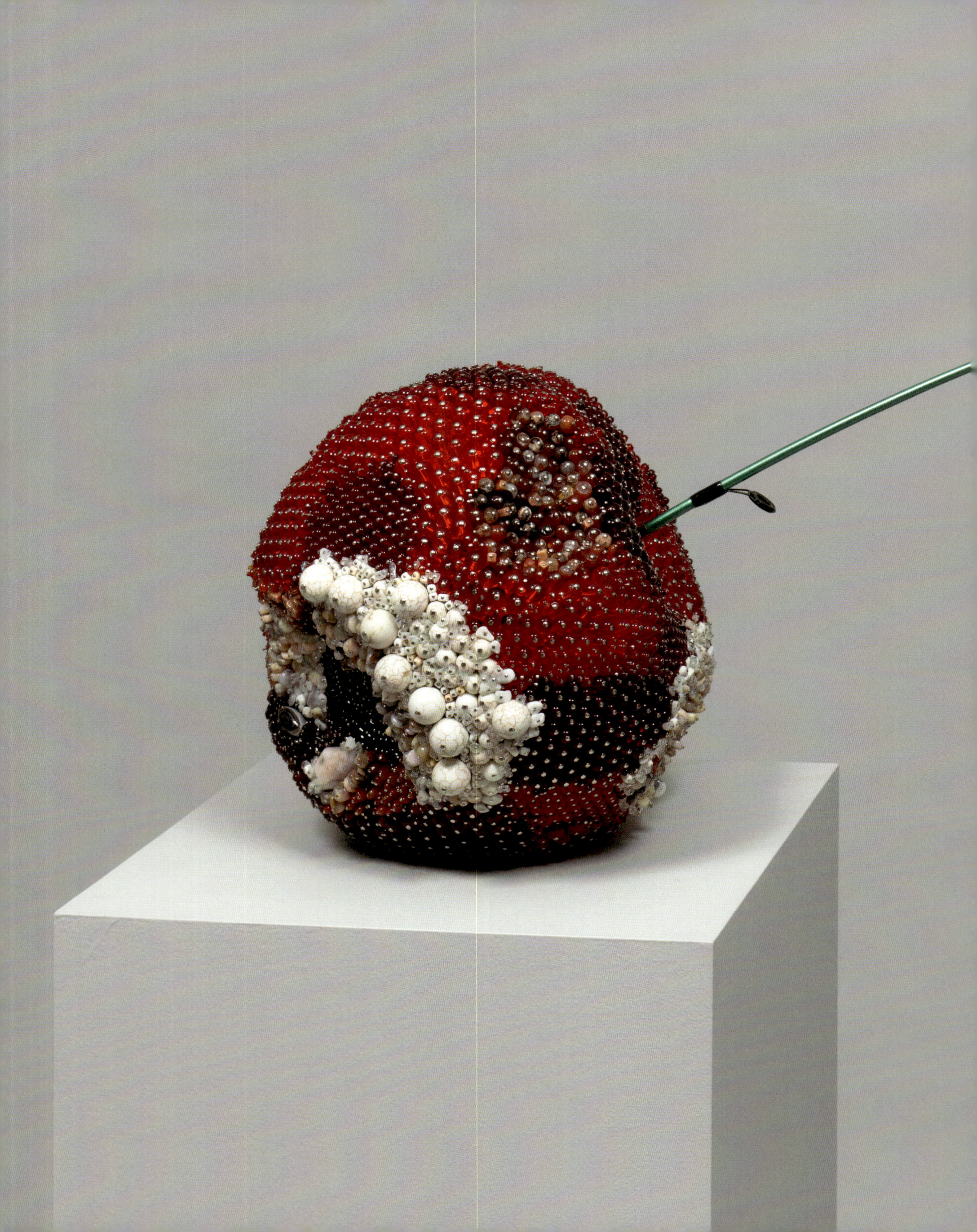

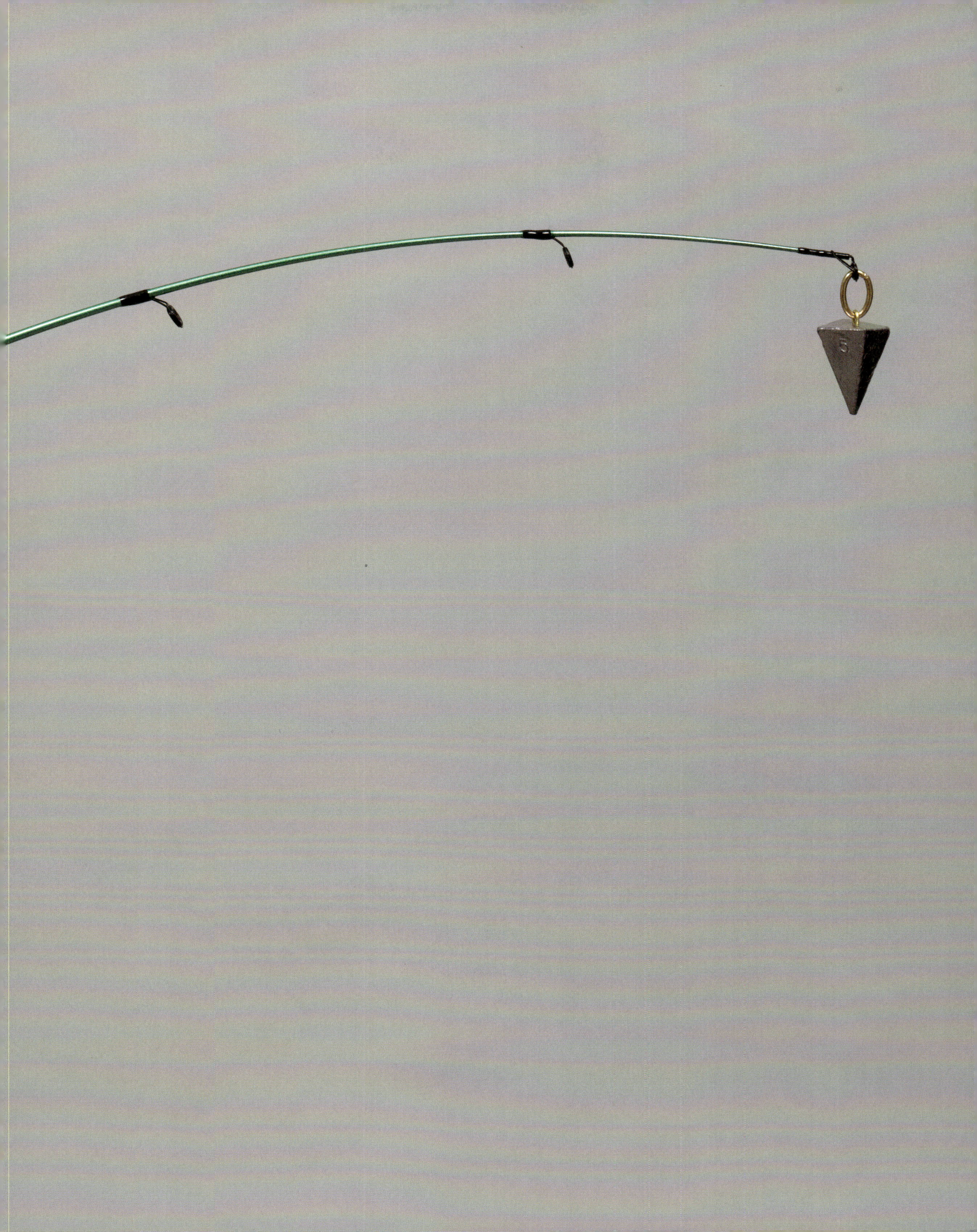

Published on the occasion
of the exhibition

Kathleen Ryan

May 6–June 18, 2021
Karma
188 E 2nd Street
172 E 2nd Street
New York, NY 10009

Edition of 1,000

Photography by Lance Brewer

ISBN 978-1-949172-74-4

AF594404

The 24-hour Coding Bootcamp:
The Only coding book that teaches content upload to the Real Web Server

CONYITHUB CORP.
(Council of NY IT Hub)
67-51 Cloverdale Lane,
Oakland Garden, NY 11364

info@codingnhosting.org
Phone:718-208-3595
ISBN 978-1-7345754-0-8

Educational facilities and other organizations that are interested in more information about special discounts available for bulk purchases should contact the author.

Printed in the United States of America
www.codingnhosting.org

PREFACE

In today's technology-dominated world, Coding (also called Programming) is an essential tool for every individual. According to the Bureau of Labor Statistics and Facebook, web development is one of the fastest-growing careers in today's economy with a projected 14% growth rate by 2023. By that time, there will over 1 million jobs related to programming and web development in the US alone by that time.

Simply put, coding is a language for the future. Schools should add coding as a separate course for middle-school students (and onwards). That way, by the time they graduate and enter their professional lives, they are equipped with one of the most essential skills of today.

However, a large majority of the people do not understand this and thus, they are not readily preparing for it. Therefore, I have written this book to change people's minds and give them a basic idea about coding and programming languages.
This book is for anyone who is interested in coding or learning about the Web.
It comprises of 5 parts that are each divided into 12 chapters, and each chapter has 3-8 sections.

It is not like traditional books. To make the book easy to understand and more interesting, I have given it a bit of a unique touch. It includes lots of pictures and charts along with jokes about programming and funny cartoons, instead of words and sentences to make it more fascinating and not boring.

For your learning, I have included in a little over 1 gigabyte of Web Hosting Space for 3 months and more than enough email addresses for your friends and family without any charges.
Also, for every dollar you spend on this book, we put in an additional one dollar will be donated to UNICEF under your name.

I hope buying this book and studying coding is one of the best choices in your life.
Likewise, knowing you through this book is the greatest blessing in my life.
Keep Dreaming!

♥ Purple you all!
from Queens, NYC

About the Author

Samuel Yunse Han

Born in S. Korea
Resident in NYC
Educated at Columbia Univ
A Relatively Young Entrepreneur

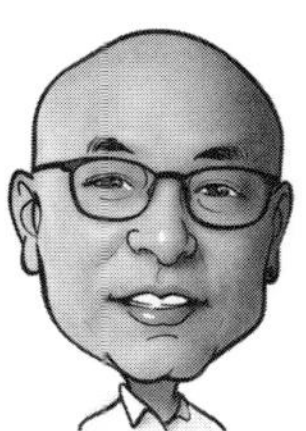

CONTENTS

PART 1. GETTING STARTED

PART 2. PAGE LAYOUT & DESIGN

PART 3 . JavaScript & PHP

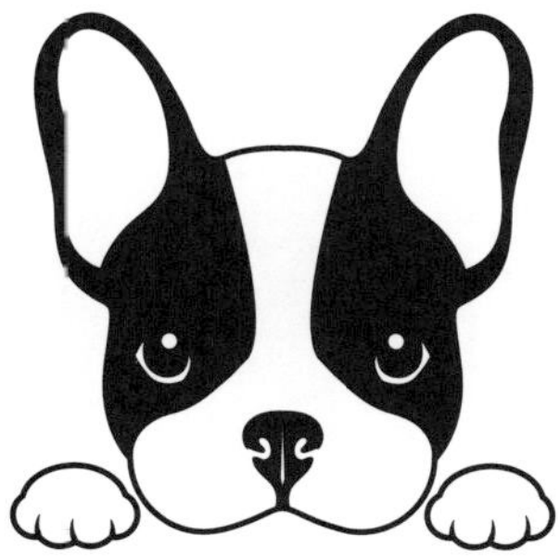

Before start, you **must** have:

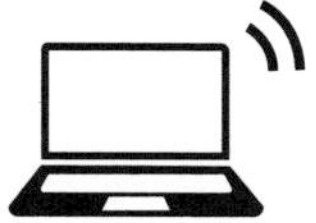

"Internet connected" laptop or desktop computer.

email address.

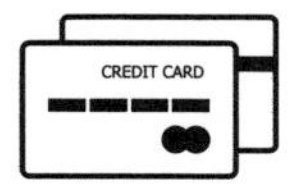

$16.95 available credit/debit card for 1-yr domain name.

"Open-mind" with pen/pencil.

PART 1

GETTING STARTED

This part will provide you with instruction on how to

- Register your own domain name.
- Create your first web page using HTML code.
- Style it using CSS.

CHAPTER 1

Web & Coding

1. What is the Web?
2. Web Languages
3. What is Coding?
4. Internet Technology
5. Development Tools

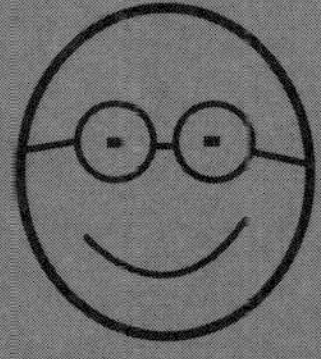

1 What is the **Web**?

Web (World Wide Web or WWW)

- A collection of websites or web pages connected to local computers through the Internet
- It is a part of *the Internet*.

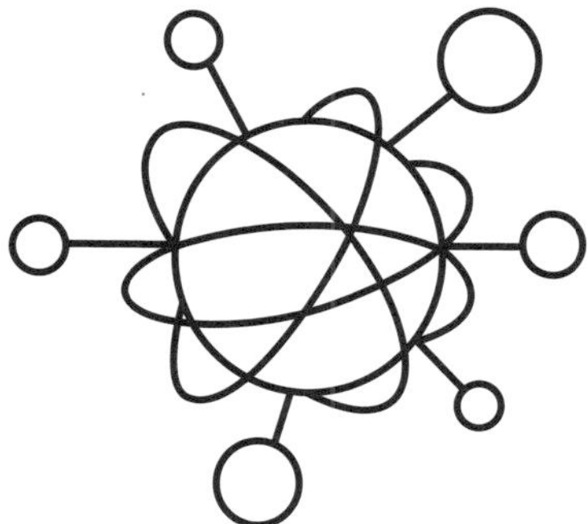

World **W**ide **W**eb
=WWW
=**W**eb

The Internet is composed of Web, FTP, Telnet, Email and others.

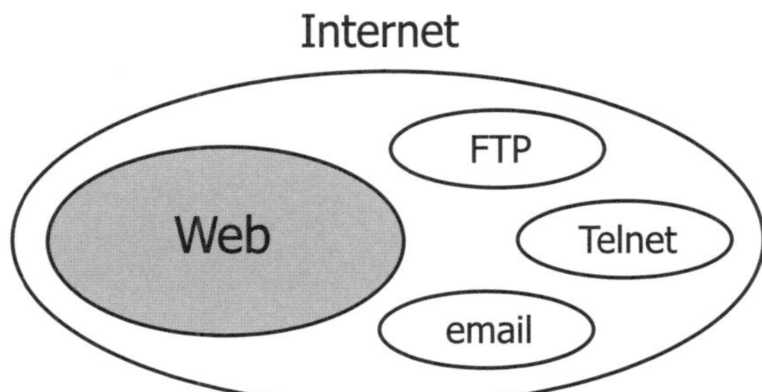

Internet

The Interconnected Network enables computers and other devices to connect and exchange information.

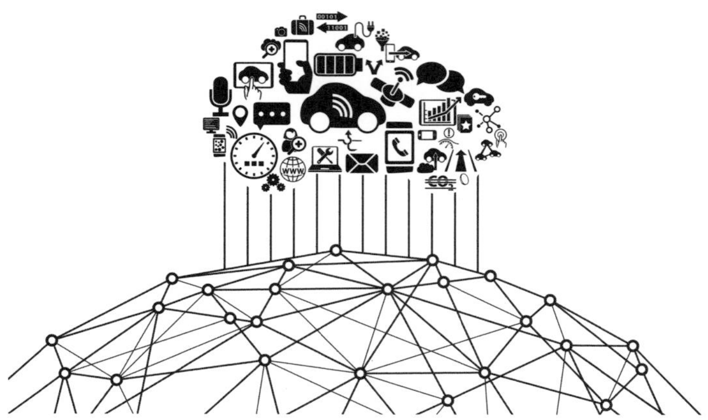

You need 5 things for the Web:

- HTML (Hyper Text Markup Language)
- URL (Uniform Resource Locator)
- HTTP (Hyper Text Transfer Protocol)
- Web Browser
- Web Server

The father of Web,
Tim Berners-Lee, created the
5 things needed for the Web.

2 Web Languages

There are 2 kinds of Web Languages based on where the language is executed:

- Client-side Language
- Server-side Language

	executed	language
client	web browser	HTML, CSS, JavaScript, etc.
server	web server	PHP, Python, Java, etc..

HTML/CSS/JavaScript

You

Client

PHP/Python

Server

Note:

There are also new languages on the server side.
Ruby, Swift, Perl etc..

Client-Side Language

- HTML (Hyper Text Markup Language)
- CSS (Cascading Style Sheets)
- JavaScript

Server-Side Language

- PHP (HyperText Preprocessor)
- Python
- Java
- Ruby

I. Client-Side Execution:

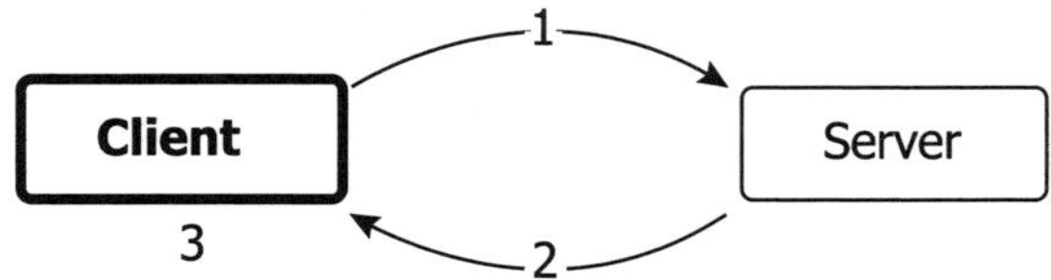

1. *Client* requests info to *Server*.
2. *Server* responds with requested info.
3. *Client Browser* interprets info and shows to *Client*.

II. Server-Side Execution:

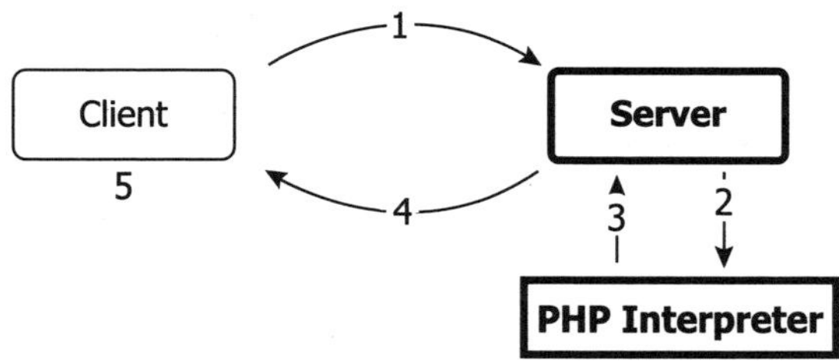

1. *Client* requests info to *Server*.
2. *Server* forwards to *PHP Interpreter* for interpretation.
3. Interpreter sends back interpreted info to *Server*.
4. *Server* responds with interpreted info.
5. *Client Browser* shows interpreted info to *Client*.

There are 1,000+ programming languages in the world

- 5% of programming languages make 95% of *application software.* *HTML, CSS, JavaScript, PHP* are among them.
- 95% of programming languages make 5% of software.

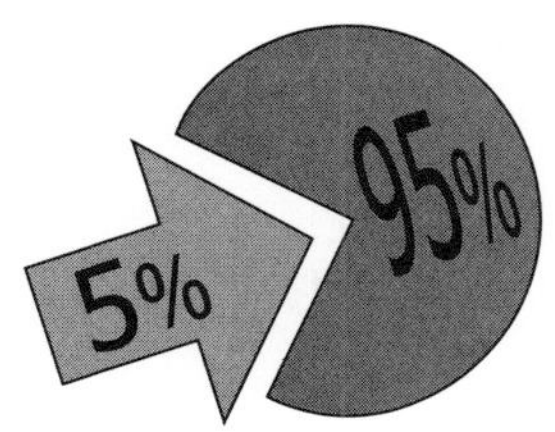

Some people say *HTML* is not a *Programming Language*. In this book I assume that *HTML* is also one of the *Programming Languages* like *PHP, Python,* and *Java.*

3 What is **Coding?**

- *Code* is instructions written in a language that the computers and devices can understand.
- Only *code* makes a computer and device work correctly.
- *Code* is now available to everyone and is an asset to anyone.

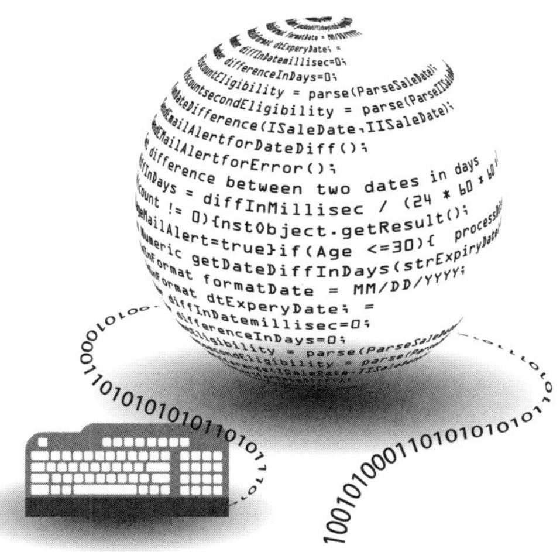

Coding is the process of writing Code.

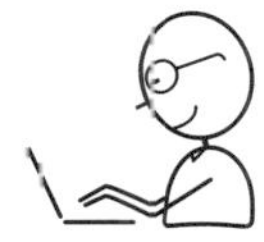

Computational Thinking

- When you learn to *code*, you learn how a computer works. *Computational Thinking* is thinking like a computer. It is a mental activity that requires a long time to understand.
- Learning how to write *code* at a young age provides a discipline that no other course can match. Successful entrepreneurs such as *Bill Gates*, founder of *Microsoft*, and *Mark Zuckerberg*, founder of *Facebook*, both started *coding* at a young age.

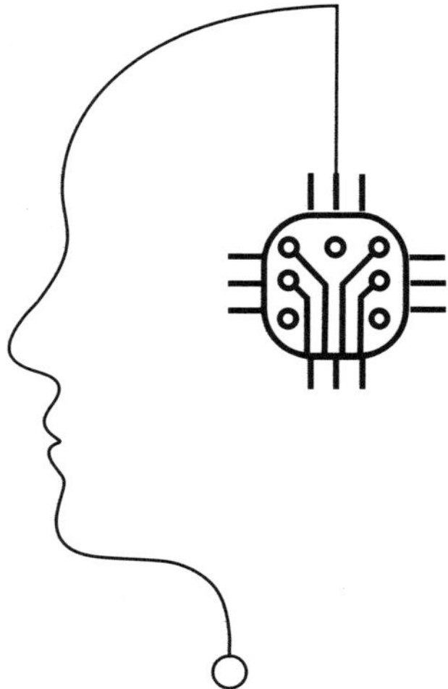

The first person who said *Computational Thinking* was *Barack Obama*'s personal coding teacher, *Jeannette Wing*.

Algorithm

- *Although* computers are capable of completing many amazing tasks, they are very unintelligent.
- Computers can only distinguish between *yes* and *no*. They need an exact *algorithm* to perform a certain task.
- A computer *algorithm* explains to your computer how to do something by using a *sequence*. Learning the *sequence* of a computer *algorithm* will help you solve complex problems easily.

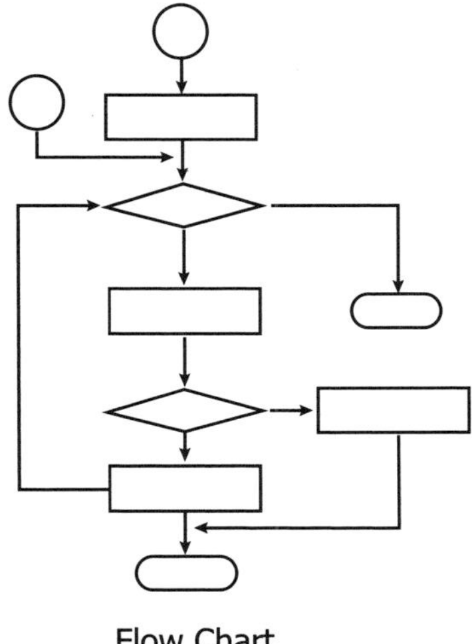

Flow Chart

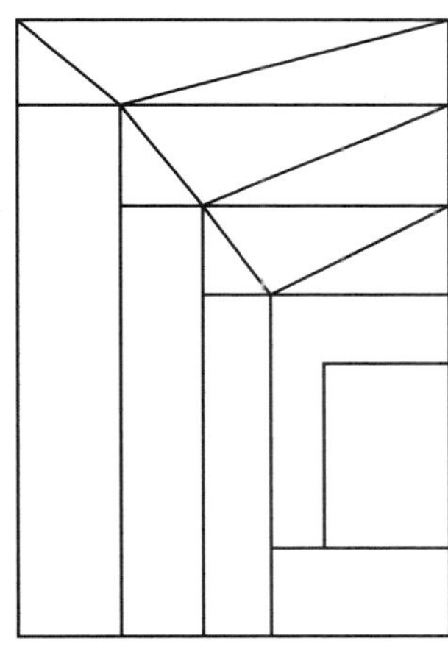

Nassi–Shneiderman Diagram

Note

This is a *flowchart* to demonstrate what a sequence may look like.
However, some programmers use something called *Nassi–Shneiderman Diagram (NSD)*

4 Internet Technology

IP Address

- An unique number that is assigned to all computers/devices when they connect to the *Internet*.
- It is like the phone number of your mobile phone.

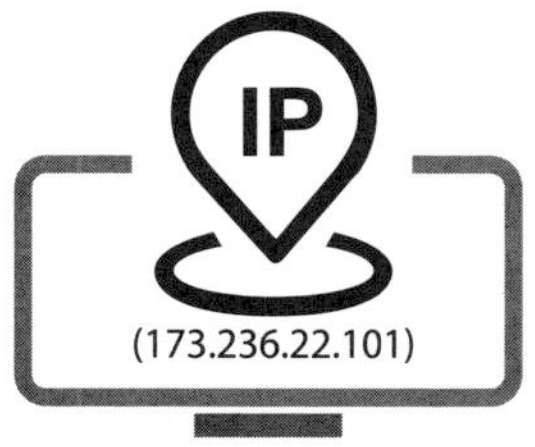

Phones have phone numbers and computers have IP addresses.

Domain Name

- It is your *website name*.
- It is the address where internet users can access your *website.*
- It has a *prefix, a sub-domain, a domain name,* and *an extension*:

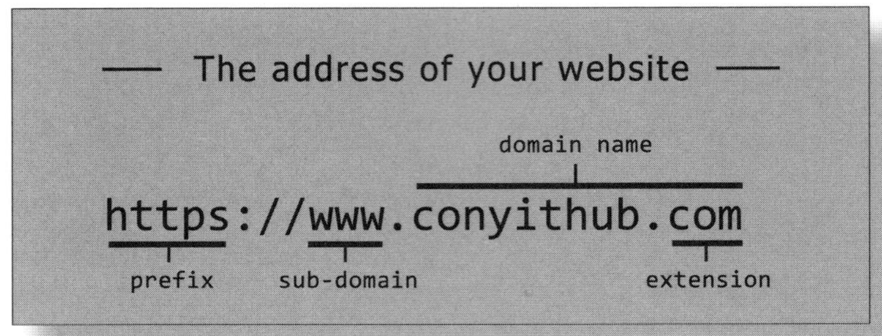

The Domain Name is much easier to remember than IP Address (173.236.22.101)

Note

There are 280 internet *domain extensions.* And 50% of them are `.COM` and `.NET`

Hosting Service

- To operate a *website*, you need to have a *server computer* connected to *the Internet* 24 hours a day, 365 days a year.
- It costs a lot of money for an individual, a company or an organization to build and operate such a *server computer* independently.
- To solve these problems, a professional company has built several *server computers* in advance, and then a certain portion of the space is rented and paid for by users, which is called a *hosting service.*

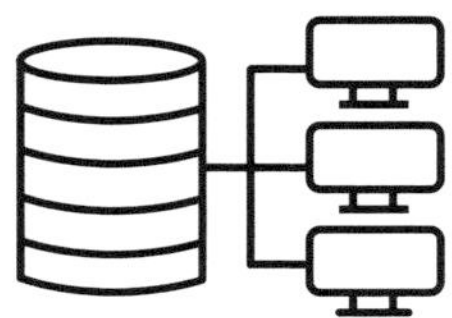

DNS (Domain Name System)

DNS is a *transfer system* between *IP Address* and *Domain Name*. All *servers* are organized and managed by *ICANN.*

1. When the *domain name* is typed, your computer (client) will ask *ICANN* for the *IP Address* that is linked to the *Domain Name Server.*
2. The *IP Address* is given,
3. Then, the connection is established between *your computer (client)* and the *Hosting Server.*

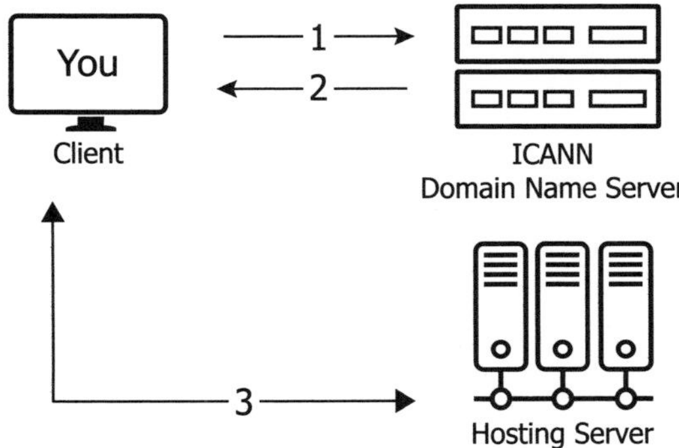

ICANN
(The Internet Corp for Assigned Names and Numbers)

ICANN controls all the *domain names*.
They have a table which has

- A list of *IP Addresses* and
- A list of *Domain Names* linked each other.

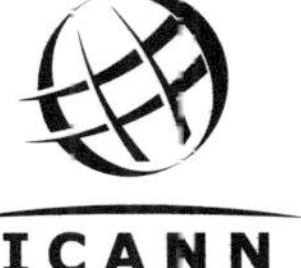

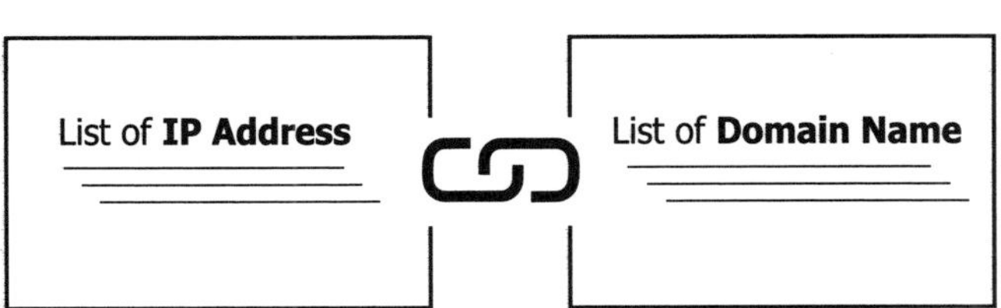

5 Development **Tools**

You need 3 *development tools* to make your *website*:

- Web Browser
- FTP Software
- Text Editor

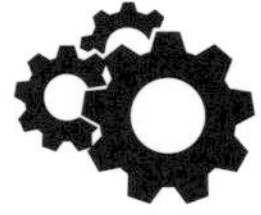

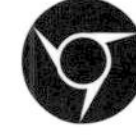 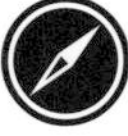 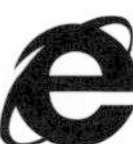  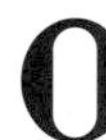

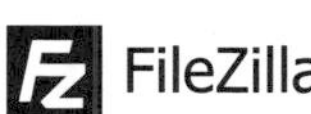

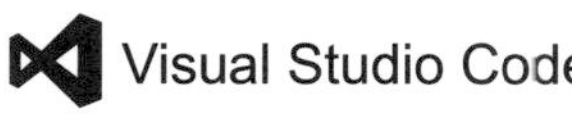

Web Browser

A *web browser* is software that allows the user to access and *interpret information* from the *web*.

Most commonly used today are:

- *Google Chrome*: developed by *Google.*
- *Safari*: default browser on *Apple* devices.
- *Internet Edge*: developed by *Microsoft,* included in *Windows* line of *Operating Systems.*
- *Firefox*: developed by *Mozilla.*
- *Opera*: by *Opera Software.*

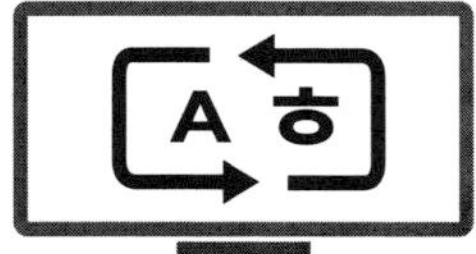

FTP Software

- *FTP (File Transfer Protocol)* is a standard *Internet protocol* that is used to transfer files between computers on a network.
- With this software, you can *upload* and *download* a file onto your *website*.
- We will use *FileZilla* as our *FTP Software* throughout this book.

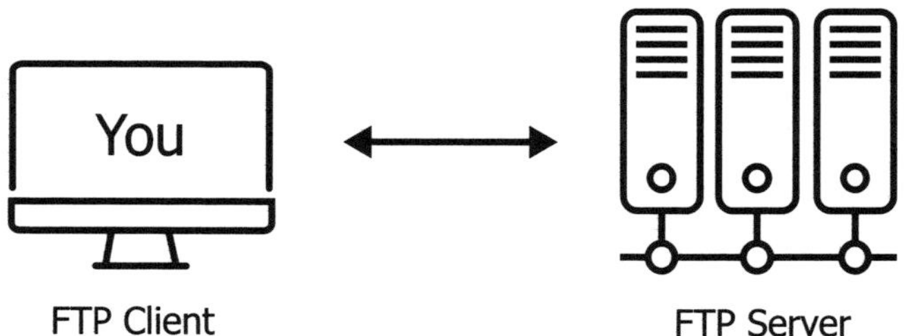

> **Note**
>
> *Web Browser, FTP Software, Text Editor.* These are 3 *development tools* to make your website.

Download FileZilla

1. Go to *www.filezilla-project.org* and
2. Select *Download FileZilla* ***Client.***

Installation

After the file download finishes, you will need to start *FileZilla Installer*. It is not complicated to install. Read and follow the instructions.

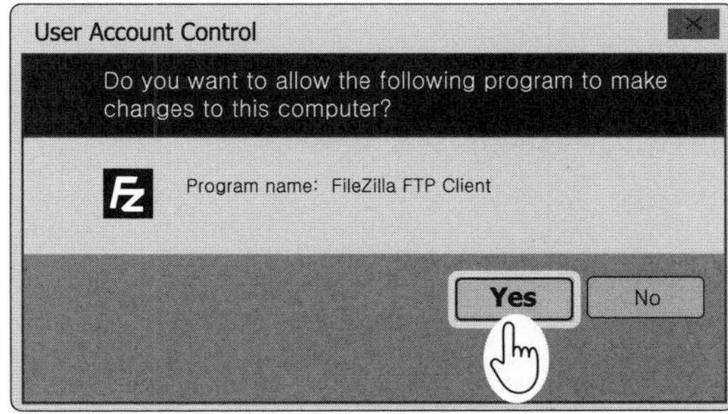

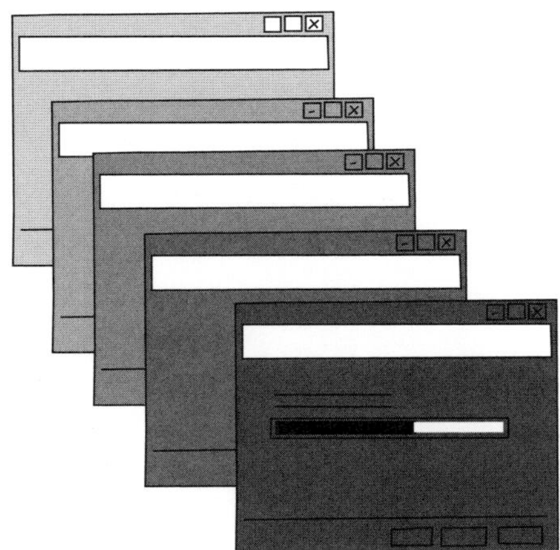

After these series of *"pop-ups"*, you will see the menu *"Choosing Components"* like on the next page of this book.

Choosing Components

When you see the pop-up, you will select the components of the *FileZilla Client* you want to install.

Make sure you check the boxes below except the *"FileZilla Client"* box and click *"Next."*

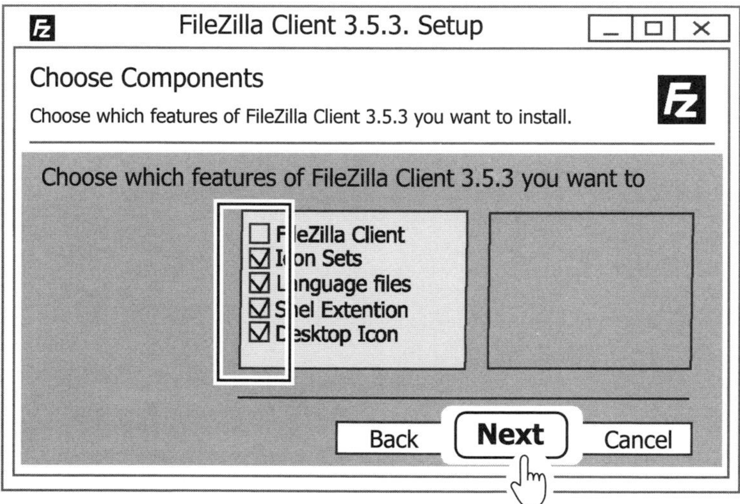

Finish Installation

Once you have completed all these steps, choose "Finish" on the next pop up.

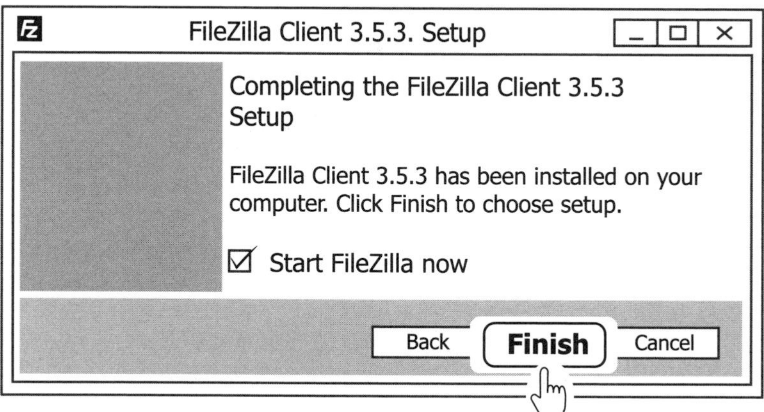

After you click Finish, you will see a screen similar to the one below. We will use this FTP software, *FileZilla*, for the rest of this book.

Windows O/S:

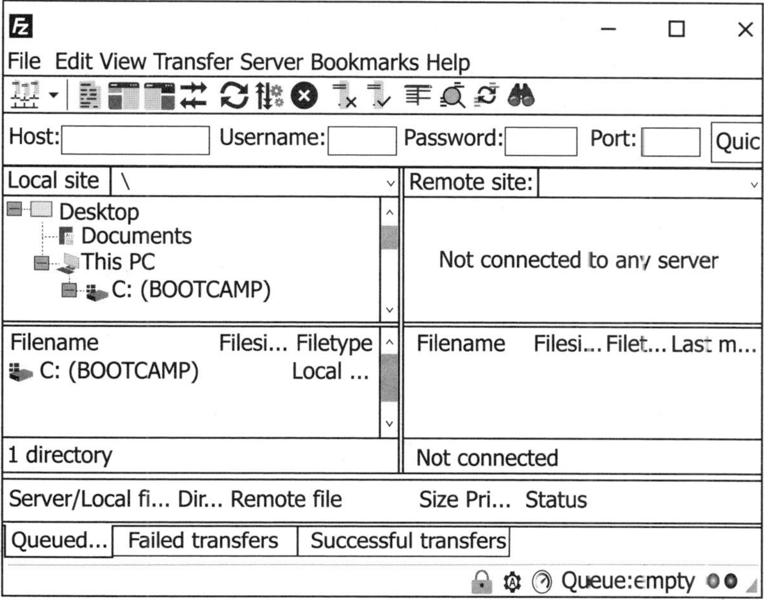

> **Note**
>
> There are several differences between the *Windows* and *Mac O/S (Operating System)* version of *FileZilla*.

Mac O/S:

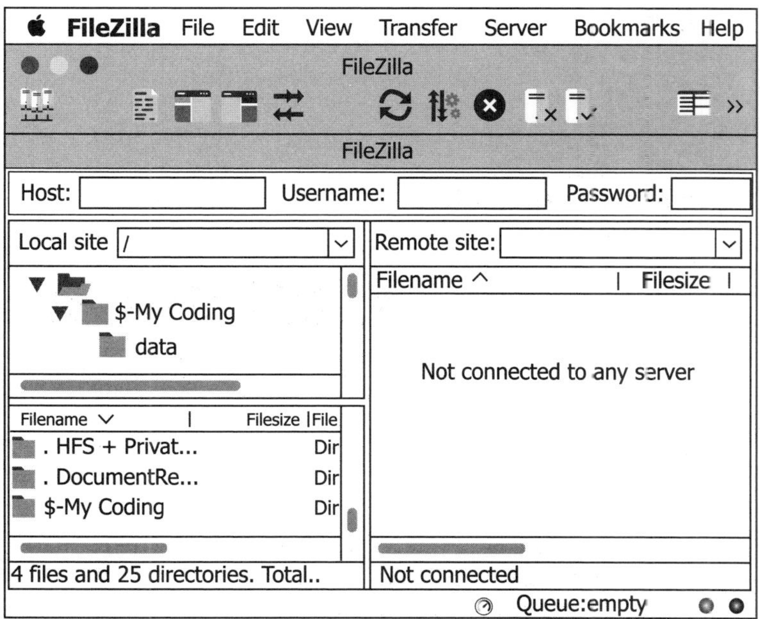

Text Editor

- A *Text Editor* is a software that allows a user to create and adjust *website code*.
- *Windows PC* has a *Text Editor* called *Notepad,* which is already installed. Likewise, *Mac PC* also has a *Text Editor* called *TextEdit*.
- We suggest and will use *Visual Studio Code* as our *Text Editor* through out this book. It is free and easy to use, just like *FileZilla*.

	editor	editor for coding
Windows	Notepad	Visual Studio Code, Sublime Text, NotePad++,..
Mac	TextEdit	Visual Studio Code, Sublime Text, Atom,..

Note

The *Downloading* and *Installation* of *Visual Studio Code,* like *FileZilla,* is not complicated.
Just follow the instructions and it is ready to use.

Download Visual Studio Code for Windows O/S

https://visualstudio.microsoft.com/downloads/

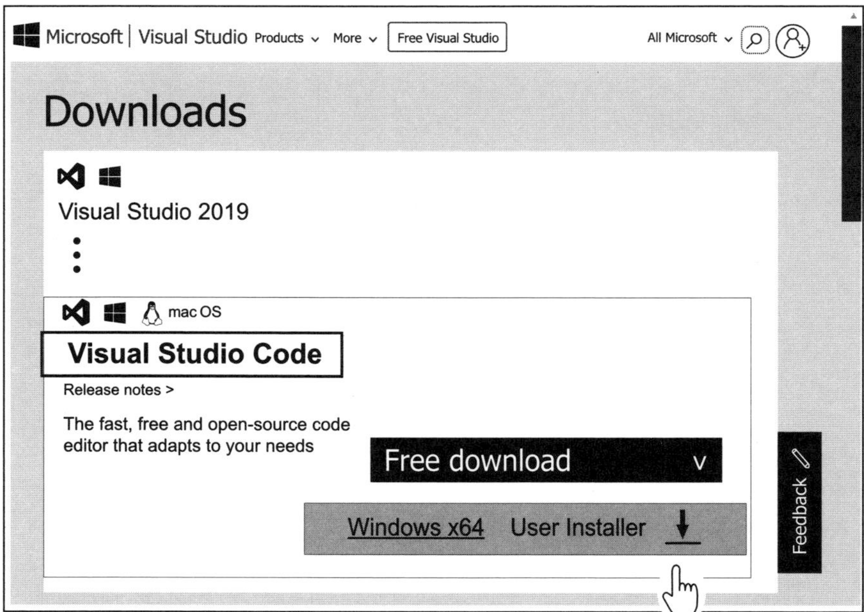

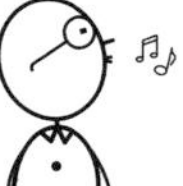

In Visual Studio Code Section, select "Free download" and "Window x64 User Installer" for free use.

Download for Mac O/S

https://visualstudio.microsoft.com/downloads/

The same as Windows O/S, except select "mac O/S Intel Package."

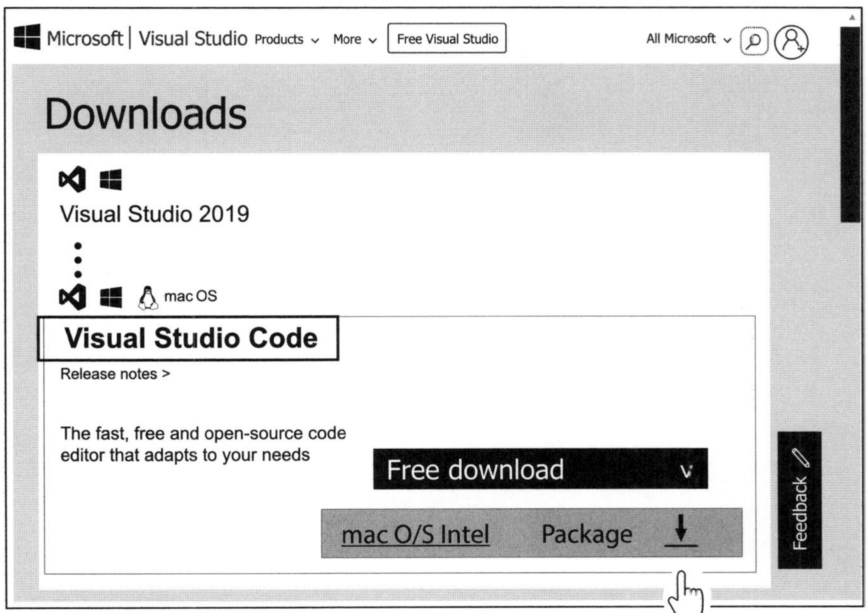

CHAPTER 2

Web Server

1. Domain Registration
   & Hosting Account Setup
2. Setting up cPanel & Email Account
3. Connect to a Server

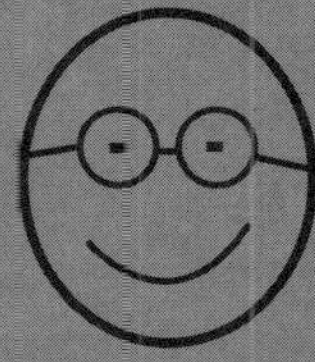

1 Domain **Registration** & **Hosting Account** Setup

To make a new Website, you need two things:

- A *Domain Name*
- A *Hosting Service*

A *Domain Name* is like the address of your home.
Hosting is the space of your house where you place your furniture and other items.

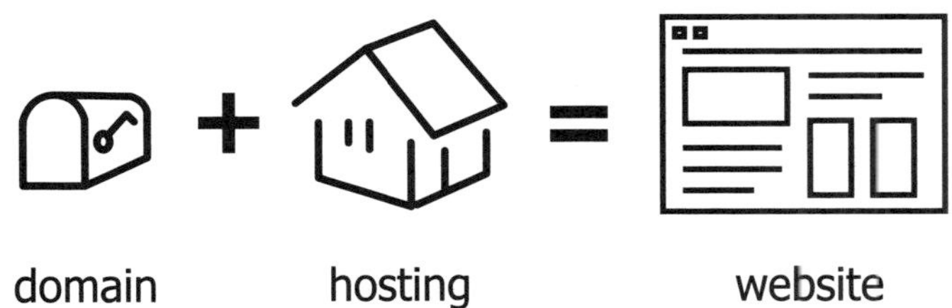

Both *Domain Registration* and *Hosting Account Setup* can be done at www.codingnhosting.org

Domain Registration & Hosting Account Setup

- This step is very simple & easy: use www.codingnhosting.org
- Read the next Flow Chart carefully and then follow the instructions of each step on your *Computer Screen* for the next 11 pages.

You need $16.95 ($16.77 + $0.18 -tax & fee) for 1-year Domain Registration and Hosting is free for 3 months.

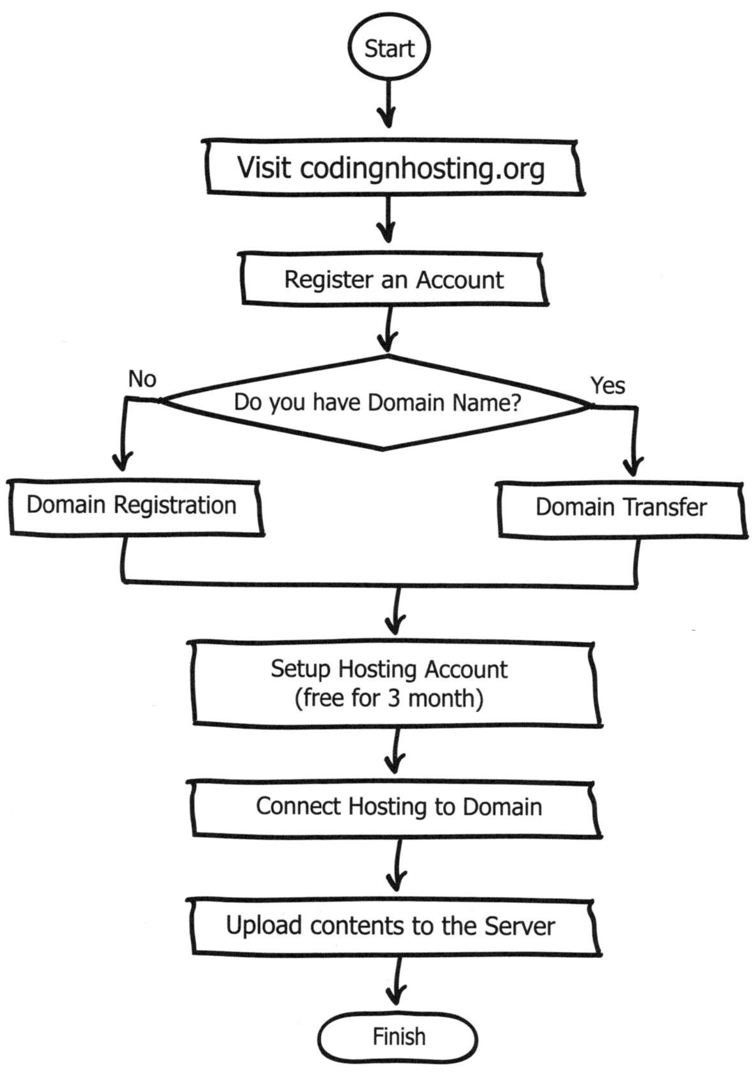

Visit Coding and Hosting site

❶ Let's go to "www.codingnhosting.org"

❷ Select "Register"

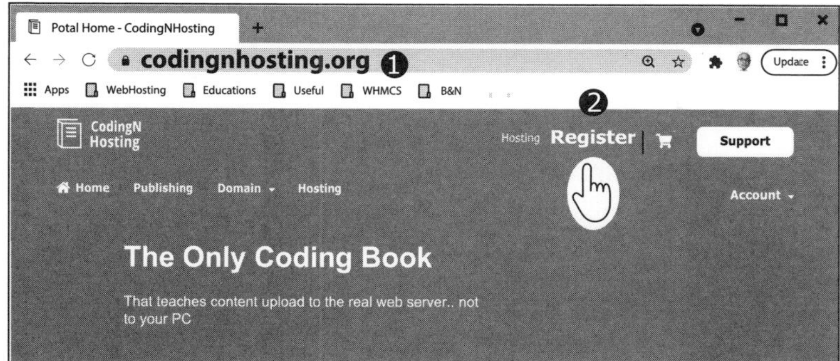

Register/Create an Account

Fill out the form and press "Register"

Your email will become your login ID/ Username

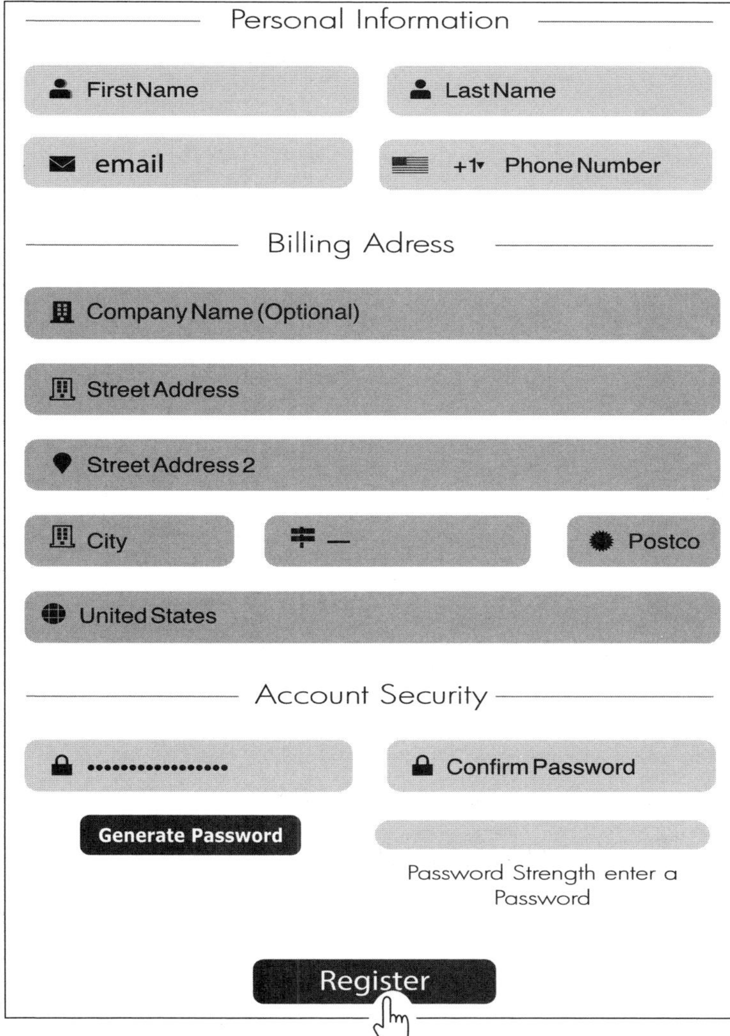

Verify email address

- You will receive 2 emails: Welcome and Email Address Verification
- Go to the "Email Address Verification" and "Click" the link:
  Verify your email address
- You will go back to www.codingnhosting.org

Select Register New Domain

Click "Domain" and select "Register New Domain"

Find a Domain Name

❶ Type in the favorite name you want to register and enter.

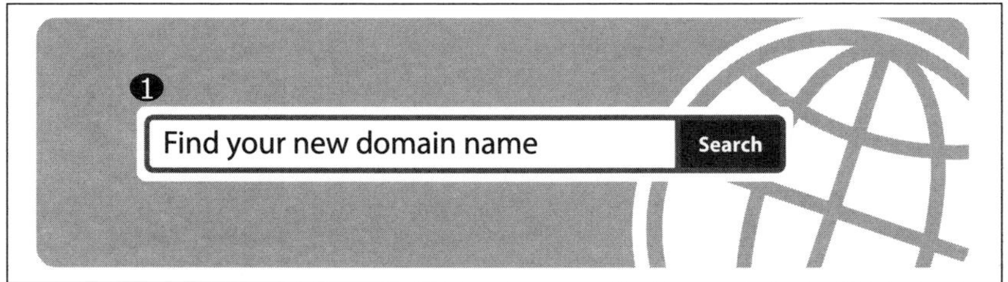

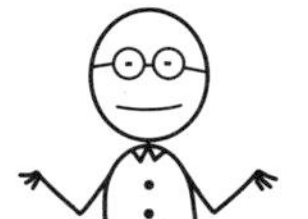

When you *register a domain name*, a lot of names are already taken. Try a different extension or put some extra numbers or characters.

❷ Let's assume that your domain name is "myDomain.com"

❸ Click "Add to Cart"

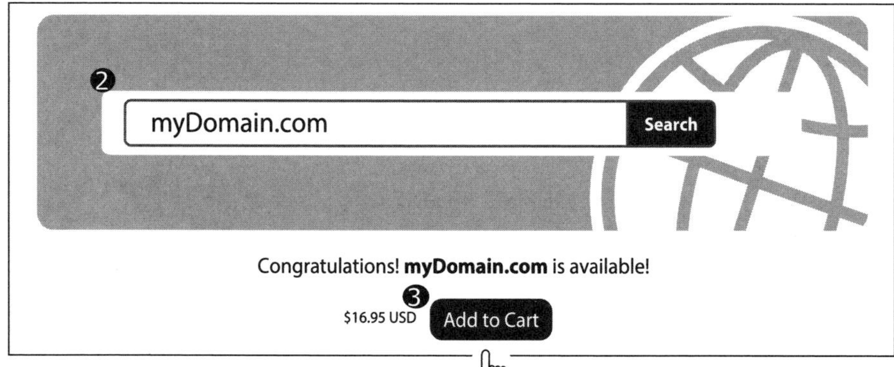

Find a Domain Name (cont')

❹ Click "Checkout"

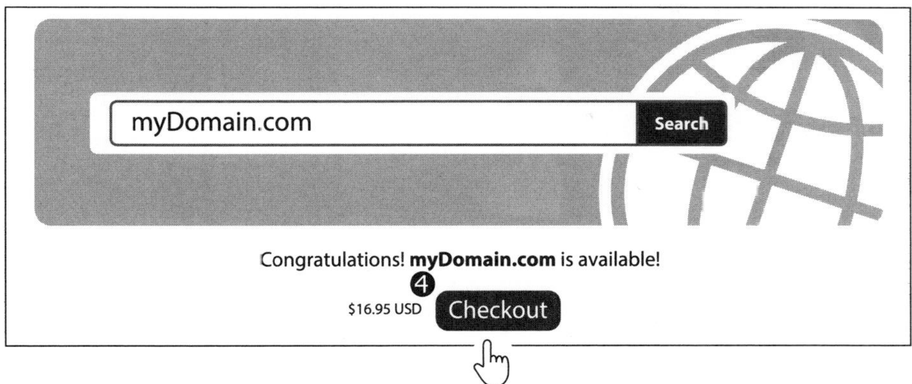

Domain Name Registration

❶ Make sure you put in the right name

❷ Click "Continue"

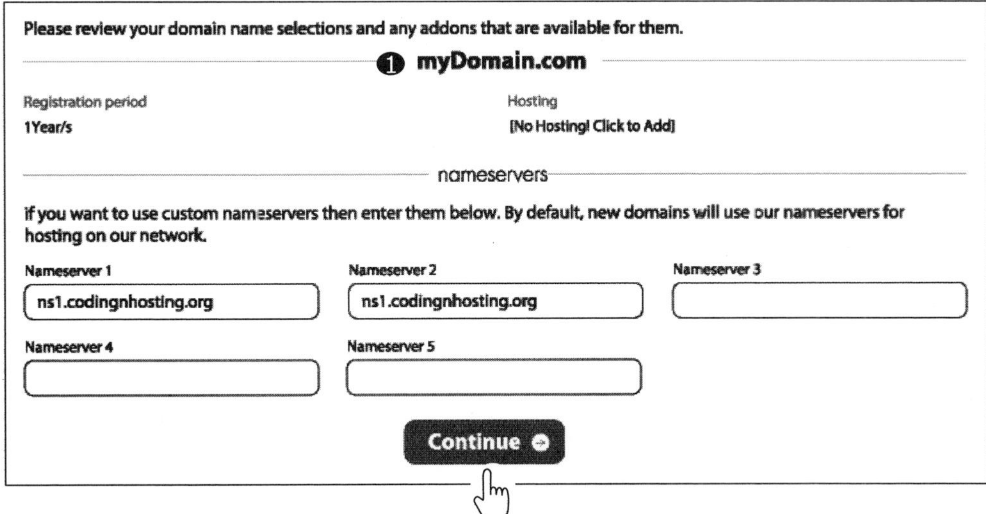

Domain Name Registration (cont')

❶ Click "Checkout"

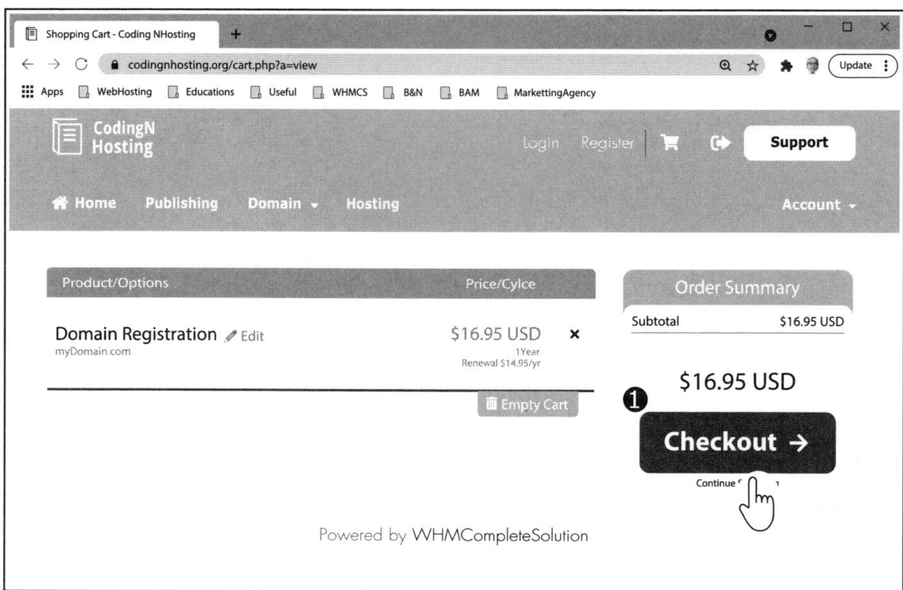

After clicking "Checkout", you will find a screen like the one below.
Do **not** click "Complete Order" and go to Hosting instead.

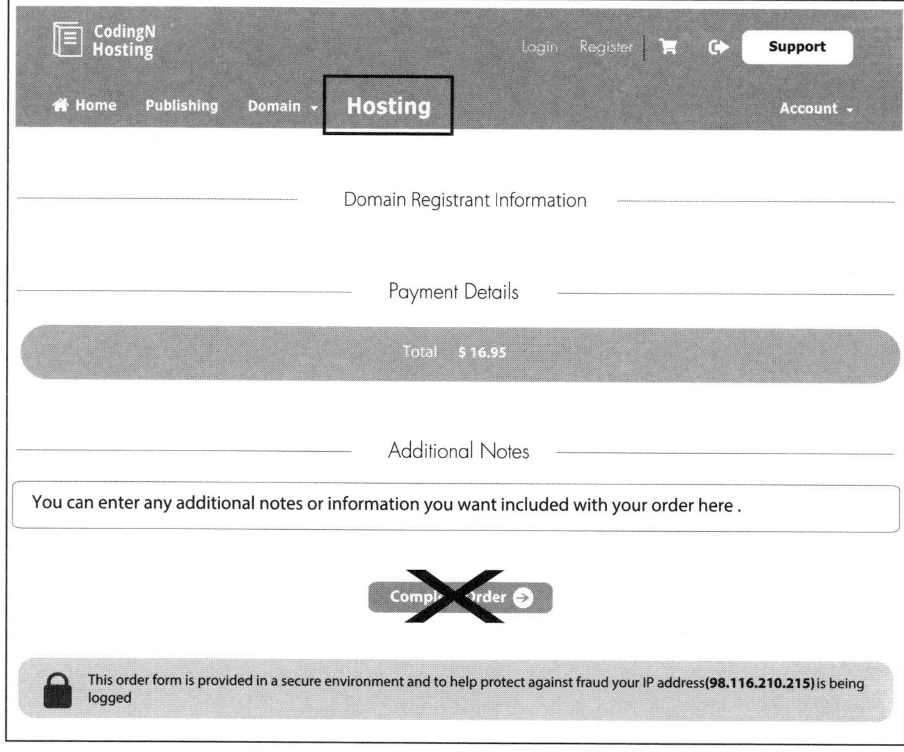

Add 3 Month Free Hosting Service

❶ Click "Hosting"

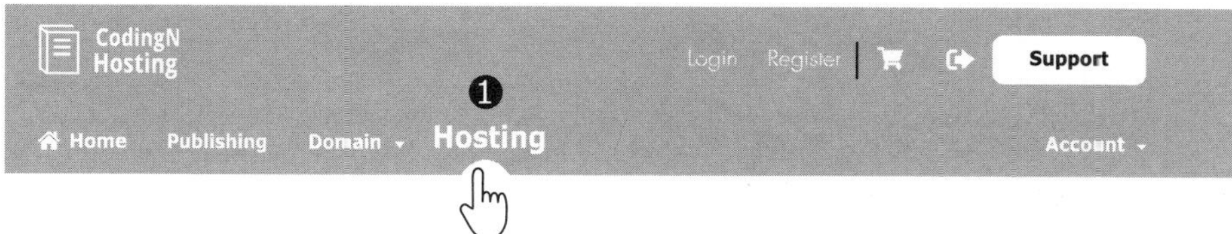

You will find the screen like the one below.

❷ Click "GET IT FOR FREE"

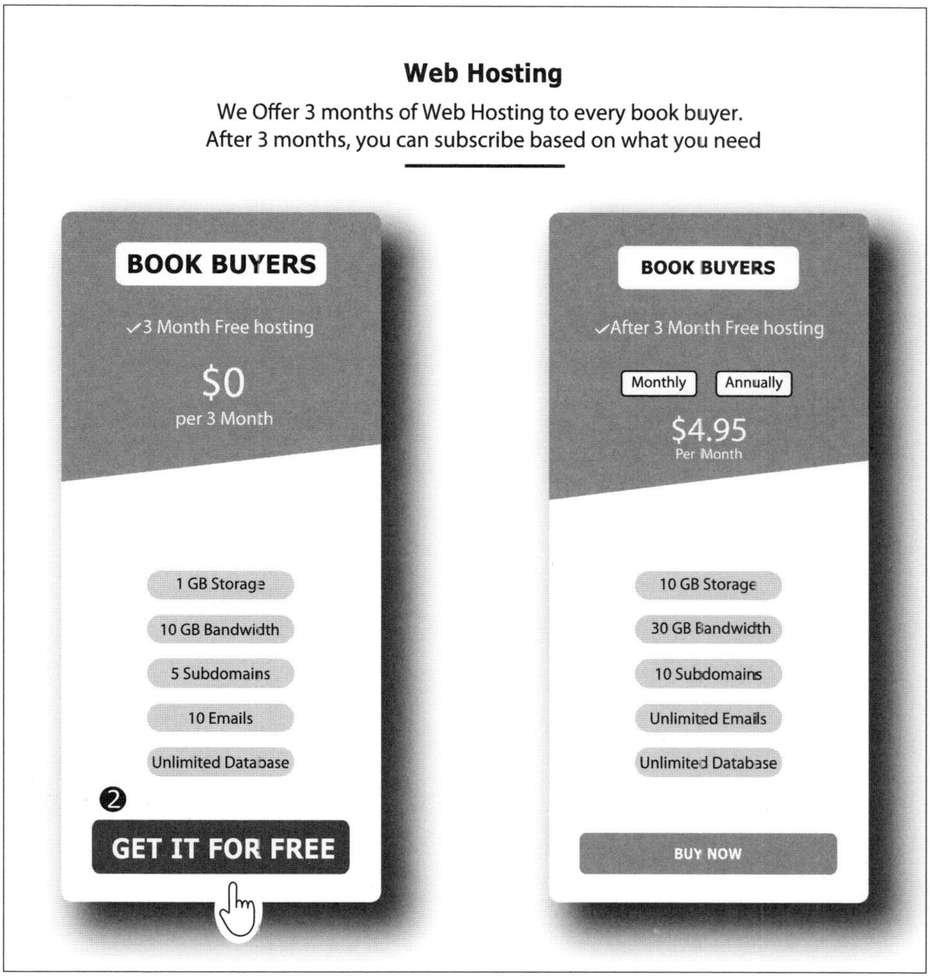

Web Hosting

We Offer 3 months of Web Hosting to every book buyer.
After 3 months, you can subscribe based on what you need

BOOK BUYERS

✓3 Month Free hosting

$0
per 3 Month

1 GB Storage
10 GB Bandwidth
5 Subdomains
10 Emails
Unlimited Database

❷
GET IT FOR FREE

BOOK BUYERS

✓After 3 Month Free hosting

Monthly | Annually

$4.95
Per Month

10 GB Storage
30 GB Bandwidth
10 Subdomains
Unlimited Emails
Unlimited Database

BUY NOW

As mentioned earlier, there are 3 months of *Web Hosting Space* are included free for learning purpose.

Checkout

❶ Select "Use a domain already in my shopping cart"

❷ Click "Use"

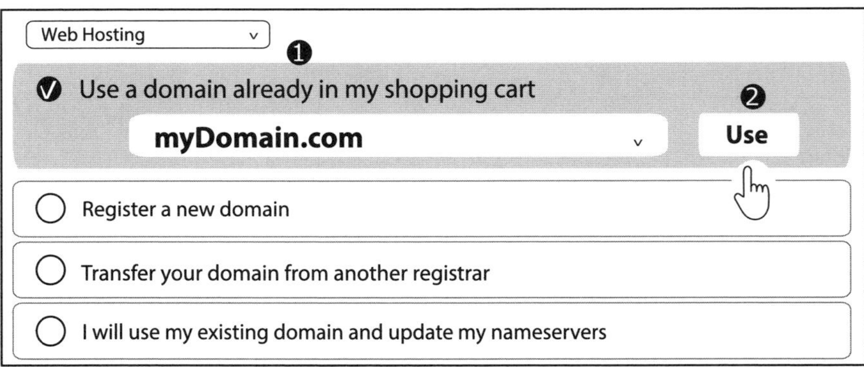

Let's checkout both Hosting and Domain Registration by clicking "Checkout"

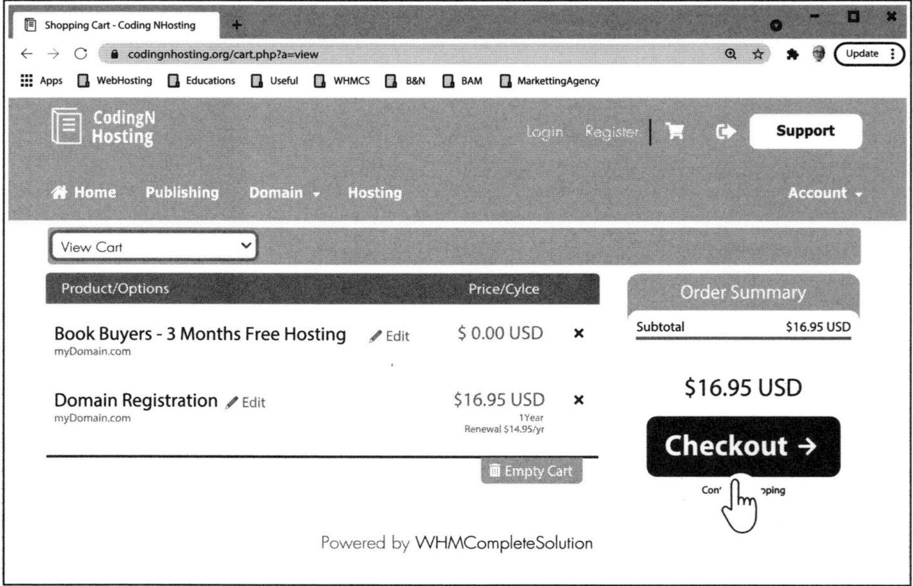

Complete Order

❸ Type in the "Credit Card Information"

❹ Click "Complete Order"

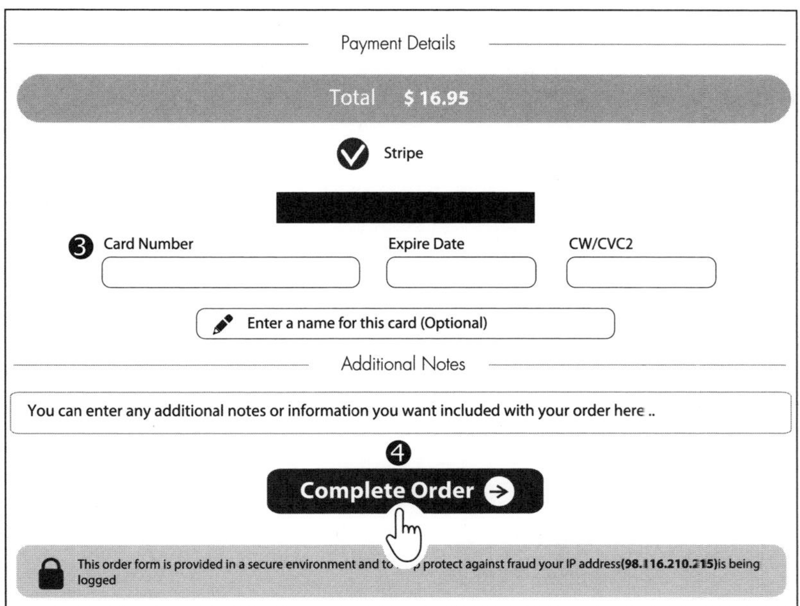

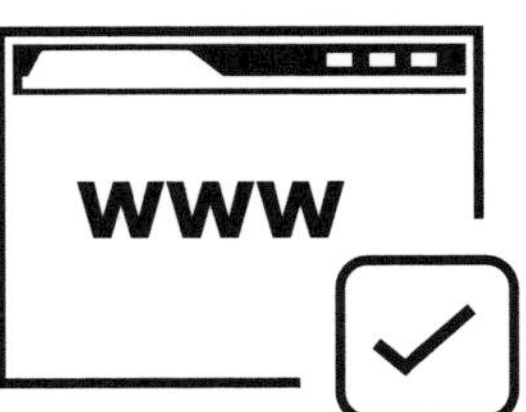

The Domain Name (myDomain.com) is yours and some portion of Web Space is yours as well.

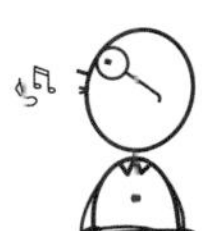

You can skip the next page (just one page), as long as you're **not** a "Domain Name Transfer" customer.

Domain Transfer

If you have a Domain Name already and transfer the name to us, you can use "Transfer Domain to Us", a sub-menu of "Domain".

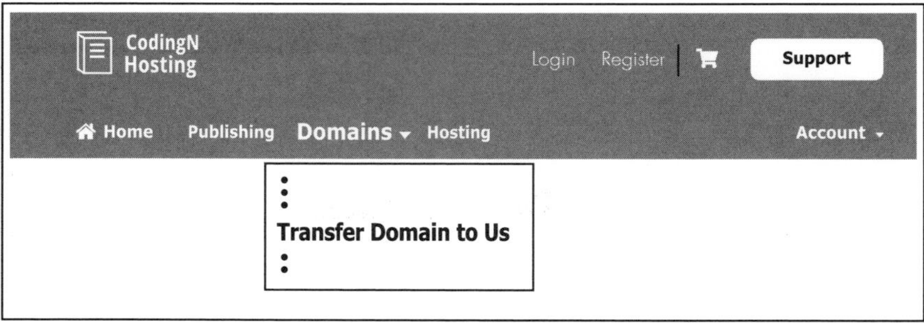

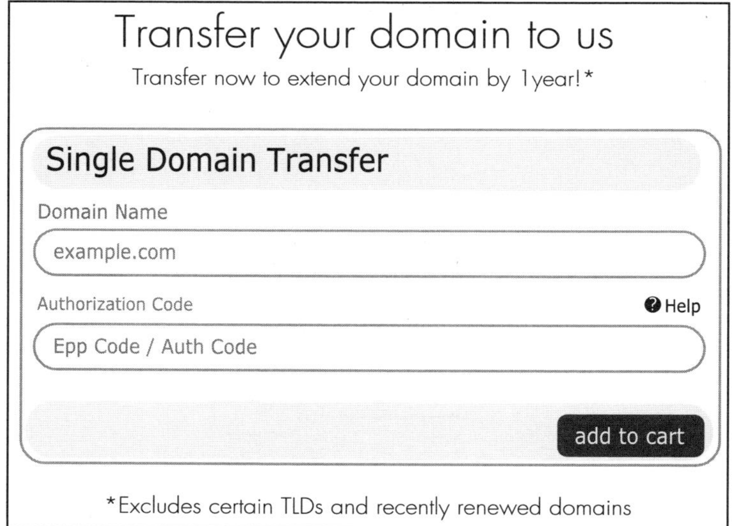

Since you registered a Domain Name before, you can do "Domain Transfer" without any problem. Right?

From pg# 47

After the order is completed, you will receive 7 more emails:

❶ Open and click the link: "http://dani1052240.myorderbox..."

❷ You will find the Username and Password in the "Login Details" section in the "New Account Information" email.
You should save the cPanel Username and Password (I suggest saving it either in your Notepad or TextEdit in your PC).
You will need this information for the next session.

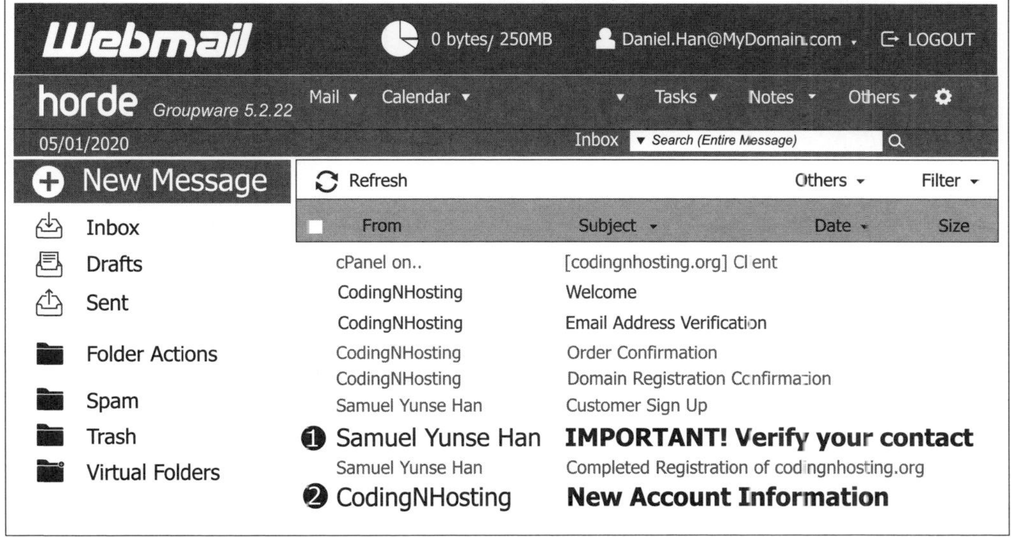

Note

Your domain name may not be visible on the internet instantly. This process is called *internet propagation* and can take up to 48 hours. But most of North American users will have a fully functional site within 30-45 minutes.

Now you have:

- Registered Domain Name.
- Hosting Space.

With these 2 major elements, you can make a Website.

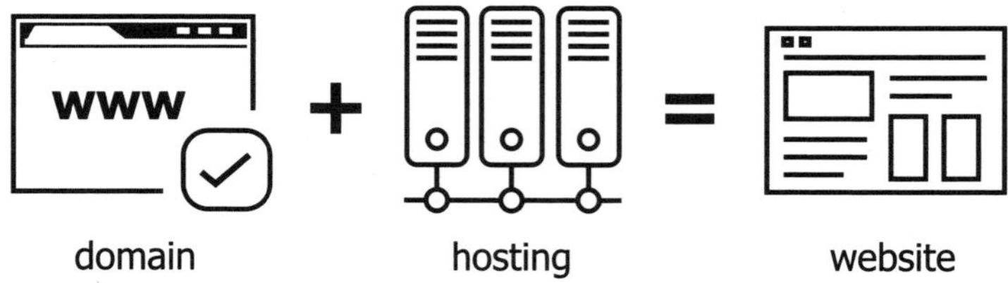

And now, how an algorithm is defined..

Algorithm(noun.)

```
Word used by programmers when..
They do not want to explain what they did.
```

2 Setting up cPannel & Email Account

Setting up cPanel (Hosting Control Panel)

- For controlling Hosting Servers, you need a web-based interface provided by a Web Hosting Service Provider.
- This interface allows users to manage and control services such as email, database, etc
- We will use *"cPanel"* as our Hosting Control Panel.

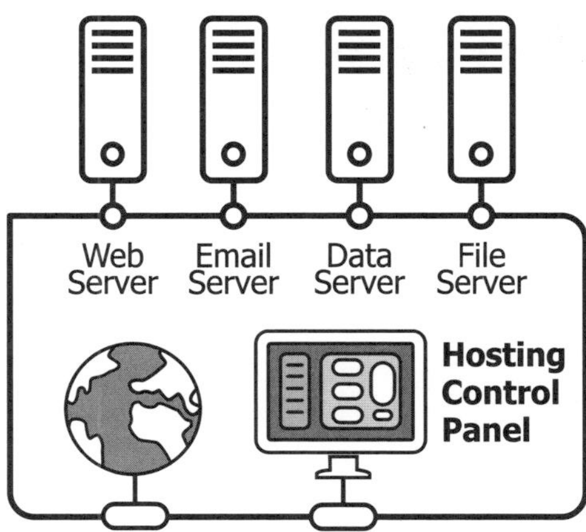

Note

You can manage all your servers with a *browser.*

Unlike *FileZilla* or *Visual Studio Code*, you don't need to install cPanel. It's already installed on our server. For access:

1. Just type in: https://www.myDomain.com/cPanel
2. Type in *Username* and *Password* also.(pg# 49)

> **Note**
> Copy(:ctrl + C, :comm + C) & Paste(:ctrl + V, :comm + V) is the fastest & easiest way to type in or key in the word/phrase into the certain targeted area.

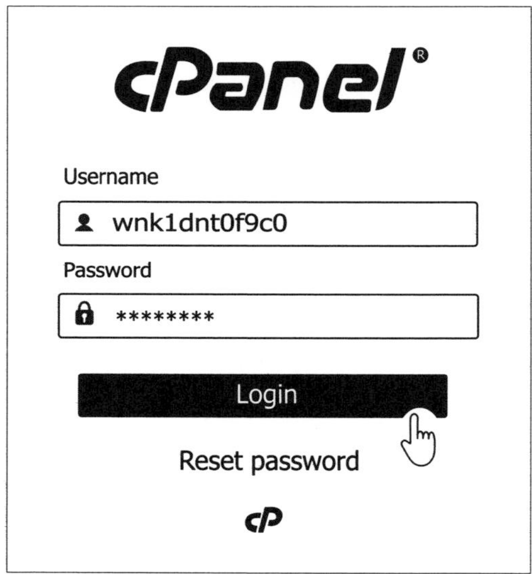

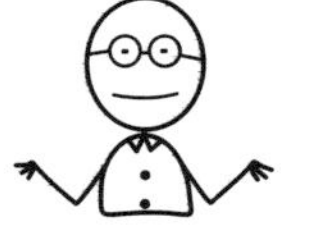

Sorry for the Cranky 12-digit cPanel Username. At this stage, I can not control that name.

Setting up an Email Account

❶ Create an email account by selecting the "Email Account" icon.

❷ Click the "CREATE" button.

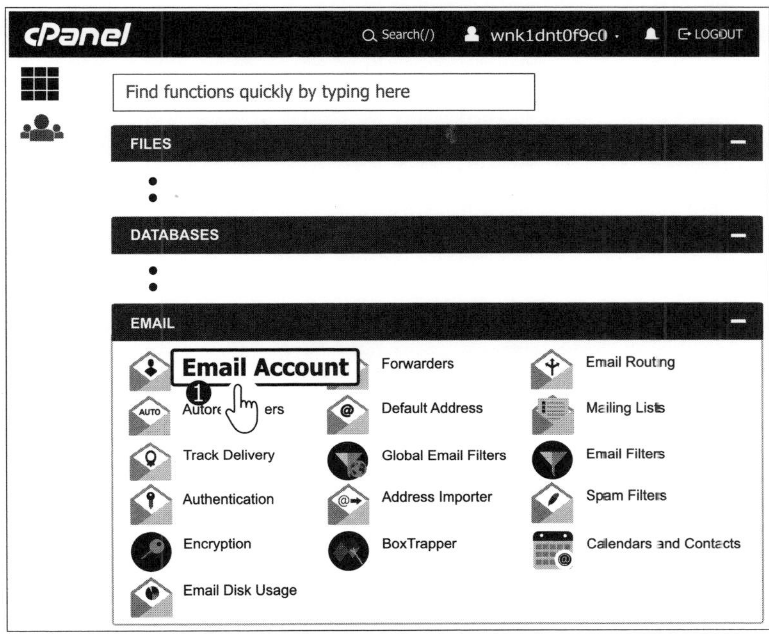

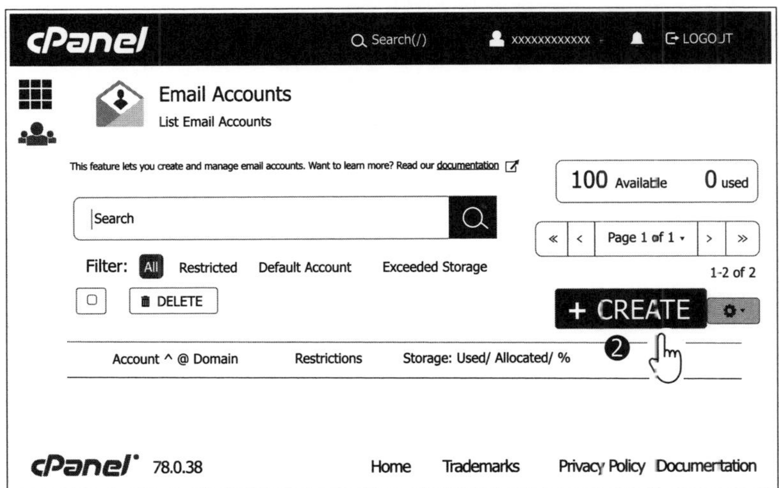

Setting up an Email Account (cont')

❸ Type in email address you want to use

❹ Type in the "Password"

❺ Click "CREATE"

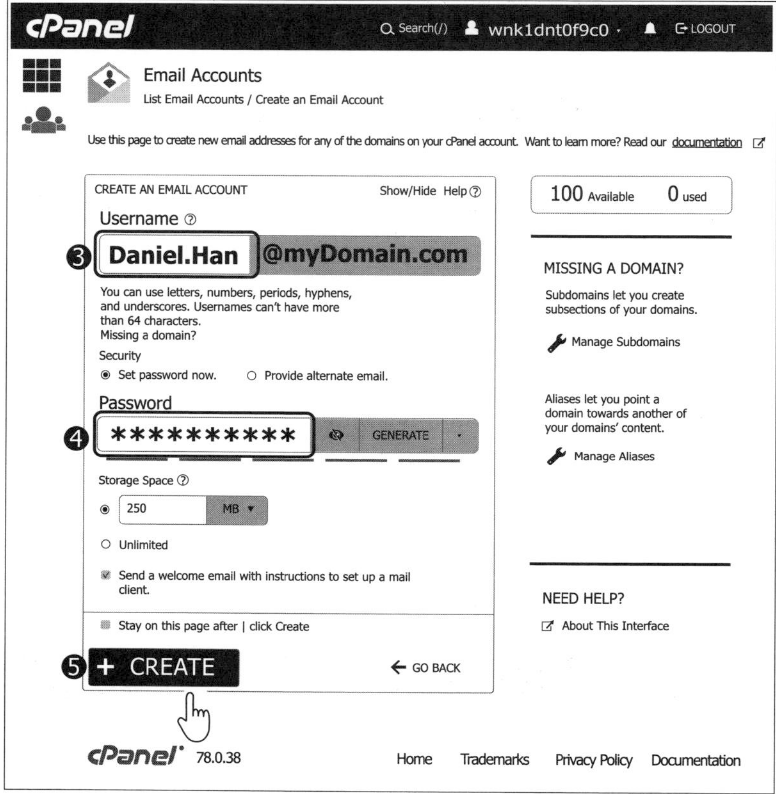

> **Note**
>
> Try to make your *password* unique and "easy to remember."

❻ Do you see the email you just created? (Daniel.Han@myDomain.com)

❼ Press "CHECK EMAIL"

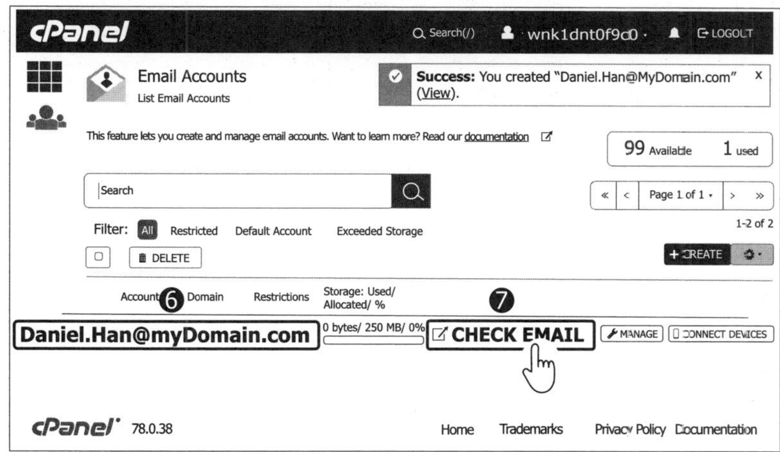

❽ Select "horde" as your Default Webmail Application

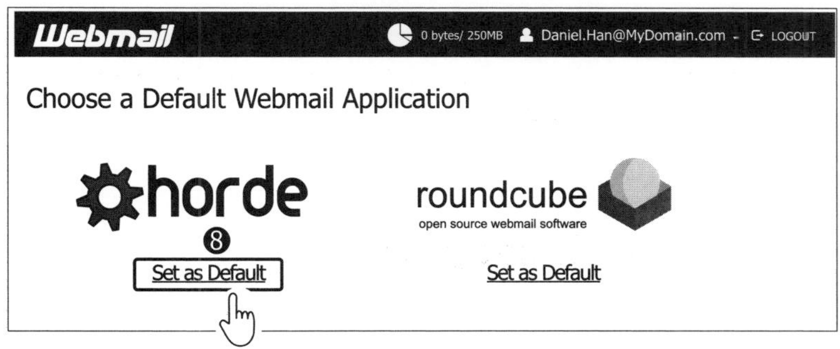

Webmail is a *Web based email system.*
So, you can access it from any-where.
Horde and *Roundcube* are *Webmail Applications* supported by cPanel.

❾ You will find a screen like the following:

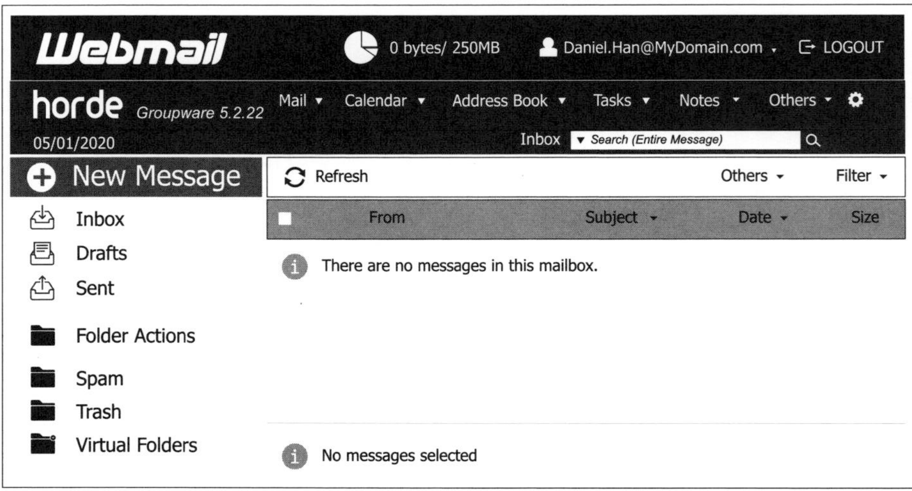

Access Webmail

Now, you can access your Webmail from anywhere by typing www.myDomain.com/webmail

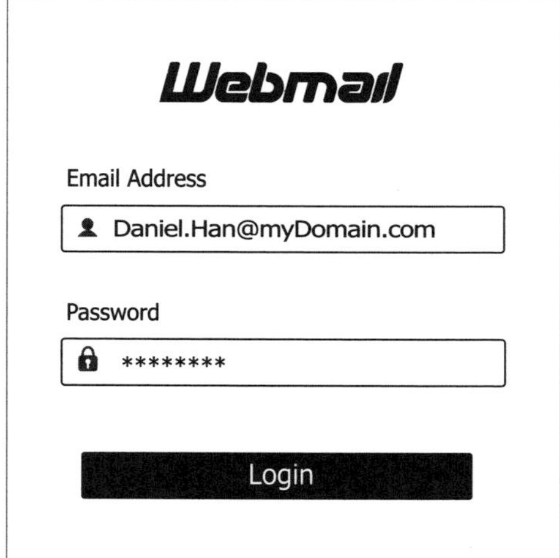

The *email Address* and *Password* are the same ones used when you created an *Email Account* on pg# 56.

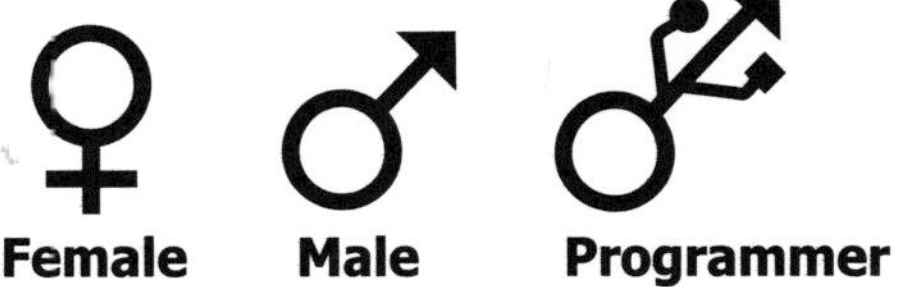
Female
Male
Programmer

3 Connect to a **Server**

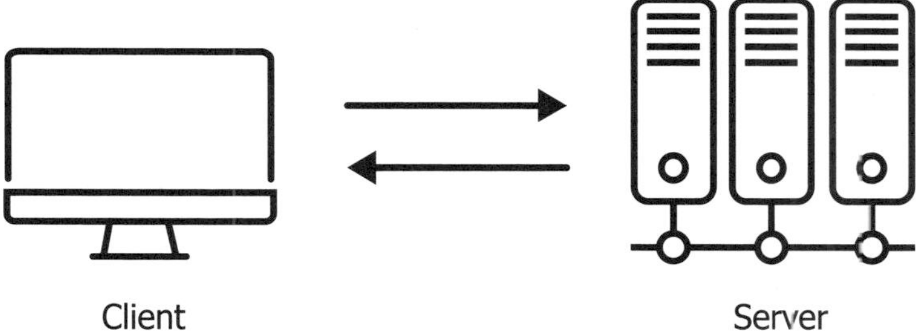

> **Note**
>
> There is no difference between a *Server Computer* and a *Client Computer*.
>
> Both are designed to run in exactly the same. You can run the same software on each of them.

You downloaded and installed *FileZilla* in Chapter 1, Section 05, pg# 31, Development Tools. Now, let's make a connection to our server.

Connect to a Server for Windows ( ) user

Open *FileZilla* by double-clicking "*FileZilla Client*":

❶ On the top left corner, hover over "*File*" and click it.

❷ Click "*Site Manager*"

❸ Select "*New Site*"

❹ Put your *Host Name* with the extension (.com or .net) which you just registered in section 01, pg# 42 : myDomain.com

❺ Make sure "*Logon type*" is "*Normal*" and type in **cPanel** "*User(name)*" and "*Password*" which I sent you by email(pg# 49)

❻ Click "*Connect*".

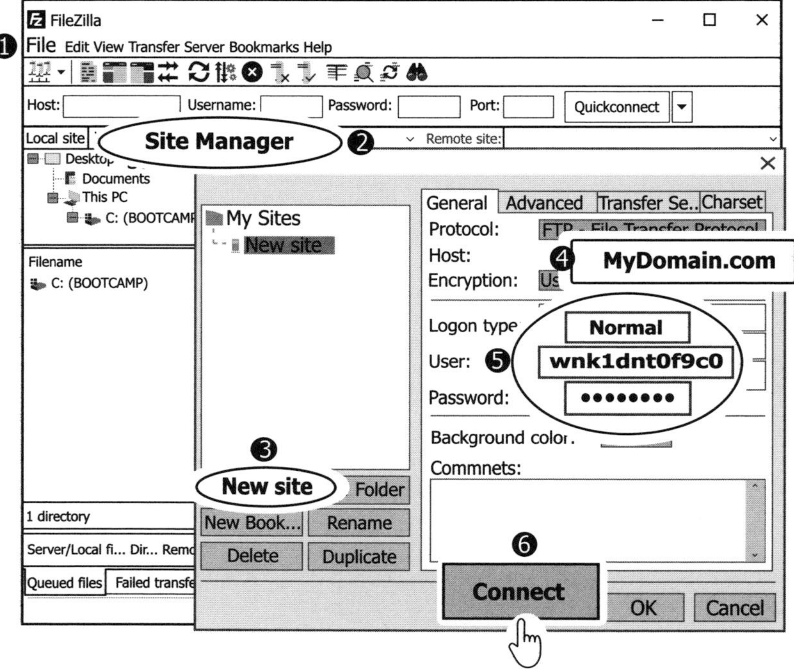

Note

If the connection is not established, the *internet propagation* is processing. Please wait 30 to 45 minutes.
If it takes more than 45 minutes, contact our customer support number (866)964-2867

Connect to a Server for Mac () user

Exactly the same as *FileZilla Windows O/S* on your left, except the *back ground menu* is slightly different.

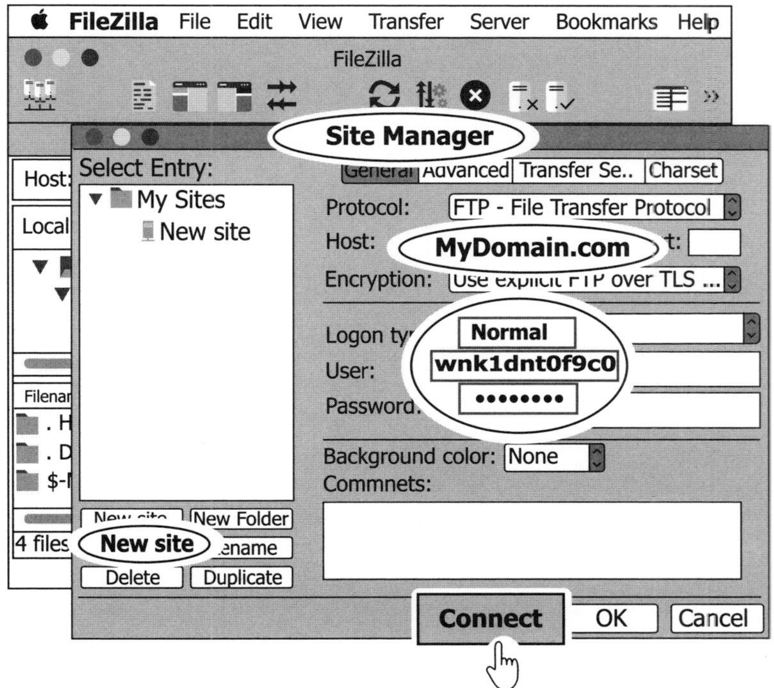

You may not be familiar with the screen above and on the left. They are from a Linux System. Don't worry: you only need to know file, directory/folder organization, and transfer.

Linux System

Linux is an *Open Source* operating system that was released on September 17, 1991 by Finnish-American, *Linus Torvalds*. Currently, it is the leading operating system on servers.

Local and Remote site Screen for Windows O/S ( ) users

- The screen is divided into two sides: "*Local site*" and "*Remote site*". The *Local site* is your PC and the *Remote site* is our (www.codingnhosting.org) server.
- We will learn and then practice *transferring files* and about *folders/directories* in Chapter 3.

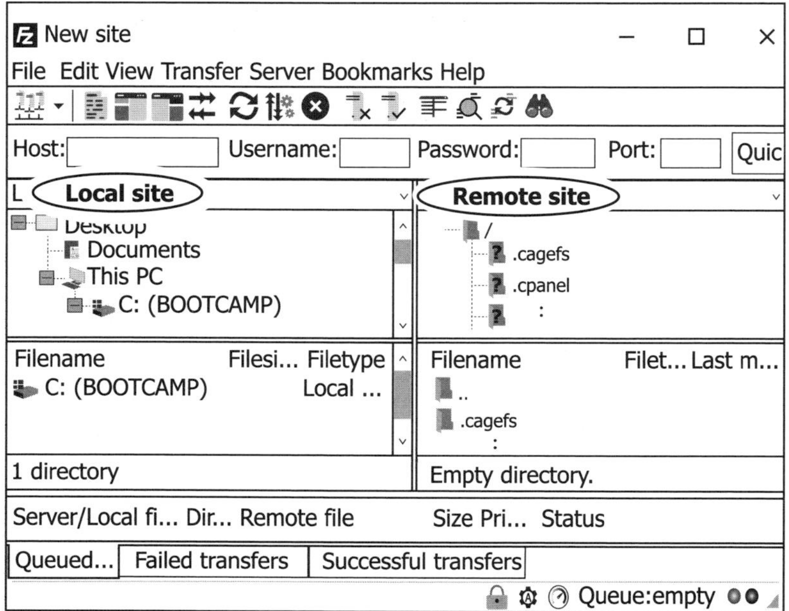

> **Note**
>
> Even though your screen shows the *Local* and *Remote site* next to each other, they can be located on opposite side of the globe.

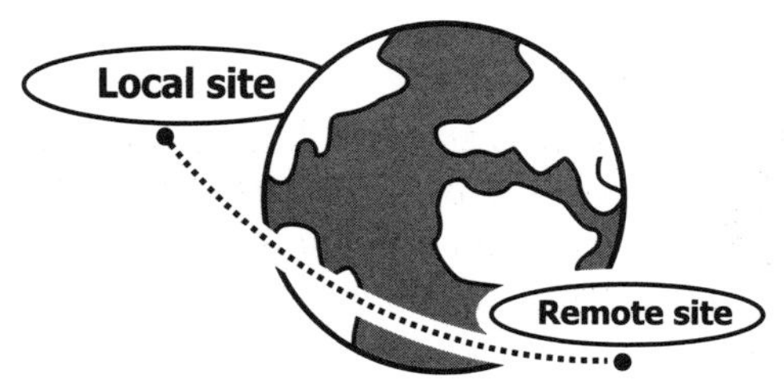

Local and Remote site Screen for Mac O/S () users

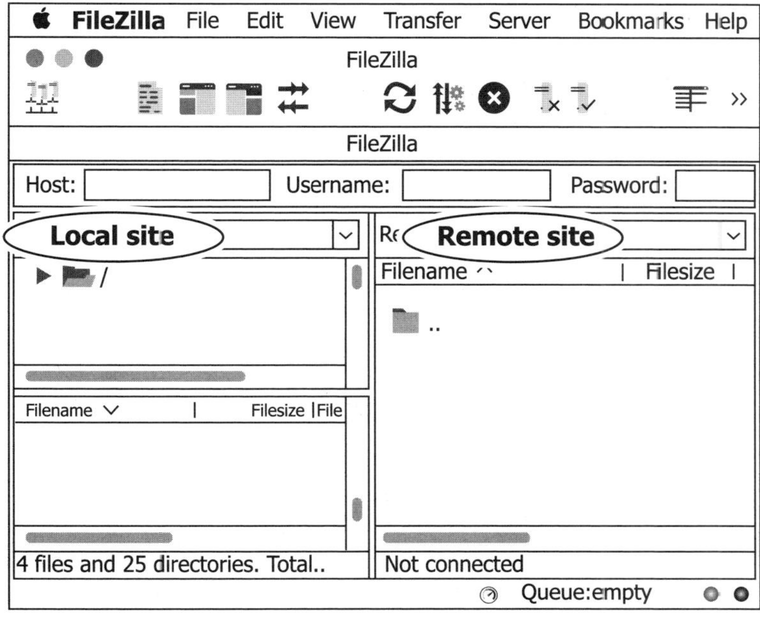

Root Directory

Unlike a *Windows user, a Mac user* may not be familiar with the concept "*Root*" or *"Root Directory"* in the PC. This is important when you do *file* and *folder/directory organizations.*

- The concept of *Root* is exactly the same as the root of the tree and it starts from the *Root* (level 0), and it branches out into levels 1, 2, 3..
- *Folder* is also the same as "*File Folder*" which holds a bunch of files.

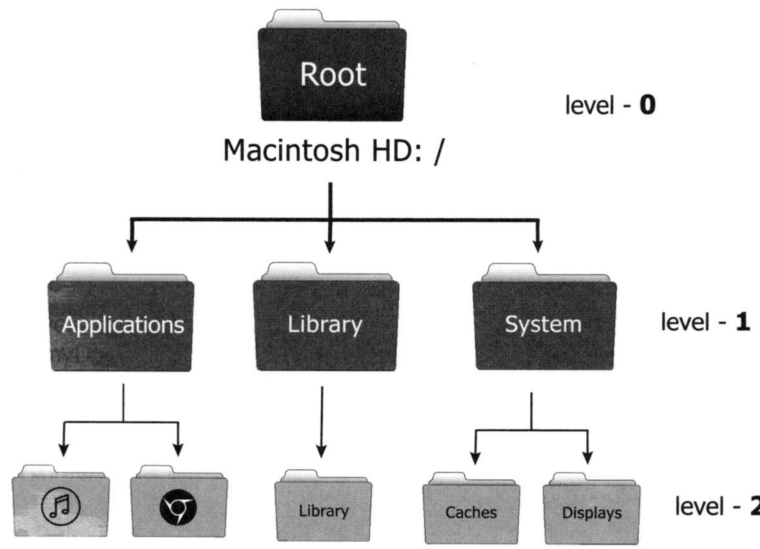

> **Note**
>
> In *Windows O/S, "C"* is the *Root Directory* and in *Mac O/S, "/"* is *Root Directory.*
> Both have a *Hard Disk Drive.* It is named "*C drive*" on a Windows O/S(⊞) and *"Mac HDD"* on a Macintosh O/S ().

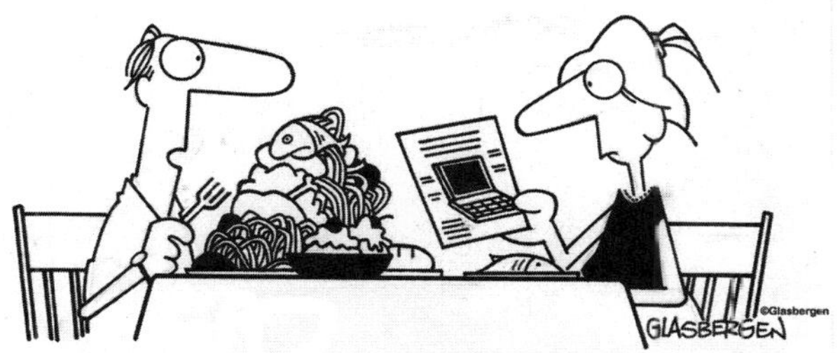

"I ordered my new laptop today. It has a 4 tera byte hard drive, 4 cores, full-size keyboard, and a 17-inch touch screen. I'm gonna need a bigger lap.."

CHAPTER 3

HTML (Hyper Text Markup Language)

1. What is HTML?
2. HTML Structure
3. Hello World!
4. Elements & Attributes
5. HTML Syntax
6. Basic Tags
7. Main Tags
8. Additional Tags

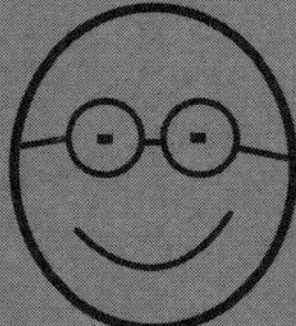

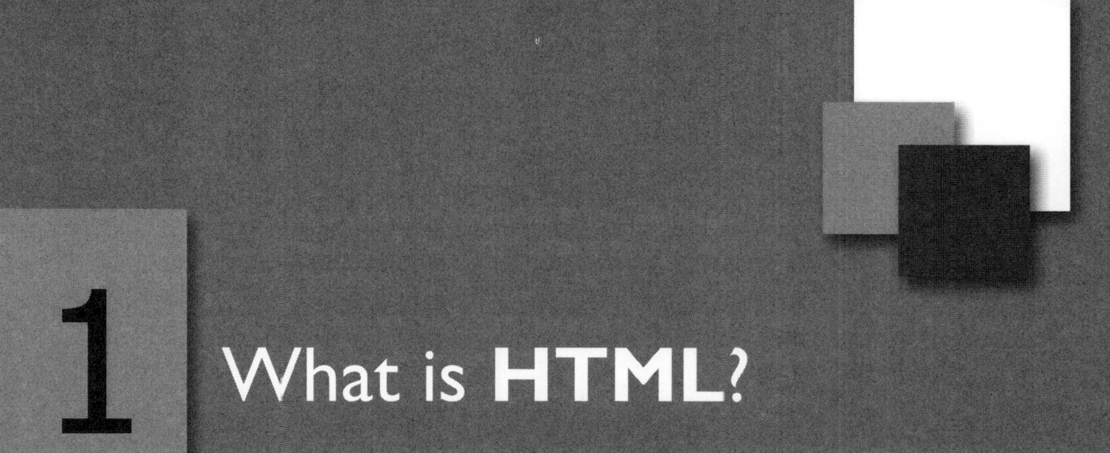

1 What is HTML?

HTML: Hyper Text Markup Language

- *Hype Text*: Text that, when clicked, it jumps from one document to another.
- *Markup*: Tags that apply layout and formatting structure to plain text.
- *Language*: A computer programming language.

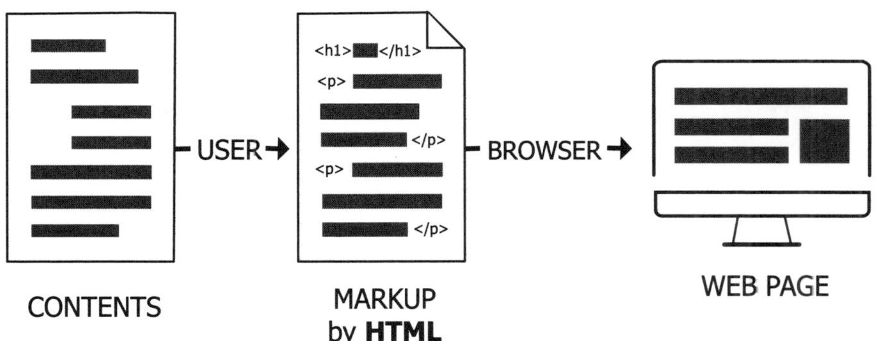

HTML is used for creating *web pages* and *web applications.*

- *HTML* is comprised of *tags*.
- *Tags* act like containers and are comprised of *angle brackets* (< >, </>)
- Most *HTML tags* have an opening and a closing *tag*, but there are *HTML tags* with no closing *tag* as well.
  Tags missing a closing tag are called *empty tags.*
  Empty tags include <br>, <img>, <li>..

> **Note**
> There are a lot of "*Brackets*" in computer programming languages. Such as < >, { }, ( ), [ ], << >>.
> Most of them used for containing information.

The first *web page* was published on August 6, 1991 by *Tim Berners-Lee.*

It ran on a *NeXT* computer at CERN.

Not surprisingly, it was a pretty basic one like the one below:

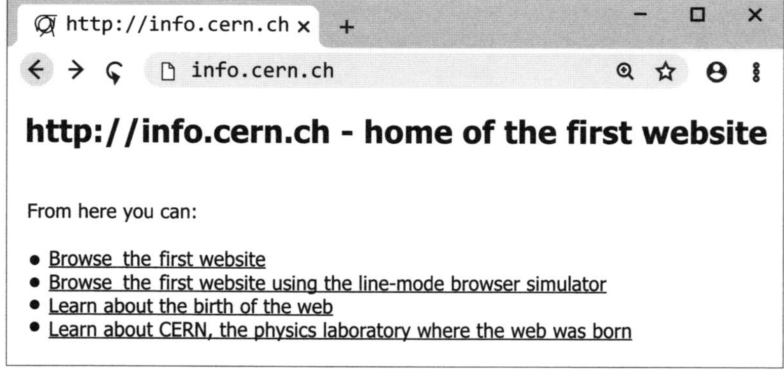

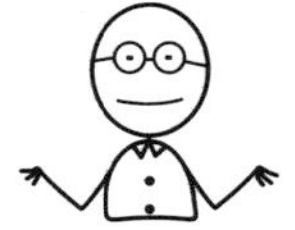

It's too simple... isn't it?
But it was "Super Sensational"
at that time.

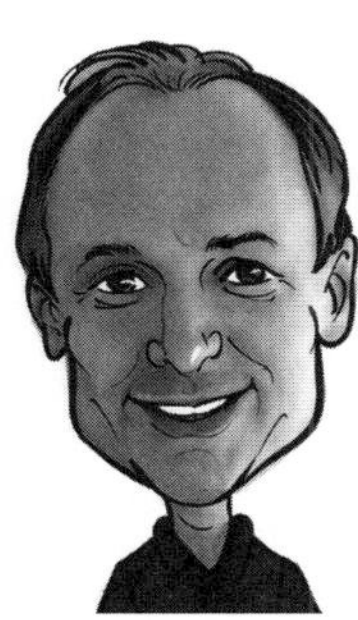

- Tim Berners-Lee, a scientist at CERN (The European Organization for Nuclear Research), developed *HTML* along with the *World Wide Web* in 1989.
- In 1991, *Tim* came out with the first *website* ever made: *www.info.cern.ch*
- You can still go to this site and learn about the birth of the web!

2 HTML Structure

There are 4 *HTML tags* you need to know for structuring a *HTML document*:

- `<!DOCTYPE html>` declares the start of a *HTML* (version5) file and appears *only* once. It is an *empty tag.*
- `<html>` describes the *web pages*. It closed with `</html>`
- <head> contains general instructions for the *browser*. It's not visible on the *web page*. It is closed with </head>
- <body> displays information on your *web page*. It is closed with </body>

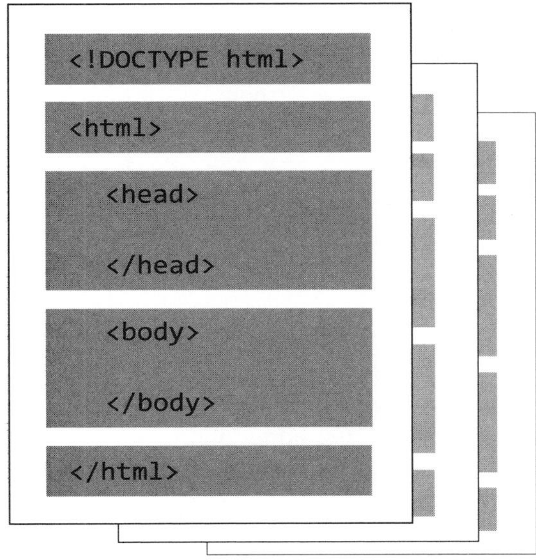

Along with *CSS (Cascading Style Sheets)* and *JavaScript, HTML* forms a major *coding language* for the web.

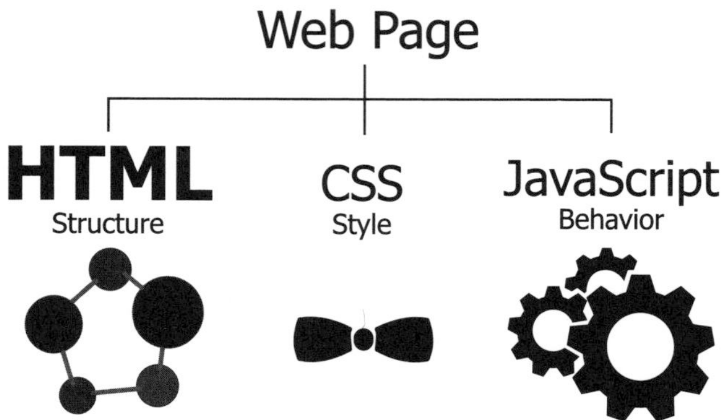

HTML Versions

Since the early days of the web, there have been many versions of HTML:

version	year
HTML 1.0	1989-1994
HTML 2.0	1995
HTML 3.2	1997
HTML 4.01	1999
XTML	2000
HTML 5	2014

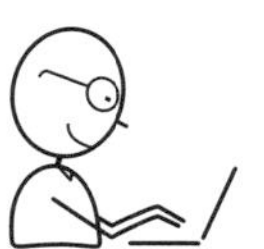

The latest version is *HTML 5* and it starts with: <!DOCTYPE html> and the rest of *HTML* versions before 5 start with: <!DOCTYPE html public... HTML X.X..>

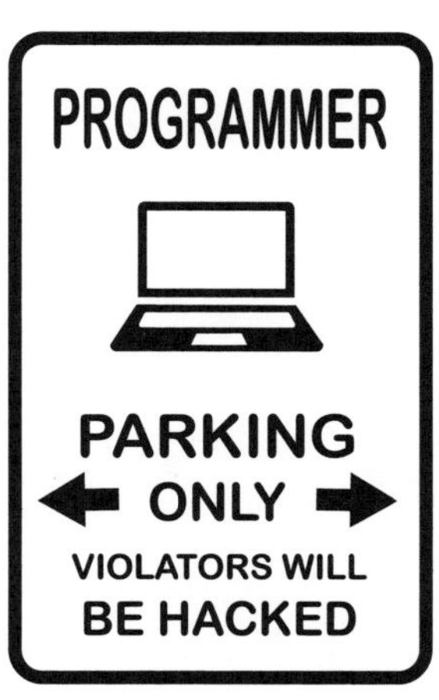
PROGRAMMER
PARKING
ONLY
VIOLATORS WILL
BE HACKED

3 Hello World!

In this section, you are going to code in your very first words ("Hello World!") onto your *Website*. To do this you will need:

- Your own *domain name* (registered in Chapter 2, Section 1, pg# 43)
- *Hosting account* (setup in Chapter 2, Section 1, pg# 45) and
- *FileZilla* (installed in Chapter 1, Section 5, pg# 32)
- *Visual Studio Code* (installed in Chapter 1, Section 5, pg# 34)
- A new *directory* which will store all your files for the *Website.*

> **"Create an index.html file and upload it to the server to show your friends all around the world !!"**

Note

"Hello World!" is traditionally, a starting programmer's (like you) "*testing word*" to test the system. Seeing these two words on the screen means their code runs correctly.

Make a New Directory for Windows O/S ( ) Users:

Open *FileZilla*

❶ Select the "C" drive and "Right Click"

❷ Select "Create Directory"

❸ Enter the name of the directory as "$-MyCoding"

This way, it shows up at **the First Line of your C drive:**

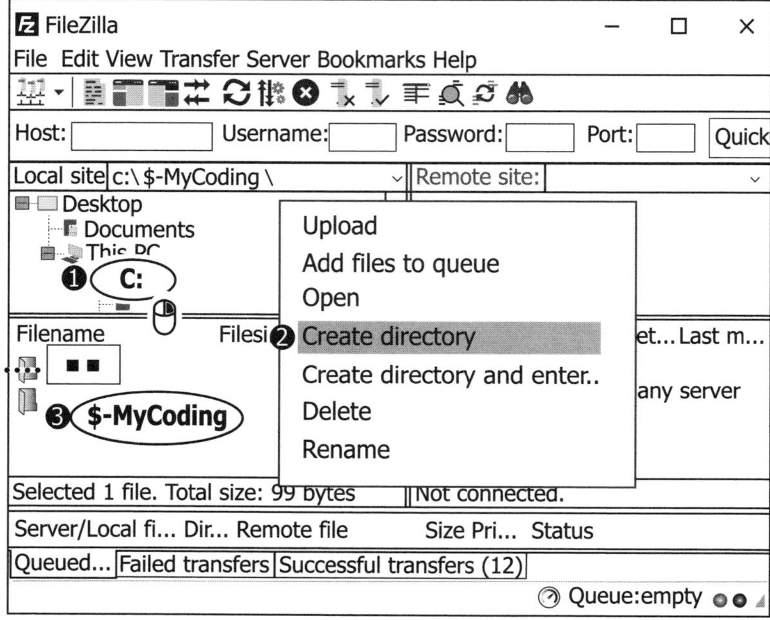

Note

There is a *Directory Name* ".." in the *Filename Section.* This is **not** a *file*. It is a "*mark*" which links to an "*upper level*" or a "*parent.*" Check pg# 66.

Unlike a *Windows O/S*, you can **not** make a directory through *FileZilla* in *Mac O/S.* In *Mac O/S,* you need to make a directory in the "*Finder*" menu.

Make a New Directory for Mac O/S () Users:

1. Go to "*Finder*"
2. Select "*Go*" in "*Menu Bar*"
3. Press "*Computer*"
4. Double Click "*Macintosh HD*"
5. *Control + Right Click* at "*Blank Space*" in the *Macintosh HD* window section.
6. Select "*New Folder*"
7. Enter the *Password* of the *MacOwner* and enter. This is the *Password* when you turn on your *Mac*. If you didn't setup a *Password,* it will not ask for the *Password.*
8. Type in "*$-MyCoding*" in "*untitled folder*"
   (It will appear at the first line under your *Macintosh HD* in *FileZilla*)
9. Now Open "*FileZilla*" and you will see a screen like the one below.

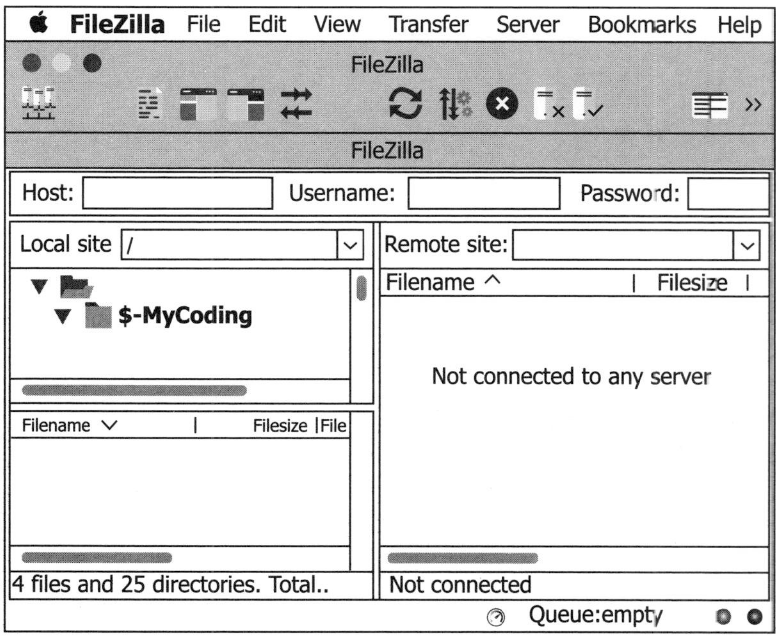

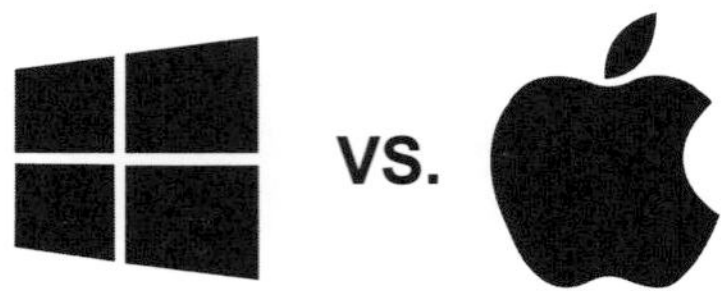

Windows vs. Mac

As you may have noticed, there are slight differences between *Windows O/S and Mac O/S.*

In particular, applications/software such as *FileZilla* differ in their *organizations* of *files* and *folders*.

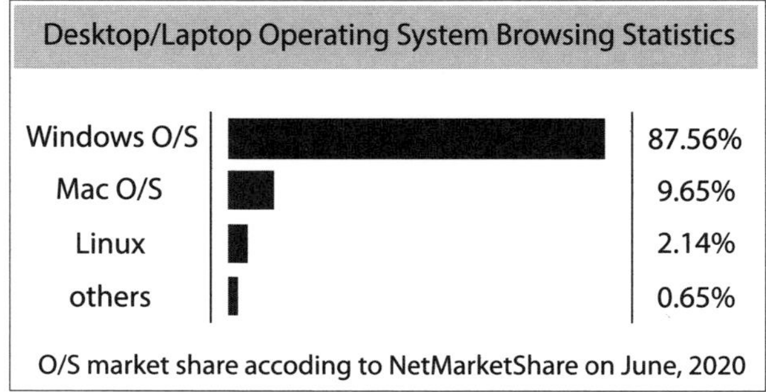

We will make an additional screen or comment for *Mac users.*

Open Visual Studio Code

- Open *Visual Studio Code* by selecting "*Visual Studio Code.*" (We installed it in Chapter 1, Section 5, pg# 34)
- Observe the front screen copy below. You will see that the *Windows O/S* is in front and the *Mac O/S* is in back.
- There are also a few differences in the "*Short Cut Key*" operations. But you will figure these out easily.

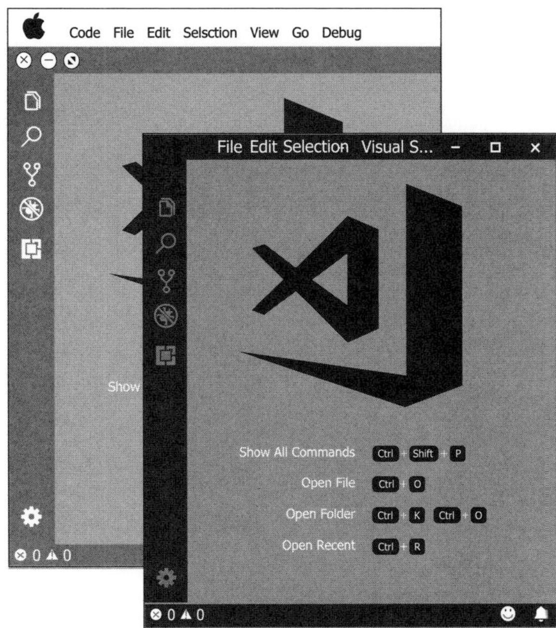

> **Note**
>
> The background color of *Visual Studio Code* will be much darker than this screen. The main reason for the black background color is it protect your eyes. It is much less tiring to view than a white background with black font.

Create a HTML file and Save

❶ Press "*File Menu*" and select "*New File*"

❷ Type in a series of code like those below:

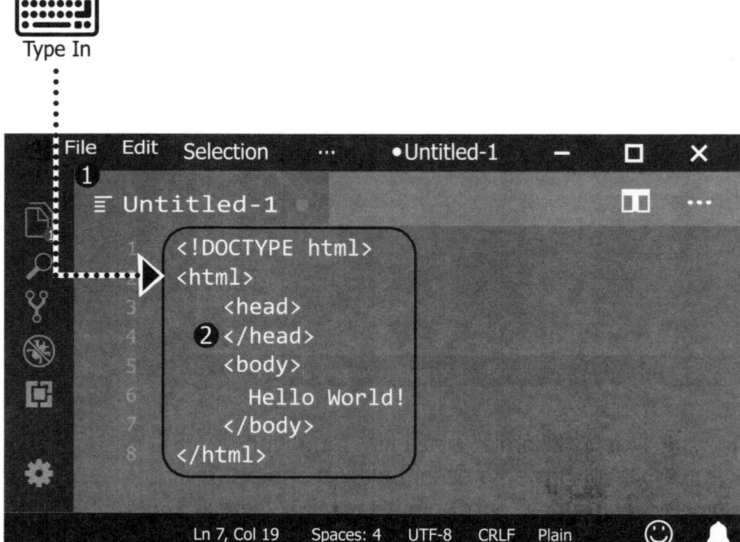

❸ Save this file under the directory name *$-MyCoding*

❹ Specify the file name as "*index*" and the file type as "*html*" so that the file will save as "*index.html.*"

❺ Click "Save"

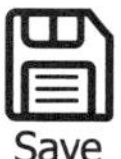

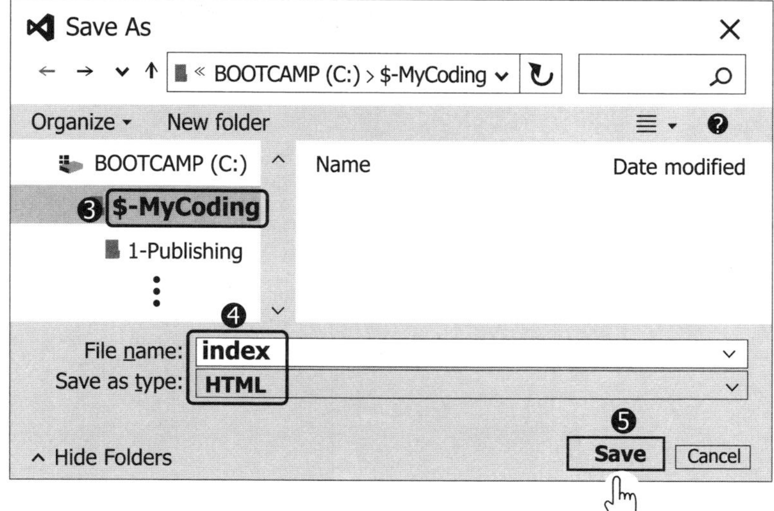

Connect to a Server

1. Open *FileZilla* by clicking "*FileZilla Client*"
2. Click "*File*"
3. Select "*Site Manager*"
4. Select "*Connect*"

The procedure for connecting to a server is explained in detail in Chapter 2 section 3 (pg# 62). Skip this and you will see the flowing *FileZilla* screen.

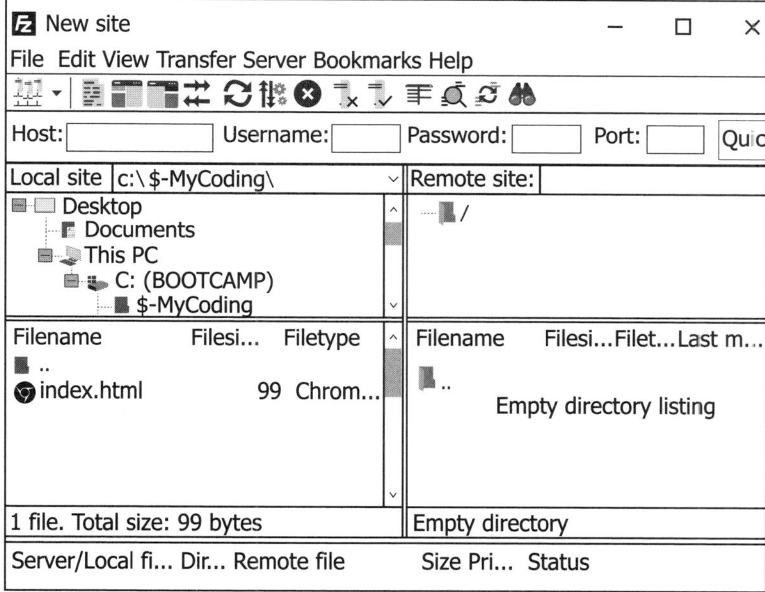

Upload file

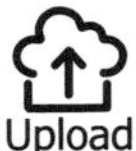

To upload your file onto the server:

❶ Open the file folder "*public_html*" in the *Remote site*.

❷ Right click (: control + right click) "*index.html*" in the *Local site*.

❸ Press "*Upload.*"

❹ The file will be *uploaded* to the *Remote site.*

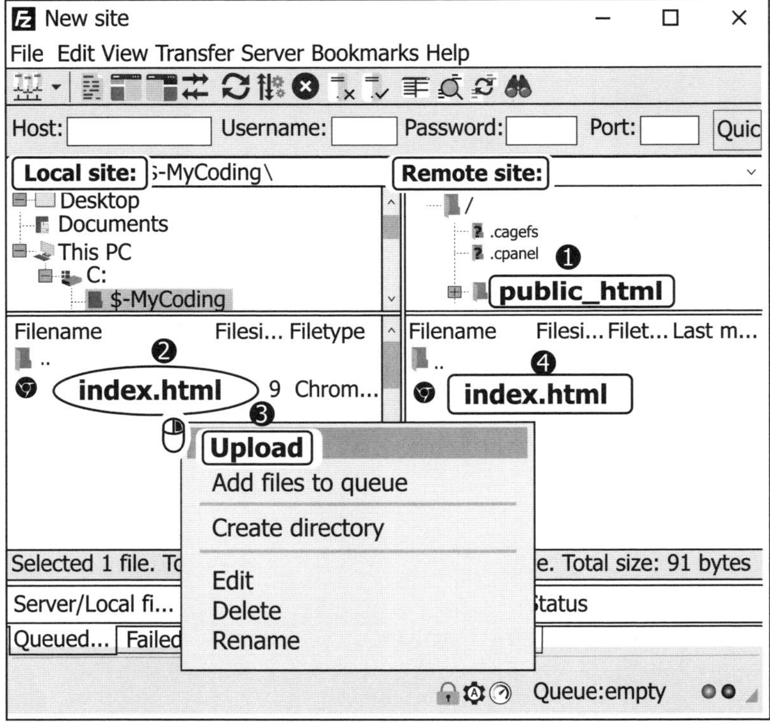

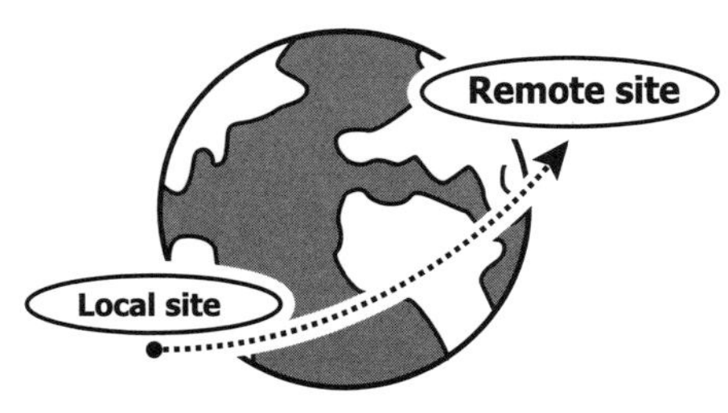

Now, let's open/reload the browser and type your domain name: *www.myDomain.com*

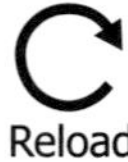

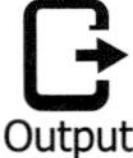

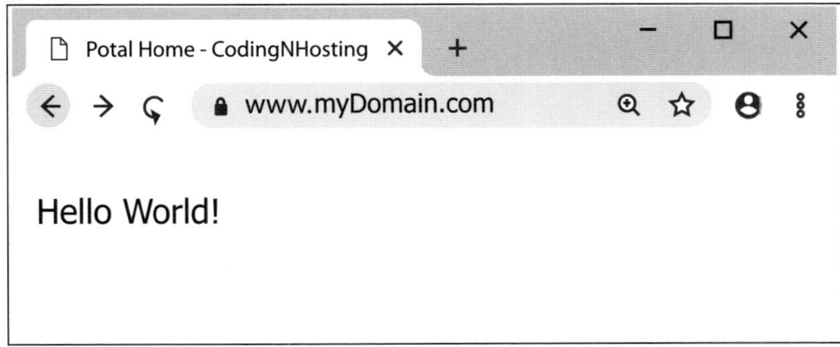

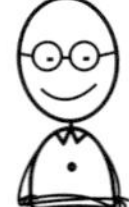

Congratulations
on your "First Website"
on the Web!

Note

"*Hello World!*" is the phrase which was influenced by Brian Kerninghan's book, "*A Tutorial Instruction to the Programming Language* **B**" published in 1972

Download file

You can *download* your files onto your PC by selecting a file you like. The method is the same as *upload*.

❶ Right click (: control + right click) "*anyfile*" in *Remote Site*.

❷ Press "*Download*"

❸ "*anyfile*" will be placed in Local site.

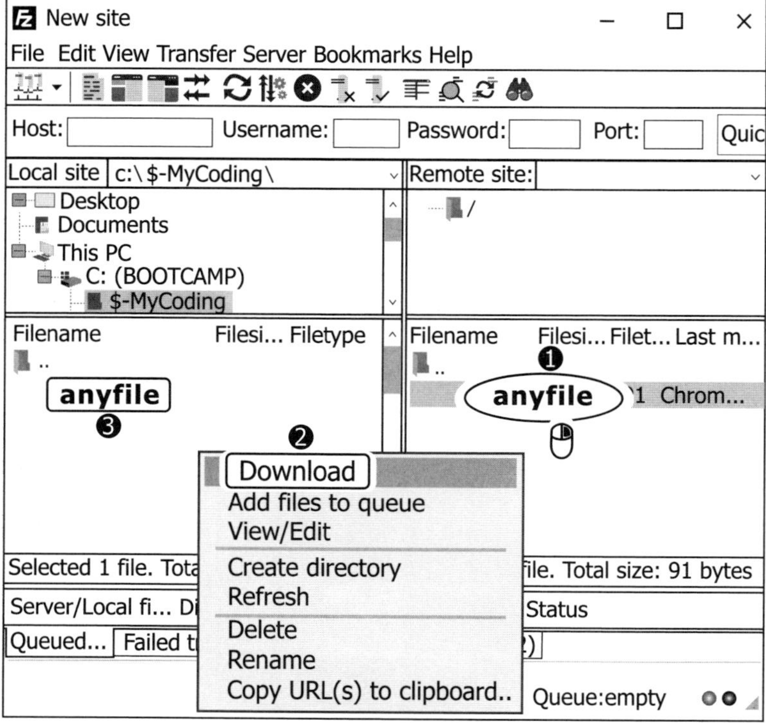

You will not have too many chances to *download* files in the early stage of your coding career.

Link to Visual Studio Code from FileZilla

- This function makes a link from *FileZilla* to *Visual Studio Code*.
- By directly connecting these two Softwares, you can save time.

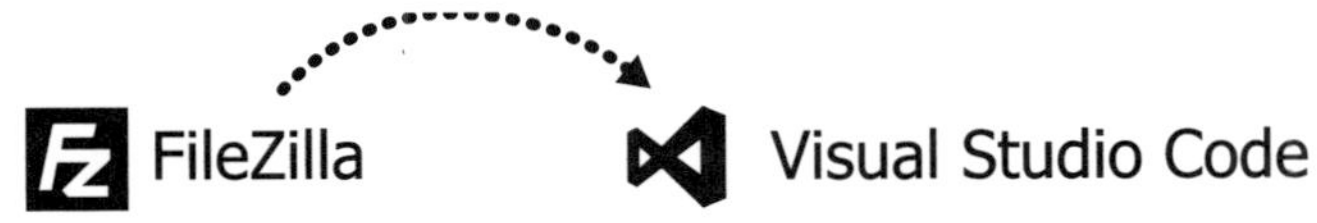

Note

When you do this step, your *FileZilla* **must be connected** to the *Server*.

It is a very convenient function when you are editing a file while *downloading/uploading that file*. To make this link:

❶ In *FileZilla*, click "*edit*" and select "*settings*"

❷ In the "*Select page*" section, press [−] sign (: ▼)

❸ The [−] button will change to a [+] sign (: ►) and you will find "*File editing*"

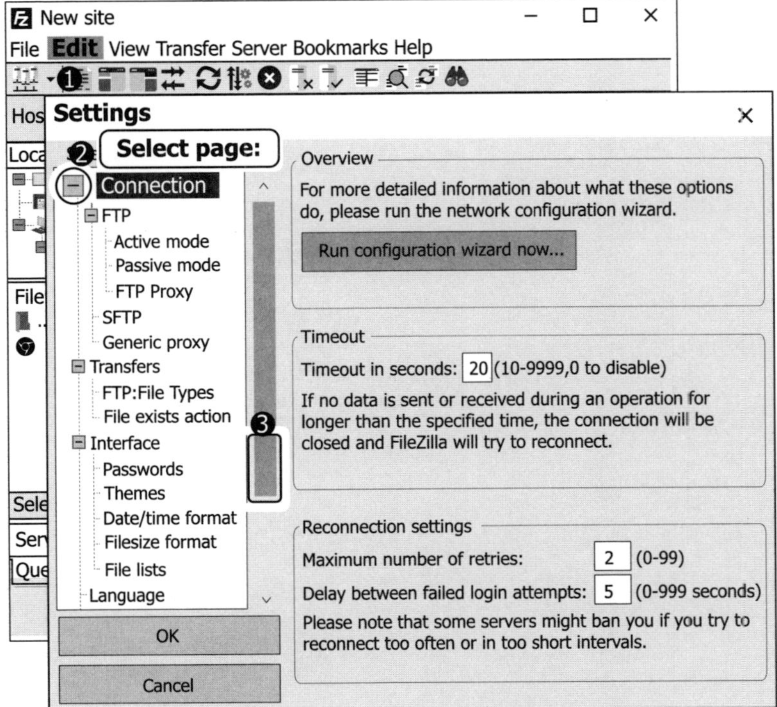

Link to Visual Studio Code - continued

❹ Click "*File editing*", you will see the screen below.

❺ Select "*Use custom editor*"

❻ Press "*Browse*"

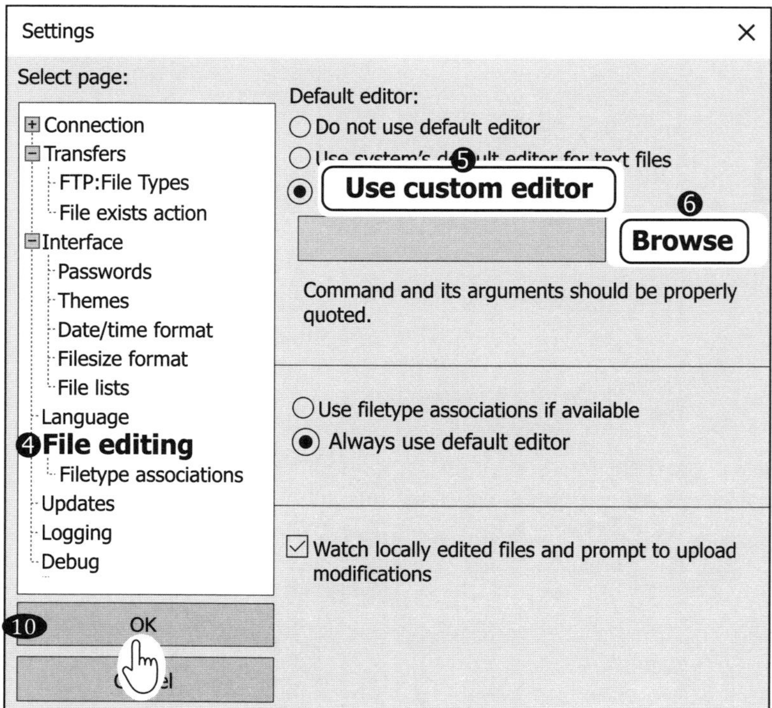

❼ Select "Desktop"

❽ Type in "Visual Studio Code"

❾ Select "Visual Studio Code" and click "Open"

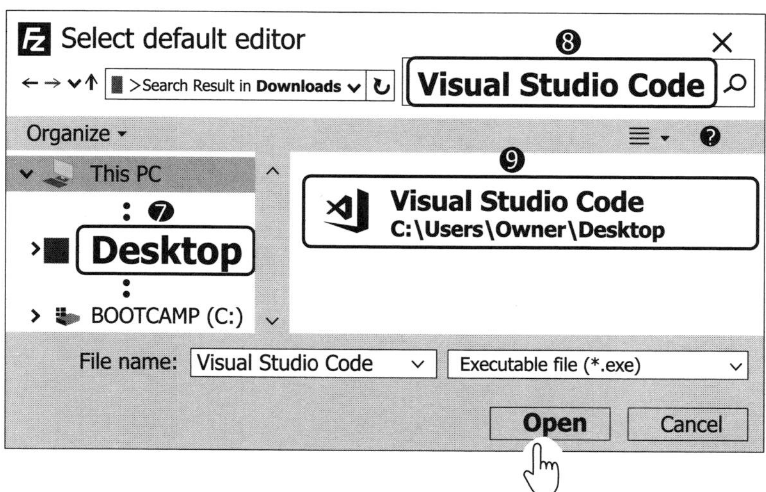

❿ Click "OK"

Let's check Link Function of FileZilla

❶ Select *index.html* file in the Local *Site*.

❷ *Right-click* (: control + right click) it and choose *Edit.*

❸ It will link to *Visual Studio Code.*

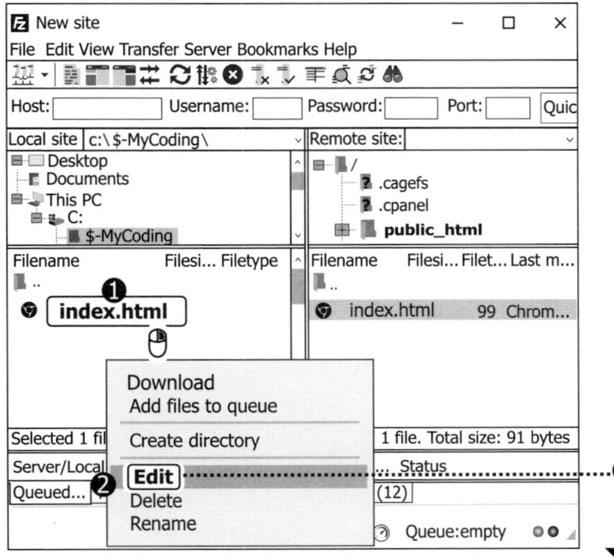

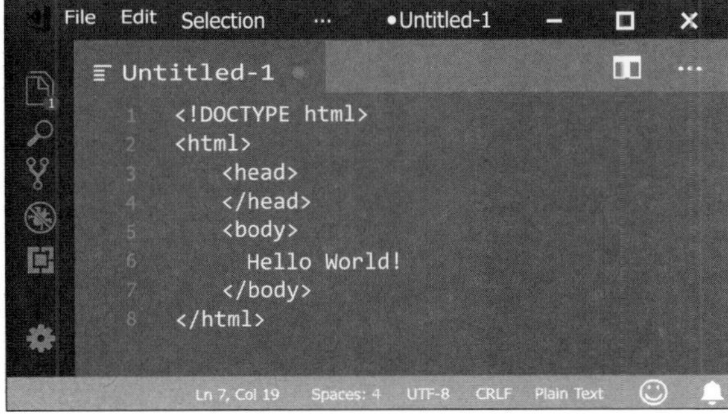

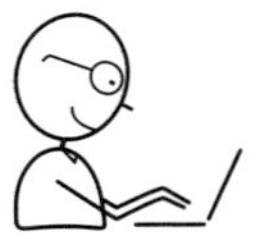

Linking is a convenience; it saves you time by reducing the times you need to mouse-click.

4 Element & Attributes

HTML Element/Tag

- *Web pages* consist of *HTML Elements*.
- *HTML Elements* mainly consist of an *opening tag* and a *closing tag* with the content inserted in between the tags.

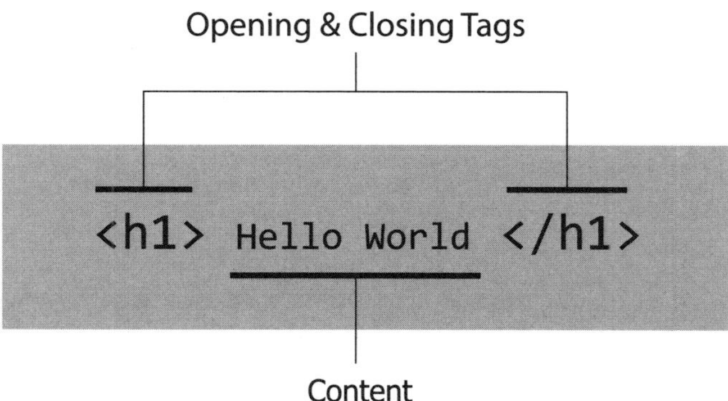

> **Note**
>
> In *HTML 5*, the words "*element,*" "*tag,*" and "*markup*" are all considered the same.

HTML Attributes

- You can put more information in the *opening tag* (between the *tag name* and *right bracket*). This is called an *attribute.*
- It is made up of two parts: *Attribute Name* and *Attribute Value,* which is surrounded by a *double quotation mark* (" ").
  These two parts are separated by an *equal sign* (=).
- *An attribute* is used when more information is added to a *tag*.

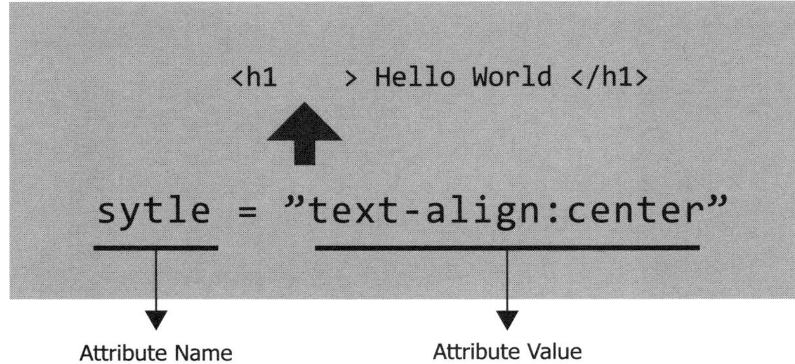

> **Note**
>
> There are *107 HTML Elements/Tags* and 164+ *Standard Attributes* in *HTML 5*. You don't need to memorize all of them. Just remember some of the *basic ones*.

Only content parts display in the screen

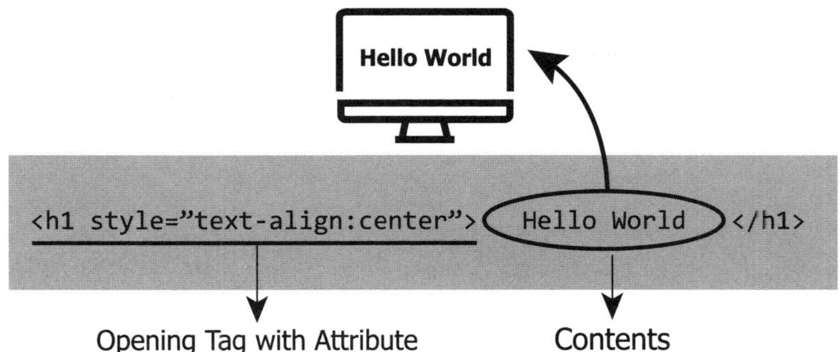

Don't worry about `h1, style, text-align` and `others`. You will learn about them later in this chapter. For now, just understand the *concept* and *structure* of *Elements/Tags* and *Attributes*.

Additional

- Some *HTML elements* are without content. These are called *empty tags* and include `<br>` tag (which indicates a *"line break"*), `<img>` tag (defines an *"image"* in an *HTML page*), and `<li>` tag (*"listed item"* used for *Navigation Section*)
- Earlier, many presentational *attributes* were used, like `align, valign, bgcolor,` etc. But now in *HTML 5*, these *attributes* are removed. *CSS* is used instead of these *attributes*.

5 HTML **Syntax**

- *HTML Syntax* is like grammar in English.
- The correct use of *programming syntax* is very important. If there is a *syntax error*, the computer will not work correctly.
- There are many *syntaxes* in *HTML,* and some of them are like the following:

Case In-sensitivity

HTML is *Case In-sensitive* in most respects:

ACamelBack = acamelback

NOTE

Attribute values are *case sensitive*. For example, `class="aa"` is **not** the same as `class="AA"`.

Comment Line

- A *comment line* in *HTML* is not visible on your *website*. It is used for providing additional information about the *code* for the *programmer*.
- *Comment lines* can be added on the *HTML command line* starting with "<!--" and ending with "-->" like this:

```
<!-- Write your comments here -->
```

Non-Breaking Space ( )

Non-Breaking Space ( ) has 2 main functions:

- Creates *multiple (white) spaces* that are visible on a *web page*. *HTML* will only display *one space* between *words*, no matter how many times you press the *space bar*. To make an *extra space* show up, type * * in the area where you want to make the *space*.
- Create a space in a line that can**not** be broken by *word wrap*. So, two words separated by * * will stick together. (see example below):

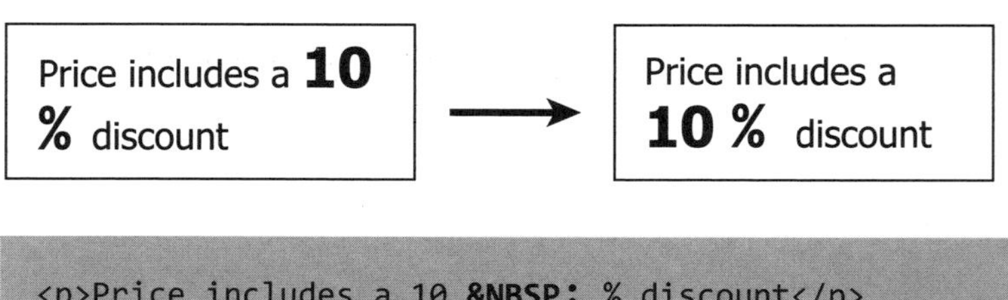


```
<p>Price includes a 10   % discount</p>
```

Looks a little weird when "*10*" and "*%*" are separated. It looks much nicer and clearer when * * is used.

Indentation

When an *element* carries more than one line of code, it is recommended to make *indentations* of the *element's contents.* This makes easy to read where the *element* and *content* begins and ends.

```
<table><tr><td>Data One</td><td>Data Two</td></tr>
<tr><td>Data Three</td><td>Data Four</td></tr></table>
```

```
<table>
  <tr>
    <td>Data One</td>
    <td>Data Two</td>
  </tr>
  <tr>
    <td>Data Three</td>
    <td>Data Four</td>
  </tr>
</table>
```

6 Basic Tags

- There are **107** *tags* in *HTML 5* up to date.
- We label **12** of these as *Basic Tags* (see table below).

12 Basic Tags

tags	description
`<!--  -->`	comment tag
`<!DOCTYPE html>`	declare the document type HTML 5
`<html>`	defines HTML document
`<head>`	information about document
`<body>`	defines the document's body
`<h1> .. <h6>`	defines HTML headings
`<p>`	defines a paragraph
` `	defines a single line break
`<hr>`	defines a horizontal ruler/line
`<b>`	defines bold text
`<a>`	defines an anchor tag
`<img>`	defines an image inserting

WHATWG

NOTE

HTML 5 was developed by *WHATWG (Web Hypertext Application Technology Working Group)* and influenced by *W3C (The World Wide Web Consortium)* which was founded by *Tim Berners-Lee.*

You don't need to type-in the codes. Just understand what each of tags means.

```
1  <!DOCTYPE html>
2  <html>
3    <head>
     </head>
4  <body>
5    <h1>This is heading 1</h1>
     <h2>This is heading 2</h2>
6     <p>Hello World!
7       <br>
        my name is
8      <b>Daniel</b>
      </p>
9     <hr>
10    <a href="https://www.google.com">Visit Google</a>
      <br>
11    <img src="images/image_river.jpg">
12 <!-- you need to download and save this img file -->
   </body>
   </html>
```

This is heading 1

This is heading 2

Hello World!

my name is **Daniel**

Visit Google

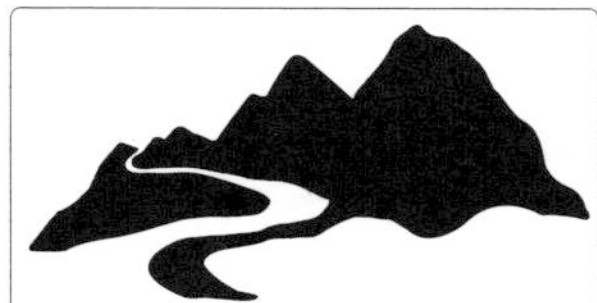

❶ `<!DOCTYPE html>` tag:

Used to declare to the browser "*This is a HTML 5 document.*" It should be the *very first thing* in the document.

❷ `<html>` tag:

Indicates that anything between this and closing `</html>` tag is *HTML code.*

❸ `<head>` tag:

Used to contain specific information about this *web page*.

❹ `<body>` tag:

Contains all the contents of this *HTML* document, such as `text, hyperlinks, images,` etc.

❺ `<h1> .. <h6>` tag:

Used to define *headings*. `<h1>` defines largest and `<h6>` smallest.

❻ `<p>` tag:

Used to define blocks of *paragraph text.*

❼ `<br>` tag:

Used to insert a line *break* or *carriage-return*.

❽ `<b>` tag:

Used to markup text as *bold.*

❾ `<hr>` tag:

Used for creating a *horizontal rule.*

⓾ `<a>` tag:

Anchor tag. Used to create a hyperlink to another location.

⑪ `<img>` tag:

Used to insert an *image* into your *HTML* document.

⑫ `<!-- -->` tags:

Used to insert *comments* in the HTML source code.

Invisible, but useful when you have a lot of codes.

These tags are **not** supported in *HTML 5* anymore, and their function is better handled by *CSS.*

12 tags that were deleted from HTML 5

<acronym>

<applet>

<basefont>

<big>

<center>

<dir>

<font>

<frame>

<frameset>

<noframes>

<strike>

<tt>

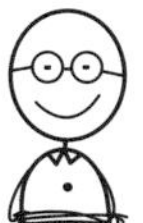

Before practicing *HTML coding*, let's create and organize our *directory, "$-MyCoding"* and download necessary files.

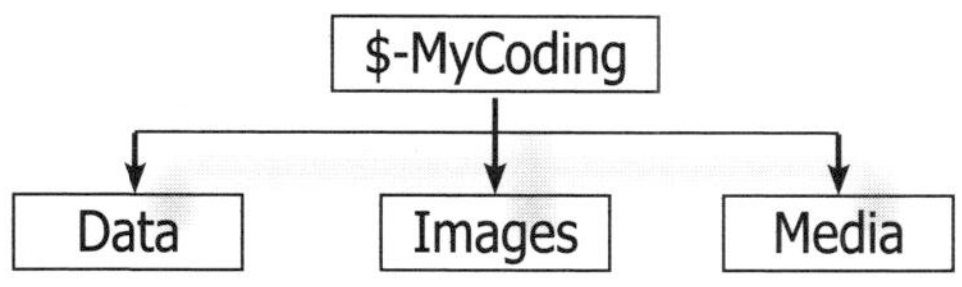

NOTE

I will use FileZilla for file/folder organization. Some of you might not be familiar with this. But don't worry just follow the instructions:

Make a new Directories

Let's make new directories named "*Data*", "*Images*", and "*Media*" *respectively* under the directory "*$-MyCoding*":

❶ Hover over *$-MyCoding* directory, right-click (: control + right click), and select "*Create Directory*"

❷ Delete ***all the characters*** ("C:\$-MyCoding\New directory") and just type in "*Data*"

Let's make 2 more directories:

Repeat ❶ and ❷ and type in "*Images*" and "*Media*"

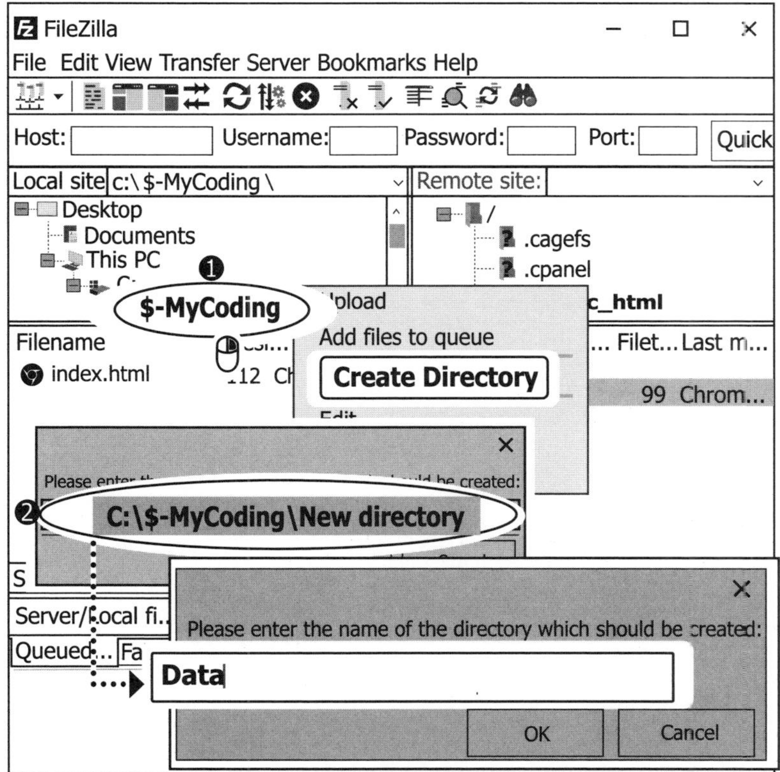

Download and save a picture file

PICTURE

1. Go to *www.pixabay.com*
2. In *search image box*, type and enter "*river*".
3. *Skip* first "*Sponsored Images iStock*" line of images.
4. Select any of the next "*Free image of river" image files.*
5. Download the *image file* by selecting the "*Free Download*" button.

: After the download is done, open and save it by clicking "*Control+S* " and name it "*image_river.jpg*" under the directory named "*Images*", which is a sub-directory of "*$-MyCoding*"

: The file is saved in the "*downloads" section* with a name that the *pixabay.com* site made. Rename it (*Control+Click*) as "*image_river.jpg*" and move it to the directory *images:*

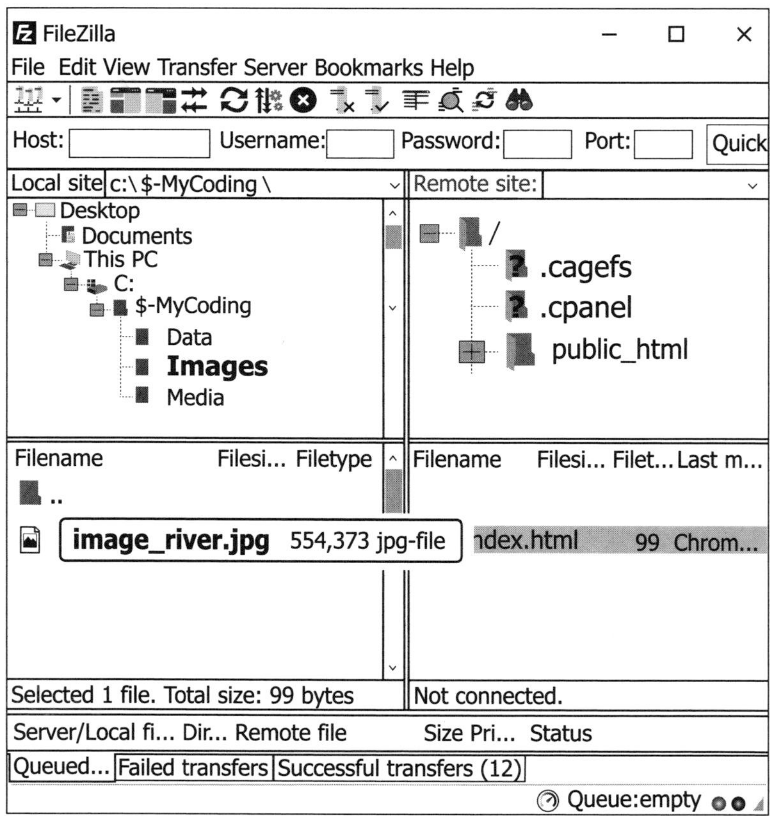

Download and save a picture file for Mac

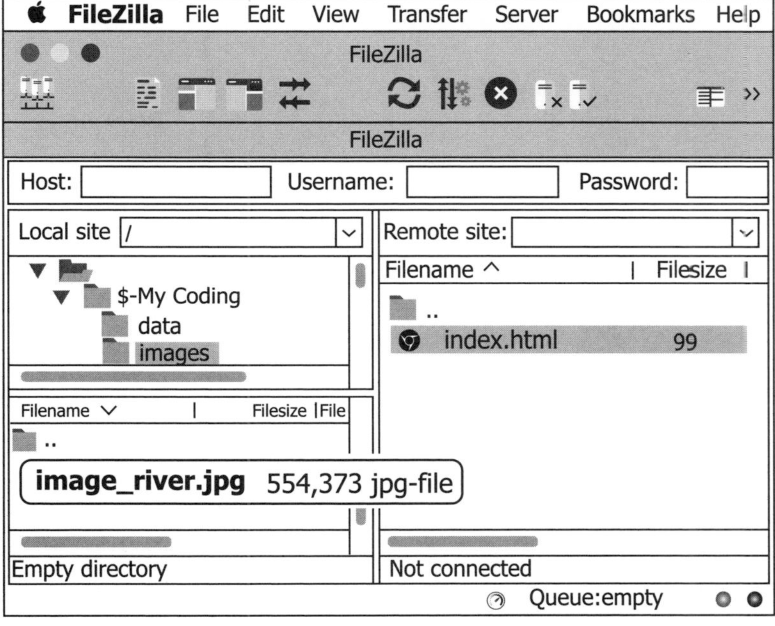

Create a HTML file

Now, let's make a simple *HTML* file using the *12 basic tags* that we just introduced. (pg# 102, 103) :

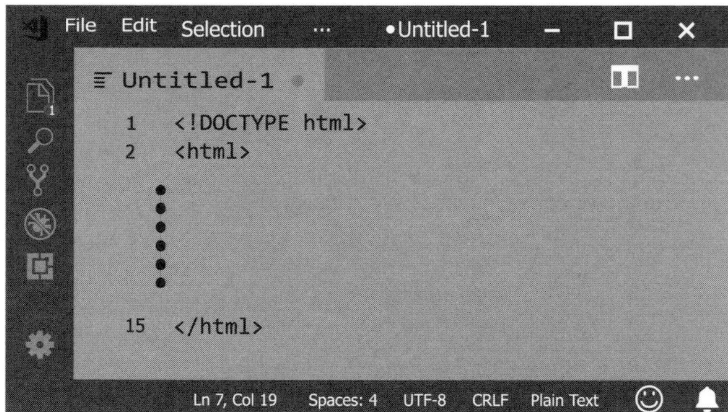

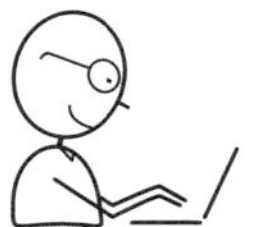

From now on, I will use a "simplified" screen like the one below: Please type exactly like this using *Visual Studio Code*.

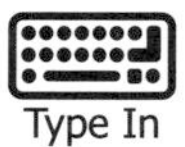

Type In

```
<!DOCTYPE html>
<html>
  <head>
  </head>
  <body>
    <h1>This is heading 1</h1>
    <h2>This is heading 2</h2>
     <hr>
     <p>Hello...
       <br>
       my name is
       <b>Daniel.</b>
     </p>
     <a href="https://www.google.com">Visit Google</a>
     <br>
     <img src="Images/image_river.jpg" width="200"
      height="100">
<!-- you need to download and save this image file -->
   </body>
</html>
```

Save and Upload file and Upload directory

Save this file as "*index.html*" in the directory *$-MyCoding* on the Local site *C* drive (: *Mac HD*)
You will have "*index.html* already exists" Pop Up.
(because, we created it in Chapter 3, Section 3, pg# 84)
Click "Yes" or Press "OK"

❶ Make sure you select directory "*public_html*" in the Remote site.

❷ Upload *index.html* to the directory by right-clicking (: control + right click) and choose *upload.*

❸ Right-click (: control + right click) the *images* directory and *upload* it to the *public_html* directory.

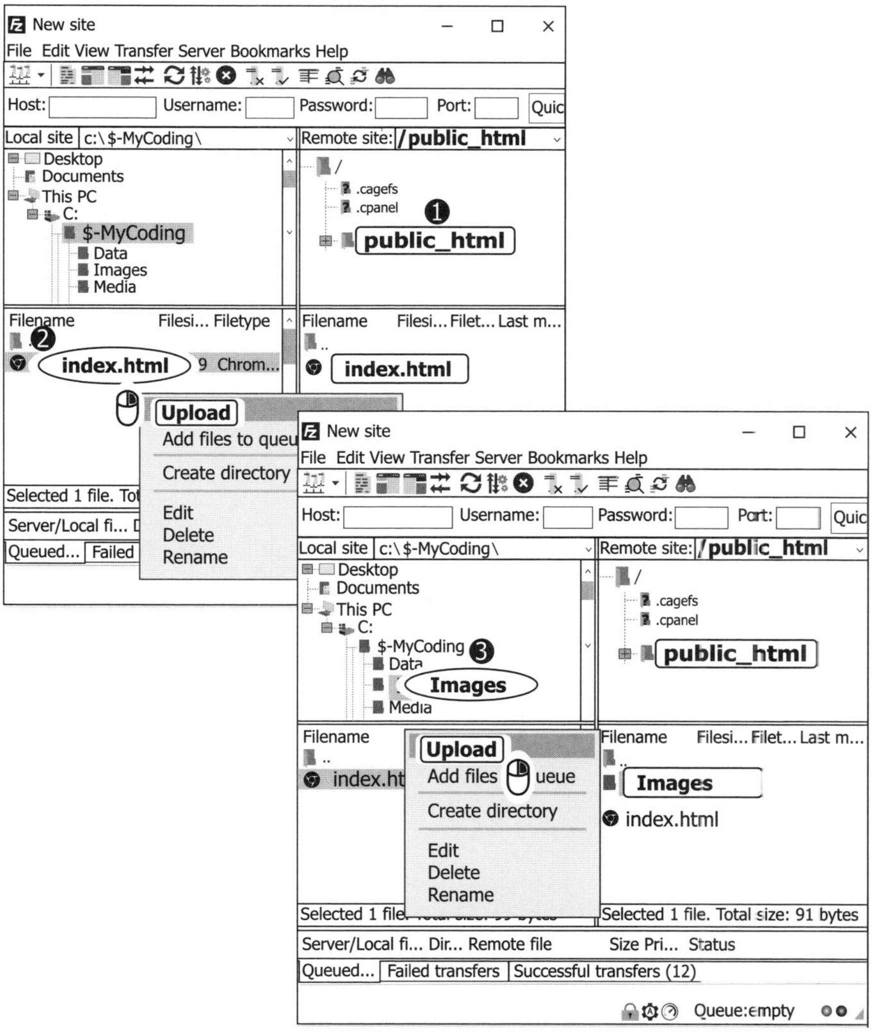

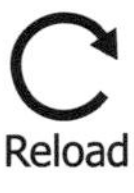

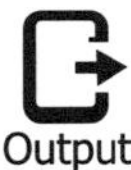

❹ *Open* or *reload* your site: *myDomain.com*

❺ *Output* will be like this:

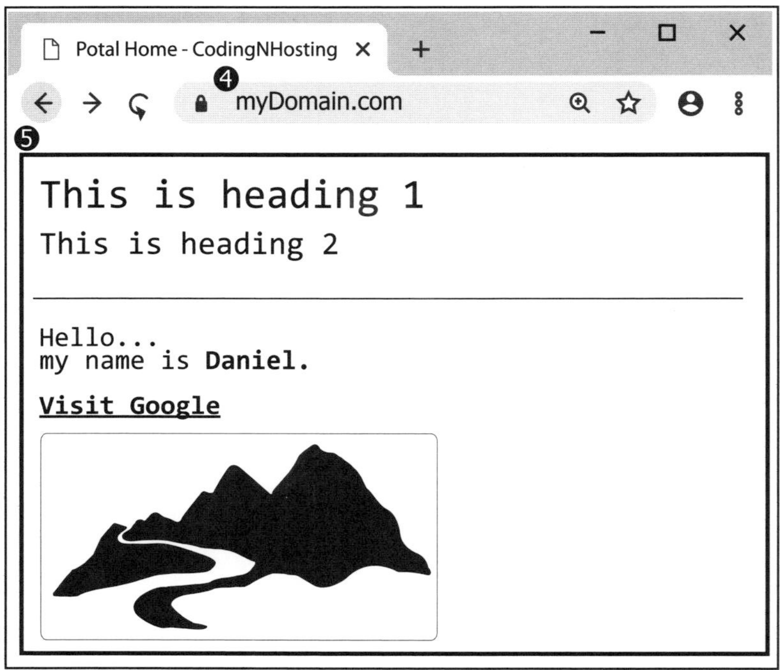

Year 2001

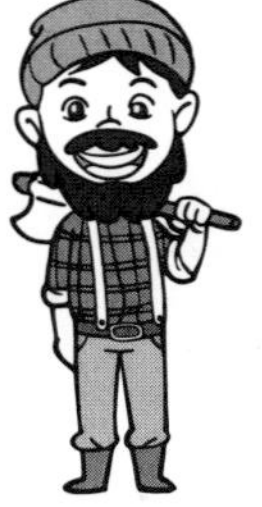

Lumberjack

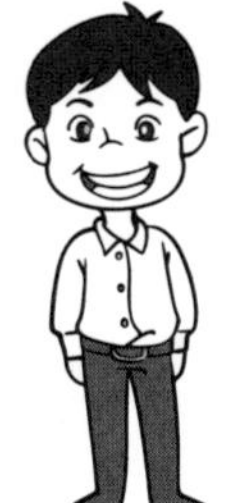

Programmer

Year 2021

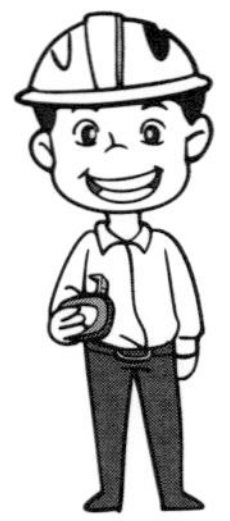

Lumberjack

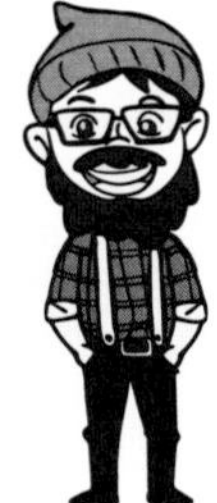

Programmer

7 Main Tags

Main tags are mainly for *structuring* the website.
They are like the *backbone* of the web.

I categorized 9 different kinds of 56 *main tags* as follows:

- Head Tags
- Layout Tags
- Semantic Tags
- List Tags
- Frame Tags
- Media Tags
- Formatting Tags
- Form Tags
- Table Tags

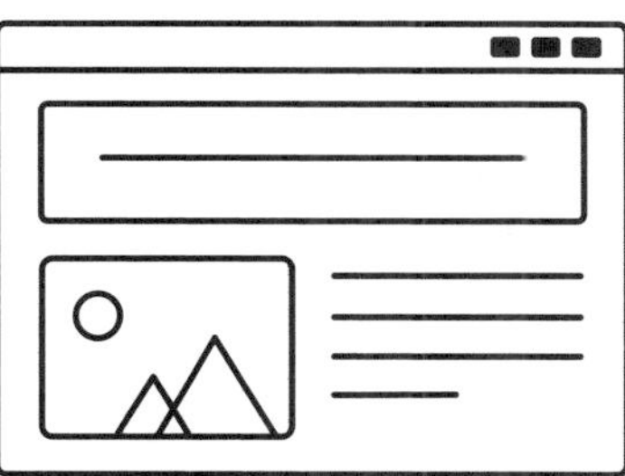

No need for you to memorize all the *HTML* tags. Just understand the meaning and concepts.

The nine different categories of tags:

Head Tags

<title>
<meta>
<link>
<style>
<script>

Layout Tags

<div>
<span>

Semantic Tags

<header>
<nav>
<article>
<aside>
<details>
<figcaption>
<figure>
<footer>
<main>
<mark>
<section>
<summary>
<time>

List Tags

<ol>
<ul>
<li>

Frame Tags

<embed>
<iframe>
<object>
<param>

Media Tags

<audio>
<video>
<source>
<track>

Formatting Tags

<del>
<em>
<i>
<ins>
<s>
<strong>
<sub>
<sup>

Form Tags

<form>
<option>
<label>
<input>
<select>
<button>
<textarea>
<fieldset>
<legend>

Table Tags

<table>
<caption>
<thead>
<tbody>
<tfoot>
<th>
<hr>
<td>

Head Tag (metadata)

The `<head>` tag is a container for all the *head elements* such as a `<title>` for the document, `<meta>` information, `<link>`, `<style>`, `<script>` and more.
We call this *"metadata"*

- <title>
- <meta>
- <link>
- <style>
- <script>

Except for the <title> tag, the contents of the <head> tag do **not** show in the browser screen.

```
<!DOCTYPE html>
<html>
  <head>
    <title>My Page Title</title>
    <meta charset="UTF-8">
    <link rel="stylesheet" type="text/css" href="sample.css">
    <style> p {text-align: center;} </style>
    <script src="javascript.js"></script>
  </head>
  <body>
    <p>Content of title tag will be displayed in
    the browser tab</p>
  </body>
</html>
```

Note:

Metadata is "what the data is."
Metadata for a music file might include the *artist's name, the album,* and *the year* it was *released*, etc.

- <title>

This tag is usually displayed in the *browser's title bar.* It is also displayed in *browser bookmarks* and *search results.* It should be 70 characters or less including spaces.

- <meta>

The <meta> tag in *HTML* provides information about the *HTML* Document such as charset, name, content, etc...

<meta> ≠ metadata

the tag <meta>
is different than
metadata

> **Note**
>
> The word *meta* is from the *Greek* meaning "*with it*" and is often used to refer to something that *refers to itself.*

- <link>

This tag is used for defining a link to an *external resource.*
Commonly used for a *CSS* file.

- <style>

This tag is used for declaring a *style sheet* within your *HTML* document.

- <script>

The <script> tag contains the *scripting statements,* or it points to an *external script file*...mainly *JavaScript.*

Note:

Learn how to:
Type in: Using *Visual Studio Code*,
Save: To C drive (Mac HDD),
Upload: To the server thru *FileZilla*,
Reload: The Browser, and
Output: To your Computer Screen.

From now on I will use icons to indicate this instead.

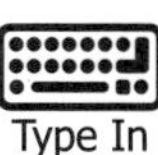
Type In

Type in, Save. Upload, Reload, and Output process is in pg# 108, 109, 110

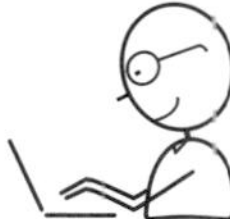

```
<!DOCTYPE html>
<html>
  <head>
    <title>My Page Title</title>
    <meta charset="UTF-8">
    <link rel="stylesheet" type="text/css" href="sample.css">
    <style> p {text-align: center;} </style>
    <script src="javascript.js"></script>
  </head>
  <body>
    <p>Content of title tag will be displayed in
    the browser tab</p>
  </body>
</html>
```

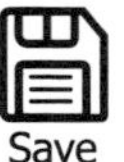
Save

Upload

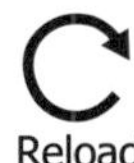
Reload

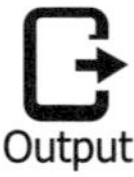
Output

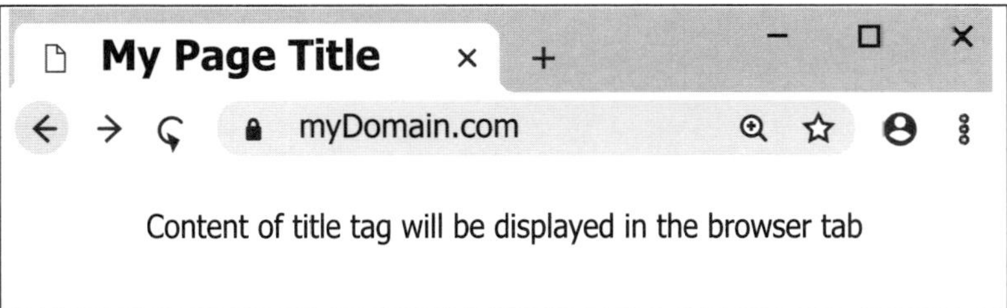

Layout Tags

Layout Tags define a display *layout* in a *browser:*

- `<div>`

Always starts on a *new line* and takes up the full width available.

- `<span>`

It doesn't start on a new line and only takes up as much width as needed. Usually inside a paragraph.

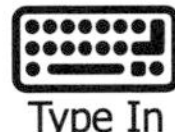

Type In

```
<!DOCTYPE html>
<html>
   <head>
   </head>
   <body>
       <div>Hello</div>
       <div>World!</div>
       <span>Hello</span>
       <span>World!</span>
   </body>
</html>
```

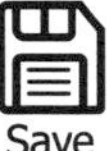

Save

Upload

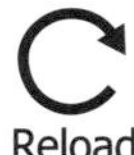

Reload

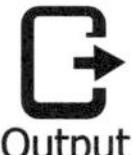

Output

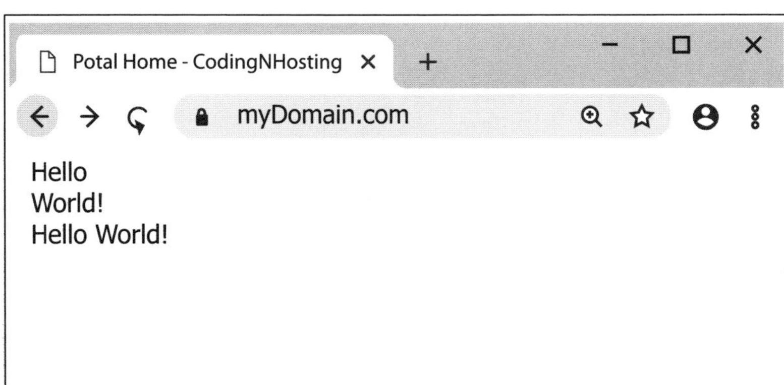

Semantic Tags

HTML 5 adds some *Semantic Tags* to define layouts that are easier to understand than what the generic `<div>` tag is capable of.
These tags make *web pages* more informative and adaptable, allowing *browsers* and *search engines* to better interpret content.

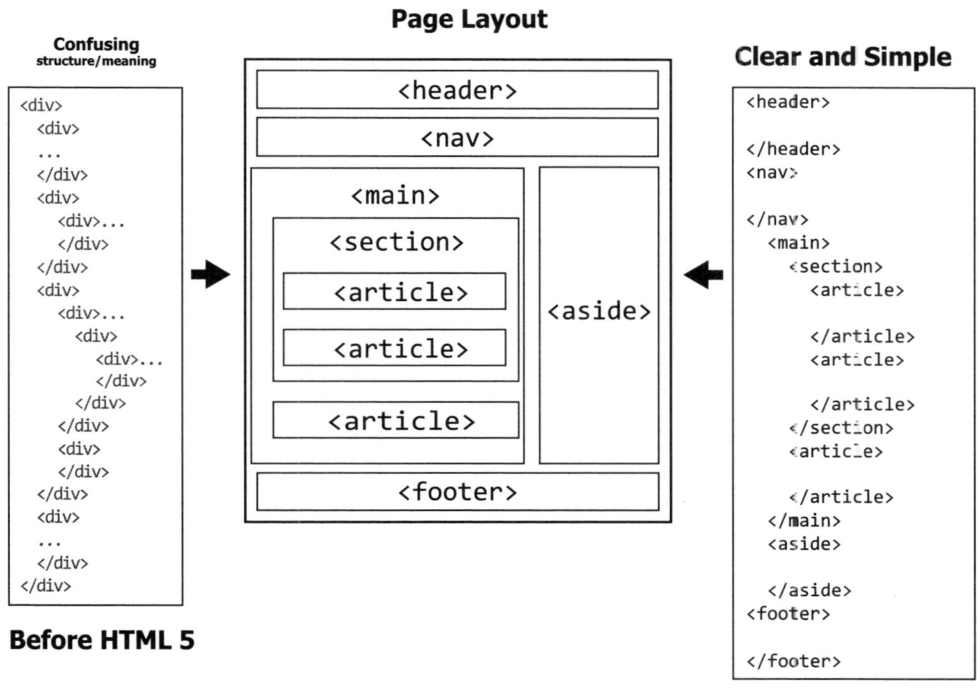

- `<header>`

The `<header>` tag defines a *header* of a web page or a section.
It contains a *logo, navigation links, login, search* and *others.*

- `<nav>`

The `<nav>`, (*navigation)* tag is used to define a *block* of *navigation links,* either within the current document or a different one.
Examples are *menu, index,* and *table of contents.*

- `<main>`

This tag specifies *the main* content in the document.
The content inside the `<main>` tag should be unique to the document.
It can **not** contain any content that is repeated across documents such as the *company logo, copyright info, navigation links* and *search forms*.
The <main> tag must be used only **once** in a document.

- `<section>`
- `<article>`

Think about a newspaper, the sports `<section>` will contain `<article>`s that are about sports while the business `<section>` will contains `<article>`s about money.

- `<aside>`

This tag has been added to *HTML 5* to define a section with additional information related to the content that is around the tag. It is generally used to enhance an *article* with additional information.

> **Note**
>
> Do not confuse the `<aside>` element with *sidebar*. The *sidebar* is just a visual element, and the `<aside>` tag is an addition to the *main* content.

- `<footer>`

The `<footer>` tag defines the *footer* of a web page or a section.
Usually, it contains *copyright information, contact details, navigation links*, etc.

There are 6 more *Semantic Tags*:

`<details>` `<figcaption>` `<figure>`
`<mark>` `<summary>` `<time>`

List Tags

There are three types of *list tags*:

<ul> *Unordered List*, <ol> *Ordered* **L***ist*, <li> *List Item*

- <ul> defines an *unordered list* of items and is displayed with *bullets(dots)*.
- <ol> tag is used to create an *ordered list,* which contains elements in a certain sequence.
- <li> is used for *list item.*

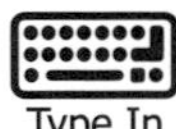
Type In

```
<!DOCTYPE html>
<html>
   <head>
   </head>
   <body>
       <nav>
       <ul>
          <li>Item 1</li>
          <li>Item 2</li>
          <li>Item 3</li>
       </ul>
       </nav>
   </body>
</html>
```

Save

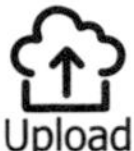
Upload

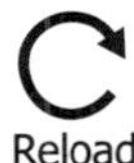
Reload

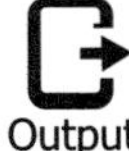
Output

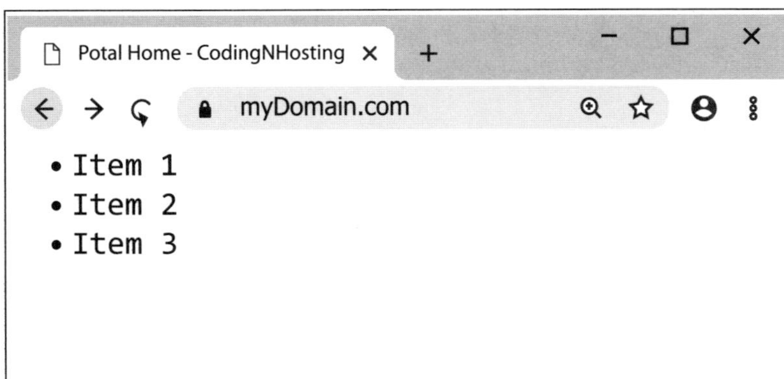

Frame Tags

A *Frame tag* is part of a *web page* that loads and displays content independently. There are 4 tags for putting a content into the *HTML document*:

- `<embed>`
- `<iframe>`
- `<object>`, `<param>`

- `<embed>`

The `<embed>` tag can be used for *embedding* an external application or interactive content, typically *multimedia content*, like *audio* or *video* into an *HTML document*.

> **Note**
>
> The `<embed>` tag has been very well supported in most web browsers for a long time.
> However, the `<embed>` tag was not a part of the *HTML 4* specification. *HTML 5* requires inclusion of this tag as a standard.

- `<iframe>`

The `<iframe>` tag defines an *Inline Frame* that contains *external objects* mainly from *other web page*. It is often used in *online advertising*, where the contents of the `<iframe>` is an ad from an *external party.*

- `<object>`
- `<param>`

The `<object>` tag defines an *embedded object* within an *HTML document*. Use this tag for *embedding multimedia* or *another web page* into your *HTML* document. You can use the `<param>` tag to pass *parameters* to plugins that have been *embedded* with the `<object>` tag.

Additional information for Frame Tags

These tags are allowed in *HTML 5* to load external *plugin* content, but they are confusingly similar in *functionality*.
Bottom line up-front, the `<iframe>` is actually more commonly used by vendors such as *YouTube* and *Spotify*.

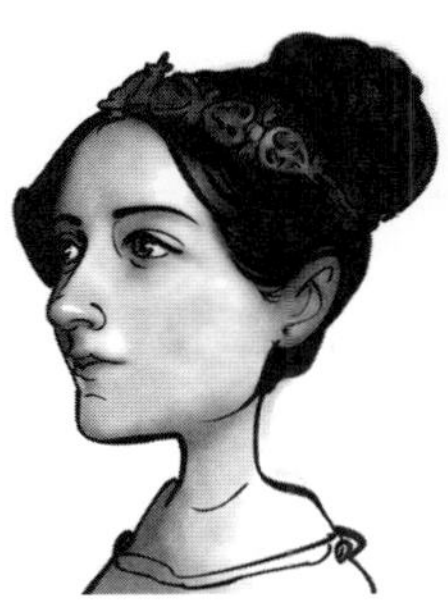

Ada Lovelace

An English mathematician and writer.
She is considered to have written instructions for the *first computer program* in the mid-1800s.
She was born in London on December 10, 1815. Ada showed her gift for mathematics at an early age.
Because she introduced many programming concepts, Ada is considered the first computer programmer.
Ada died on November 27, 1852.

Media Tags

In *modern browsers*, adding a *video/audio* file to your website is as easy as adding an *image*. You don't have to deal with special *plugins* or need crazy *markups* any more. You can do it with a *single* element.

- `<audio>`
- `<source>`
- `<video>`
- `<track>`

- <audio>
- <source>

The `<audio>` tag is used to embed *sound content* in documents.
It may contain one or more *audio source*, each represented by the `src attribute` and the `<source>` tag. The *browser* will choose the most suitable one.

- `<video>`

The `<video>` tag specifies *video*, such as a *movie clip* or other *video streams*. Currently, the `<video>` element supports 3 video formats: *MP4, WebM,* and *Ogg*.

- `<track>`

The `<track>` tag defines *captions, description, subtitles,* and *chapters* for the two *media tags*, `<audio>`, and `<video>`.

Download and save a Video File

1. Go to *www.pixabay.com*
2. Select "*Videos*"
3. Pick any Video which is less than 15 seconds long.
4. Click "Free Download", select the lowest resolution, and select "Download".
5. After download has completed, press the upper arrow (^, Google Chrome Browser) and select "Show in Folder."

Download and save a Video File (cont')

6. You will find the mp4 file (could be any name) in the "Downloads" folder; *Right Click*(:Control + Right Click) on that file.
7. "Copy" and "Paste" that file on the "Media" directory which is a sub-directory of "$-MyCoding" on the Local site *C* drive (: *Mac HD*)
8. Type in the following code:

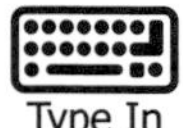

Type In

```
<!DOCTYPE html>
<html>
   <head>
   </head>
   <body>
     <video width="400" controls>
       <source src="http://myDomain.com/Media/AnyName.mp4">
     </video>
   </body>
</html>
```

9. Save as "*index.html*" and upload it to the *public_html* directory by right-clicking (: control + right click) and choose *Upload.*
10. Right-click (: control + right click) the *Media* directory and Upload it to the *public_html* directory.

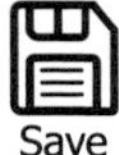

Save

Upload

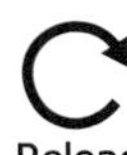

Reload

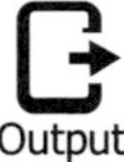

Output

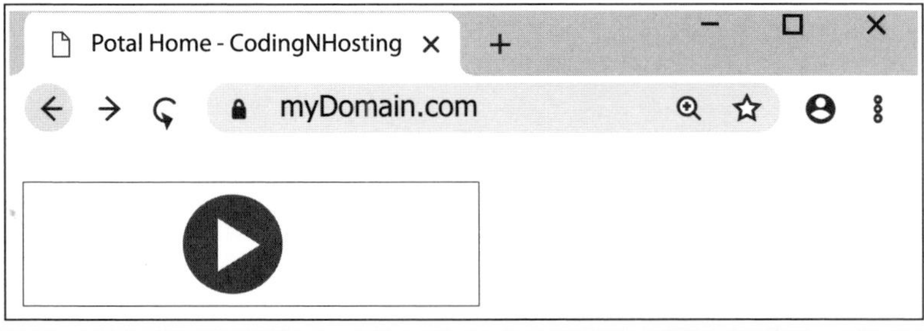

Formatting Tags

These tags are designed to *display special types of text.*

tags	descriptions
`<del>`	delete text
`<em>`	emphasized text
`<i>`	italic text
`<ins>`	inserted text
`<s>`	strike-through text
`<strong>`	important text
`<sub>`	subscript text
`<sup>`	superscript text

> **Note**
>
> `<s>` tag represents content that is no longer *accurate* or *relevant*.
> `<del>` tag represents *deleted/removed* text.

Browsers will normally strike a line through *deleted* text (`<del>`) and underline *inserted* text (`<ins>`).

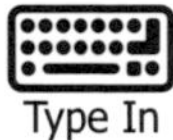
Type In

```
<!DOCTYPE html>
<html>
  <head>
  </head>
  <body>
    <p>The movie ticket is
       <del>$10</del> <ins>$7</ins>
    </p>
      <em>This is emphasized text</em>
      <i>This is italic text</i>
    <p>My favorite flower is <ins>tulip</ins>
    </p>
      <strong>This is strong text</strong>
    <p>This is <sub>subscripted</sub> text</p>
    <p>This is <sup>superscripted</sup> text</p>
  </body>
</html>
```

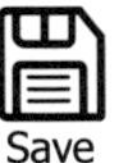
Save

Upload

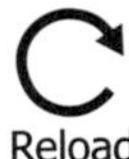
Reload

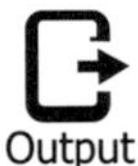
Output

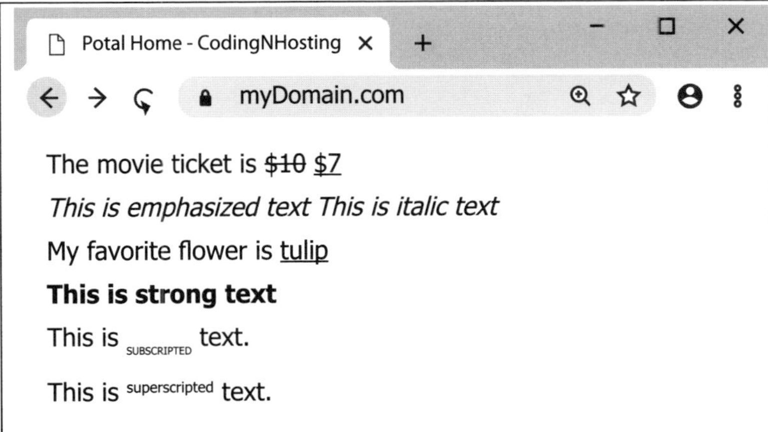

Form Tags

Form tags are used for creating a *form for user input.*
A form can contain *textfields, checkboxes, radio-buttons* and more.
Forms are used to pass *user-data* to a *specified server.*

tags	descriptions
<form>	create a form for user input
<fieldset>	groups related elements in a form
<legend>	defines a caption for the <fieldset> element
<input>	defines user control within a form
<textarea>	defines a multiline input control (text area)
<label>	defines a label for an <input> element
<select>	defines a drop-down list
<optgroup>	defines a group of related options in a drop-down list
<option>	defines an option in a drop-down list
<button>	defines a clickable button
<datalist>	specifies a list of pre-defined options for input controls
<output>	defines the result of a calculation

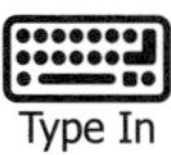


```
<!DOCTYPE html>
<html>
<body>
  <form>
    <fieldset>
      <legend> What is your favorite Pixar movie? </legend>
         <select>
            <optgroup>
               <option> Finding Nemo </option>
               <option> Up </option>
               <option> Monsters Inc. </option>
               <option> The Incredibles </option>
               <option> Soul </option>
               <option> Inside Out </option>
               <option> Coco </option>
               <option> Cars </option>
               <option> Luca </option>
               <option> Wall-E </option>
               <option> Ratouille </option>
               <option> Toy Story </option>
            </optgroup>
         </select>
     </fieldset>
   </form>
</body>
</html>
```

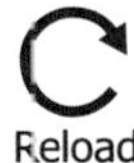

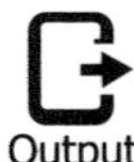

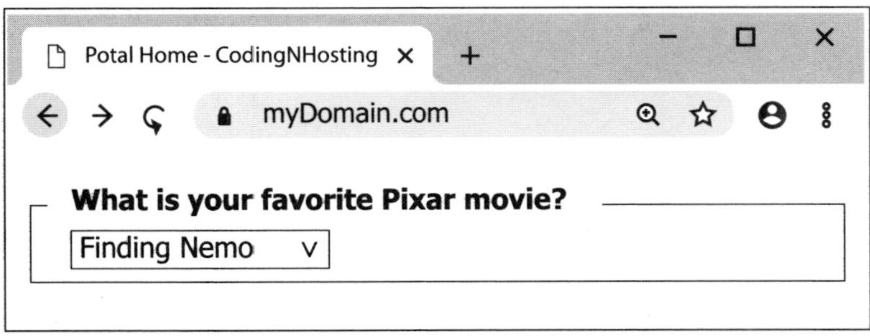

Table Tags

Table tags define *tabular data*; the information is presented in a two-dimensional table comprised of rows and columns of cells containing data.

tags	descriptions
`<table>`	defines a two-dimensional table
`<caption>`	used for creating table captions
`<thead>`	table head, used to group head content in a table
`<tbody>`	groups the body content in a table
`<tfoot>`	table foot, groups the foot content in a table
`<th>`	defines header cell
`<tr>`	table row, defines a row in a table
`<td>`	table data, defines a cell in a table

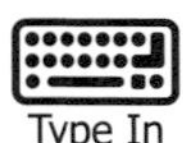
Type In

```
<!DOCTYPE html>
<html>
<body>
   <caption> <b> Top 5 Highest Grossing Pixar Movies </b>
   </caption>
   <br><br>
     <table>
        <thead> <b> Pixar Movie</b> </thead>
               
        <thead> <b> Year </b> </thead>
         
        <thead> <b> Billions </b> </thead>
           <tbody>
              <tr>
                 <td> The Incredibles 2 </td>
                 <td> 2018 </td>
                 <td> 1.242 </td>
              </tr>
              <tr>
                 <td> Toy Story 4 </td>
                 <td> 2019 </td>
                 <td> 1.073 </td>
              </tr>
              <tr>
                 <td> Toy Story 3 </td>
                 <td> 2010 </td>
                 <td> 1.066 </td>
              </tr>
              <tr>
                 <td> Finding Dory </td>
                 <td> 2016 </td>
                 <td> 1.028 </td>
              </tr>
              <tr>
                 <td> Finding Nemo </td>
                 <td> 2003 </td>
                 <td> 0.871 </td>
              </tr>
           </tbody>
      </table>
   <br>
   <a href = "https://disney.fandom.com/f/p/4400000000000004799">
    Click here to learn more </a>
</body>
</html>
```

Save
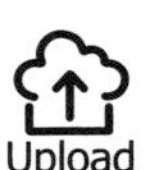
Upload
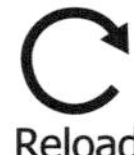
Reload
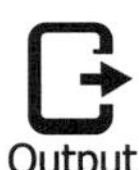
Output
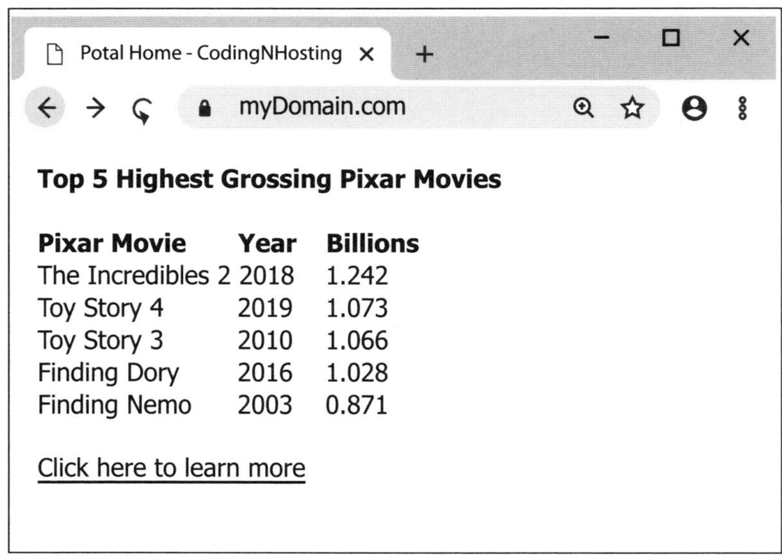
Potal Home - CodingNHosting
myDomain.com
Top 5 Highest Grossing Pixar Movies
Pixar Movie Year Billions
The Incredibles 2 2018 1.242
Toy Story 4 2019 1.073
Toy Story 3 2010 1.066
Finding Dory 2016 1.028
Finding Nemo 2003 0.871
Click here to learn more

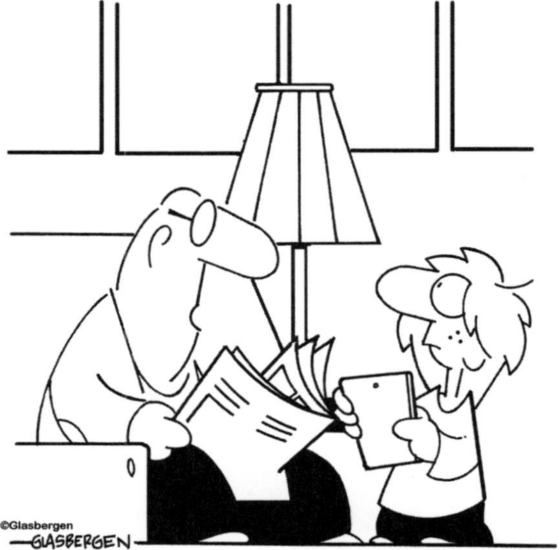

"Newspapers may not be as cool as the Internet, but they're still the best way to read 50 year old comics and yesterday's news."

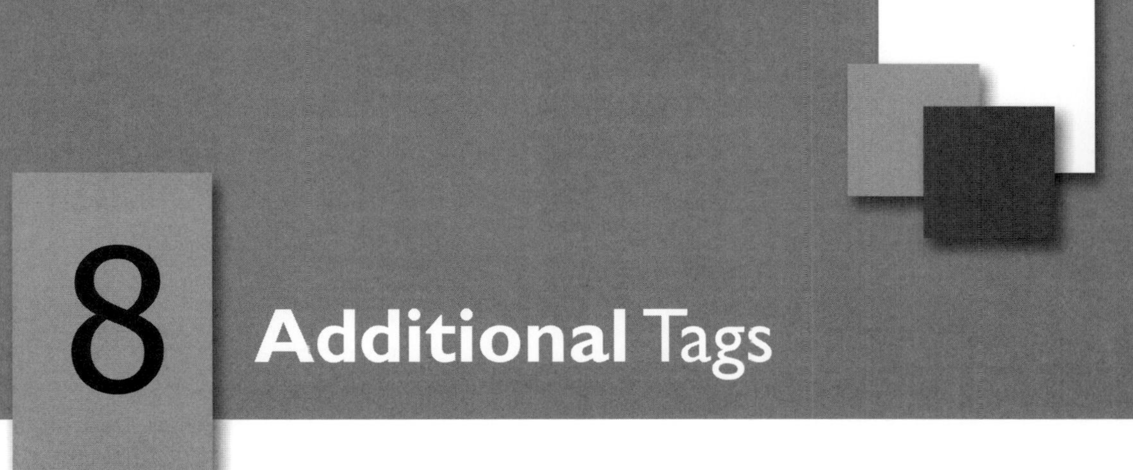

8 Additional Tags

So far, we have learned about *12 basic tags* and *56 main tags*.
In this section, I list the *39 additional tags*; these are the 3rd most important tags.
As mentioned earlier, you don't need to memorize these.
Entire lists are in Part V of the Index & Appendix.

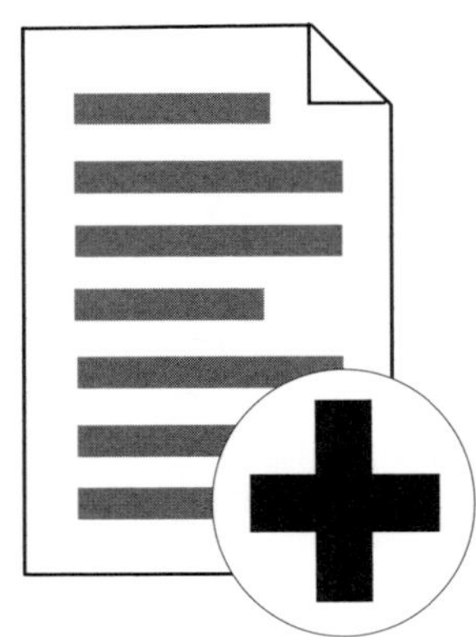

<abbr>
<address>
<area>
<base>
<bdi>
<bdo>
<blockquote>
<canvas>
<cite>
<code>
<col>
<colgroup>
<data>
<datalist>
<dd>
<dfn>
<dialog>
<dl>
<dt>
<kbd>
<map>
<meter>
<noscript>
<optgroup>
<output>
<picture>
<pre>
<progress>
<q>
<rp>
<rt>
<ruby>
<samp>
<small>
<svg>
<template>
<u>
<var>
<wbr>

I have created the *Basic, Main,* and *Additional Tags* categorized for your understanding. So, when you search the web for further studying, type in the *Tag Name* instead of *Basic, Main, or Additional Tags*.

What's a computer's favorite beat?

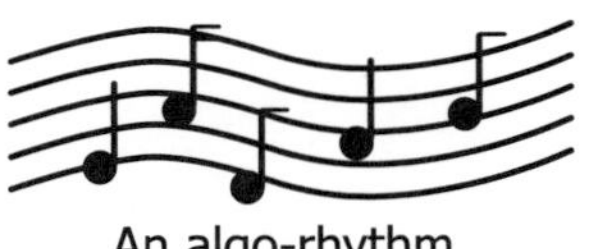

An algo-rhythm.

CHAPTER 4

CSS (Cascade Style Sheets)

1. What is CSS?
2. CSS Type
3. CSS Syntax
4. CSS Selectors
5. CSS Properties
6. CSS Reset

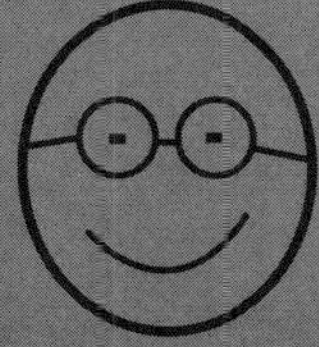

1 What is **CSS**?

CSS (Cascading Style Sheets), like HTML, is another markup language.

- With *CSS* you can style how you want your *HTML* tags to be presented on your *website*. It is like putting your own style of make up on it. This way, the website looks better.
- Like *HTML* and *JavaScript*, it forms one of the major *coding language* for the Web.

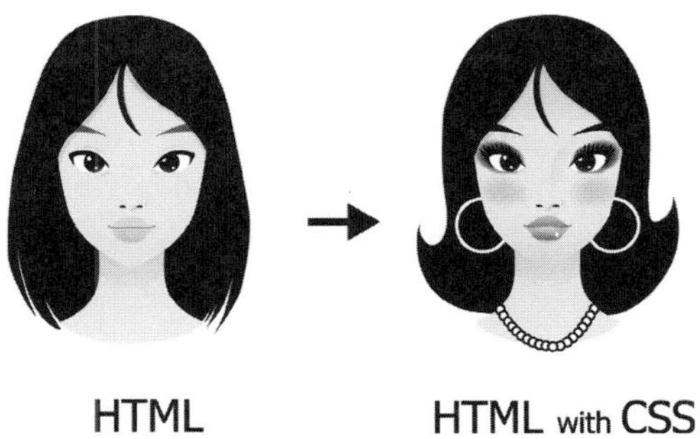

	HTML	CSS
made for	building web page structure	styling and/or decorating a web page built by HTML
relationship	can use CSS in HTML file	can **not** use HTML in CSS file
component	consists of tags surrounding contents	consists of selectors followed by a declaration block
main function	to create a semantic web page with tags, media objects, geo location, web storage, and web accessibility	to style a web page with properties, selectors, and to build a Responsive Web Site

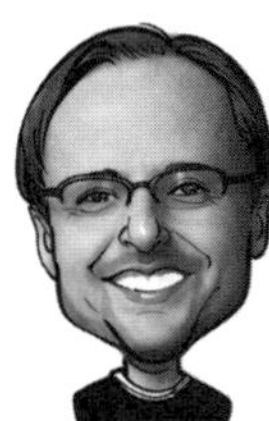

Håkon Wium Lie (born July 16, 1965)

A Norwegian computer scientist and web pioneer. He is best known for developing *Cascading Style Sheets (CSS)* while working with *Tim Berners-Lee* at *CERN* in 1994. He was the *Chief Technology Officer* of *Opera Software,* one of the five major *Web Browser Developing Companies,* from 1998 until 2016.

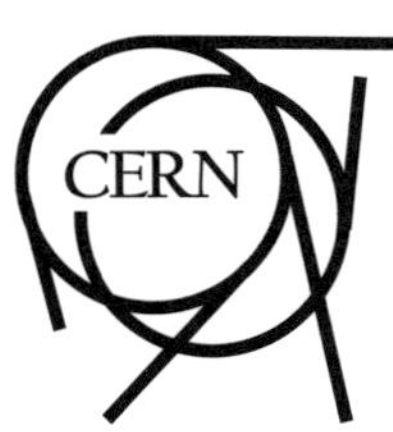

CERN (European Organization for Nuclear Research) is a European research organization that operates the largest particle physics laboratory in the world. Established in 1954, the organization is based in a northwest suburb of Geneva. It is an official *United Nations Observer.*

CSS is responsible for the design and style of the *website* or *web page* including the *layout, visual effects,* and *background*.

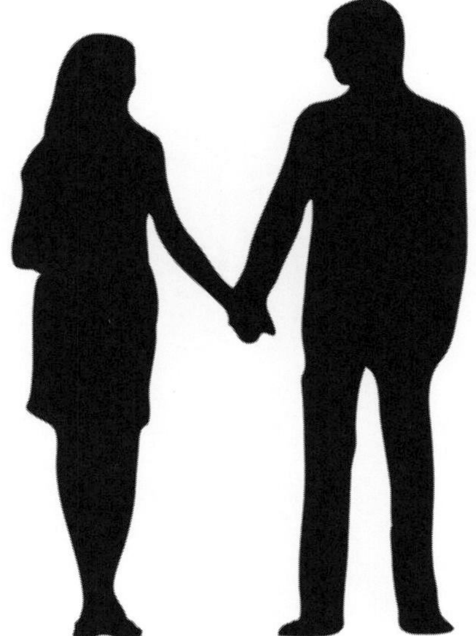
You are the
CSS in my
HTML

2 CSS Type

CSS can be used to define *text styles, background color, table sizes,* and *other aspects* of web pages.

There are three different ways to insert a *Style Sheet* into a *HTML* file:

- *Internal Style Sheet.*
- *Inline Style Sheet.*
- *External Style Sheet.*

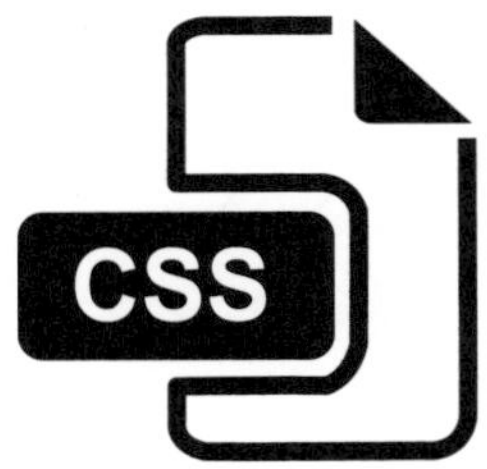

Internal Style Sheet

- It is wrapped in the *HTML* `<style>` tag.
- It is located in the `<head> or <body>` *section* of the *HTML* page.

```
<!DOCTYPE html>
<html>
   <head>
      <style>
         h1 {font-style:italic;}
      </style>
   </head>
   <body>
      <h1>Hello World!</h1>
   </body>
</html>
```

Internal

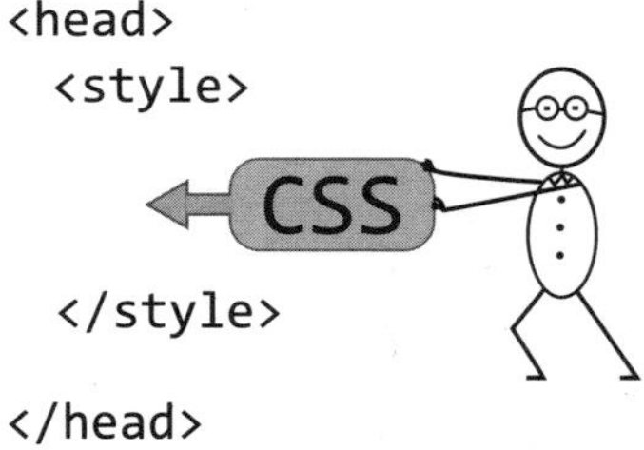

> **Note**
>
> The `<style>` tag can be placed in the `<head>` *or* `<body>` of the *HTML* file.

Inline Style Sheet

- It is *inside* of an *HTML* tag, using the *style attribute.*
- It is used to apply style to a *single element.*

```
<!DOCTYPE html>
<html>
  <head>
  </head>
  <body>
    <h1 style="font-style:italic;>Hello World!</h1>
  </body>
</html>
```

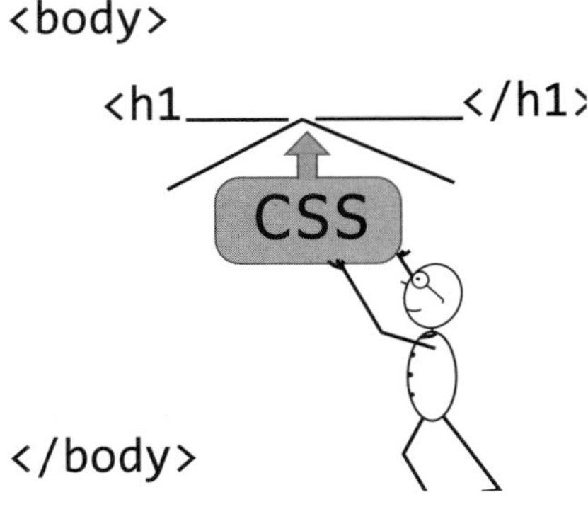

External Style Sheet

- It allows you to define a *style sheet* as a separate document and import it into your *web pages*.
- This *style sheet* contains only *CSS code* and saves with a *".css" file extension*.
- With this *CSS* file, you can change the look of an *entire website* simply by changing one file.
- This *CSS* file is then referenced in your *HTML* using the `<link>` tag instead of `<style>`.

> **Note**
>
> If you need to use your *style sheet* for various pages, then it's always recommended to define an *External Style Sheet* in a separate file.

The `<link>` tag is used for defining a *link* to an external resource.
It is placed in `<head>` tag and should have *three attributes*:

- `rel`: specifies the *relationship* between the *current* document and the *linked* document.
- `type`: specifies the *type* of `<input>` element to display.
- `href` *hypertext reference:* specifies the *URL* of the page opened after you click on the link.

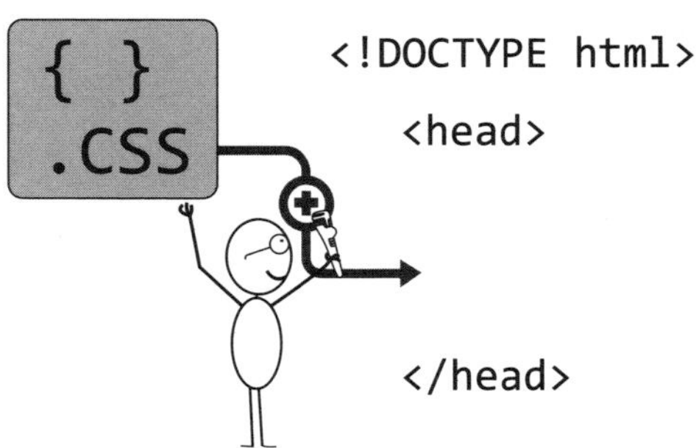

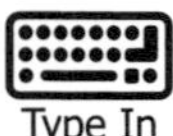


```
<!DOCTYPE html>
<html>
   <head>
      <link rel="stylesheet" href="mystyle.css">
   </head>
   <body>
      <h1>Hello World!</h1>
   </body>
</html>
```

Type in the following CSS document, save as "mystyle.css", and upload it to the directory ("public_html"), where index.html is located.

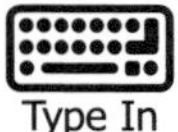


```
body {font-style: italic;}
```

The codes above each use *CSS* to produce the same output:

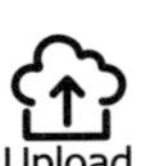

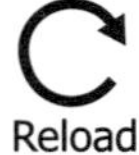

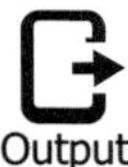

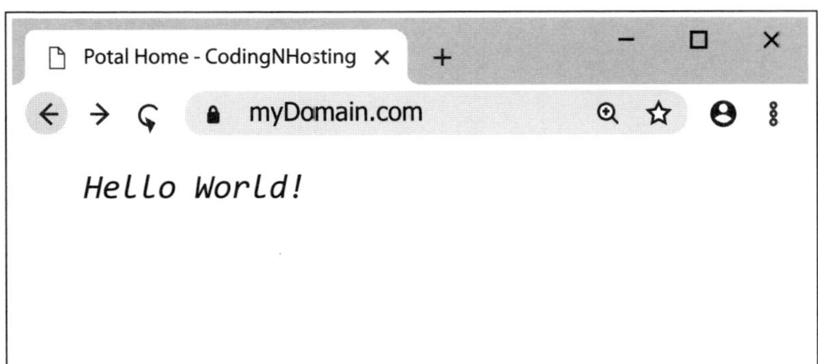

3 CSS **Syntax**

CSS Syntax

- It is made up of a *selector* and a *declaration block*.
- The *selector* is the *HTML* element you want to style.
- The entire *declaration block* is always surrounded by *curly braces*.
- The *declaration* is made up of a *property* and a *value*; these two are separated by a colon.

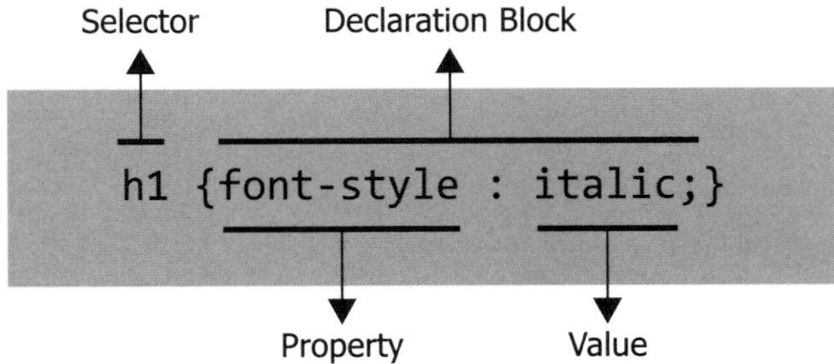

- The *property* defines what *characteristic* to style and the *value* defines how you want to style it.
- You can have *multiple declarations* in a *declaration block,* and they each are separated by and end with a semicolon (;).

Case In-sensitivity

CSS is *case in-sensitive* for *HTML selectors*.

head = HEAD

CamelBack = camelback

CSS Comments

With *CSS*, you can write *comments* on your *text editor* to provide information.

The concept is the same as *HTML comments* and they will not show up on your actual *website*.

It starts with "/*" and ends with "*/"

```
/* your comment here */
```

Grouping Selectors

If your *declaration block* has the same style *properties* and *value*, you can group the *HTML selectors*, each separated by a comma, together to simplify the code.

● {text-align : ce..}

■ {text-align : ce..} → ●, ■, ▲ {text-align : ce..}

▲ {text-align : ce..}

```
<!DOCTYPE html>
<html>
   <head>
   <style>

     h1 {text-align : center; color : red;}
     h2 {text-align : center; color : red;}
     p  {text-align : center; color : red;}
```

```
<!DOCTYPE html>
<html>
   <head>
   <style>

   h1,h2,p {text-align:center; color:red;}

   </style>
   </head>
   <body>
       <h1>Hello World!</h1>
       <h2>How are You?</h2>
       <p>My name is Samuel</p>
   </body>
</html
```

4 CSS **Selectors**

There are 3 ways to select *HTML elements* to be styled in *CSS*.

- *User Defined Selectors (*`class, ID`*)*
- *Tag Selector.*
- *Universal Selector.*

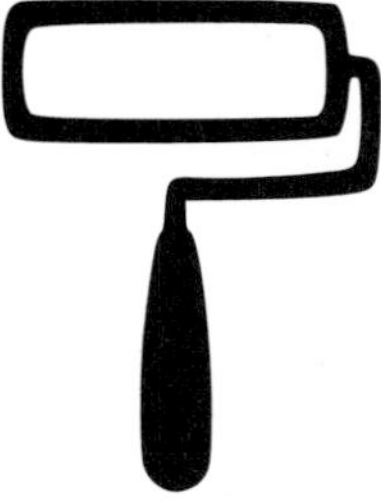

User Defined Selectors

There are 2 kinds of *user defined selectors*: `class` and `ID`.
With these, you can define your own *selectors* according to the syntax they offer.

Class Selector

This *selector* selects *HTML elements* with a specific `class` *attribute*. To do this, write a *dot* (.), followed by a user defined `class` name.

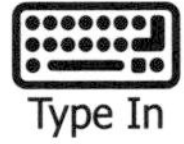

Type In

```
<!DOCTYPE html>
<html>
   <head>
      <style>
      .whoiam {font-style: italic;
      }
      </style>
   </head>
   <body>
      <h1>Hello World!</h1>
      <div class="whoiam">
        <p>My name is Samuel</p>
        <p>I am living in NYC</p>
      </div>
   </body>
</html>
```

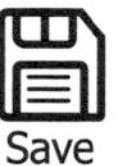

Save

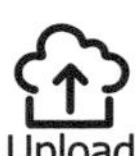

Upload

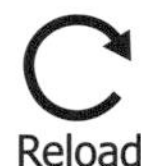

Reload

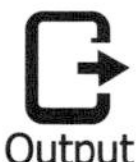

Output

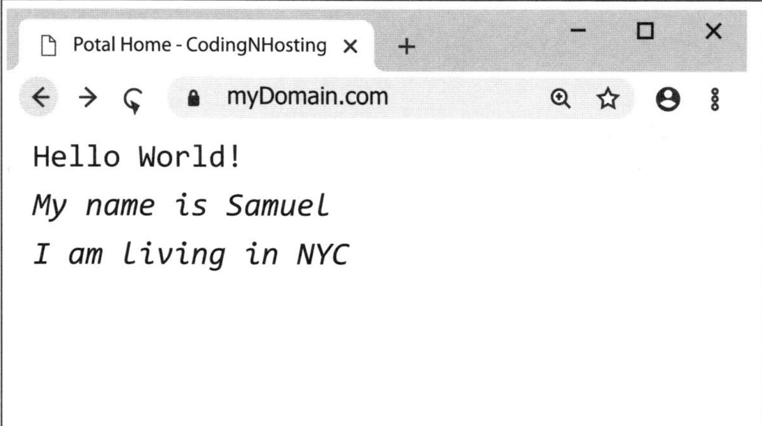

ID Selector

You can also style an *HTML element* with the `ID` *attribute*.
It works the same way as the `class` *selector* except:

- it is used to *select* one unique element.
- you use a *hash* (#) sign instead of *dot* (.) before the `ID` name.

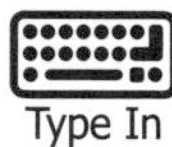

Type In

```
<!DOCTYPE html>
<html>
   <head>
       <style>
       #cityHeader {font-style: bold;
       }
       .NYCity {font-style: italic;
       }
       </style>
   </head>
   <body>
       <h1 id="cityHeader">NY City 5 Boroughs</h1>
       <div class="NYCity>
         <p>Queens</p>
       </div>
       <div class="NYCity">
         <p>Manhattan</p>
       </div>
       <div class="NYCity">
         <p>Brocklyn</p>
       </div>
       <div class="NYCity">
         <p>Bronx</p>
       </div>
       <div class="NYCity">
         <p>Staten Island</p>
       </div>
   </body>
</html>
```

Note

The difference between an `ID` and a `class` is that an `ID` can be used to identify only *one* element, whereas a `class` can be used to identify *more than one element*.

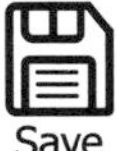

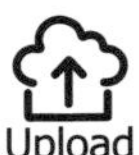

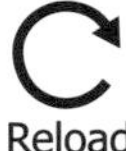

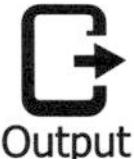

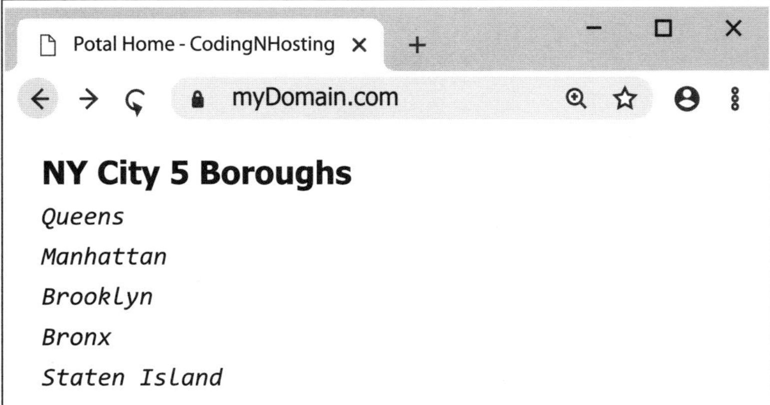

Tag Selector

It is the actual *HTML Tag name* and points to the *HTML Tag* you want to style.

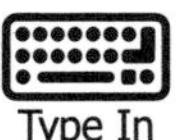


```
<!DOCTYPE html>
<html>
   <head>
      <style>
         h1 {font-style: italic;}
      </style>
   </head>
   <body>
      <h1>Hello World!</h1>
   </body>
</html>
```

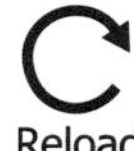

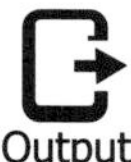

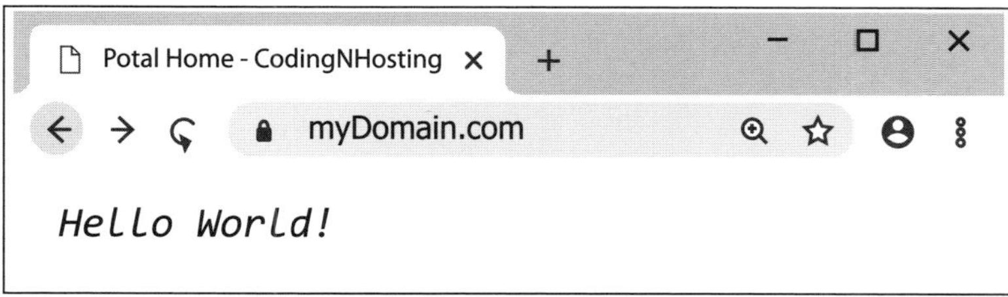

Universal Selector (*)

The *CSS universal selector* selects all the elements on a web page.

```
<style>
   * {font-style: italic;}
</style>
```

This single line of code surrounded by the *curly braces* will affect *all the elements* present on the *HTML* page.

We declare an *universal selector* with the help of an *asterisk* (*) at the beginning of the *curly brace*.

bracket	name	used for
< >	angle bracket	HTML tag
{ }	curly brackets or braces	CSS declaration
( )	parentheses or braces	JavaScript function
[ ]	square brackets or box brackets	PHP/JavaScript array

5 CSS **Properties**

- *CSS properties* are elements that create styles.
- For example, if you make a font style *italic*, the `font-style` is a *property* and `italic` is the *value* of that property.

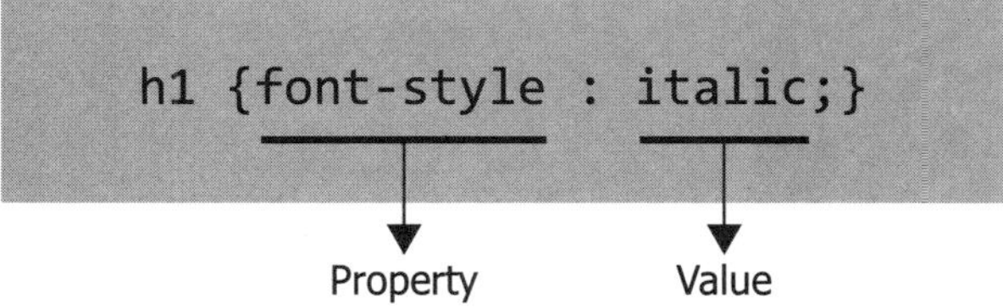

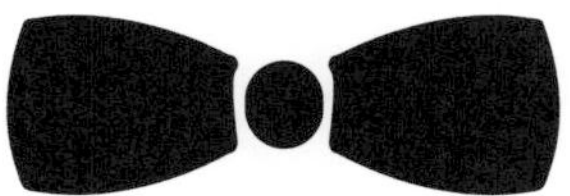

Currently, there are *over 500 properties*. You do not have to memorize all of them. Just understand their meanings. They are on the next page.
And 220 frequently used property are listed in Part V (Appendix).

Frequently used CSS properties:

CSS Properties	descriptions
`font/text`	both properties serve to set the appearance of individual font in a word or line of text
`border/margin/ padding (box model)`	adds content of a box, border, margin, and/or padding built up around one another
`background`	allows you to control the background of any element; such as background-color and background-size
`display`	specifies how a certain HTML element should be displayed: block, inline, inline-block, and others
`float/clear`	places an element on the left/right side of the container, allowing text and inline elements to wrap around each other
`height/width`	sets the height/width of an element

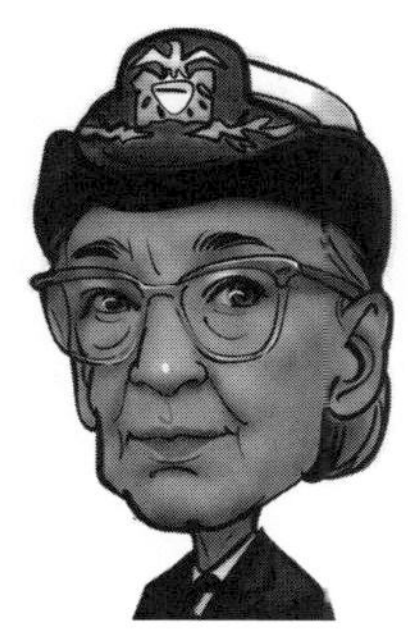

Grace Hopper

American *computer scientist* and *US Navy Officer*. *Grace* helped develop a *compiler* that was a precursor to the widely used *COBOL language*. *Grace* joined the U.S. Navy during World War II and was assigned to program the *Mark I* early-stage computer developed by Harvard University staff in 1944. She continued to work in computing after the war, leading the team that created the first computer language *compiler* which translates one language into another.

She resumed active naval service at the age of 60, becoming a *rear admiral* before retiring in 1986. On New Year's Day 1992, *Grace* died in her sleep of natural causes at her home in Arlington, Virginia. She was 85 years old.

6 CSS **Reset**

- Every *web browser* has its own *default setting* for styling different *HTML elements.*
- *CSS reset* (reset style sheet) is a collection of *CSS commands*.
  It is on the next page.
- A *CSS reset* can force every browser to have all its styles reset to *null*, thus avoiding *cross-browser differences*.

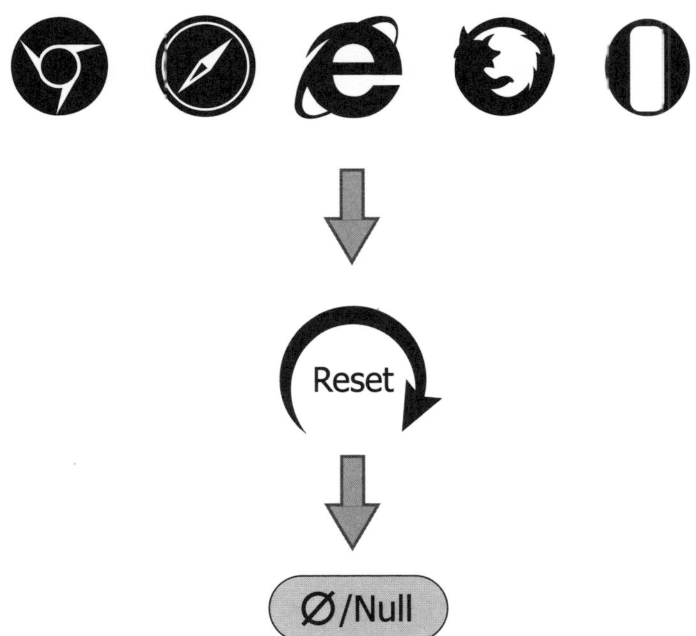

CSS Reset Code:

```
/* http://meyerweb.com/eric/tools/css/reset/
   v2.0 | 20110126
   License: none (public domain)
*/

html, body, div, span, applet, object, iframe,
h1, h2, h3, h4, h5, h6, p, blockquote, pre,
a, abbr, acronym, address, big, cite, code,
del, dfn, em, img, ins, kbd, q, s, samp,
small, strike, strong, sub, sup, tt, var,
b, u, i, center,
dl, dt, dd, ol, ul, li,
fieldset, form, label, legend,
table, caption, tbody, tfoot, thead, tr, th, td,
article, aside, canvas, details, embed,
figure, figcaption, footer, header, hgroup,
menu, nav, output, ruby, section, summary,
time, mark, audio, video {
	margin: 0;
	padding: 0;
	border: 0;
	font-size: 100%;
	font: inherit;
	vertical-align: baseline;
}
/* HTML5 display-role reset for older browsers */
article, aside, details, figcaption, figure,
footer, header, hgroup, menu, nav, section {
	display: block;
}
body {
	line-height: 1;
}
ol, ul {
	list-style: none;
}
blockquote, q {
	quotes: none;
}
blockquote:before, blockquote:after,
q:before, q:after {
	content: '';
	content: none;
}
table {
	border-collapse: collapse;
	border-spacing: 0;
}
```

Note

One of the pioneers of the *CSS Reset Method*, *Eric Meyer*, created a Reset Style Sheet that is still in use on millions of websites today. Most people use it in its unedited form.

```
Q: What do you call a programmer
   from Finland?
A: Nerdic
```

Timeline of World's Famous Computer Programmers

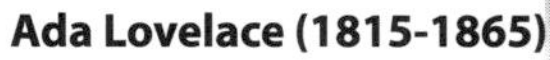

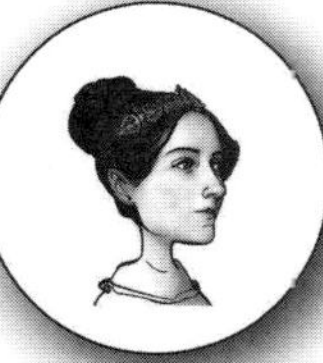

Ada Lovelace (1815-1865)
Wrote the World's First Computer Program in 1843

Grace Hopper (1906-1992)
Created the World First Computer Compiler, a program that turns "human readable" code to computer code

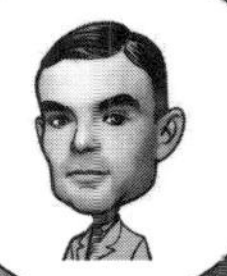

Alan Turing (1912-1954)
A mathematical who established the foundation of modern computer science

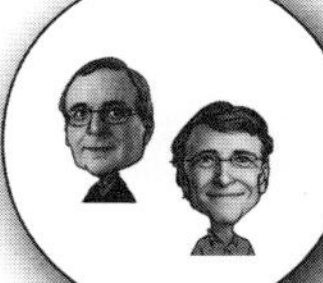

Paul Allen (1953-2018)
Bill Gates (1955-)
Co-founded the Microsoft corporation and created the Microsoft Operation System

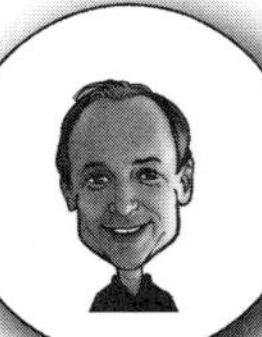

Tim Berners-Lee (1955-)
Computer Scientist who invented the World Wide Web and the HTML programming language

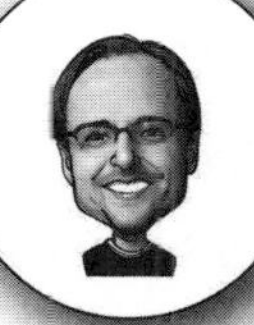

Hakon Wium Lie (1967-)
A computer scientist, influenced by Tim Berners-Lee, who invented CSS

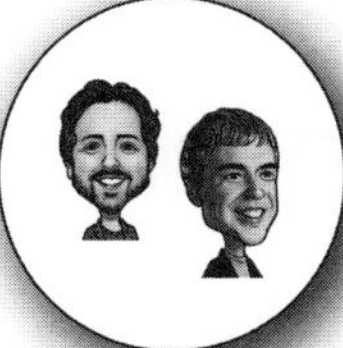

Sergey Brin (1973-)
Larry Page (1973-)
Both are computer scientists and internet entrepreneurs who co-founded the Google

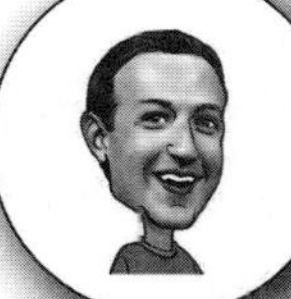

Mark Zuckerberg (1984-)
A computer scientist and internet entrepreneur who co-founded Facebook

Review Section: By now you should be familiar with the following terms:

1. Difference between the Internet and the World Wide Web.
2. Server, Website, and Domain Name.
3. IP address.
4. Local Site and Remote Site.
5. Upload and Download.
6. HTML tags (include list of tags, e.g. `<head>, <p>, <body>` and others)
7. Basic Tags, Main Tags, and Additional Tags.
8. Elements and Attributes for HTML code.
9. Property and Value for CSS styling.
10. Syntax.

PART 2

PAGE LAYOUT & DESIGN

This part, you will learn how to

- Organize the layout of your website by dividing it into the three areas.
- How to style text and elements in a box using CSS.
- How web page layout adapts to different devices.

From Chapter 6 thru Chapter 8, I will use sample code very simple. Just read through and try to understand the concept.

CHAPTER 5

Area & Sections

1. Header Area Layout
2. Center Area Layout
3. Footer Area Layout

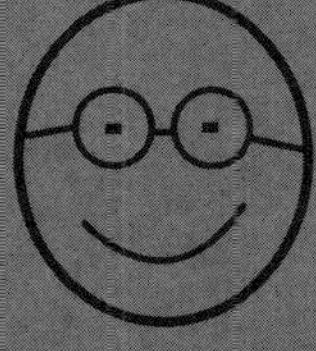

1 Header Area Layout

Every *website* has a `<header>` area.
The `<header>` area will frequently appear throughout all the pages of your *website*. In this area, we can use the two `semantic` tags:

- `<header>` tag represents opening content, typically a group of *introductory* or *navigational* aids.
- `<nav>` tag defines a set of *navigation links*.

> **Note**
>
> We learned about `semantic` tags in Chapter 3, Section 7, *HTML Main Tag* (pg# 119)

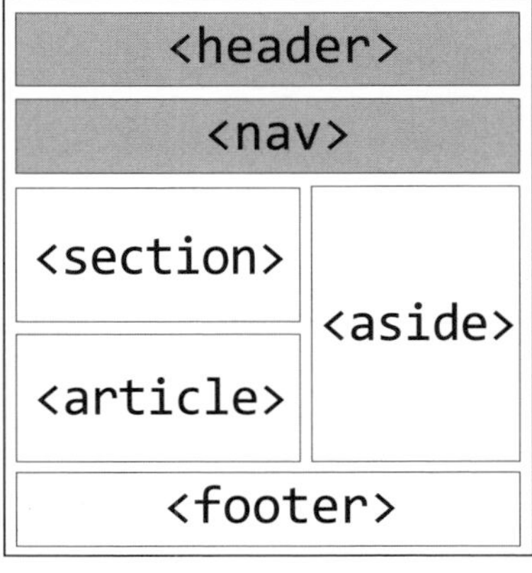

Header Area

Center Area

Footer Area

The <header> tag typically contains:

- *logo* or *icon*
- *login*, *search* or *authorship* information.
- one or more *heading elements* (<h1> - <h6>)
- others.

The <header> area is one of the most valuable sections of your entire *website*. Visitors should be able to recognize your brand and understand what your company does as soon as they land on your *website*. The <header> is one of the most important tools to make sure that happens.

Note

Do not confuse the <header> tag with <head> tag.
The <head> tag is one of main tags and contains metadata and is not shown to the user (Chapter 3, Section 7, pg# 115)

The <nav> tag is new in *HTML 5* and defines a set of *navigation links*.

A document may have several <nav> tags; for example, one for *site navigation* and one for *intra-page* (same page) *navigation*.

The <header> area serves as a signboard and map for information on the *website.*

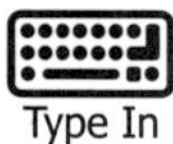
Type In

```
<!DOCTYPE html>
<html>
    <head>
    <style>
      li {
        display: inline-block;
        margin-right: 10px;
      }
    </style>
    </head>
    <body>
    <header>
      <h1>Welcome to our page</h1>
      <hr>
    </header>
    <nav>
      <li>Home</li>
      <li>About us</li>
    </nav>
    </body>
</html>
```

Save

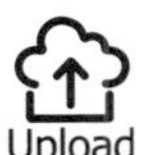
Upload

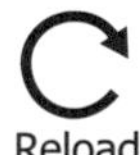
Reload

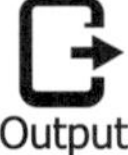
Output

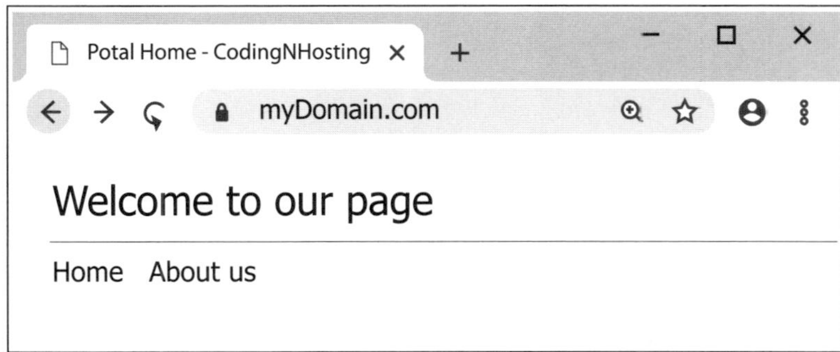

2 Center Area Layout

The *center area* contains all the content for the specific *web page.* It is the largest area in the page layout.
The center area has:

- `<section>`
- `<article>`
- `<aside>`
- `<main>`
- others

With *HTML 5,* we can use the new <section> tag to contain all of our content for the specific *web page*. The content contained in the <section> tags should always differ for each *web page*.

Center Area is different from the `<center>` tag in *HTML 4* and earlier versions. The `<center>` tag is not supported in *HTML 5.* Use *CSS* instead.

<header> <nav>	**Header Area**
<section> <article> <aside>	**Center Area**
<footer>	**Footer Area**

Note

Center Area Tags, such as `<section>` and `<aside>` are explained in *Semantic Tags (Chapter 3, Section 7, pg# 119,120)*

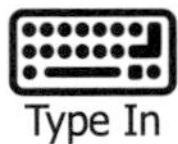
Type In

```
<!DOCTYPE html>
<html>
  <head>
    <style>
      li {
        display: inline-block;
        margin-right: 10px;
      }
    </style>
  </head>
  <body>
    <header>
        <h1>Welcome to our page</h1>
        <hr>
    </header>
    <nav>
        <li>Home</li>
        <li>About us</li>
    </nav>
    <section>
        <h2>The section title</h2>
        <p>The text paragraph.</p>
    </section>
    <article>
        <h2>Article name</h2>
        <p>Article contents</p>
    </article>
    <aside>
        <h2>Aside Info</h2>
        <p>Contents aside.. additional</p>
    </aside>
  </body>
</html>
```

Save
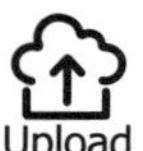
Upload
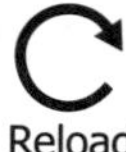
Reload

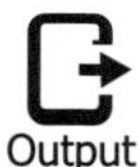
Output

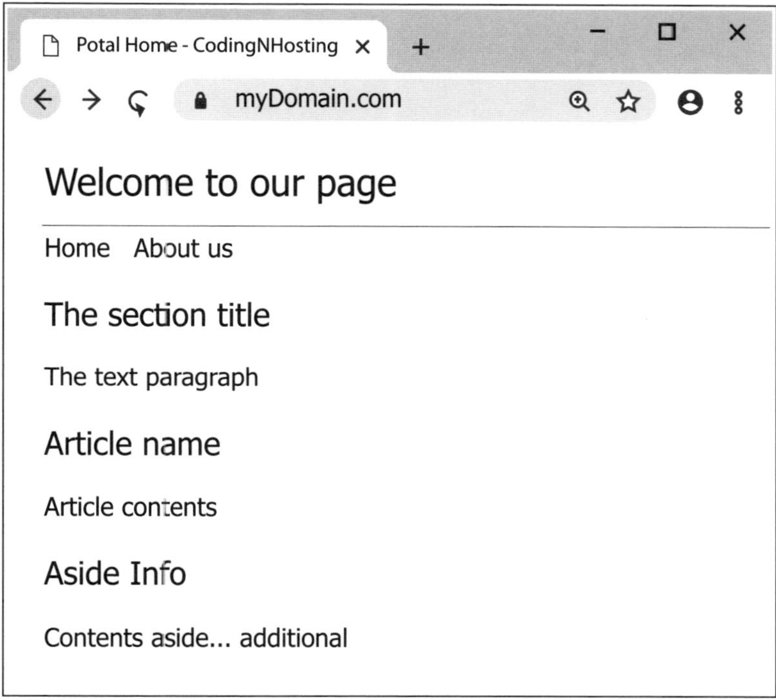
Potal Home - CodingNHosting
myDomain.com
Welcome to our page
Home About us
The section title
The text paragraph
Article name
Article contents
Aside Info
Contents aside... additional

3 **Footer Area** Layout

With *HTML 5*, we can now use the new *semantic tag* `<footer>` to give our web pages a *Footer Area*.

The *footer area* is located at the bottom of your web page. It displays the same content throughout the different pages of your *website.*

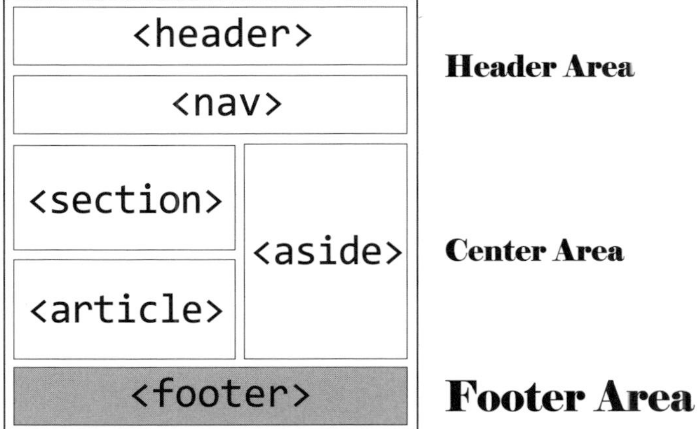

Most of the <footer> tag contains:

- *copyright information*
- *business name*
- *terms of use*
- *author of web site*
- *business address*
- *others*

You can have several <footer> tags on a web page. For example, you can place a <footer> inside the <article> tag to store information related to *the article* (links, footnotes, etc.).

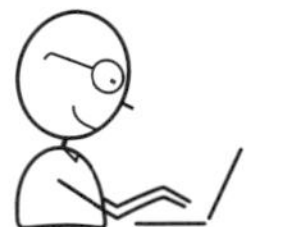

The <footer> tag, like other *semantic* tags (e.g. <header>, <nav>, <section>, etc) was introduced in *HTML 5* .

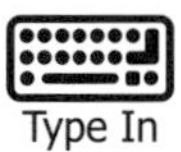

Type In

```
<!DOCTYPE html>
<html>
  <head>
    <style>
      li {
        display: inline-block;
        margin-right: 10px;
      }
    </style>
  </head>
  <body>
    <header>
      <h1>Welcome to our page</h1>
      <hr>
    </header>
    <nav>
       <li>Home</li>
       <li>About us</li>
    </nav>
    <br>
    <br>
    <footer>
        © 2021 MyDomain Corporation
    </footer>
  </body>
</html>
```

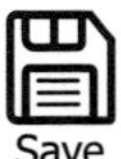
Save
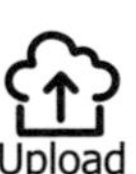
Upload
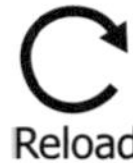
Reload
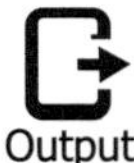
Output
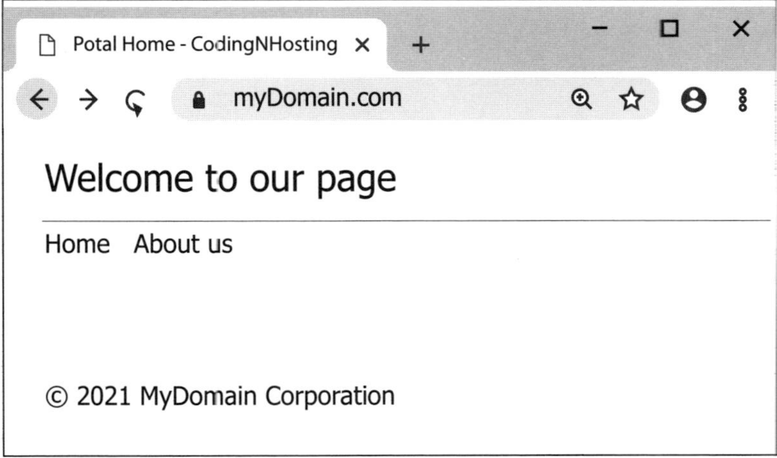
Potal Home - CodingNHosting
myDomain.com
Welcome to our page
Home About us
© 2021 MyDomain Corporation

CHAPTER 6

Font & Text

1. CSS Font Property
2. CSS Text Property

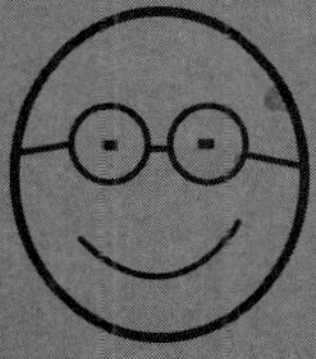

1 CSS **Font Property**

CSS font property sets the appearance of the specific font.

It defines:

- `font-family`
- `font-size`
- `font-style`
- `font-weight` (boldness)

font	descriptions
`font-family`	specifies the font family a text
`font-size`	sets the size of a text
`font-style`	specifies the font style of a text
`font-weight`	specifies the weight of a text

Note

The *HTML* `<font>` tag specifies the *font face, font size*, and *color of a text*.

But the `<font>` tag is **not** supported in *HTML 5.* Use *CSS* instead.

Font Families

The `font-family` is the font you want to use for your content. It is a good idea to have a couple of extra *font* in the `font-family` property so that it can be displayed if the first font does not work.

The syntax for the `font-family` property:

```
p {font-family: arial, "Times New Roman", serif;}
```

- The *extra values* are separated by *commas (,).*
- If the name of `font` contains more than one word, put it inside *quotation marks* (*"Times New Roman"*).

Font Size

The `font-size` is the size you want your font to be displayed.
The `font-size` has two types: *absolute size* and *relative size.*

- *Absolute size*

Absolute size uses a fixed size. This means that the font will be the same size regardless of what the *browser* used.
An example of a `font-size` with the *absolute size* is *px*.

The syntax for the *absolute size* in *px* and *%*:

```
div a {font-size: 12px;}
div b {font-size: 80%;}
```

- *Relative size*

Relative size is not a fixed size. The size is *relative* to the surrounding elements.
Using *relative size* allows the text size to change depending on the *browser* used.

The syntax for the *relative size:*

```
div c {font-size: medium;}
div d {font-size: x-large;}
```

> **Note**
> *px (pixel)*, is the smallest area in a display.
> If a monitor has 200 *ppi (pixels per inch)*, then there are 200 pixels in any given area per *square inch.*

Font Style

The `font-style` property is used to specify *italic* or *oblique* faces. There are three values for the `font-style` property:

- `normal` - The text is shown normally.
- `italic` - The text is shown in *italics.*
- `oblique` - The text is very similar to *italic*, but *less* supported.

```
p {font-style: italic;}
```

Font Weight

The `font-weight` property is used to specify the *weight* or *boldness* of the text.

The `font-weight` property has 5 values:

- `normal`
- `bold`
- `bolder`
- `lighter`
- `100-900 (700 is regular size)`

```
div normal {font-weight: normal;}
div thick {font-weight: bold;}
```

As mention earlier, I will use sample code very simple like above until the end of Chapter 8. Just read thru and try to understand the concept if you can.

2 CSS Text Property

Another way for decorating characters in *CSS* is *Text Property*.

In this *Text Property* section, I will just explain two frequently used properties: `color` and `text-align`.

The *Color* of a text can make a huge difference in your *website.*

property	descriptions
`text-align`	specifies the horizontal alignment of text
`color`	sets the color of the text
`direction`	specifies the text direction/writing direction
`letter-spacing`	increases/decreases the space between characters in a text
`line-height`	sets the height of a line
`text-decoration`	specifies the decoration added to the text
`text-indent`	specifies the indentation of the first line in a text-block
`text-shadow`	specifies the shadow effect added to the text
`text-transform`	controls the capitalization of text
`text-overflow`	specifies how overflowed content that is not displayed should be signaled to the user
`unicode-bidi`	used together with the direction property to set or return whether the text should be overridden to support multiple languages in the same document
`vertical-align`	sets the vertical alignment of an element
`white-space`	specifies how white-space inside an element is handled
`word-spacing`	increases/decreases the space between words in a text

Text Align

The `text-align` property specifies the *horizontal alignment* of text in an element.

```
p {text-align: center;}
```

value	descriptions
`left`	aligns the text to the left
`right`	aligns the text to the right
`center`	centers the text
`justify`	stretches the lines so each line has an equal width
`initial`	sets this property to its default value
`inherit`	inherits this property from its parent element

Text Color

The `color` property is used to set the `color` of the *text*.
The `color` is specified in 3 ways:
color name, HEX (Hexadecimal), RGB (Red Green Blue)

```
P {color: red;}
```

value	descriptions
color name	`red, blue, etc..`
HEX value	`#ff0000, #0000ff`
RGB value	`rgb (255,0,0), rgb (0,0,255)`

Note

The HEX value is a triplet specifying the amounts of Red, Green, and Blue (#RRGGBB). Unlike RGB value, TWO characters are needed to specify the amount of Red and each these characters is one of the 16 symbols from the hexadecimal number system.

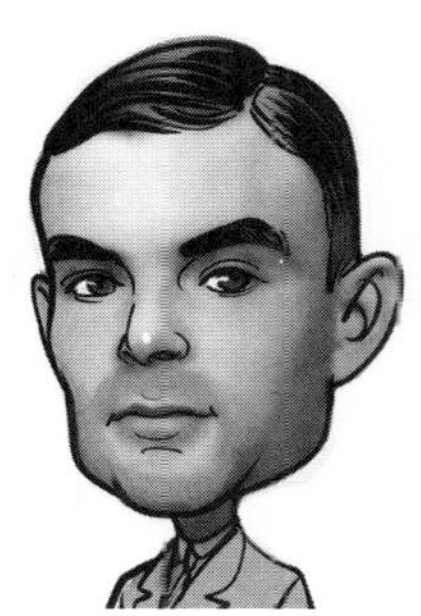

Alan Turing

An English *mathematician* and *computer scientist*. Alan Turing was born on June 23, 1912, in Maida Vale, London, England.

Alan, a famed *code-breaking* war hero, now is considered the father of *computer science* and *artificial intelligence*.

Alan died on June 7, 1954.

CHAPTER 7

CSS **Box Model**

1. What is a Box Model?
2. Measurement Unit & Shorthand Property
3. CSS Box Model-Border
4. CSS Margin & Padding
5. CSS Box-Sizing

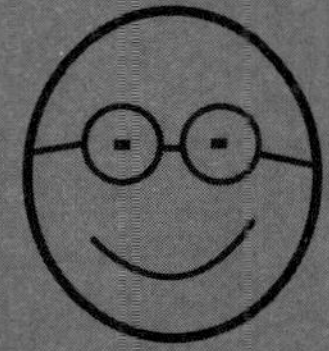

1 What is a **Box Model**?

- The *CSS box model* is the foundation of *layout* on the Web.
- Each element is represented as a rectangular box, with the box's *border, margin, padding,* and *content* like a *New York Times* website below.

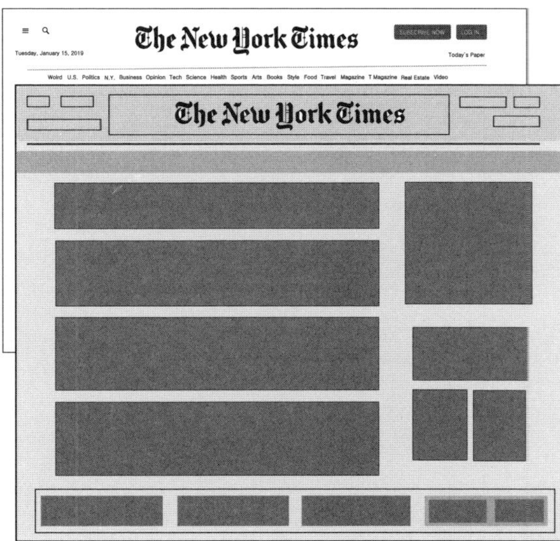

Box Model

You can style these boxes with *CSS* by selecting the *HTML* tags or by selecting the `class` or ID name that you have given them.

```
div {
  width: 300px;
  border: 15px solid green;
  padding: 50px;
  margin: 20px;
}
```

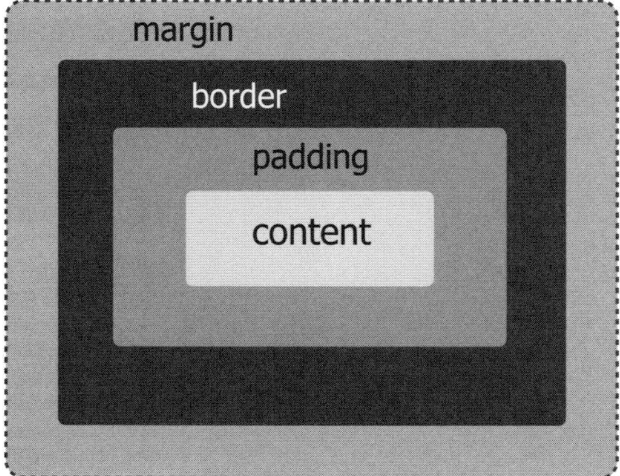

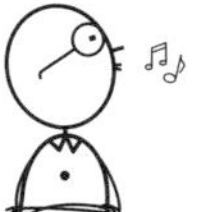

Unlike the border of a picture, the *border* of a *CSS* box does not hug the edge of the content (the *padding* does). In the *CSS* box model, the *border* is BETWEEN the *padding* and the *margin*.

Note

According to Microsoft's *"CSS usage on the web platform"*, 8 of the 10 mostly used properties are *"box related"* ones. For this reason, the *Box Model* is very important.

Height and Width

These properties define the `height` and `width` of an element.

There are three ways to define these properties:

- *Auto (default value)*
- *Length (*`px, cm`*, etc.)*
- *Percentage (%)*

```
div {
    height: 100px;
    width: 500px;
}
```

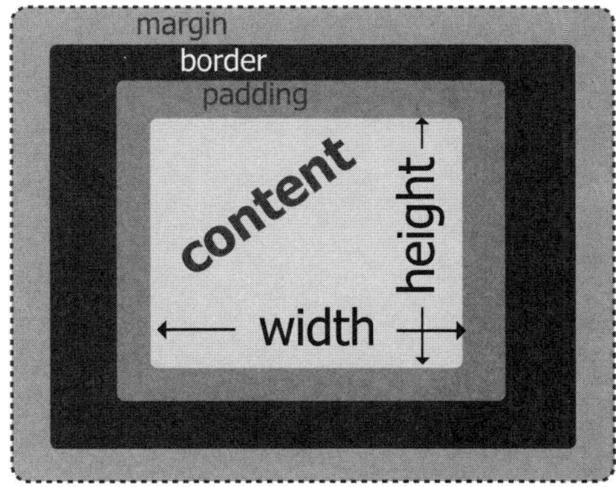

value	descriptions
auto	calculated by the browser automatically
length	specifies a height/width in `px, pt, cm`, etc.
%	specifies a height/width in % of the width of the element

The height and width properties do **not** include borders, margins ,or paddings

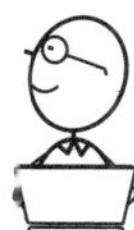

2 Measurement **Unit** & **Shorthand** Property

Before we start the next *Box Model* sections, let's spend some time figuring out what they are:

- *Measurement Unit*.
- *CSS Shorthand Property*.

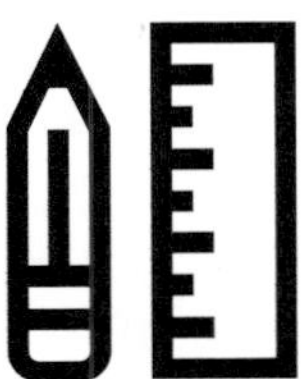

COMMA
↓
CMA

The standard *font size* of every *web browser* is 16px (pixel)

Measurement Unit

CSS 3 supports two kinds of *measurement units:*

Absolute and *Relative*.

- **Absolute Unit**

unit	name	equals to
`px`	pixels	1 px = 1/96th of 1 inch
`cm`	centimeters	1 cm = 37.8 px
`mm`	millimeters	1 mm = 1/10th of 1 cm
`q`	quarter millimeters	1 Q = 1/4th of 1 mm
`in`	inches	1 in = 2.54 cm = 96 px
`pc`	picas	1 pc = 1/6th of an inch
`pt`	points	1 pt = 1/72nd of an inch

Note

These values are more useful when used for print, rather than screen output.

For example, we don't typically use `cm` (centimeters) on screen.

The only value that you will commonly use is `px` (pixels).

- **Relative Unit**

unit	description
em	relative to the current font-size of the element (2 em means 2 times the size of the current font)
rem	stands for Root EM, font-sized of the root element
ex	relative to the x-height (height of lowcase x) of the current font
ch	advanced measure (width) of the character "0"
lh	the line height of the element
*vw	** 1 % of the viewport's width
*vh	1 % of the viewport's height
*vmin	1 % of the viewport's smaller dimension
*vmax	1 % of the viewport's larger dimension

Note

The *em* and *rem* units are practical in creating perfectly scalable layouts.

* `viewport` = the browser's window size
(you will learn about the `viewport` in the next chapter)

** If the `viewport` is 50 *cm* wide, 1 *vw* = 0.5 *cm*

em is an old *typographic unit*, known as an *em square* or *mutton*. An *em square* is a square blank type, where the length of each side was the same as the width of an uppercase “M”.

CSS Shorthand Properties

`border`, `margin`, and `padding` are all *shorthand properties* that can include all four side values.
A *Shorthand property* saves a lot of time and works well.
You can include 1, 2, 3 or 4 values for the *border property.*
Syntaxes for the *border shorthand property* are:

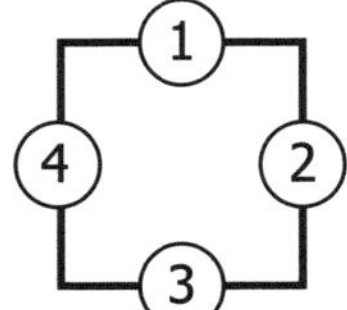

4 values: the 1st number defines the *border-top* property, the 2nd number defines the *border-right* property, the 3rd number defines the *border-bottom* property, and the 4th number defines the *border-left* property.

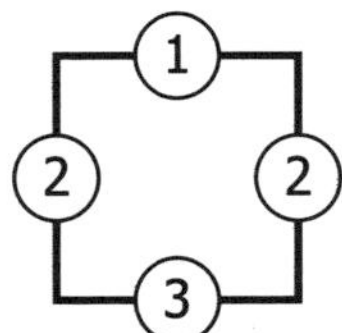

3 values: the 1st number defines the *border-top* property, the second number defines the *border-right* and *border-left* properties, and the 4th number defines the *border-bottom* property.

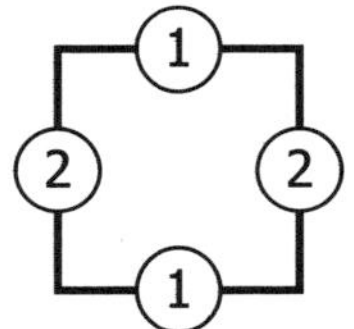

2 values: the 1st number defines the *border-top* and *border-bottom* properties and the 2nd number defines the *border-right* and *border-left* properties.

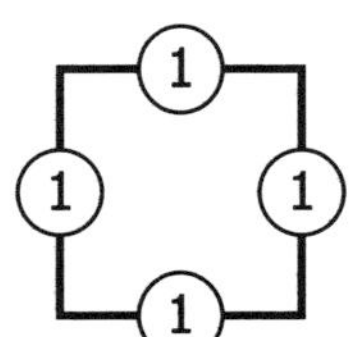

1 value: the 1 number defines the border property of *all four* sides.

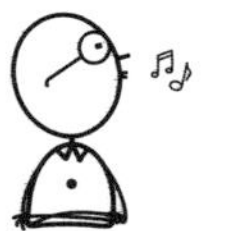

Think of a clock,
starting at *mid-day* and moving
clockwise.

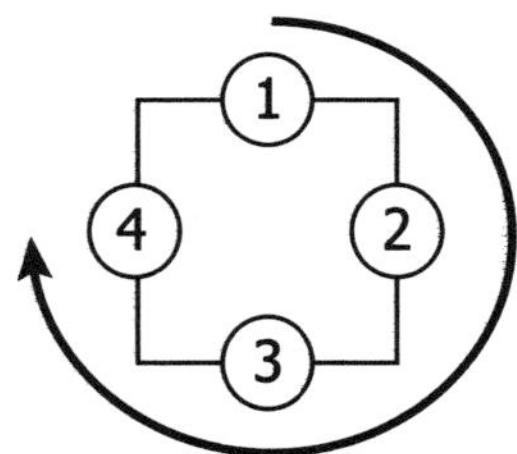

```
{border-top: 10px;
 border-right:20px;
 border-bottom:5px;
 border-left:15px;
}
```

```
{border: 10px 20px 5px 15px;}
```

```
{border-top: 10px;
 border-right:20px;
 border-bottom:5px;
 border-left:20px;
}
```

```
{border: 10px 20px 5px;}
```

```
{border-top: 10px;
 border-right:20px;
 border-bottom:10px;
 border-left:20px;
}
```

```
{border: 10px 20px;}
```

```
{border-top: 10px;
 border-right:10px;
 border-bottom:10px;
 border-left:10px;
}
```

```
{border: 10px;}
```

Note

Other programming languages also have their own *Shorthand Property.*

3 CSS Box Model-**Border**

Border is the Base of Box Model

`Border` properties allow you to define the `style`, `width`, and `color` of a `border` and it's `radius`:

- `border-style`
- `border-width`
- `border-color`
- `border-radius`

The `border` property has 4 elements/borders:

- `border-top`
- `border-right`
- `border-bottom`
- `border-left`

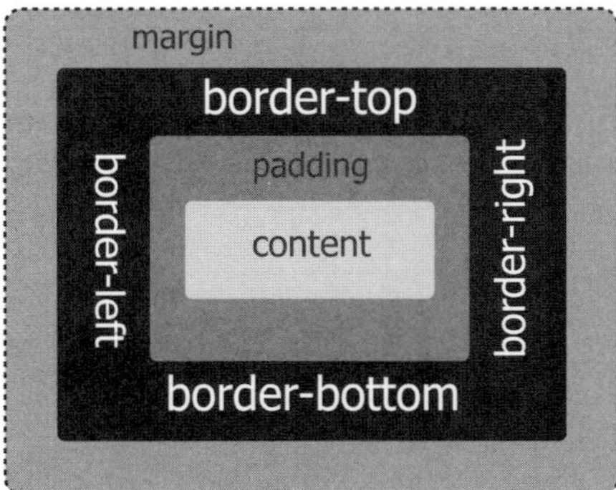

Border Style

```
p {border-style: dotted;}
```

The `border-style` property defines the style of the four borders. The style can be specified by these values:

value	description
`dotted`	dotted border
`dashed`	dashed border
`solid`	solid line border
`doubled`	double lined border
`groove`	3D groove border
`ridge`	3D ridge border
`inset`	3D inset border
`outset`	3D outset border
`none`	no border

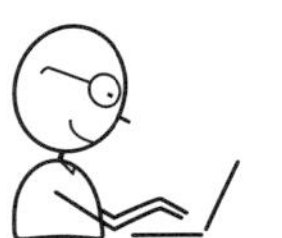

You need to define the `border-style` **first**. If you don't, the rest of the *border* properties will not work; they will be invisible.

Border Width

```
p {border-width: 2px;}
```

The property can have from one to four values: `top`, `right`, `bottom` and `left border`.

value	descriptions
length/size	`px, em, pt, cm, etcs`
3 thicknesses	`thin, medium, thick`
initial	sets to it's default value
inherit	inherits from its parent element

Border Color

```
p {border-color:red;}
```

The `border-color` property sets the color of an element's 4 borders (`top, right, bottom, left`)

The color can be set by:

value	descriptions
color name	`red, blue, etc..`
HEX value	`#ff0000, #0000ff`
RGB value	`rgb (255,0,0) rgb (0,0,255)`
HSLA value	`hsla (60, 90%, 50%, .8)`
transparent	clear looking

HSLA value:

H: Hue is a degree on the color wheel from 0 to 360. 0 is red, 120 is green, and 240 is blue.

S: Saturation is a percentage value, 0% means a shade of gray, and 100% is the full color.

L: Lightness is also a percentage value, 0% is black, and 100% is white.

A: Alpha is a number between 0.0 (fully transparent) and 1.0.

Note

The `border-color` property does **not** work if it is used alone. Use the `border-style` property to set the *borders* first.

Border Radius

```
p {border-radius: 0px 50px 20px 100px;}
```

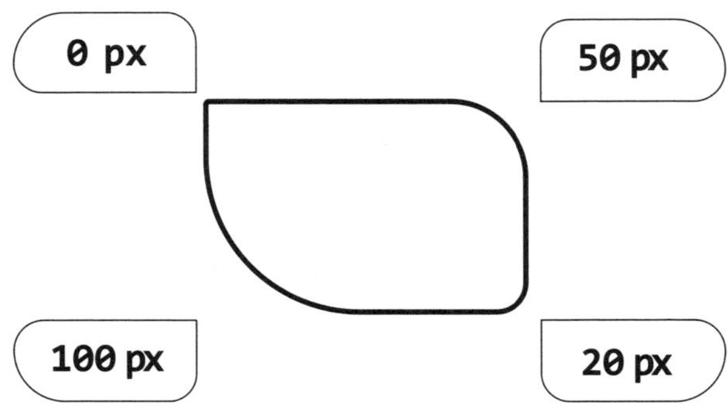

The `border-radius` property defines the style of the four cornerrs:

- `top-left`
- `top-right`
- `bottom-right`
- `bottom-left`

There are different ways to specify its value:

unit	descriptions
length	specifies the shape of corners in length(`px, pt, cm`, etc)
%	specifies the shape of the corners in %
inherit	inherited from the parent element

Border Radius Shorthand Property

You can use the `border-radius` *Shorthand Property* to style the corners of the *box model*.
This property allows you to *round* corners.
You can specify the borders with up to four corner *values*:

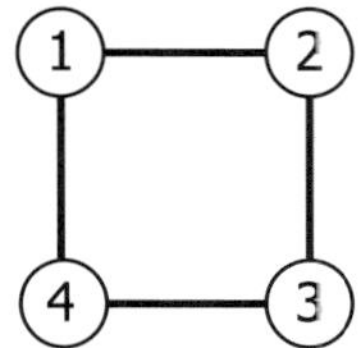

4 *values*: the 1st value defines the `top-left` corner, the 2nd value defines the `top-right` corner, the 3rd value defines the `bottom-right` corner, and the 4th value defines the `bot-tom-left` corner

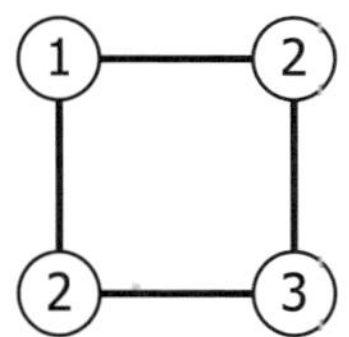

3 *values*: the 1st value defines the `top-left` corner, the 2nd value defines the `top-right` and `bottom-left` corners, and the 3rd value defines the `bottom-right` corner

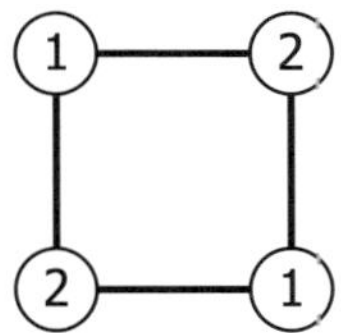

2 *values*: the 1st value defines the `top-left` and `bottom-right` corner, the 2nd value defines the `top-right`, and `bottom-left` corner

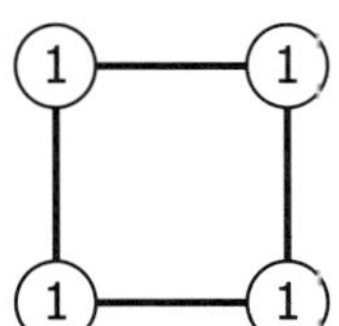

1 *value*: 1 value defines *all four* corners

The 3 border properties (`style, width, color`), like the `border-radius`, have *shorthand properties*.

4 CSS Margin & Padding

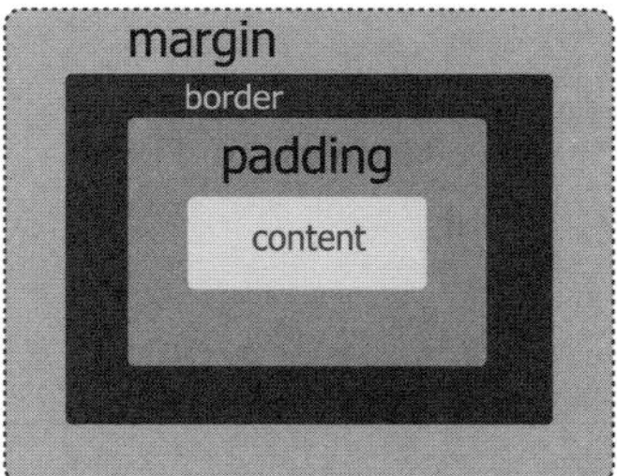

Lorem ipsum dolor sit amet, consectetuer adipiscing elit, sed diam nonummy nibh euismod

Lorem ipsum dolor sit amet, consectetuer adipiscing elit, sed diam nonummy nibh euismod

Without Margin & Padding

Lorem ipsum dolor sit amet, consectetuer adipiscing elit, sed diam nonummy nibh euismod

Lorem ipsum dolor sit amet, consectetuer adipiscing elit, sed diam nonummy nibh euismod

With Margin & Padding

The box to your left looks *"unbalanced and weird,"* right? That's why we need Margins & Paddings with Borders

Margin

This property defines the space around elements.

`Margin` values can be set with `auto, lengths, and percentages`
There are four properties to define the *value* of each side.

- `margin-top`
- `margin-right`
- `margin-bottom`
- `margin-left`

unit	descriptions
auto	calculated by the browser automatically
length	specifies a margin in `px, pt, cm`, etc
%	specifies a margin in % of the width
inherit	should be inherited from the parent element

Shorthand Property for Margin

`Margin` is also a *shorthand property* and a simple example is below:

```
{margin-top: 100px;
 margin-right:50px;
 margin-bottom:80px;
 margin-left:40px;
}
```

```
{margin: 100px 50px 80px 40px;}
```

Padding

The `padding` property defines the space between the `content` and the `border`.
`Padding` values can be set with `lengths` or `percentages`.
Like the `margin` property, there are four properties to define the space of each side.

- `padding-top`
- `padding-right`
- `padding-bottom`
- `padding-left`

unit	description
length	specifies a padding in px, pt, cm, etc
%	specifies a padding in % of the width of the element
inherit	should be inherited from the parent element

Other Shorthand Property

`Padding` is a also *shorthand property*, let's check other *Shorthand Properties* in this section. Let's review the other *Shorthand Properties* in this section:

property	structure & example
border	{border: border-width | border-style | color;
	{border: 1px dotted #ff0000;}
border-top	{border-top: border-width | border-style | color;}
	{border-top: 1px dotted #ff0000;}
padding	{padding: padding-top | padding-right | padding-bottom | padding-left;}
	{padding: 1em 2em 3em 4em;}
background	{background: background-color | background-image | background-repeat | background-attachment | background-position;}
	{background: #ff0000 url("MyDomain.com") no-repeat | center | left;}
font	{font: font-style | font-variant | font-weight | font-size | line-height | font-family;}
	{font: italic small-caps normal 13px 150% Arial;}

5 CSS **Box-Sizing**

Box Sizing

`Box-sizing` defines how the `width` and `height` of an element are calculated.

value	descriptions
`border-box`	width and height properties include content, padding and border
`content-box`	width and height properties include only the content; border and padding are not included

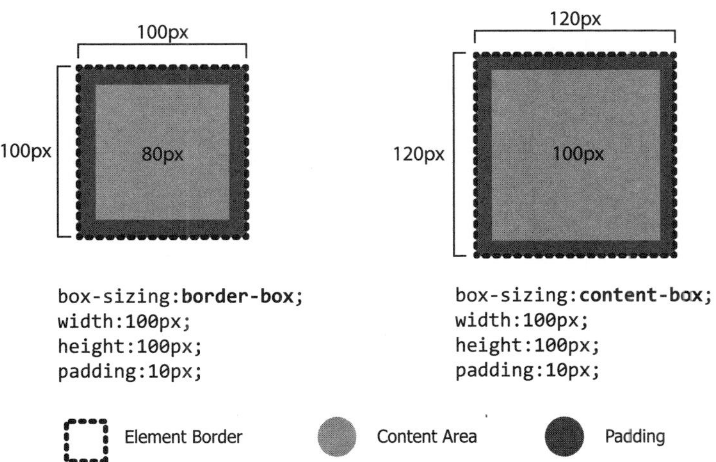

It makes dealing with the sizes of elements much easier, and generally eliminates a bunch of headaches you will have while laying out your content.

CHAPTER 8

RWD (Responsive Web Design) & Positioning

1. What is Media Query?
2. What is RWD?
3. What is Viewport?
4. What is Positioning?

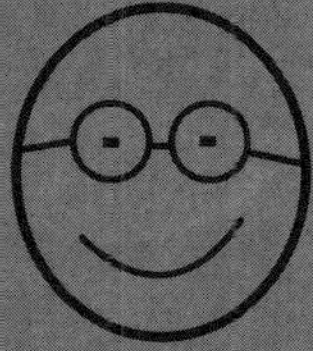

1 What is **Media Query**?

- *Media Query* is a *CSS 3* module allowing content rendering to adapt to the types and conditions of different devices and screen sizes.
- It is a fundamental part of *Responsive Web Design (RWD)* and made up of a *media type* that can be true or false.
  If it is true, the *media query* is applied.

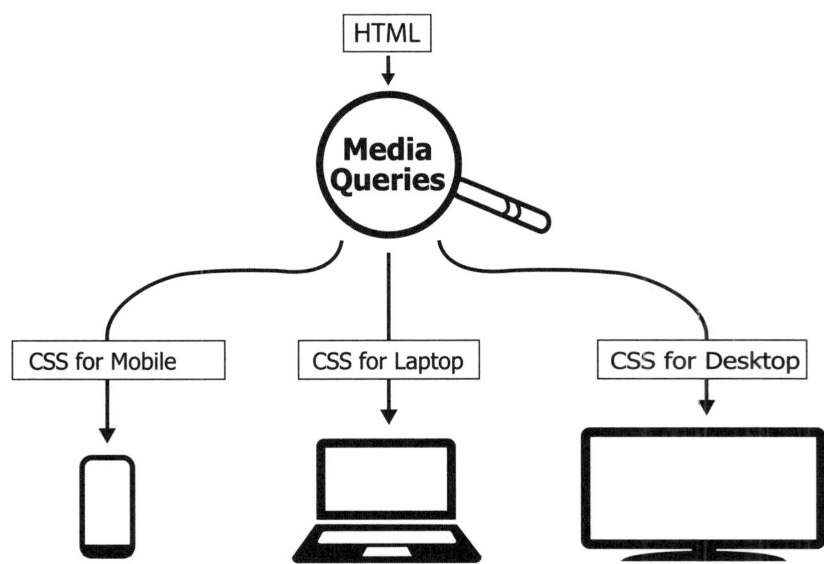

Note

Media Query is useful when you want to modify your *website* depending on a *device's type* (printer vs. screen) or specific *characteristics* and *parameters (screen resolution* or *browser viewport* width*).*

Breakpoint

*Breakpoint*s are browser widths with specific numbers that change the layout of your *website* if the browser fits the declared width. The table below shows the standard *media query breakpoints.*

600px ▼	1024px ▼	1400px ▼	1920px ▼	
cell phone	tablet	laptop	desktop	TV & others
600	601-1024	1025-1400	1401-1920	1921

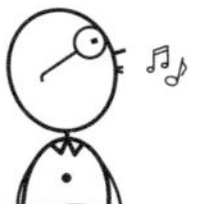

Breakpoints allow the layout to adjust accordingly to provide the best experience for the user.

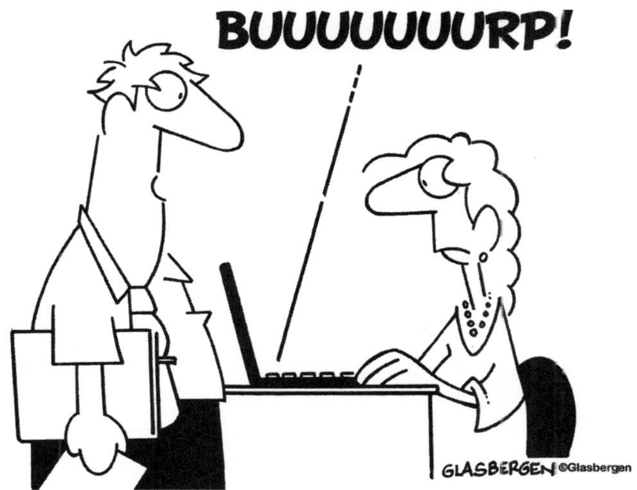

"sounds like your hard drive is getting full"

2 What is **RWD**?

- *RWD (Responsive Web Design)* makes a *web page* look good on all devices.
- The *content* of the *web page* will be the same no matter what device is being used, but the *layout* of the *web page* will differ.
- In 2010, web designer *Ethan Marcotte* first used the term *Response Web Design* to refer to a web design approach that builds on the basics of *fluid design*. His goal of *RWD* is that content is easy to view, read, and navigate, regardless of the device type and size on which it is viewed.

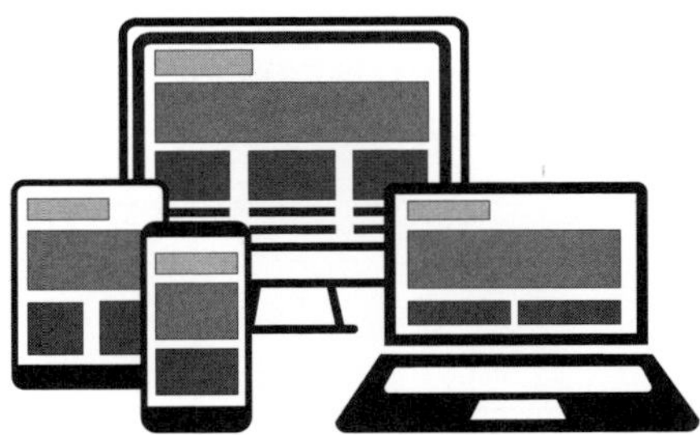

Responsive Web Design is about using *HTML* and *CSS* to automatically resize, hide, shrink, or enlarge a *website* to make it look good on all devices (desktops, tablets and smartphones)

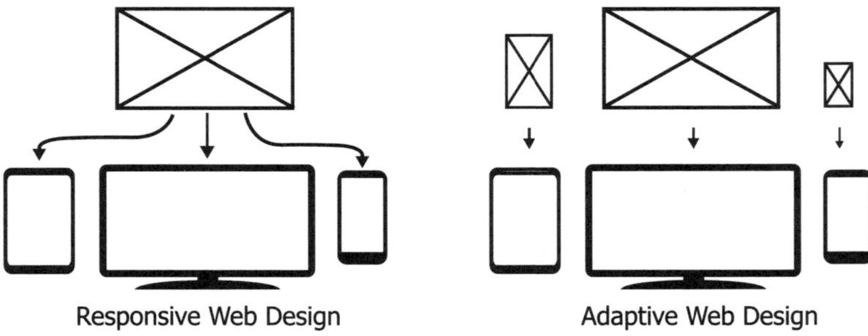

RWD vs. **AWD (Adaptive Web Design)**

AWD is similar to *RWD* in the sense that they both are meant to change the layout of the *web page* for different sized devices.

The big difference between these two methods is:

- *RWD* adapts to the size of the screen no matter what the target device/screen size is. The layout is *fluid* and uses CSS media to change styles. This *fluid grid* enables the page to resize its width and height to adapt to different screen sizes and show correctly.
- *AWD* detects the type of device being used **first** before providing the pre-set layout for that device.

> **Note**
>
> In some aspect, you can say "*RWD* is *browser* based and AWD is *device* based."

	RWD	AWD
support & adoption	✓	
flexibility	✓	
e-commerce		✓
speed		✓
example	apple.com	amazon.com

An easy way to understand the difference is by comparing *amazon.com* and *apple.com.*

- Visit *apple.com* and minimize the screen. The website changes according to the size of the *browser*. This is *RWD*.
- Now, try the same procedure with *amazon.com*. Minimizing the website will not change the layout of the web page. However, if you view *amazon.com* on your phone, the layout will appear completely different. This is called *AWD*.

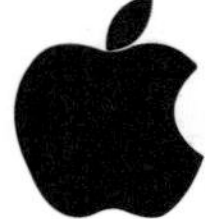

3 What is Viewport?

The *viewport* is the user's visible area of a *web page*.

- It is a <meta> tag contained in the <head> section.
- It tells the *browser* how the *web page* should be displayed.
- No matter what device is being used, the *website* will vary with the device.

With this new <meta> element, the *website* scales to the width of the device.

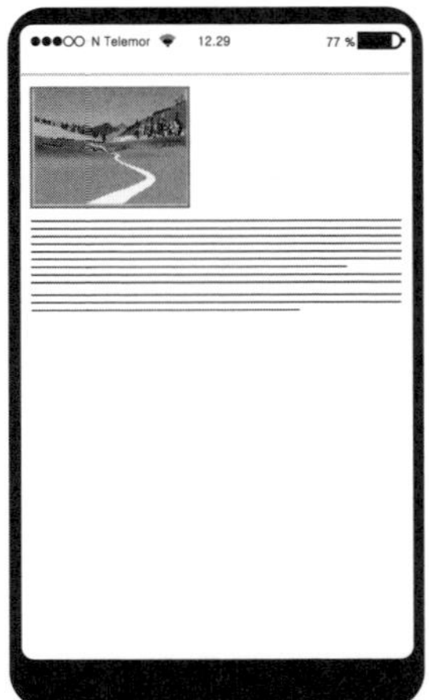

Without Viewport <meta> tag

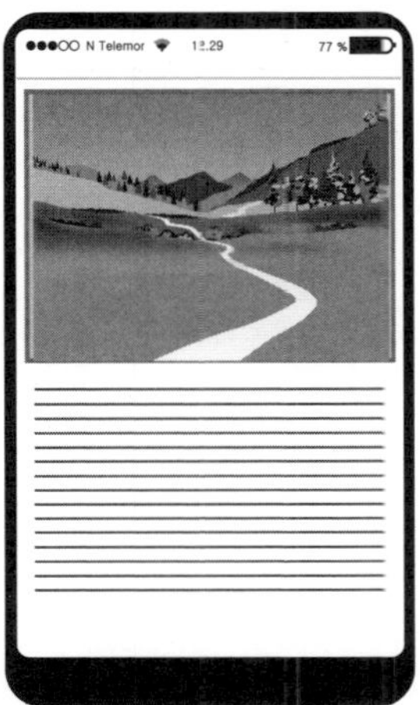

With Viewport <meta> tag

A *web page* can be made to be seen properly on different size screens by configuring the *viewport.*

Before *smartphone* became popular, *websites* were designed to be displayed on a computer screen.

People on *smartphones* would have a bad experience when visiting *websites* because the content would show up to be too small for the average person to see clearly.

Users would have to scroll vertically instead of horizontally when visiting a website. The user would have to pinch the screen to zoom in and zoom out and have to scroll horizontally to read or see the content. It was troublesome.

With this new `<meta>` element, the *website* scales to the width of the device.

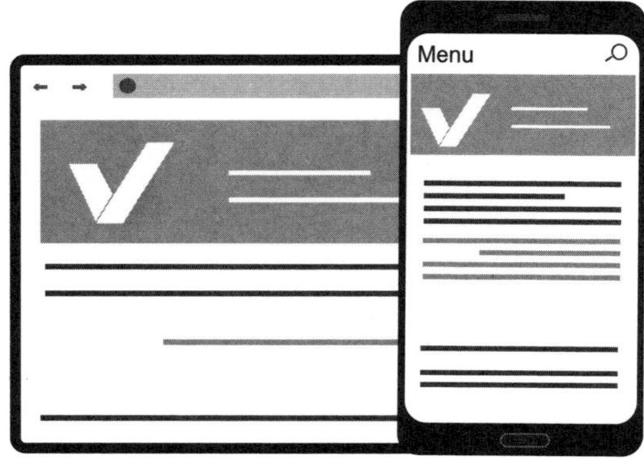

With a line of *HTML* `<meta>` tag, websites have contents that are clearly visible and comfortable to see no matter what device is used.

```
<meta name="viewport" content="width=device-width,
initial-scale=1.0">
```

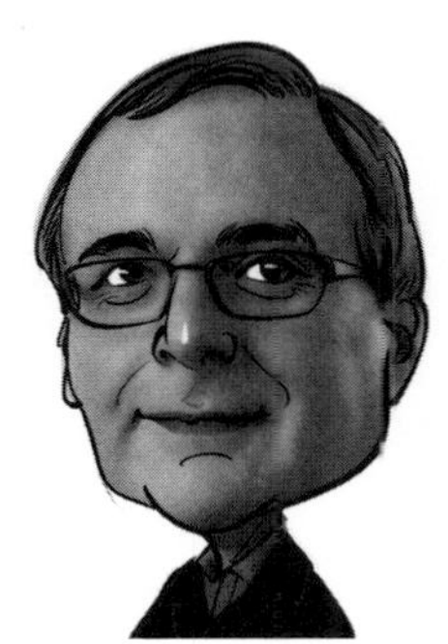

Paul Allen

An American *Entrepreneur* and *Investor* best known for being one of the co-founders of *Microsoft* along with *Bill Gates*.

Born on January 21, 1953, in Seattle, Washington, Paul Allen met fellow Lakeside School student and computer enthusiast Bill Gates when Allen was 14 and Gates was 12. Less than a decade later, in 1975, college drop-outs Allen and Gates founded *Microsoft*. Allen resigned after being diagnosed with Hodgkin's disease in 1983 and continued to pursue other business, research, and philanthropic opportunities.

He died on October 15, 2018. He was 65 years old.

4 What is **Positioning**?

- *CSS Positioning* allows you to control how elements are positioned on a *web page*, including *positioning* an element behind or next to another.
- In order to make more complex layouts, it is important to get a better understanding of *CSS Positioning*.
- You can *position* elements with the following properties (except when using static): top, bottom, left, and right.

value	descriptions
`static`	elements render in order, as they appear in the document flow
`relative`	moves the elements box relative to its original position in the flow
`absolute`	enables to set the exact position of an element on a page
`fixed`	element is positioned relative to the browser window
`z-index`	controls stacking order priority

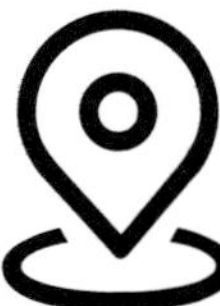

Note

Elements are positioned using the top, bottom, left, and right properties. However, these properties will **not** work unless the positioning property is set first.

Static

The *CSS property*, `static`, is a default value.
It is always positioned according to the normal *flow of the page.*
It is **not** affected by the top, bottom, left, and right properties.

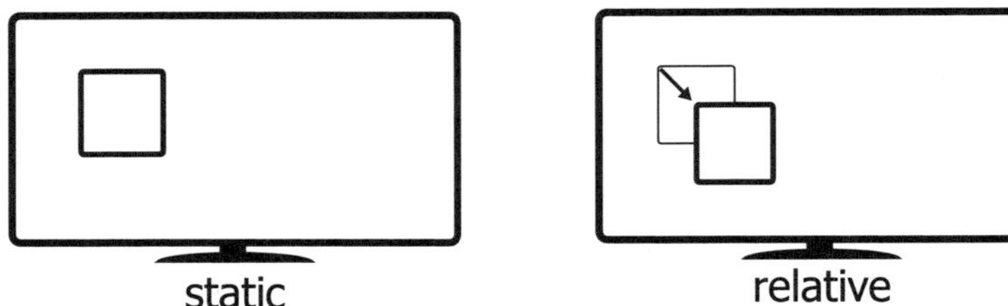

Relative

It moves elements around `relative` to where they would normally appear in the `static` flow of the page.
Setting the top, left, bottom, and right properties of a *relatively-positioned* element will cause it to be adjusted away from its normal position.

```
{
position: static;
width: 200px;
height: 200px;
border: 5px solid black;
}


{
position: relative;
top: 100px;
left: 100px;
width: 200px;
height: 200px;
border: 5px solid red;
}
```

Absolute

The elements are removed from the document flow entirely and positioned with respect to a containing element.

Consider this the most manual way to lay out an element, cause there's no longer any relationship with the `static` flow of the page.

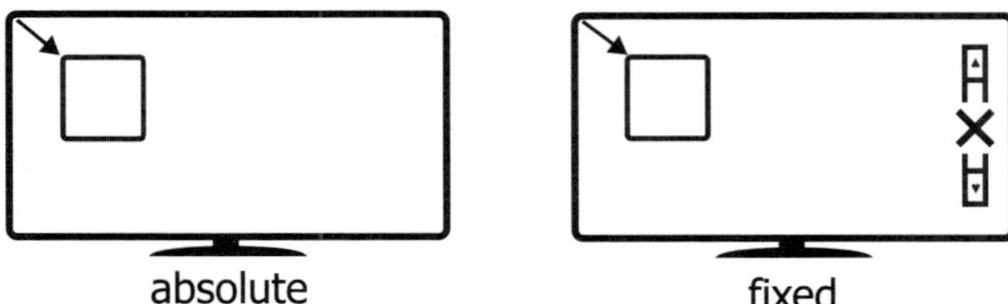

Fixed

`Fixed` *position* elements always stay in the same place even if the page is *scrolled*. The top, right, bottom, and left properties are used to position the element.

```
{
position: absolute;
top: 100px;
left: 100px;
width: 200px;
height: 200px;
border: 5px solid blue;
}


{
position: fixed;
top: 100px;
left: 100px;
width: 200px;
height: 200px;
border: 5px solid red;
```

z-index

The `z-index` property in *CSS* controls the *vertical stacking order* of elements that overlap. The higher the number, the closer it is to you.

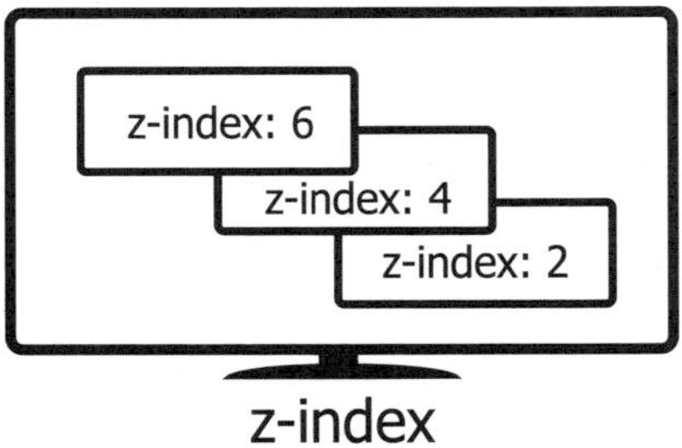

z-index

```
{
position: relative;
z-index: 2;
border: solid;
}


{
position: absolute;
z-index: 4;
border: solid;
}


{
position: absolute;
z-index: 6;
border: solid;
}
```

If two positioned elements overlap without a `z-index` specified; the element positioned last in the *HTML* code will be shown on top.

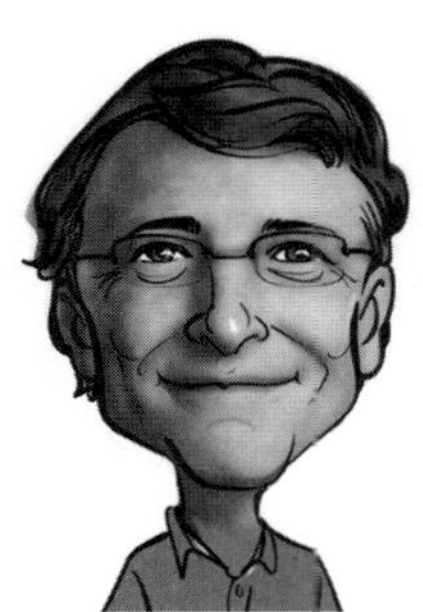

Bill Gates

An american *business entrepreneur*, *software developer*, and *investor*. Bill founded the world's largest software business, *Microsoft*, with Paul Allen, and subsequently became one of the richest men in the world. In February 2014, Gates announced that he was stepping down as *Microsoft's* chairman to focus on charitable work at his foundation, the *Bill and Melinda Gates Foundation*.

Review Section: You should be familiar with the following terms:

1. Header, Center, and Footer Area.
2. Box-Model: Border, Padding, and Margin.
3. Short-Hand Property.
4. RWD
5. Viewport

PART 3

JavaScript & PHP

In this part, you will learn

- How JavaScript can make your web page come to life using functions and loops.
- How PHP organizes functions and variables.

CHAPTER 9

JavaScript

1. What is JavaScript?
2. JavaScript Event & Function
3. JavaScript Variables
4. Data Type & Operators
5. Conditional & Loop Statement
6. Where to Place?

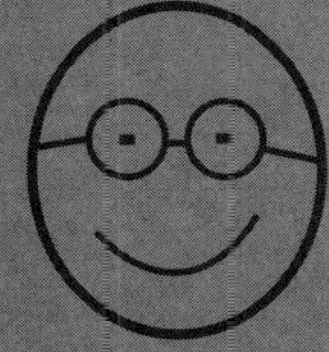

1 What is **JavaScript**?

- *JavaScript* is a *programming language* that is used to create dynamic and interactive effects on a *website*.
- *HTML, CSS,* and *JavaScript* are the three core *programming languages* for *web development.*
- It is case-sensitive so all the letters must be consistent with all the *JavaScript code*.
- *JavaScript* is the mostly used *script language* in the world.

HTML CSS JavaScript

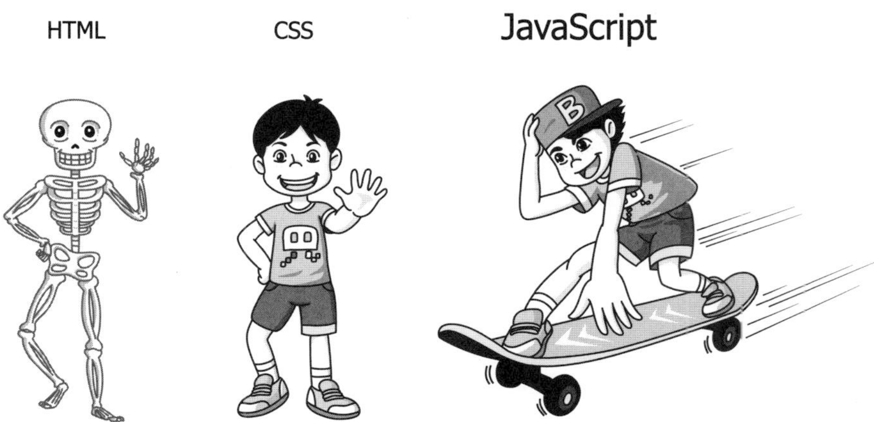

Java and *JavaScript* are different programming languages. *Java* and *JavaScript* are written, *assembled*, and *executed* differently. Each has dramatic differences when it comes to what it is capable of doing.

Let's make a simple *JavaScript* within the *HTML* document first and see if it works.

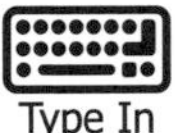
Type In

```
<!DOCTYPE html>
<html>
  <body>
    <input type="button" onclick="alert('Hello World!')"
    value="Hello World!"/>
  </body>
</html>
```

> **Note**
>
> Bold part is *JavaScript code* and it's inserted in *HTML* like *CSS.*

Save

Upload

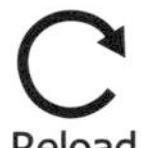
Reload

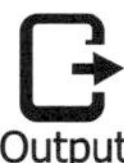
Output

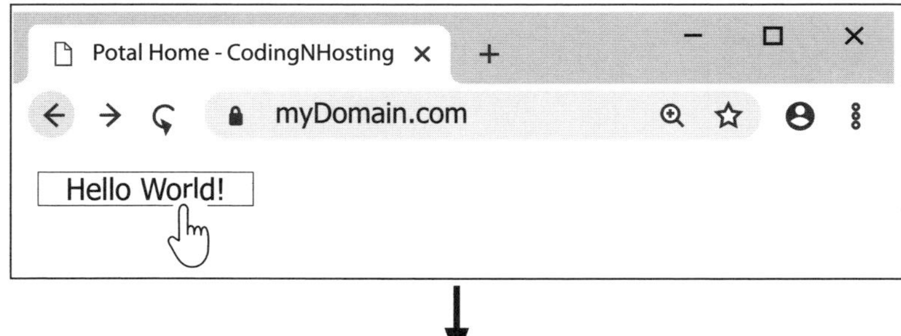

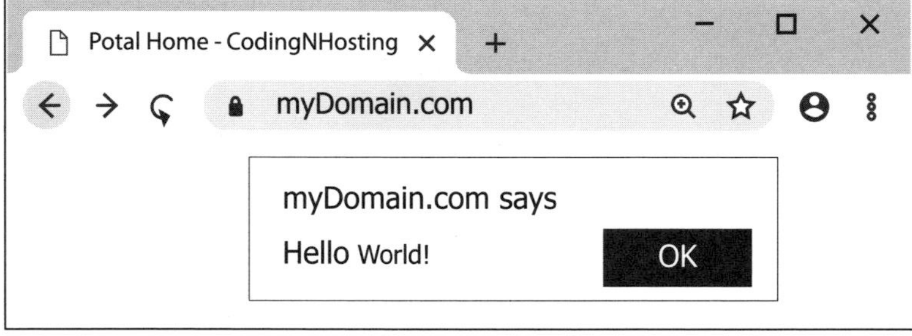

By inserting a line of *JavaScript code*, you can communicate (right now very basically) with the *website* you just made.

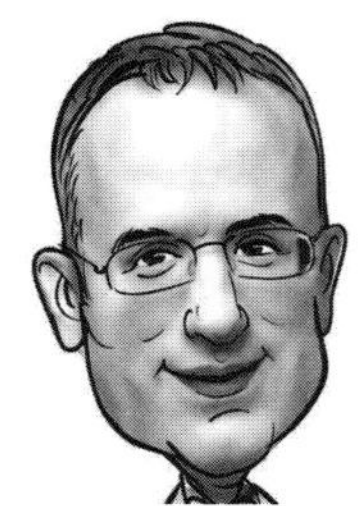

Brendan Eich, an American technologist, created the *JavaScript programming language*.
He co-founded the *Mozilla Project* which developed *Firefox*, one of the five major web browsers.

What can *JavaScript* do?

- Change HTML *content.*
- Change HTML *attributes.*
- Change the CSS *style.*
- Hide HTML *elements.*
- Show *hidden* HTML *elements.*

Case Sensitivity

Unlike HTML or CSS, *JavaScript* is *Case Sensitive*. Whatever the *JavaScript command* or *variable* you are using, you need to make sure of the difference between *upper* and *lower* case characters.

JavaScript ≠ JAVASCRIPT

Comment Line

The *JavaScript comment line* is the same as the CSS (multi-line) and the *PHP* (single line)

// : Single Line Comment

/*··*/ : Multi-line comment

	single line comment	multi-line comment
JavaScript	//	/* */
HTML	<!-- -->	
CSS	/* */	
PHP	//, #	/* */

2 JavaScript **Event & Function**

JavaScript Event

A *JavaScript Event* occurs when the user or the browser performs a specific task in the web browser. This is how *JavaScript* is able to interact with HTML.

Examples of events:

- When a user *click*s a mouse.
- When a user *presse*s a button.
- When a user *resize*s the window.
- When a web page has *load*ed completely.

When these *events* occur, *JavaScript* is able to execute code.

Hello World!

Commonly used HTML Attributes / JavaScript Events

event	descriptions
onclick	user clicks an HTML tag
onchange	an HTML tag has been changed
onmouseover	the user moves the mouse over an HTML tag
onmouseout	the user moves the mouse away from an HTML tag
onkeydown	user pushes a keyboard key
onkeyup	user releases a keyboard key

```
<!DOCTYPE html>
<html>
  <body>
    <button onclick="document.write('Hello World!')"> click me
    </button>
  </body>
</html>
```

<button>: *HTML form* tag. It is one of the *main tags*.

onclick: HTML *Attribute / JavaScript Event.*

document.write: *JavaScript code*, writes a string of text ("Hello World!") to *HTML document*.

click me: Just *contents*.

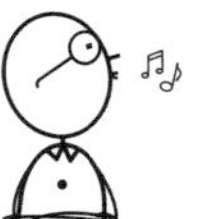

The *HTML statement* from the above and right page work in exactly the same way except for the right side is using the *JavaScript function*. *JavaScript* code `document.write` and `alert` is mostly used for testing the *code*.

JavaScript Function

- The *JavaScript function* is a set of *JavaScript statements* that perform a task.
- It is reusable by other code and it is one of the most important parts of *JavaScript.*
- It is **not** executed until it is called.
- It is composed of the word `function`, followed by the *function name*. There is always *parenthesis* after the *function name*, followed by a *curly bracket*. *JavaScript code* is inside of a *curly bracket.*

```
<!DOCTYPE html>
<html>
  <body>
     <button onclick="myFunction()">Click me.
     </button>
     <script>
        function myFunction() {
            document.write("Hello World!");
        }
     </script>
  </body>
</html
```

`<script>`, `</script>`: *HTML* `JavaScript` *opening/closing tag*

`function`: `Function` *declaration* for `JavaScript`

`myFunction()`: Name of the `function`

`{ }`: *Opening/closing* of *function statement* and `JavaScript` *code* inside

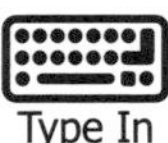


```
<!DOCTYPE html>
<html>
  <body>
     <button onclick="myFunction()">Click me.
     </button>
     <script>
        function myFunction() {
            document.write("Hello World!");
        }
     </script>
  </body>
</html
```

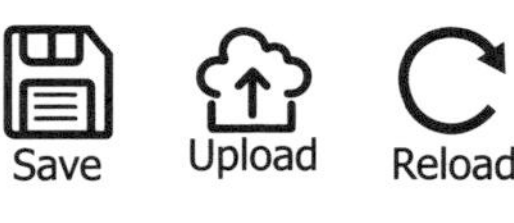

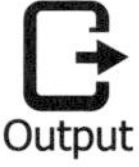

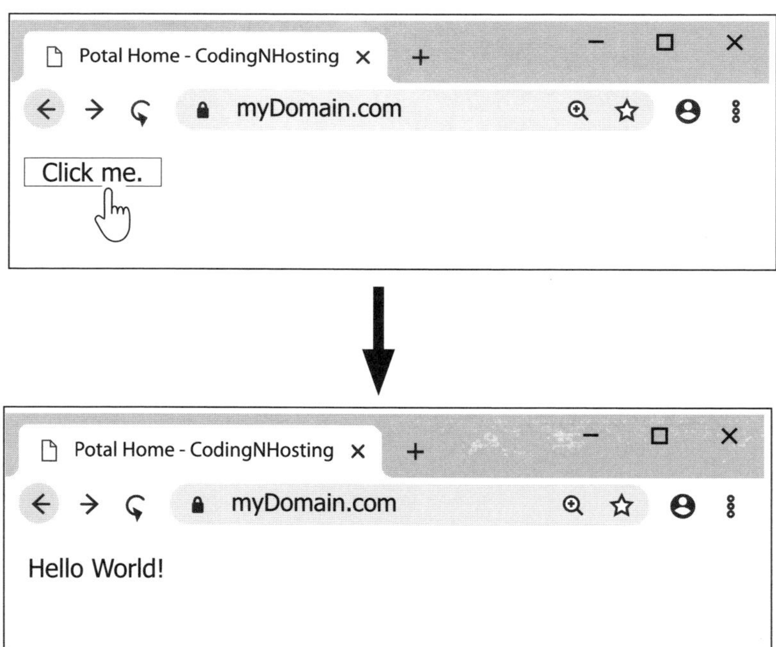

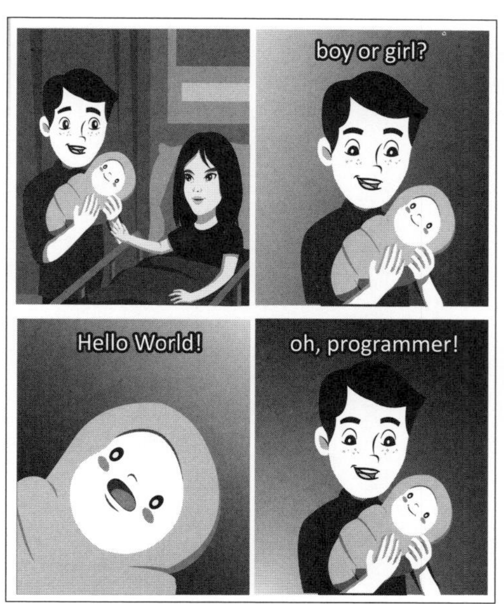
boy or girl?
Hello World!
oh, programmer!

3 JavaScript **Variables**

Variables

The mathematical meaning of *variable* is anything that can vary.

- *Variables* in *JavaScript* are containers for storing *data value.*
- *JavaScript* uses *reserved keywords* `var`, `let` and `const` to declare a *variable*.
- A *variable* must have a unique name.
- *Variables* should be declared before use.
- You can assign a value to a *variable* using the equal to (=) *operator* when you declare it or before you use it.

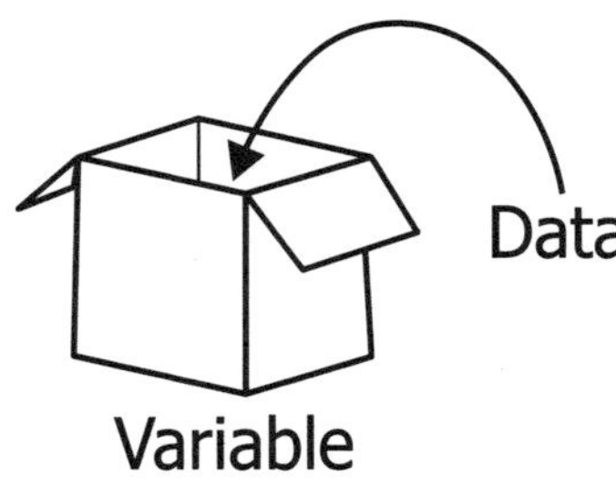

JavaScript variables can contain *numbers, text strings* and *other values.* For example, the following statement creates a *variable* called `danielHan` and assigns it the *value* `21`.

```
let danielHan = 21;
```

The Equal (=) *sign* in a programming language does **not** have the same meaning in an *arithmetic operation*. It assigns the *value* on the right-hand side to the *variable* you entered on the left.

Every *variable* has a unique name of your choice. However, there are rules you must follow when choosing a *variable name*:

- *Variable* names can **not** be a *keyword* such as `if, while, var` etc.
- *Variable* names can include upper or lower case *alphabet letters,* numbers 0-9, and the *underscore* (_) character.
- *Variable* name can **not** include space or any other *punctuation character.*
- The first character must be either a *letter* or an *underscore*.
- There is no official limit on the length of a *variable name*, but it must fit on one line.

Note

Choose friendly or easy to read/remember names. After spending a couple of days away from the *coding*, you mostly won't understand your *variable names* without a supporting document.

`var` vs. **`let`** vs. **`const`**

- `var`

`var` declarations are for the *entire file*. It is useful when you want your *entire file* to have access to *basic data* such as `user-id, session, etc.`

- `let`

Unlike `var` declarations, `let` declarations are *locally scoped* and can **not** be re-declared. The *values* can be updated but only within the *scope*. This solves the problem of the unintentional declaration of an *existing variable.*

- `const`

Its *value* remains `constant` during *program runtime* and can not be changed by the program. It can neither be *redefined* nor *updated*.

	scope:portion of code	redefine/update
`var`	global	can be redefined and updated
`let`	local	can not be redefined, can be updated
`const`	local	can neither be redefined nor be updated

good and valid examples of *variable names:*

```
let myVariableName;
var invoiceNumber_1120;
let _validID;
```

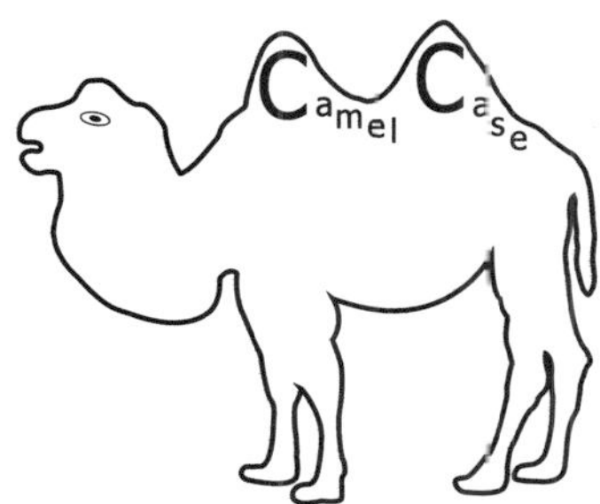

camelCase is a naming convention in which each word within a compound word is capitalized except for the first word.
It makes compound names more readable.

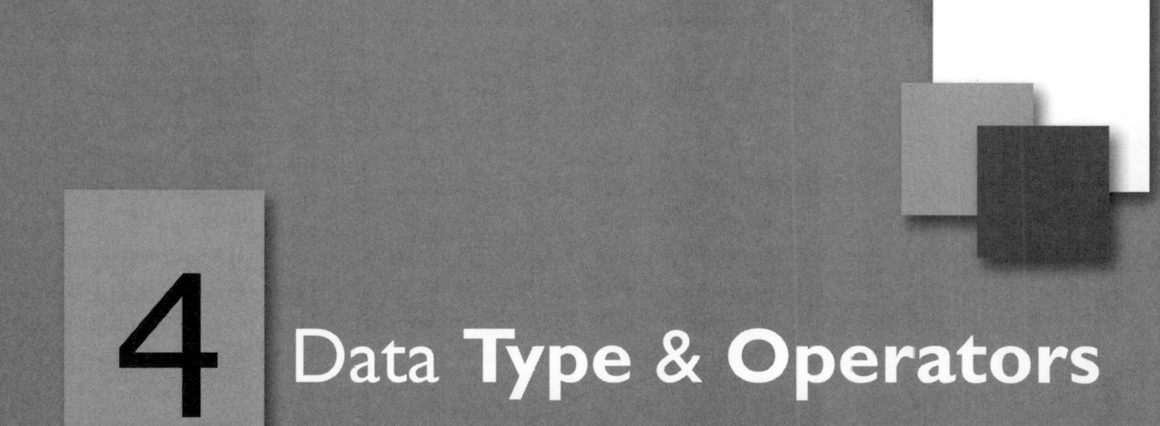

4 Data Type & Operators

In many programming languages, *Data Type* and it's *Operator* is an important concept and it makes a program operate correctly.

Data Type

There are 2 types of Data Type in JavaScript:

- *Primitive Types*
- *Reference Types*

Primitive Type

data type	descriptions
number	represents both integer & floating point numbers
string	character string. must be surrounded by quotes
boolean	only two values. with true or false
null	null value: doesn't belongs to any of above
undefined	a variable declared, but not assigned
symbol	for unique identifiers

- ***Number***

Number type is mainly for arithmetic operations such as:

  * *Multiplication* (*)
  * *Division* (/)
  * *Addition* (+)
  * *Subtraction* (-)
  * Others

- ***String***

The sequence of characters. In *JavaScript*, there are 3 types of *quotes*:

  * *Double quotes: "Hello"*
  * *Single quotes: 'Hello'*
  * *Backticks: `Hello`*

- ***Boolean***

This type is commonly used to store `true` or `false` values:

  * `true`: *yes* or *correct.*
  * `false`: *no* or *incorrect.*

- ***Null***

In *JavaScript*, `null` is **not** *"a reference to a non-existing object"* or a *"null pointer"* like in some other languages.
It's just a special *value* that represents *"nothing", "empty",* or *"value unknown".*

- ***Undefined***

The meaning of `undefined` is *"value is not assigned."*
If a *variable* is declared, but not assigned, then its *value* is `undefined`.

- ***Symbol***

Just like their Primitive Data Type (Number, String, Boolean), they can be created using the function Symbol() which returns a Symbol.

Reference Type

data type	descriptions
`array`	used to store multiple values in a single variable
`object`	like an array but multiple types of value in a single variable

- ***Array***

Creates and stores a list of multiple items in a single variable.
It is useful when creating ordered collections of the same type of data.

- ***Object***

This is used to represent *something* in your code. It can be defined by a set of characteristics. These are called *properties* that consist of a *key* and a *value*.

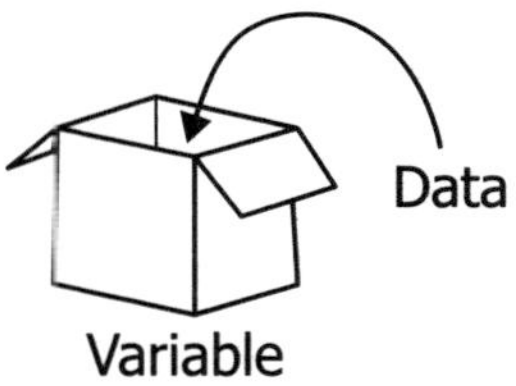

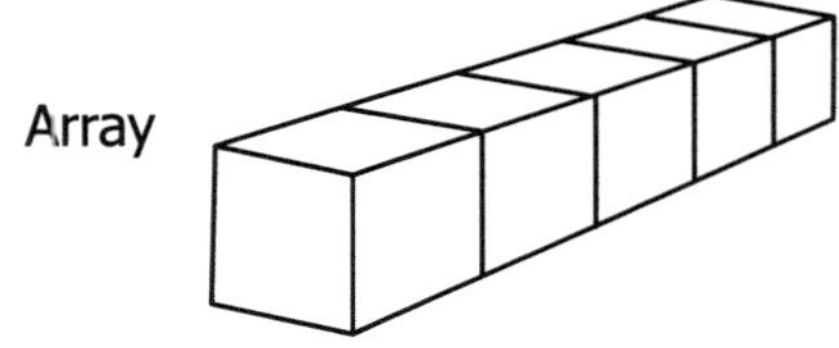

JavaScript Operators

JavaScript operators are used to perform arithmetic operations, assign operators, compare operators, and more.

- **Arithmetic Operators**

These operators are used to perform arithmetic between variables and/or values.
Below, y is set to y = 2

	operator	operation	meaning	result
	+	x=y+2	addition	x=4
	-	x=y-2	subtraction	x=0
	*	x=y*3	multiplication	x=6
	/	x=3/y	division	x=1.5
**	%	x=7%y	division remainder	x=1
	++	x=y++	increment	x=3
	--	x=y--	decrement	x=1

```
    3
6 ) 19
  - 18
  ----
     1  <-- Division Remainder  **
```

- **Assign Operators**

These are used to assign values to JavaScript variables.
Below, x,y, and z are set to x=1, y=2, z=3

	operator	operation	meaning	result
	=	x=y+z	x=y+z	x=5
	+=	x+=y	x=x+y	x=3
	-=	x-=y	x=x-y	x=-1
	*=	x*=y	x=x*y	x=2
	/=	x/=y	x=x/y	x=0.5
**	%=	z%=y	z=z%y	z=1

- **Comparison Operators**

These are used in logical statements to determine equality or difference between variables or values.
Below, x,y,v, and z are set to x=5, y=2, v="2", z=3

operator	operation	meaning	result
==	x==y	equal to	false
===	x===v	equal to (value & Type)	false
!=	x!=y	not equal to	true
<=	x<=y	less than equal to	false
>=	x>=y	greater than equal to	true
<	x<y	less than	false
>	z>y	greater than	true

5 Conditional & Loop Statement

Conditional Statement

- *Conditional statements* are used to perform different actions based on different *conditions*.
- If a condition is `true`, you can perform one action. If the condition is `false`, you can perform another action.

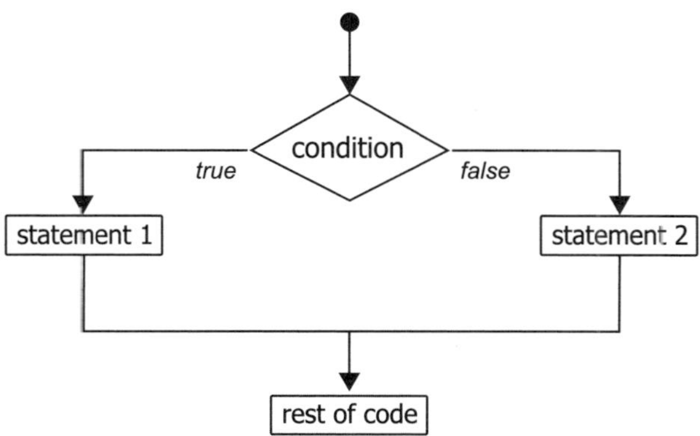

There are mainly three types of *conditional statements* in *JavaScript*:

- `if` statement
- `if, else` statement
- `if, else if, else` statement

Variables and *expression* with *operators*, *conditional* and *loop statements* are key for programming code.

`if` **statement**

If `(condition)` is `true`, { **`block of JavaScript code`** } executes.

```
if (condition) {
// block of code to be executed if the condition is true
}
```

> **Note**
>
> `if` is in lowercase letters. Uppercase letters (`If` or `IF`) will generate a JavaScript error.

`if else` **statement**

If `(condition)` is `true`, { **`block 1 of JavaScript code`**} executes.
If `(condition)` is `false`, { **`block 2 of JavaScript code`** } executes.

```
if (condition) {
  //  block 1 of code to be executed if the condition is true
} else {
  //  block 2 of code to be executed if the condition is false
}
```

`if else if else` **statement**

If `(condition1)` is `true`, { **`block 1 of JavaScript code`** } executes.

If `(condition1)` is `false` and `(condition2)` is `true`,
{ **`block 2 of JavaScript code`** } executes.

If `(condition1)` is `false` and `(condition2)` is `false`,
{ **`block 3 of JavaScript code`** } executes.

```
if (condition1) {
  // block of code to be executed if condition1 is true
} else if (condition2) {
  // block of code to be executed if the condition1 is
false and condition2 is true
} else {
  // block of code to be executed if the condition1 is
false and condition2 is false
}
```

Loop Statement

Loops are used to execute a *block of code* a specified number of times or while a specified condition is `true`.
In *JavaScript* there are two different kinds of *loops*:

- `while`
- `for`

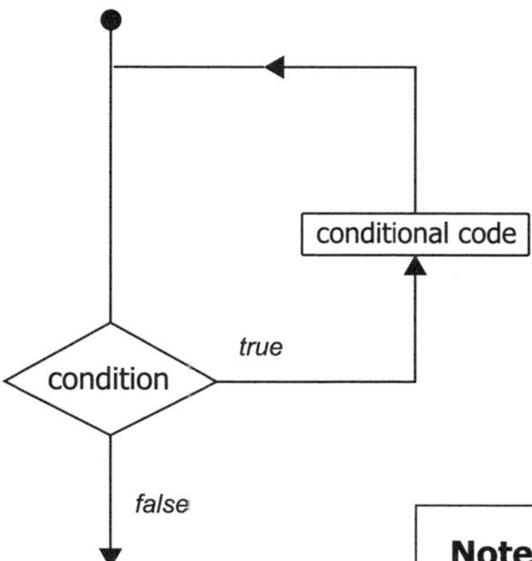

> **Note**
>
> Make sure you increase the *variable* used in the *condition*; otherwise the *loop* will never end and this will *crash* your browser

`while` *loop*

The `while` *loop* will execute the code block first, before checking `if` the *condition* is `true`, then it will repeat the *loop* as long as the *condition* is `true`.

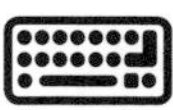
Type In

```
<!DOCTYPE html>
<html>
<body>
   <script language="javascript">
   var i=0
   while (i<=10)
   {
   document.write("The number is " + i);
   document.write("<br />");
   i=i+1;
   }
   </script>
</body>
</html>
```

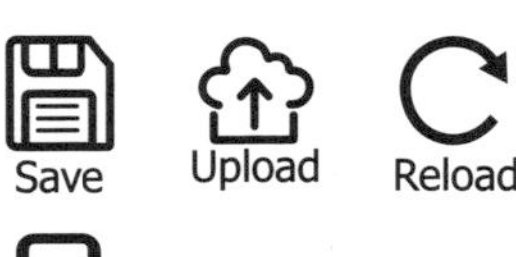

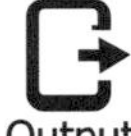

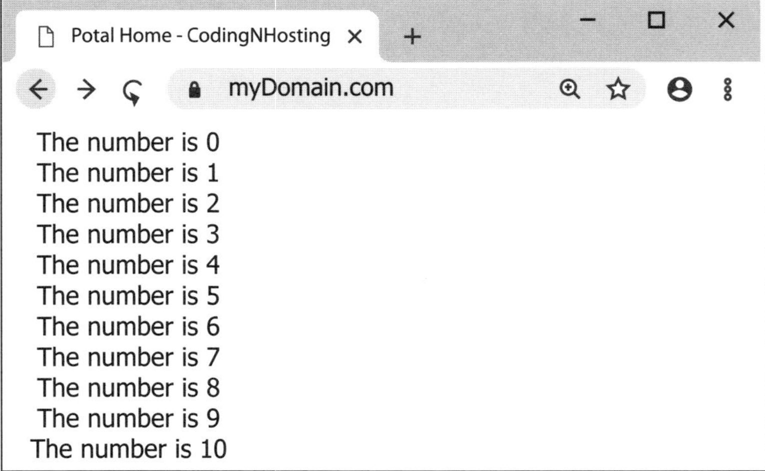

`for` *loop*

The `for` *loop* will execute the code block first, before checking `if` the *condition* is `true`, then it will repeat the *loop* as long as the *condition* is `true`.

"Output" is the same as above.

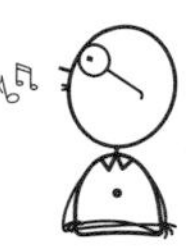

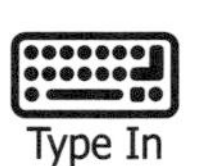


```
<!DOCTYPE html>
<html>
<body>
   <script language="javascript">
   var i=0
   for (let i=0; i<=10; i++)
   {
   document.write("The number is " + i);
   document.write("<br />");
   }
   </script>
</body>
</html>
```

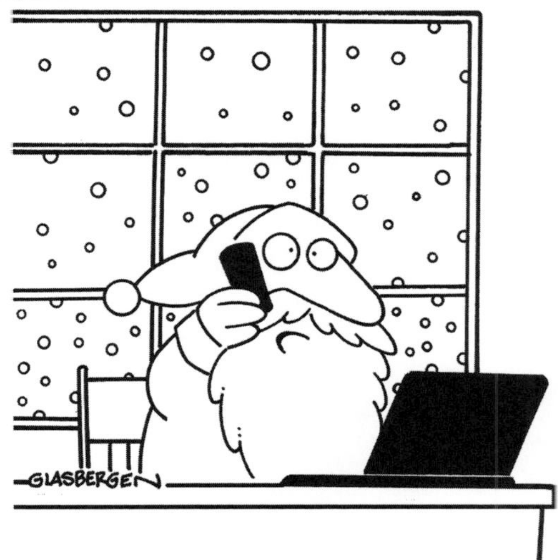

"We're staying home Christmas Eve.
This year every kid will be downloading
digital games from the cloud!"

6 Where to **Place?**

You can place *JavaScript* into your *HTML* file in four different ways:

- <body> *section*
- <head> *section*
- Both <body> & <head> *sections*
- *External JavaScript*

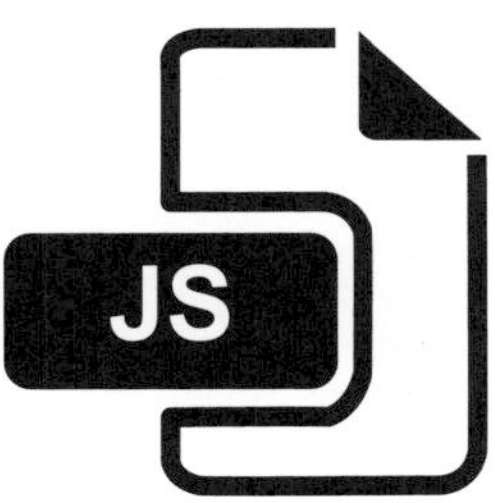

Body Section

JavaScript can be placed in the **<body>** *section* of an *HTML* file. It must be contained in **<script>** tags.
In this example, a *JavaScript* `function` is placed in the **<body>** *section* of an *HTML* document. The `function` is *invoked* when a **<button>** is clicked

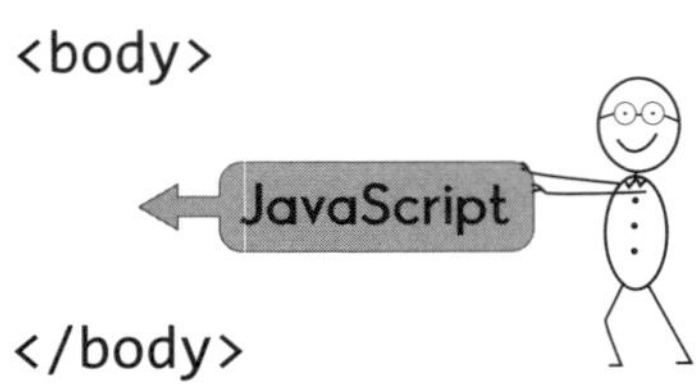


```
<!DOCTYPE html>
<html>
  <head>
  </head>
  <body>
    <button onclick="myFunction()">Click me
    </button>
    <script>
      function myFunction() {
        document.write("Hello World!");
      }
    </script>
  </body>
</html>
```

> **Note**
>
> Try to put *JavaScripts* at the bottom of the <body> tag. With this it improves the display speed, because *script interpretation* slows down the display.

Head Section

JavaScript `functions` can be placed in the **<head>** *section* of an *HTML* document.
It must be contained in **<script>** *HTML* tags like in the *Body Section*.
The *code* inside the *JavaScript* `function` is enforced when the `function` is called. In this example, a **<button>** is *clicked* to call the function.

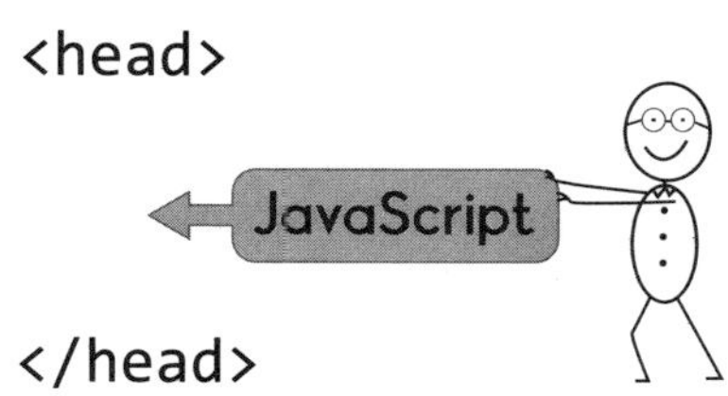

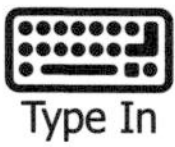
Type In

```
<!DOCTYPE html>
<html>
  <head>
    <script>
      function myFunction() {
        document.write("Hello World!");
      }
    </script>
  </head>
  <body>
    <button onclick="myFunction()">Click me</button>
  </body>
</html>
```

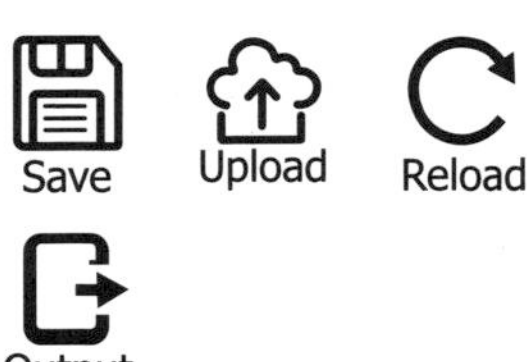

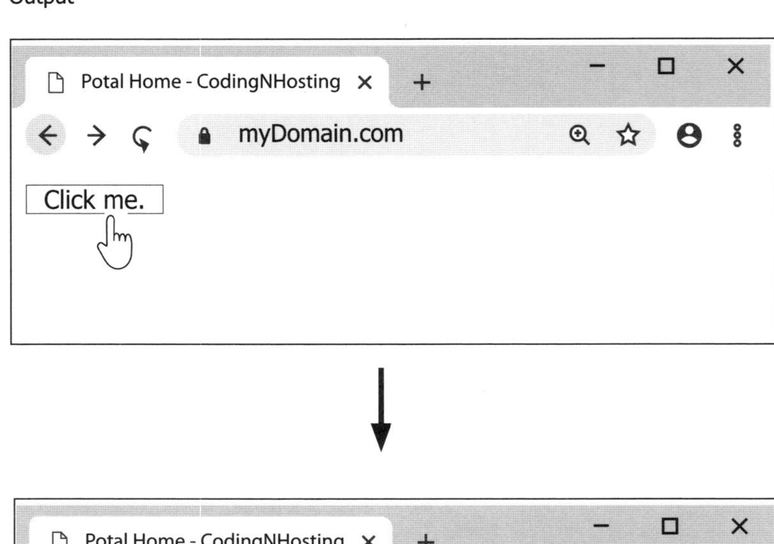

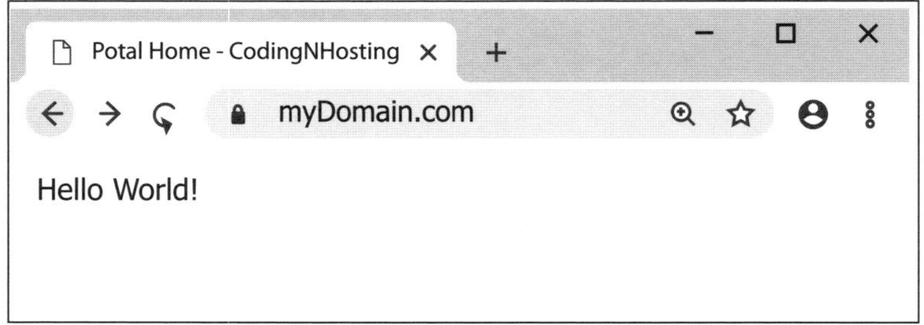

> **Note**
>
> Like a *CSS*, *JavaScripts* are practical when the same *code* is used in many different *web pages.*

External JavaScript

JavaScript can be placed in a separate file and then named. It is named *myScript.js* in this example.
The *code* inside the separate file does **not** need to be contained in `<script>` tags.
You can use the external *JavaScript* file by using the **`src`** *attribute* in the **`<script>`** tag.

External

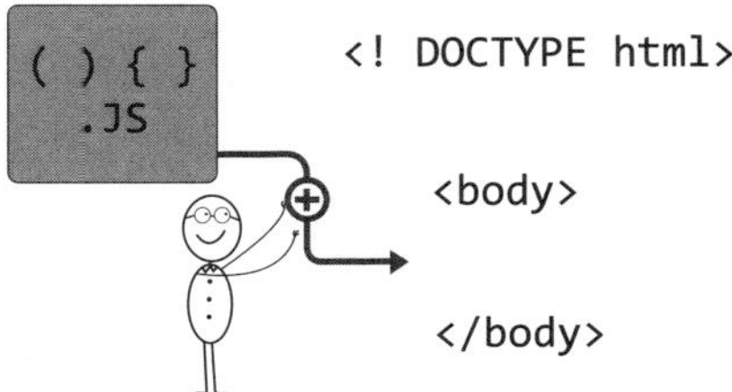

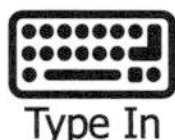
Type In

```
<!DOCTYPE html>
<html>
  <head>
  </head>
  <body>
    <script src="myscript.js"></script>
  </body>
</html>
```

Type in the following JavaScript document, save as "myscript.js", and upload it to the directory ("public_html"), where index.html is located.

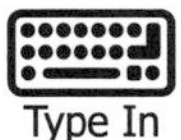
Type In

```
//this is myscript.js file

    document.write("Hello World!");
```

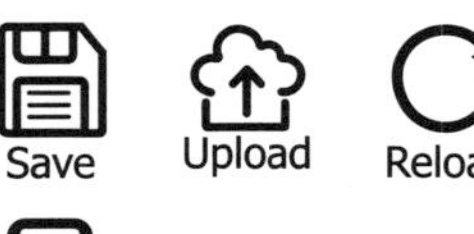
Save
Upload
Reload

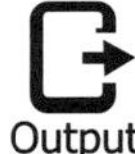
Output

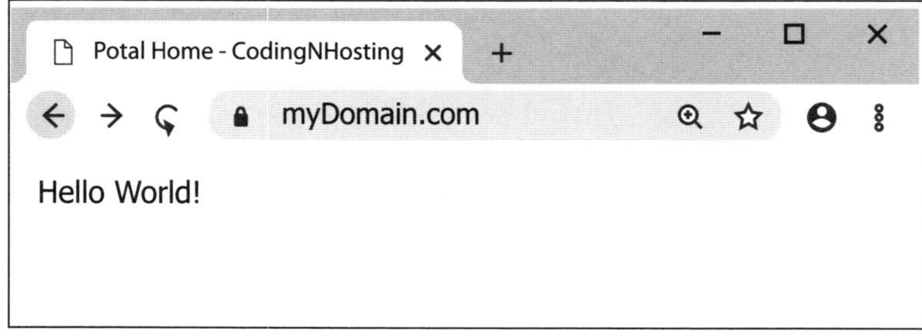
Potal Home - CodingNHosting
myDomain.com
Hello World!

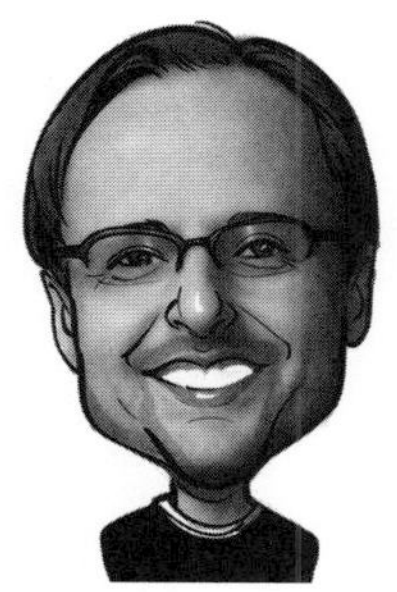

Håkon Wium Lie

Håkon is a Norwegian *computer scientist* and *web pioneer.*

He is best known for developing *Cascading Style Sheets (CSS)* while working with Tim Berners-Lee at CERN in 1994.

Along with his work on the *CSS specifications,* Håkon has been an activist for standards in general. He challenged *Microsoft* to improve their support for standards in *Internet Explorer* and proposed the *Acid2* test, which was later developed and published by the *Web Standards Project.*

He was the *Chief Technology Officer of Opera Software* from 1998 until 2016.

CHAPTER 10

PHP (Personal Home Page)

1. What is PHP?
2. PHP Syntax
3. Variable & Data Type
4. PHP Function

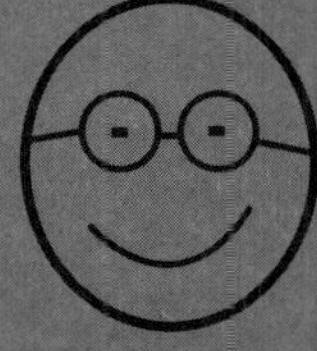

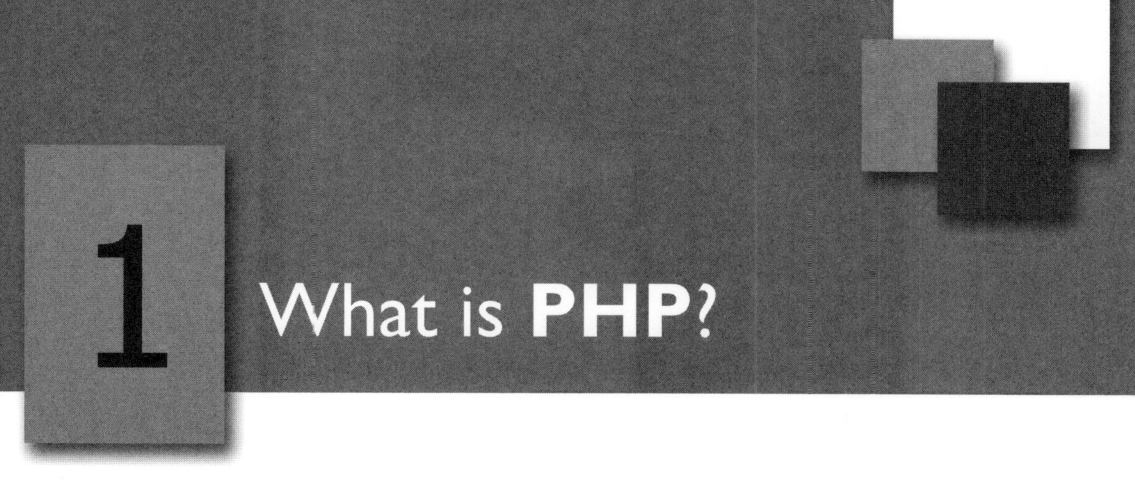

1 What is PHP?

PHP (*Personal Home Page/Hypertext Preprocessor)* is a widely-used *open source, server side script language.*

- It is especially well-suited for web development.
- It is *interpreted* and *executed* on a *server* that has *PHP* installed. (It is already installed in our server)
- It can be *embedded* into *HTML*.
- *PHP* files can be identified by the *.php* extension.

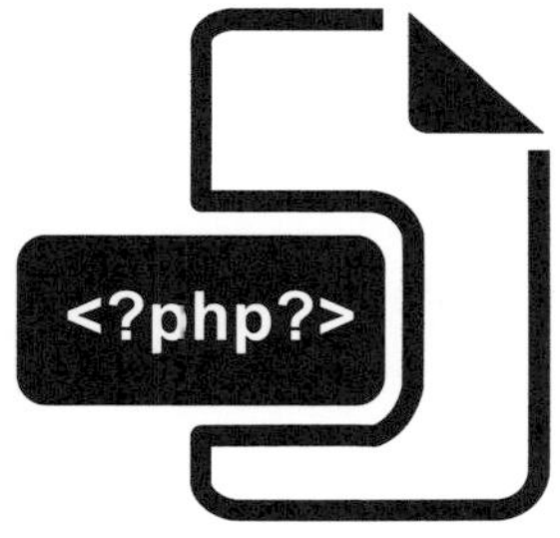

Ramus Lerdorf is a Danish-Canadian *Computer programmer.* He created the *PHP scripting* language in 1994.

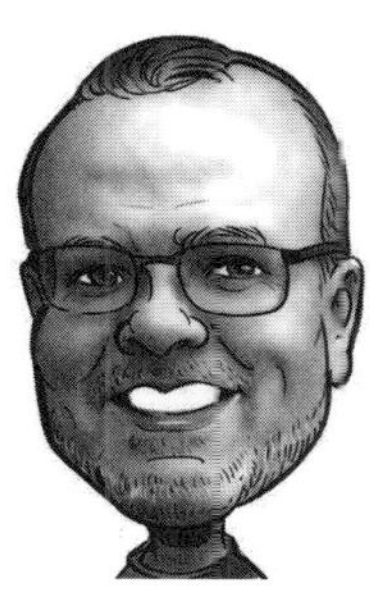

PHP vs. JavaScript

- *JavaScript* is an example of a *client side script* that is *interpreted* by the *client browser.*
- *PHP* is a *server side script* that is *interpreted* on the *server*.
- Both *PHP* and *JavaScript* can be *embedded* into *HTML* pages.

I. Client Side Execution:

1. Client requests info to the Server thru the Internet.
2. Server responds with requested info thru the Internet.
3. Client browser run/interprets the info and shows to Client.

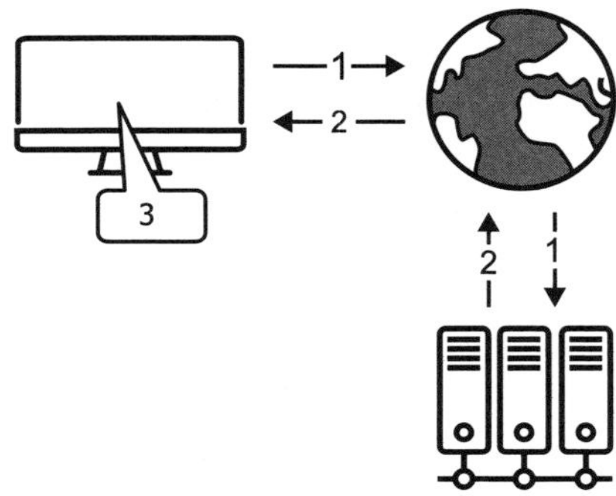

II. Server Side Execution:

1. Client requests info to Server thru the Internet.
2. Server forwards to PHP Interpreter for Interpretation.
3. PHP Interpreter sends back Interpreted info to the Server.
4. Server responds with interpreted info to Client thru the Internet.
5. Client browser shows interpreted info to Client.

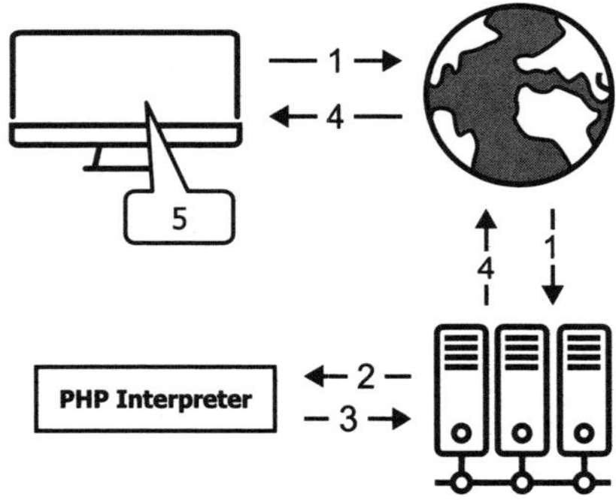

❶ Type in the following PHP document and save as "index.**php**".

❷ Upload it to the directory ("**public_html**") at the **Remote site.**

❸ Delete *index.html* in the **Remote site.**

```
<!DOCTYPE html>
<html>
   <head>
      <title>A Simple PHP File</title>
   </head>
   <body>
      <h1><?php echo "Hello World!"; ?></h1>
   </body>
</html>
```

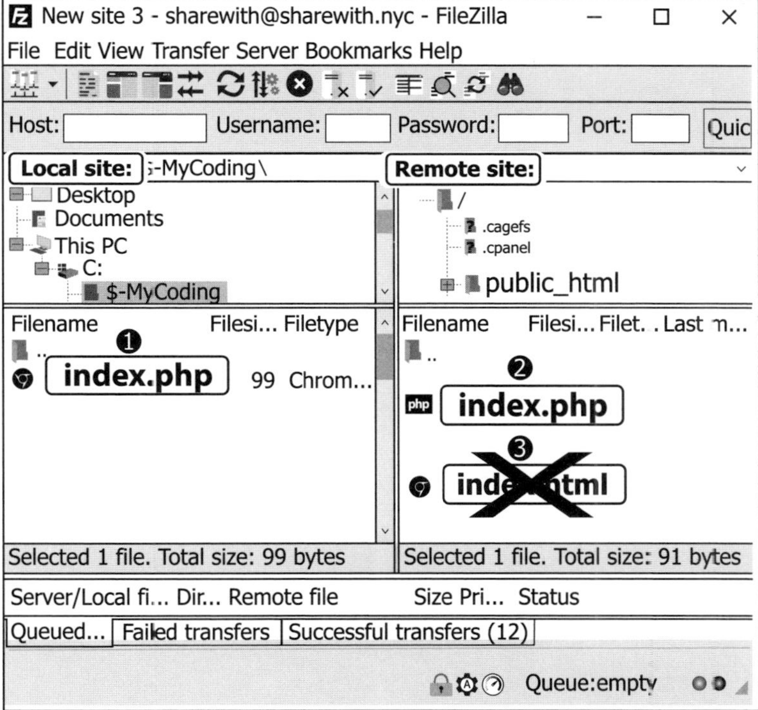

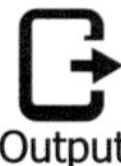

Output

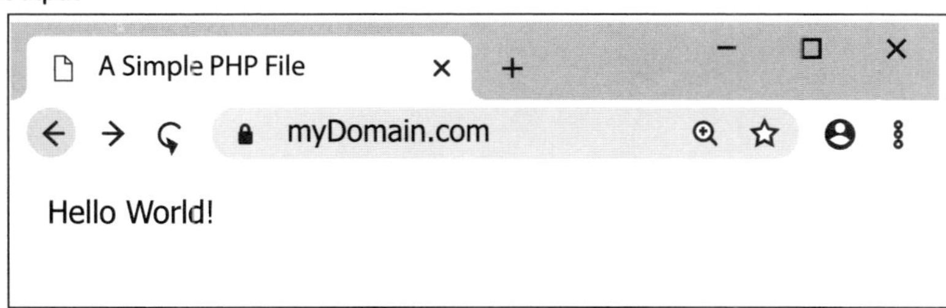

2 PHP **Syntax**

- A *PHP script* starts with the `<?php` tag and ends with the `?>` tag.
- The *PHP* delimiters `<?php` and `?>` in the following example simply tell the *PHP engine* to treat the enclosed *code block* as *PHP code*, rather than simple *HTML*.
- `echo` is *PHP code* to display/print the strings inside the quote (" ") and ends with a semi-colon (;)

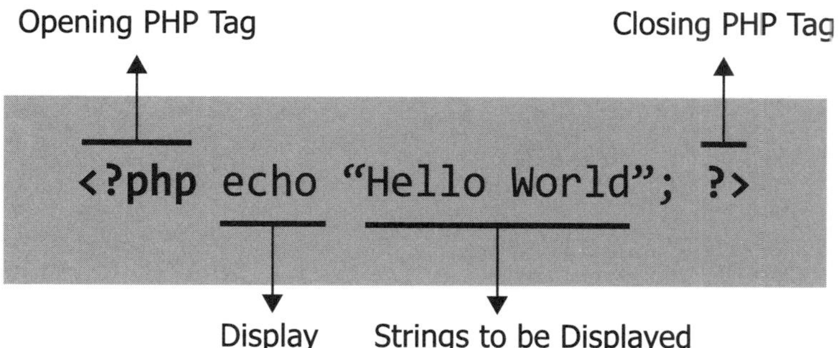

Embedding PHP within HTML

PHP files are plain text files with the *.php* extension.
Inside a *PHP* file you can write *HTML* code like regular *HTML* pages.
The *HTML* pages put *PHP* codes for server side execution.

Case Sensitivity in PHP

Lilke *JavaScript, PHP command* and *variable names* are *Case Sensitive.*
As a result the *variables* **`$color, $Color and $COLOR`** are treated as three different *variables.*

PHP Comments

PHP supports a *single line comment* as well as *multi-line comments.* To write a *single-line comment,* start the line with either *two slashes (//)* or a *hash symbol (#).* The code for a *multi-line comment* is the same as in *CSS* and *JavaScript*:

	single line comment	multi-line comment
PHP	//, #	/* */
HTML	<!-- -->	
CSS	/* */	
JavaScript	//	/* */

```
<!DOCTYPE html>
<html>
  <body>
    <?php
      // This is a single line comment
      # This is also a single line comment
      /*
      This is a multiple line comment block
      that spans across more than one line
      */
      echo "Hello World!";
    ?>
  </body>
</html>
```

PHP is used for many different kinds of *web sites* such as:

- *Facebook*: The most visited *Social Networking Site.*
- *Wikipedia*: Free *Online Encyclopedia.*
- *Yahoo*: Internet *Portal Site.*
- *WordPress*: *Website* Managing Software.

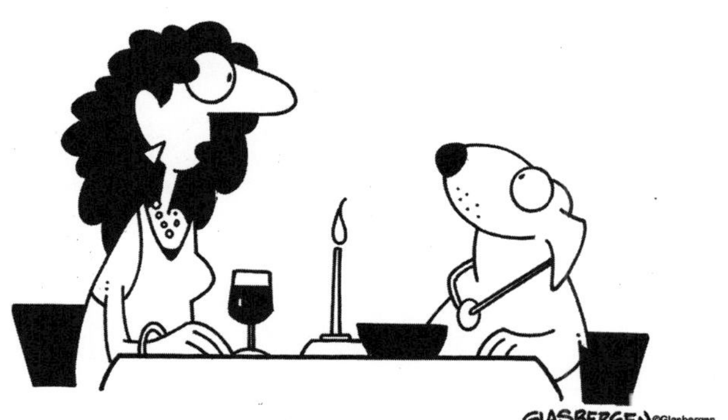

"for 18 months, we chatted online
and you never mentioned that you're a dog"

3 Variable & Data Type

Variable

Variables are used to store *data*, like a *string of text, numbers*, etc.

- Unlike *JavaScript*, a variable does **not** need to be declared before adding a *value* to it. *PHP* automatically converts the *variable* to the correct *data type*, depending on its *value*.
- After declaring a *variable*, it can be reused throughout the *code*.
- You need to put **"$"** first followed by a *variable name*.
- The *assignment operator* (**=**) is used to assign a value to a *variable*.

```
$php = "PHP variable";
```

	description	definition & usage
PHP	$variableName	contain, define and hold a value such as number, string, objects
JavaScript	let variableName	

Data Type

data type	descriptions
integer	non-decimal numbers
float	numbers with a decimal point or exponential form
string	sequence of characters, such as "Hello World!"
boolean	2 possible states: true or false
array	stores multiple values in one variable
object	stores data/information on how to process that data
null	variable that has no value assigned to it
resource	storing of a reference to functions and resources

Variable is one of the most useful and fundamental features in most *programming languages*.
It has the ability to store the *data* in a *structured format.*

```
<!DOCTYPE html>
<html>
  <body>
    <?php
      $z="Hello World!";
      $x=10;
      $y=20;
      echo $z;
      echo "<br>";
      echo $x;
      echo "<br>";
      echo $y;
    ?>
  </body>
</html>
```

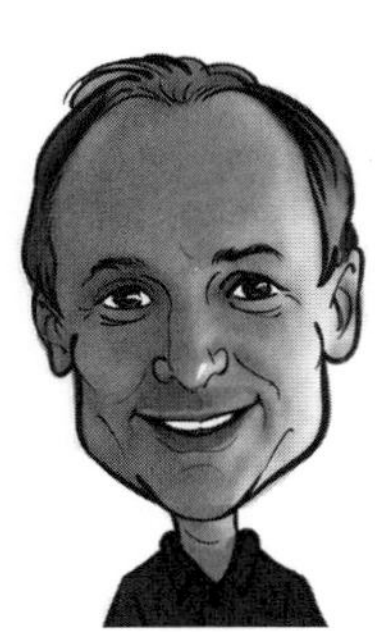

Tim Berners-Lee

An English *engineer* and *computer scientist*, best known as the *inventor* of the W*orld Wide Web* and *HTML*.
Tim proposed an *information management system* on 12 March 1989, and then implemented the first successful communication between a *Hypertext Transfer Protocol (HTTP) client* and a *server* via the *internet* in mid-November, 1989
He is the director of the *World Wide Web Consortium* that he founded in 2001.
He became a *Fellow* of the *Royal Society* in 2004 and he was *knighted*.
In 2016, he joined the *Department of Computer Science at Oxford University* as a professorial research fellow.

4 PHP **Function**

- *PHP functions* are similar to *JavaScript*.
- A *function* is a piece of code that takes *input* and *returns* a *value*.
- They are over 10,000 built-in *functions*, you also can create your own *functions*.

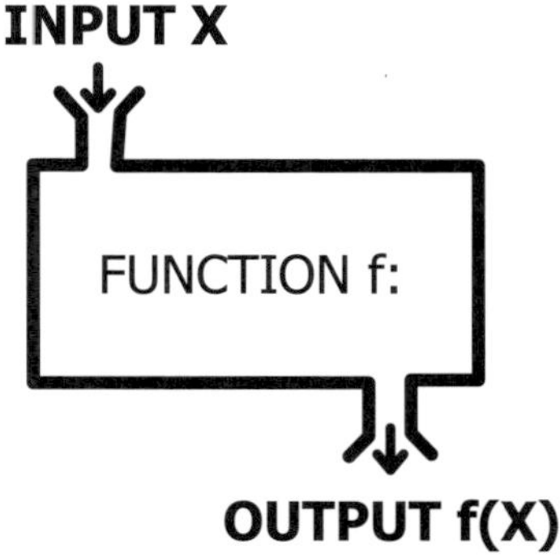

There are 2 kinds of *PHP functions:*

1. Built-in *functions*
2. User defined *functions*

Example of Built-in Functions

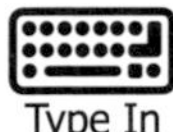
Type In

```
<!DOCTYPE html>
<html>
  <head>
     <title>A Simple PHP File</title>
  </head>
  <body>
    <?php
      /*string length or
      number of characters function
      */
      $str = "Hello World!";
      echo strlen($str);

      echo "<br>";

      #arithmetic operator
      $x=5;
      $y=10;
      $z=$x+$y;
      echo $z;
    ?>
  </body>
</html>
```

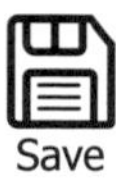
Save

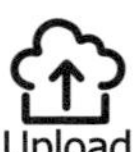
Upload

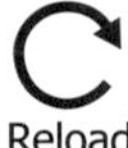
Reload

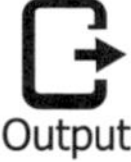
Output

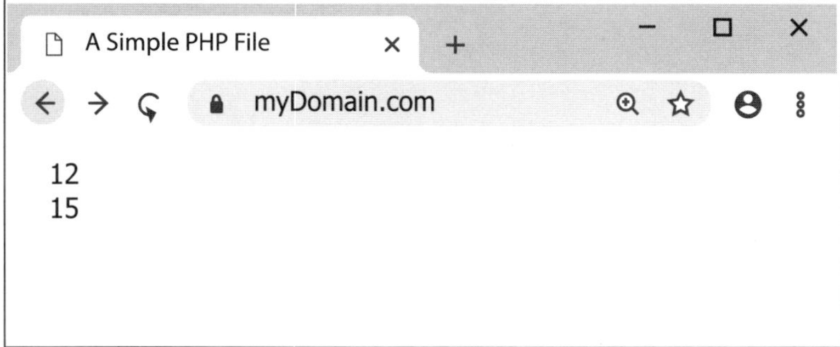

Example of User defined functions

```
<!DOCTYPE html>
<html>
<body>
   <?php
       function writeMsg() {
       echo "Hello World!";
       }
       writeMsg();
   //writeMsg() is user defined function
   ?>
</body>
</html>
```

Why use Functions in PHP?

reusable	once a function is defined, it can be called by several scripts in PHP files. This saves a lot of time.
code organization	functions allow us to group blocks of related code that perform a specific task together.
maintenance	updates to the system only need to be mace in one place.

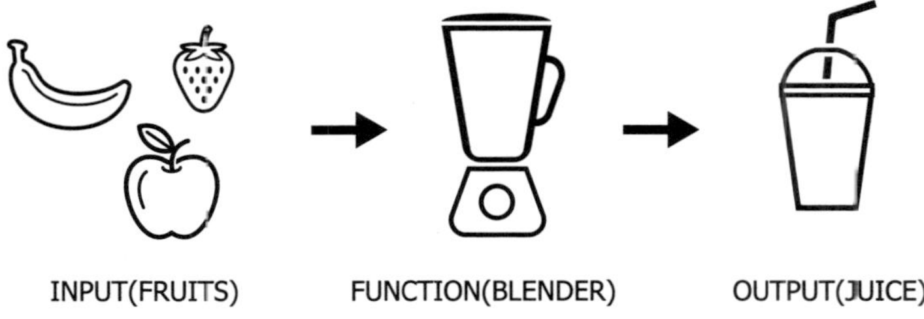

frequently used 25 PHP Functions

function	descriptions
`ceil()`	returns the next highest integer value by rounding up
`count()`	counts all elements in an array or something in an object
`die()`	output a message and terminate the current script
`echo()`	output all parameters. no additional new line is appended
`empty()`	determine whether a variable is empty
`exit()`	same as die()
`file_get_contents()`	read entire file into a string
`file_put_contents()`	write data to a file
`getenv()`	gets the value of an environment variable
`header()`	send a raw HTTP head
`htmlentitles()`	convert all applicable characters to HTML entitles
`include()`	includes and evaluates the specific file
`ini_set()`	sets the value of the given configuration option
`isset()`	determines if a variable is declared and if it is different than NULL
`mail()`	sends an email
`md5()`	calculates the md5 hash of a string
`mkdir()`	makes a directory specified by path name
`phpinfo()`	outputs information about PHP's configuration
`preg_match()`	performs a regular expression match
`print_r()`	displays information about a variable in a way that's readable
`rand()`	generates a random integer
`require()`	identical to include except upon failure, it also produce a fatal error
`str_replace()`	replaces all occurrences of the search string with the replacement string
`strlen()`	returns the length of the given string
`trim()`	returns a string with white space stripped from its beginning and end.

List of *PHP Functions*/11,038 (March, 2020):

https://www.php.net/manual/en/indexes.functions.php

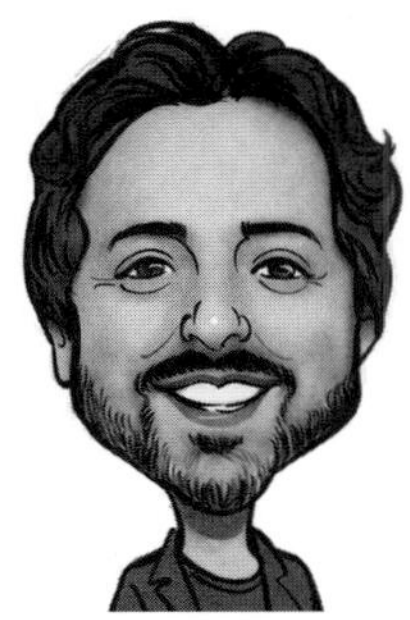

Sergey Brin

An American computer scientist and entrepreneur. He met Larry Page at Stanford University, and the two created a search engine (Google) that would sort web pages based on popularity. Google became the most popular search engine in the world after launching in 1998. They call the search engine Google after the mathematical term "googol". The meaning of "googol" is a 1 followed by 100 zeros. This represented their mission of organizing the immense amount of information available on the Internet.

Sergey was the president of Google's parent company, Alphabet Inc, until stepping down from the role on December 3, 2019.

Review Terms: You should now be familiar with the following terms:

- JavaScript, Event & Function
- Variable
- For and While Loop
- if & if, else & if , elseif, else
- PHP, Event, Function, and Variables

PART 4

GETTING IT DONE WITH PRACTICAL INFO

In this, you will learn

- How to keep your website up-to-date with current trends.
- Optimize your website so that searching the web will be able to easily find your site.
- Understand the difference between a front-end and back-end development.

CHAPTER 11

Practical Information

1. Search Engine Optimization (SEO)
2. What is DevTools?
3. What is Mobile First?

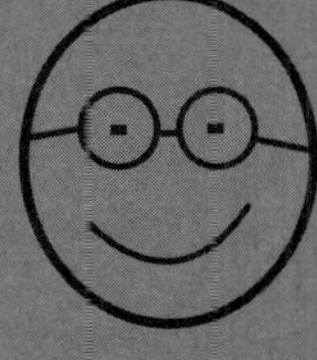

1 Search Engine Optimization

Search Engines

- A *search engine* is *web-based software* that is developed to *search* and *locate* relevant information on the *web*.
- *Search engines* generally answer the *queries* entered by the users and give them a list of *search results*.

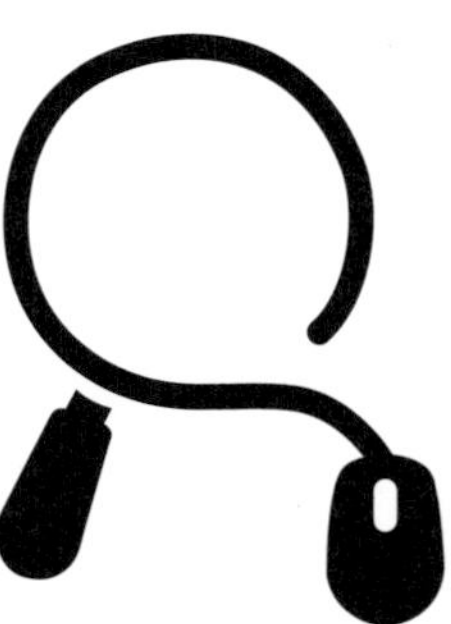

Top Search Engines in the World

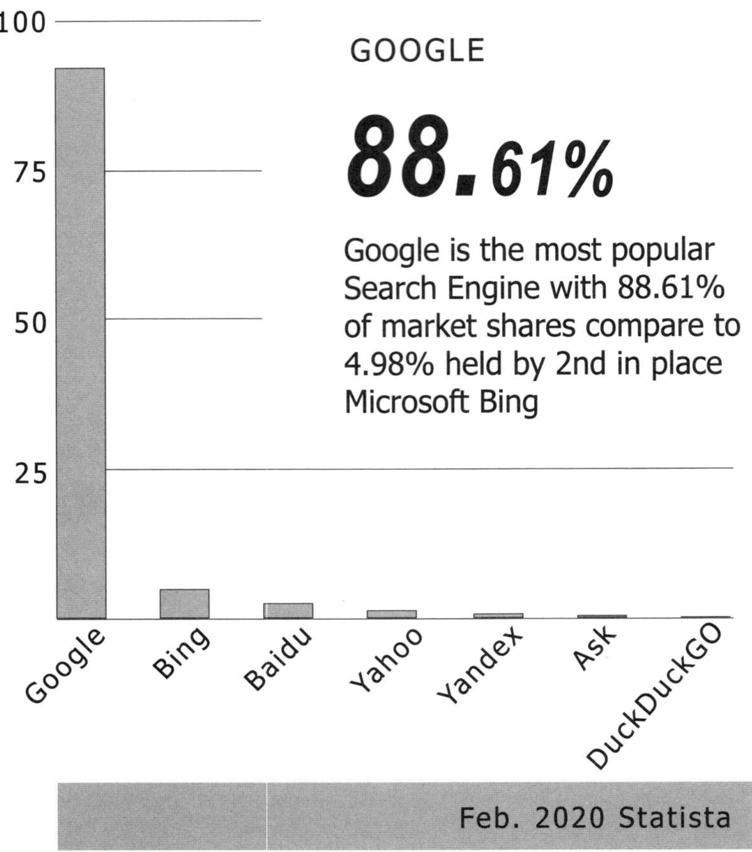

SEO (Search Engine Optimization)

One major parts of developing a *website* is getting its search engine ready. While not all sites rely on search engines for traffic, the majority do. It's a good idea to understand the basic of *search engine optimization (SEO)* so you don't make mistakes that will hurt your traffic.

What you need to do is make sure that your site provides the correct information, so that both your *audience* and *search engines* can find your site.

There are dozens of *search engines* out there, and they all use a different method for determining what site show up first in the results. There are a few things you can do that will help improve your site's ranking regardless of which *search engine* your audience uses.

- Interesting Content

This is the most important feature of a search *engine-friendly site*. You need to have text, multimedia, and images that people want to read and view.

- Convenient Navigation

You want your visitors to stay on your site as long as possible, no matter what page they end up on.

- Mobile Friendliness

Mobile-friendly sites are critical for search engine placement. More and more people use mobile devices, and Google (along with other search engines) prioritize mobile devices and *mobile-friendly pages*. If your pages are break, hard to read, or look bad on a mobile device, your site will not be ranked well in *search engines.*

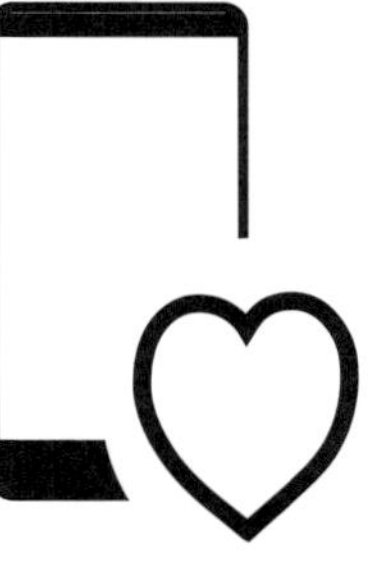

The best *search engines* such as *Google, Bing*, and even *Baidu* change the *algorithms* which control their search results frequently.

2 What is DevTools?

DevTools

DevTools stands for *Developer Tools,* which allow developers to test and *debug* their code.

It comes as a built-in feature in most *browsers*.

DevTools allow developers to work with a variety of web developing tools for *HTML, CSS, JavaScript,* such as inspecting the *network traffic, memory usage* among others.

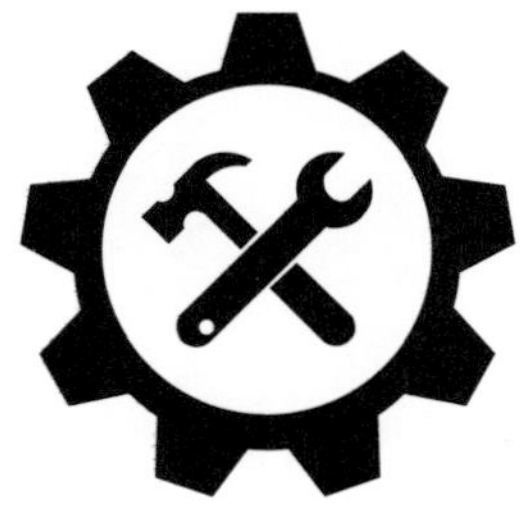

Debugging HTML & CSS Code

It doesn't matter if you're a beginner or an expert, bugs happen. So, don't worry about the bugs, just focus on locating where they are and fixing them.

In your *Google Chrome Browser*, press

- shift + control + i (window o/s)
- alt + command + i (mac o/s)

and you will see a screen like the one below.

Left bottom is *HTML* and right bottom is *CSS*.

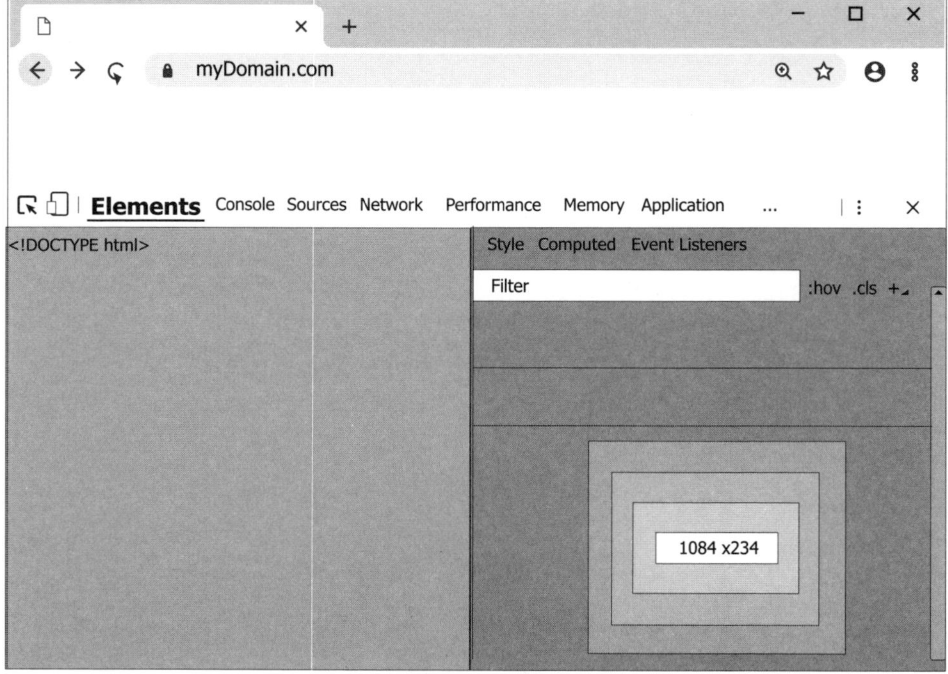

You can use the *Elements panel* for a variety of tasks:

- inspect the *HTML* & *CSS* of a web page.
- test different layouts.
- live-edit *CSS*.
- others

Note

How to call *DevTools* on other browsers.:

- *Firefox*: Shift + Control + i (**inspector**)
- *Safari*: Alt + Command + i (element)
  Alt + Command + c (JS console)
- *Explorer/Edge*: F12/ Shift + Control + i (element)
- *Opera*: Shift + Control + i (element)

Firefox is the only browser that calls the *HTML/CSS element* panel *inspector.*

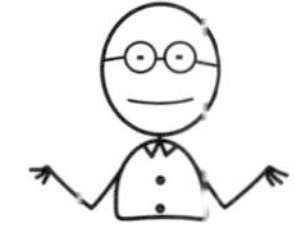

Debugging JavaScript Code

The *JavaScript Console* is an incredibly useful tool for *debugging* the code that isn't working as expected.
It allows you to run lines of *JavaScript* code against the page currently loaded in the browser, and reports the errors encountered as the browser tries to execute your code.

Another useful tool for *JavaScript Console* is the ability to check the code by entering *snippets* of *JavaScript* command into the *console*. So, you don't need to type in the *window* and upload it to the server.

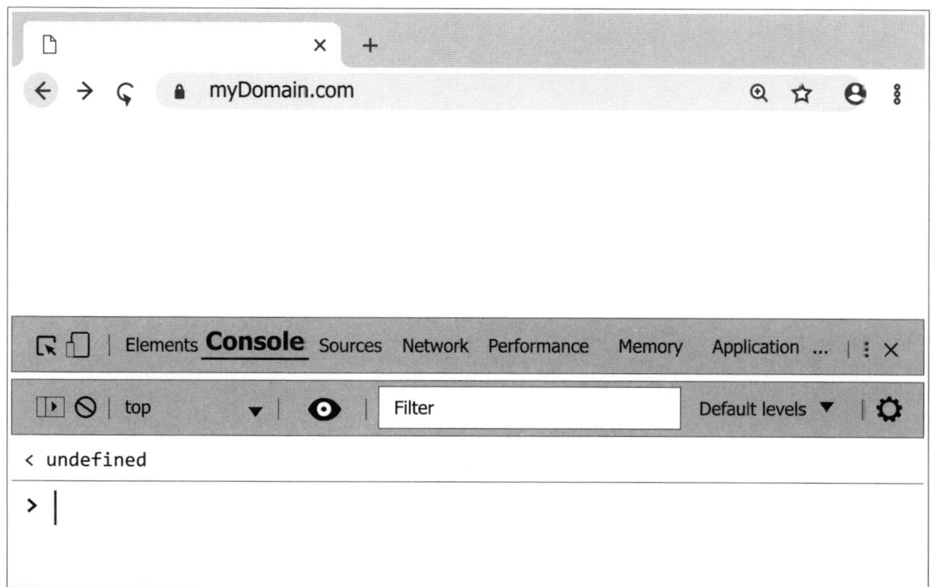

Origin of Term "Debugging"

In 1947 (the very early days of computing) a team of Navy computer programmers led by *Grace Hopper* ran into a problem with the *mainframe*. They spent many hours checking out the software. Finally, they opened up the computer and found a dead moth on the *main circuit board* blocking a *relay*.

This was the first *computer bug*. It was a real bug, an insect, not a *coding error*.

Since then, errors in computer systems, particularly in software code, have been called "bugs."

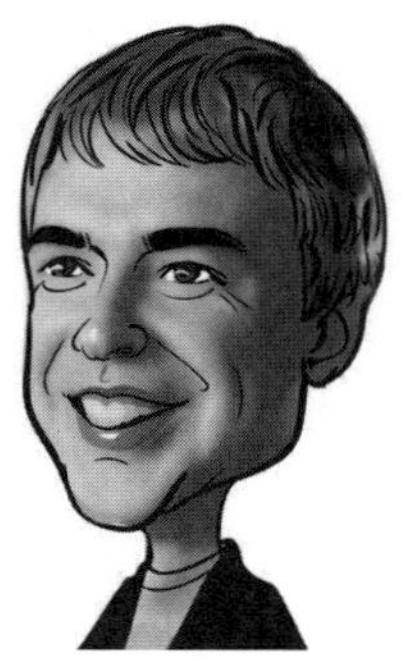

Larry Page

Larry is an internet entrepreneur and computer scientist.

Larry is best known for being one of the co-founders of Google along with Sergey Brin.

The duo developed a search engine that listed results according to the popularity of the pages.

With Larry as CEO, Google became the world's most popular search engine after launching in 1998.

Along with Sergey, Larry later took charge of Google's new parent company, Alphabet; he stepped down from the company's everyday roles in late 2019.

3 What is **Mobile First?**

What is Mobile First ?

- *Mobile First* or *Mobile First Design* was one of the hottest key words in the past decade. It is safe to say that it will also be a hot key word in our current decade (the 2020s).
- In the good old days, websites were planned and designed for desktop or laptops first and then modified for mobile phones later. So, structure, *UX (user interface)*, and even contents were based on the desktop version.
- As of April, 2020, 57.64% of all internet traffic happens on a mobile device and the number is growing. That's why we need to consider *Mobile First Design.*

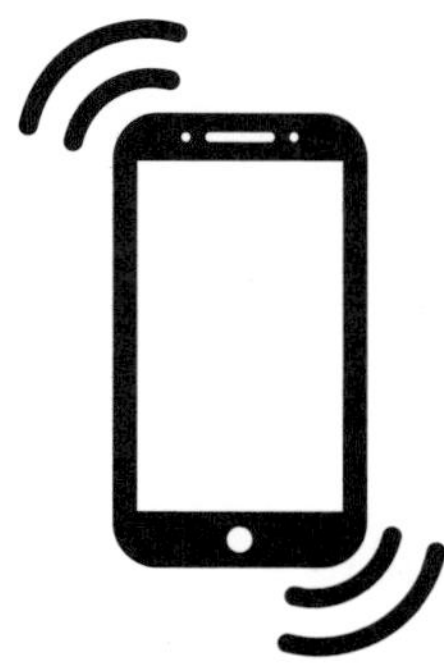

Mobile First shifts the Paradigm of a Website User Experience

Users are now viewing websites that have been created specifically for their mobile phone instead of just viewing desktop versions of the websites on their mobile phones with some adjustments.

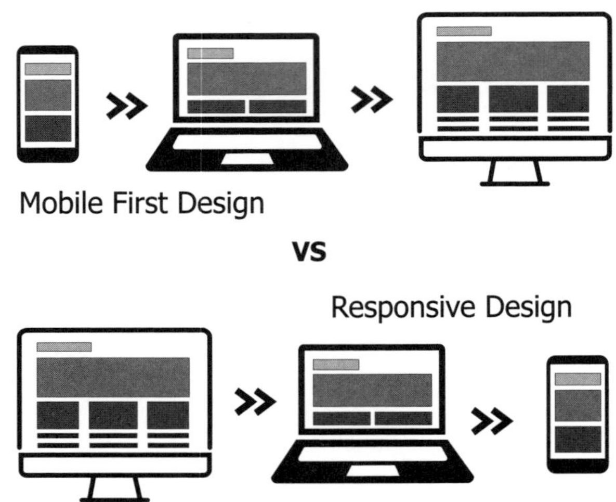

As a beginner, you need to learn the basics of web design and programming. Once you have the basics down, you should apply that process to the modern trends; ***Mobile First***

> **Note**
>
> Here are some tips for *Mobile First Design*:
>
> 1. Make it *Simple*
> 2. *Contents* First
> 3. Consider the *Download Speed*

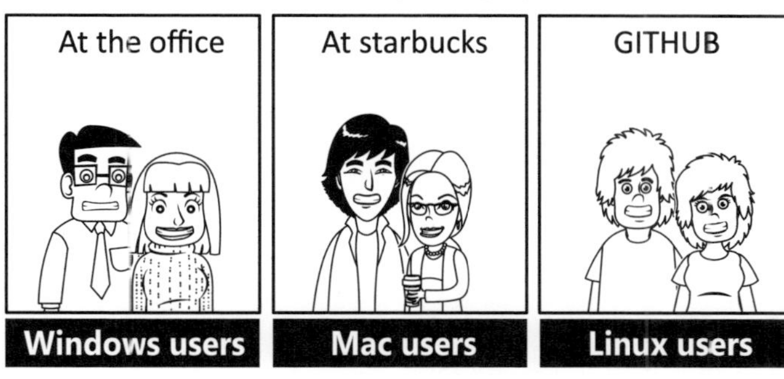

Note

GitHub is a software development *version control* service provider. It is a subsidiary of Microsoft. In 2018, Microsoft acquired the company for 7.5 billion US dollars.

CHAPTER 12

Getting Done

1. Web Development of Front-end & Back-end
2. What is Database & Big Data?
3. Web Design Trends in the Year 2020s

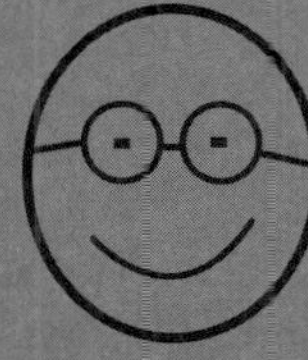

1 Web Development of Front-end & Back-end

Front-end vs. **Back-end Web Development**

This is a job function of web development of a specific website.

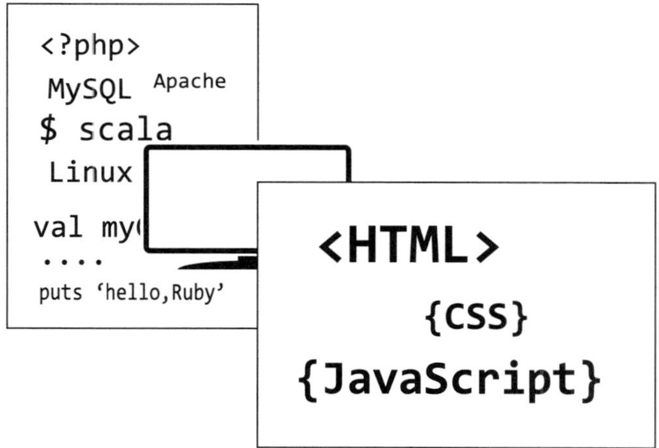

Apart from *front-end* and *back-end development*, you can go for *full stack development. Full stack developers* are familiar with both front-end and back-end development. Nevertheless, they may not have the same depth of knowledge.

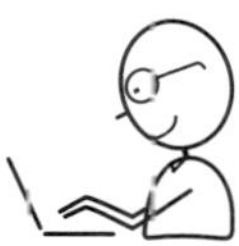

Front-end

When we discuss the *front-end* of the web, what we're really talking about is the part of the web that you can see and interact with.

The *front-end* usually consists of two parts:

- *Web design*
- *Front-end web development*

When we discuss the term *web design*, we're really talking about designs that work with *Photoshop* and *Fireworks*, and those that code using *HTML, CSS, and JavaScript.*

Everything that you see when using the web is a combination of *HTML, CSS*, and *JavaScript,* all being controlled by your computers' browsers.

Back-end

The *back-end* consists of three parts: Server, Application, and Database.

- Server

If you book a flight or buy concert tickets, you usually open a website and interact with the *front-end.*

- Application

Once you've entered that information, the application stores it in a *database* that was created on a *server.*

- Database

Just think about a *database* as a giant excel spreadsheet on server computer. Remember, though, the *server* computer is located somewhere in Arizona.

All information stays on the *server.* When you log into the account to print your tickets, you will see that the information is still in the account.

We call a person that builds all of this technology to work together as a *back-end* developer. *Back-end* technologies usually consist of languages like *PHP, Python, Ruby*, etc.

	front-end development/er	back-end development/er
job description	design the website, and keep modifying it through testing	develop software and build *database architecture* that supports the *front-end*
project goal	make sure that the website or app is accessible to all users, and responsive in all views-mobile and desktop	build an application around the front-end and provide all the support that it needs, and make sure that the site or app always functions properly
programming languages	*HTML, CSS, JavaScript*	*PHP, Python, SQL, Java, Ruby, .NET, Perl*
average basic salary	$77,908 *(Glassdoor, 15 July, 2020)*	$117,284 *(Glassdoor, 12 June, 2020)*

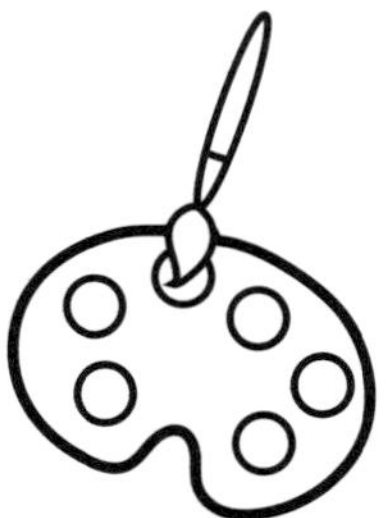

2 What is **Database** & **Big Data?**

Database

Any collection of data, or information, that is specially organized for rapid searching and retrieving by a computer system.

Big Data

Big Data refers to large amounts of data that are pouring in from various data sources and have different formats.

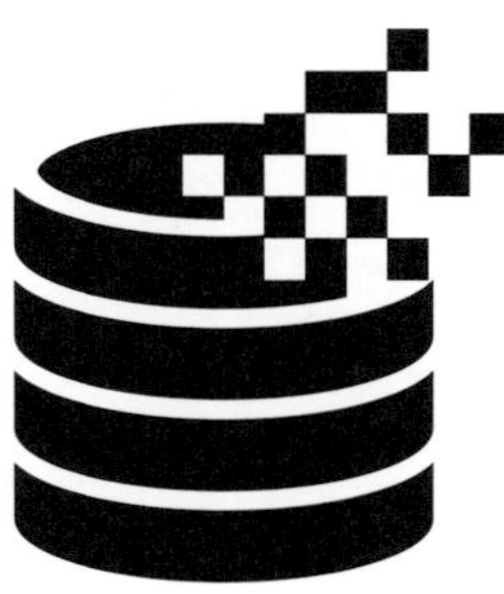

Database and DBMS (Database Management System)

- A *database* is a structured collection of data, generally stored and accessed electronically from a computer system.
- Where databases are more complicated, they are often developed using formal design and modeling techniques.
- The database management system (DBMS) is the software that interacts with end users, applications, and the *database* itself to capture and analyze the data.
- Often the term *database* is also used loosely to refer to any part of the *DBMS*, the *database* system, or an application associated with the *database*.

> **Note**
>
> Don't confuse *DBMS* and *SQL* (Structured Query Language).
> *DBMS* is a *system* and *SQL* is a *language*.
> We use the *DBMS* along with *SQL* for querying data in the *database.*

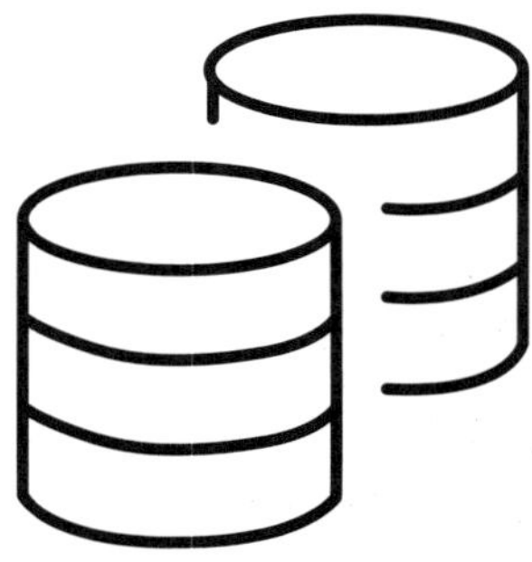

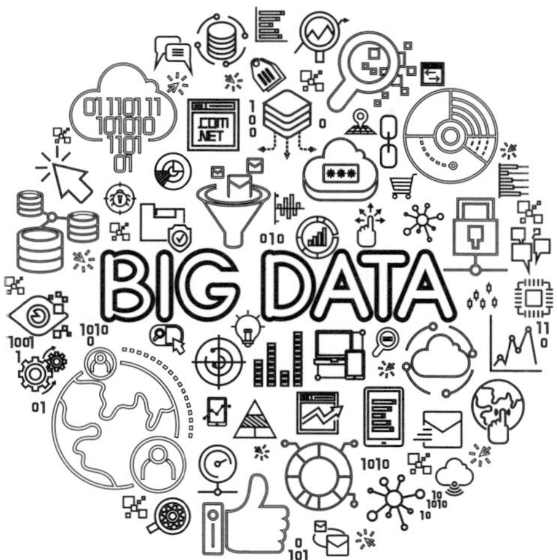

Big Data

Big data is larger, more complex data sets, especially from new data sources. These data sets are so voluminous that traditional data processing software can't manage them. But these massive volumes of data can be used to address business problems you wouldn't have been able to tackle otherwise.

There are 5 Vs of Big Data

5 Vs	description
volume	it refers to the size of the data; this data is generated in an incredible amount each second through *cell phones, social media, online transactions*, etc
velocity	it is the speed at which data is generated, collected, and analyzed
variety	this represents the different types of *big data*; it could be structured or un-structured
value	it means how much data is useful and meaningful value refers to the ability to turn your data into practical applications for your business
veracity	it means the trustworthiness of data in terms of quality and accuracy; extracting loads of data is not useful if the data is messy and of poor quality

3 Web Design **Trends** in the **2020s**

Design Trend

- As times goes by, what is hot in *web design* changes over the years. Not keeping up with certain *design trends* can instantly make your site look like a very old-fashioned one.
- Keeping up with *web design trends* every year will help you keep your site looking modern and professional.

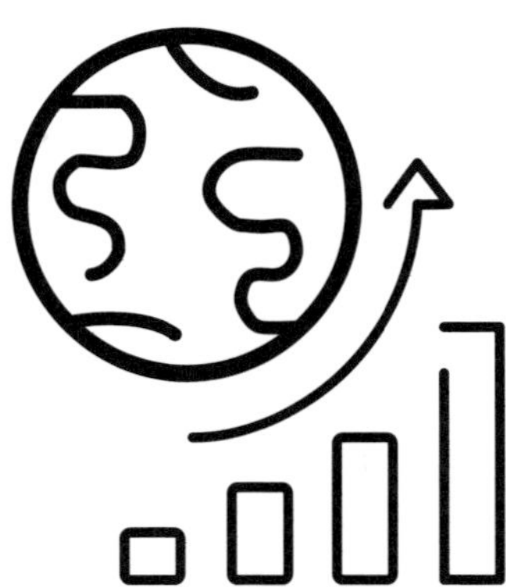

The year 2021 and 2020s Web Design Trends

As a beginner, knowing the trend of the industry is very important. *Web Design* is the same.

If you have some talent for art or design, you can create your own web pages without any outside help. Otherwise, it is a good idea to look at other websites, pick your favorite, and base your design off of it.

For copying the right site, you need to know the trend.

Year 2021

- *Minimalism/flat Design*
- *Bold Color*
- *Organic Shaped*
- *Asymmetric Layouts*
- *Hand Drawings*
- *Chatbot*

Year 202x (Mainly *Mobile First)*

- *Responsive Web Design (RWD)*
- *Motion Design/UI (user interface)*
- *Voice Interface*
- *Using Well Collected Video*
- *Considers Load Speed*
- *Thumb-friendly Design*

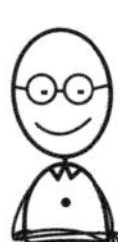

"Good artists copy, Great artists steal"
P. Picasso

"The immature poet imitates and the mature poet plagiarizes"
T.S. Eliot

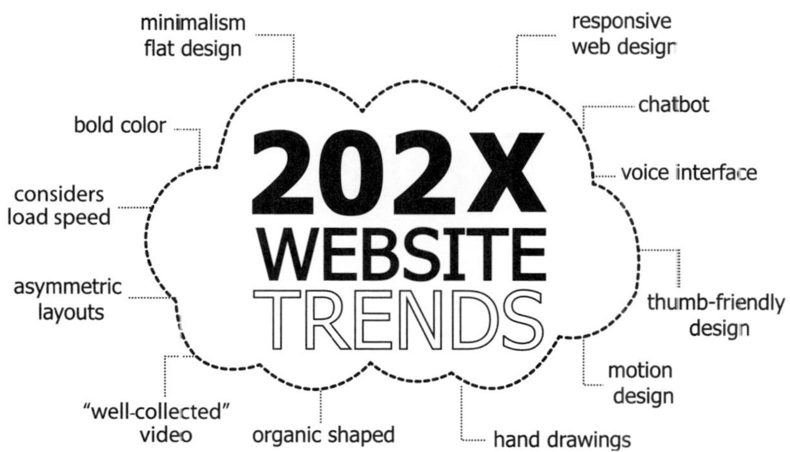

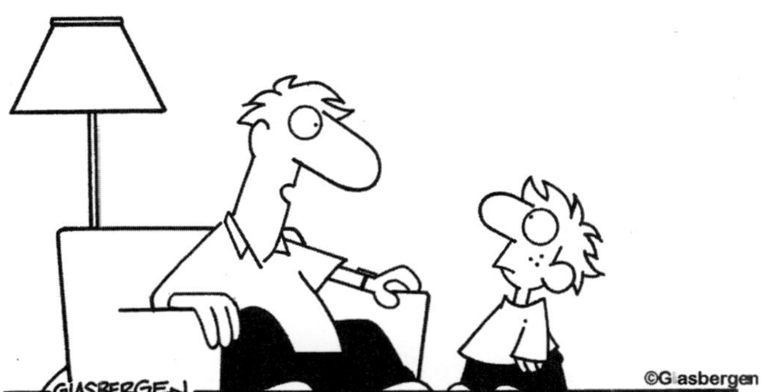

"My side of the family is full-blooded DOS and Windows. But you're one-quarter Mac with a little Linux and Amiga on your mother's side"

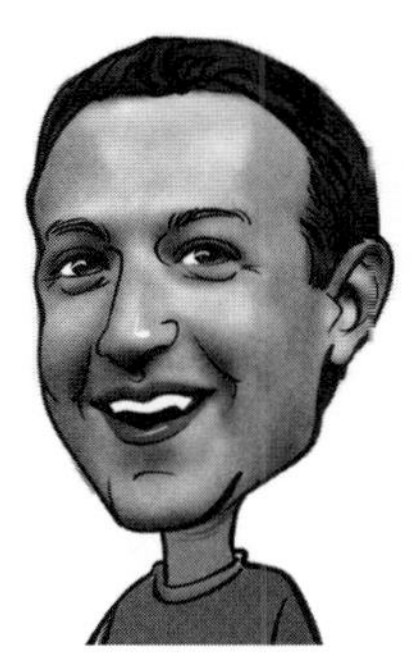

Mark Zuckerberg

Mark is an American *internet entrepreneur, computer scientist,* and *philanthropist.* Mark is a co-founder and CEO of the *social networking website Facebook*, as well as one of the world's youngest billionaires. Since amassing his sizeable fortune, Mark has used his millions to fund a variety of philanthropic causes. The most notable example came in September 2010, when he donated $100 million to save the failing Newark Public Schools' system in New Jersey. In September 2016, Mark Zuckerberg and his wife Priscilla Chan announced the *Chan Zuckerberg Initiative (CZI)*. Through the initiative, the company puts a large amount of their *Facebook* market shares into investing at least $3 billion into scientific research over the next decade to help "*cure, prevent, and manage all diseases in our children's lifetime*." The *renowned neuroscientist* of The R*ockefeller University, Cornelia Bargmann,* was named the President of Science at *CZI.*

Review Section: You should be familiar with the following terms:

1. DevTools.
2. Console.
3. SEO/Network Traffic.
4. Mobile First Design.
5. Front-End and Back-End.
6. Big Data and the 5 Vs.
7. Current Web Design Trends (asymmetric layouts, RWD, chatbot, organic shaped, hand drawings, etc).

PART 5

INDEX & APPENDIX

Index

Symbols

A

B

C

D

E

F

G

H

I

J

K

L

M

N

O

P

Q

R

S

T

U

V

W

X

Y

Z

Appendix

HTML Tags/Elements [107]

<!--...-->	Defines a comment
<!DOCTYPE>	Defines the document type
<a>	Defines a hyperlink
<abbr>	Defines an abbreviation or an acronym
<address>	Defines contact information for the author/owner of a document
<area>	Defines an area inside an image-map
<article>	Defines an article
<aside>	Defines content aside from the page content
<audio>	Defines sound content
<b>	Defines bold text
<base>	Specifies the base URL/target for all relative URLs in a document
<bdi>	Isolates a part of the text that might be formatted in a different direction from other text outside it
<bdo>	Overrides the current text direction
<blockquote>	Defines a section that is quoted from another source
<body>	Defines the document's body
 	Defines a single line break
<button>	Defines a clickable button
<canvas>	Used to draw graphics, on the fly, via scripting (usually JavaScript)
<caption>	Used for creating table captions
<cite>	Defines the title of a work
<code>	Defines a piece of computer code
<col>	Specifies column properties for each column within a <colgroup> element
<colgroup>	Specifies a group of one or more columns in a table for formatting
<data>	Links the given content with a machine-readable translation
<datalist>	Specifies a list of pre-defined options for input controls
<dd>	Defines a description/value of a term in a description list
<del>	Defines text that has been deleted from a document

<details>	Defines additional details that the user can view or hide
<dfn>	Represents the defining instance of a term
<dialog>	Defines a dialog box or window
<div>	Defines a section in a document
<dl>	Defines a description list
<dt>	Defines a term/name in a description list
<em>	Defines emphasized text
<embed>	Defines a container for an external (non-HTML) application
<fieldset>	Groups related elements in a form
<figcaption>	Defines a caption for a <figure> element
<figure>	Specifies self-contained content
<footer>	Defines a footer for a document or section
<form>	Defines an HTML form for user input
<h1> to <h6>	Defines HTML headings
<head>	Defines information about the document
<header>	Defines a header for a document or section
<hr>	Defines a thematic change in the content
<html>	Defines the root of an HTML document
<i>	Defines italic text
<iframe>	Defines an inline frame
<img>	Defines an image
<input>	Defines an input control
<ins>	Defines a text that has been inserted into a document
<kbd>	Defines keyboard input
<label>	Defines a label for an <input> element
<legend>	Defines a caption for a <fieldset> element
<li>	Defines a list item
<link>	Defines the relationship between a document and an external resource (most used to link to style sheets)
<main>	Specifies the main content of a document
<map>	Defines a client-side image-map
<mark>	Defines marked/highlighted text
<meta>	Defines metadata about an HTML document
<meter>	Defines a scalar measurement within a known range (a gauge)
<nav>	Defines navigation links
<noscript>	Defines an alternate content for users that do not support client-side scripts

<object>	Defines an embedded object
<ol>	Defines an ordered list
<optgroup>	Defines a group of related options in a drop-down list
<option>	Defines an option in a drop-down list
<output>	Defines the result of a calculation
<p>	Defines a paragraph
<param>	Defines a parameter for an object
<picture>	Defines a container for multiple image resources
<pre>	Defines preformatted text
<progress>	Represents the progress of a task
<q>	Defines a short quotation
<rp>	Defines what to show in browsers that do not support ruby annotations
<rt>	Defines an explanation/pronunciation of characters (for East Asian typography)
<ruby>	Defines a ruby annotation (for East Asian typography)
<s>	Defines text that is no longer correct
<samp>	Defines sample output from a computer program
<script>	Defines a client-side script
<section>	Defines a section in a document
<select>	Defines a drop-down list
<small>	Defines smaller text
<source>	Defines multiple media resources for media elements (<video> and <audio>)
<span>	Defines a section in a document
<strong>	Defines important text
<style>	Defines style information for a document
<sub>	Defines subscripted text
<summary>	Defines a visible heading for a <details> element
<sup>	Defines superscripted text
<svg>	Defines a container for SVG graphics
<table>	Defines a table
<tbody>	Groups the body content in a table
<td>	Defines a cell in a table
<template>	Defines a template
<textarea>	Defines a multiline input control (text area)
<tfoot>	Groups the footer content in a table

<th>	Defines a header cell in a table
<thead>	Defines a set of rows defining the head of the columns of the table
<time>	Defines a date/time
<title>	Defines a title for the document
<tr>	Defines a row in a table
<track>	Defines text tracks for media elements (<video> and <audio>)
<u>	Defines text that should be stylistically different from normal text
<ul>	Defines an unordered list
<var>	Defines a variable
<video>	Defines a video or movie
<wbr>	Defines a possible line-break

HTML Attributes [168]

attribute name	tags	descriptions
accept	<input>	Specifies the types of files that the server accepts (only for type="file")
accept-charset	<form>	Specifies the character encodings that are to be used for the form submission
accesskey	Global Attributes	Specifies a shortcut key to activate/focus an element
action	<form>	Specifies where to send the form-data when a form is submitted
align	Not supported in HTML 5	Specifies the alignment according to surrounding elements. Use CSS instead
alt	<area>, <img>, <input>	Specifies an alternate text when the original element fails to display
async	<script>	Specifies that the script is executed asynchronously (only for external scripts)
autocomplete	<form>, <input>	Specifies whether the <form> or the <input> element should have autocomplete enabled
autofocus	<button>, <input>, <select>, <textarea>	Specifies that the element should automatically get focus when the page loads
autoplay	<audio>, <video>	Specifies that the audio/video will start playing as soon as it is ready
bgcolor	Not supported in HTML 5	Specifies the background color of an element. Use CSS instead
border	Not supported in HTML 5	Specifies the width of the border of an element. Use CSS instead
charset	<meta>, <script>	Specifies the character encoding
checked	<input>	Specifies that an <input> element should be pre-selected when the page loads (for type="checkbox" or type="radio")
cite	<blockquote>, <del>, <ins>, <q>	Specifies a URL which explains the quote/deleted/inserted text
class	Global Attributes	Specifies one or more class names for an element (refers to a class in a style sheet)
color	Not supported in HTML 5	Specifies the text color of an element. Use CSS instead
cols	<textarea>	Specifies the visible width of a text area

attribute name	tags	descriptions
colspan	<td>, <th>	Specifies the number of columns a table cell should span
content	<meta>	Gives the value associated with the http-equiv or name attribute
contenteditable	Global Attributes	Specifies whether the content of an element is editable or not
controls	<audio>, <video>	Specifies that audio/video controls should be displayed (such as a play/pause button etc.)
coords	<area>	Specifies the coordinates of the area
data	<object>	Specifies the URL of the resource to be used by the object
data-	Global Attributes	Used to store custom data private to the page or application
datetime	<del>, <ins>, <time>	Specifies the date and time
default	<track>	Specifies that the track is to be enabled if the user's preferences do not indicate that another track would be more appropriate
defer	defer	Specifies that the script is executed when the page has finished parsing (only for external scripts)
dir	Global Attributes	Specifies the text direction for the content in an element
dirname	<input>, <textarea>	Specifies that the text direction will be submitted
disabled	<button>, <fieldset>, <input>, <optgroup>, <option>, <select>, <textarea>	Specifies that the specified element/group of elements should be disabled
download	<a>, <area>	Specifies that the target will be downloaded when a user clicks on the hyperlink
draggable	Global Attributes	Specifies whether an element is draggable or not
dropzone	Global Attributes	Specifies whether the dragged data is copied, moved, or linked, when dropped
enctype	<form>	Specifies how the form-data should be encoded when submitting it to the server (only for method="post")
for	<label>, <output>	Specifies which form element(s) a label/ calculation is bound to

attribute name	tags	descriptions
form	<button>, <fieldset>, <input>, <label>, <meter>, <object>, <output>, <select>, <textarea>	Specifies the name of the form the element belongs to
formaction	<button>, <input>	Specifies where to send the form-data when a form is submitted. Only for type="submit"
headers	<td>, <th>	Specifies one or more headers cells a cell is related to
height	<canvas>, <embed>, <iframe>, <img>, <input>, <object>, <video>	Specifies the height of the element
hidden	Global Attributes	Specifies that an element is not yet, or is no longer, relevant
high	<meter>	Specifies the range that is considered to be a high value
href	<a>, <area>, <base>, <link>	Specifies the URL of the page the link goes to
hreflang	<a>, <area>, <link>	Specifies the language of the linked document
http-equiv	<meta>	Provides an HTTP header for the information/value of the content attribute
id	Global Attributes	Specifies a unique id for an element
ismap	<img>	Specifies an image as a server side image map
kind	<track>	Specifies the kind of text track
label	<track>, <option>, <optgroup>	Specifies the title of the text track
lang	Global Attributes	Specifies the language of the element's content
list	<input>	Refers to a <datalist> element that contains pre-defined options for an <input> element
loop	<audio>, <video>	Specifies that the audio/video will start over again, every time it is finished
low	<meter>	Specifies the range that is considered to be a low value
max	<input>, <meter>, <progress>	Specifies the maximum value
maxlength	<input>, <textarea>	Specifies the maximum number of characters allowed in an element

attribute name	tags	descriptions
media	<a>, <area>, <link>, <source>, <style>	Specifies what media/device the linked document is optimized for
method	<form>	Specifies the HTTP method to use when sending form-data
min	<input>, <meter>	Specifies a minimum value
multiple	<input>, <select>	Specifies that a user can enter more than one value
muted	<video>, <audio>	Specifies that the audio output of the video should be muted
name	<button>, <fieldset>, <form>, <iframe>, <input>, <map>, <meta>, <object>, <output>, <param>, <select>, <textarea>	Specifies the name of the element
novalidate	<form>	Specifies that the form should not be validated when submitted
onabort	<audio>, <embed>, <img>, <object>, <video>	Script to be run on abort
onafterprint	<body>	Script to be run after the document is printed
onbeforeprint	<body>	Script to be run before the document is printed
onbeforeunload	<body>	Script to be run when the document is about to be unloaded
onblur	All visible elements.	Script to be run when the element loses focus
oncanplay	<audio>, <embed>, <object>, <video>	Script to be run when a file is ready to start playing (when it has buffered enough to begin)
oncanplaythrough	<audio>, <video>	Script to be run when a file can be played all the way to the end without pausing for buffering
onchange	All visible elements.	Script to be run when the value of the element is changed
onclick	All visible elements.	Script to be run when the element is being clicked
oncontextmenu	All visible elements.	Script to be run when a context menu is triggered

attribute name	tags	descriptions
oncopy	All visible elements.	Script to be run when the content of the element is being copied
oncuechange	<track>	Script to be run when the cue changes in a <track> element
oncut	All visible elements.	Script to be run when the content of the element is being cut
ondblclick	All visible elements.	Script to be run when the element is being double-clicked
ondrag	All visible elements.	Script to be run when the element is being dragged
ondragend	All visible elements.	Script to be run at the end of a drag operation
ondragenter	All visible elements.	Script to be run when an element has been dragged to a valid drop target
ondragleave	All visible elements.	Script to be run when an element leaves a valid drop target
ondragover	All visible elements.	Script to be run when an element is being dragged over a valid drop target
ondragstart	All visible elements.	Script to be run at the start of a drag operation
ondrop	All visible elements.	Script to be run when dragged element is being dropped
ondurationchange	<audio>, <video>	Script to be run when the length of the media changes
onemptied	<audio>, <video>	Script to be run when something bad happens and the file is suddenly unavailable (like unexpectedly disconnects)
onended	<audio>, <video>	Script to be run when the media has reach the end (a useful event for messages like "thanks for listening")
onerror	<audio>, <body>, <embed>, <img>, <object>, <script>, <style>, <video>	Script to be run when an error occurs
onfocus	All visible elements.	Script to be run when the element gets focus
onhashchange	<body>	Script to be run when there have been changes to the anchor part of the the URL
oninput	All visible elements.	Script to be run when the element gets user input
oninvalid	All visible elements.	Script to be run when the element is invalid

attribute name	tags	descriptions
onkeydown	All visible elements.	Script to be run when a user is pressing a key
onkeypress	All visible elements.	Script to be run when a user presses a key
onkeyup	All visible elements.	Script to be run when a user releases a key
onload	<body>, <iframe>, <img>, <input>, <link>, <script>, <style>	Script to be run when the element is finished loading
onloadeddata	<audio>, <video>	Script to be run when media data is loaded
onloadedmetadata	<audio>, <video>	Script to be run when meta data (like dimensions and duration) are loaded
onloadstart	<audio>, <video>	Script to be run just as the file begins to load before anything is actually loaded
onmousedown	All visible elements.	Script to be run when a mouse button is pressed down on an element
onmousemove	All visible elements.	Script to be run as long as the mouse pointer is moving over an element
onmouseout	All visible elements.	Script to be run when a mouse pointer moves out of an element
onmouseover	All visible elements.	Script to be run when a mouse pointer moves over an element
onmouseup	All visible elements.	Script to be run when a mouse button is released over an element
onmousewheel	All visible elements.	Script to be run when a mouse wheel is being scrolled over an element
onoffline	<body>	Script to be run when the browser starts to work offline
ononline	<body>	Script to be run when the browser starts to work online
onpagehide	<body>	Script to be run when a user navigates away from a page
onpageshow	<body>	Script to be run when a user navigates to a page
onpaste	All visible elements.	Script to be run when the user pastes some content in an element
onpause	<audio>, <video>	Script to be run when the media is paused either by the user or programmatically
onplay	<audio>, <video>	Script to be run when the media has started playing
onplaying	<audio>, <video>	Script to be run when the media has started playing

attribute name	tags	descriptions
onpopstate	<body>	Script to be run when the window's history changes.
onprogress	<audio>, <video>	Script to be run when the browser is in the process of getting the media data
onratechange	<audio>, <video>	Script to be run each time the playback rate changes (like when a user switche to slow motion or fast forward mode).
onreset	<form>	Script to be run when a reset button in a form is clicked.
onresize	<body>	Script to be run when the browser window is being resized.
onscroll	All visible elements.	Script to be run when an element's scrollbar is being scrolled
onsearch	<input>	Script to be run when the user writes something in a search field (for <input="search">)
onseeked	<audio>, <video>	Script to be run when the seeking attribute is set to false indicating that seeking has ended
onseeking	<audio>, <video>	Script to be run when the seeking attribute is set to true indicating that seeking is active
onselect	All visible elements	Script to be run when the element gets selected
onstalled	<audio>, <video>	Script to be run when the browser is unable to fetch the media data for whatever reason
onstorage	<body>	Script to be run when a Web Storage area is updated
onsubmit	<form>	Script to be run when a form is submitted
onsuspend	<audio>, <video>	Script to be run when fetching the media data is stopped before it is completely loaded for whatever reason
ontimeupdate	<audio>, <video>	Script to be run when the playing position has changed (like when the user fast forwards to a different point in the media)
ontoggle	<details>	Script to be run when the user opens or closes the <details> element
onunload	<body>	Script to be run when a page has unloaded (or the browser window has been closed)
onvolumechange	<audio>, <video>	Script to be run each time the volume of a video/audio has been changed

attribute name	tags	descriptions
onwaiting	<audio>, <video>	Script to be run when the media has paused but is expected to resume (like when the media pauses to buffer more data)
onwheel	All visible elements.	Script to be run when the mouse wheel rolls up or down over an element
open	<details>	Specifies that the details should be visible (open) to the user
optimum	<meter>	Specifies what value is the optimal value for the gauge
pattern	<input>	Specifies a regular expression that an <input> element's value is checked against
placeholder	<input>, <textarea>	Specifies a short hint that describes the expected value of the element
poster	<video>	Specifies an image to be shown while the video is downloading, or until the user hits the play button
preload	<audio>, <video>	Specifies if and how the author thinks the audio/video should be loaded when the page loads
readonly	<input>, <textarea>	Specifies that the element is read-only
rel	<a>, <area>, <link>	Specifies the relationship between the current document and the linked document
required	<input>, <select>, <textarea>	Specifies that the element must be filled out before submitting the form
reversed	<ol>	Specifies that the list order should be descending (9,8,7...)
rows	<textarea>	Specifies the visible number of lines in a text area
rowspan	<td>, <th>	Specifies the number of rows a table cell should span
sandbox	<iframe>	Enables an extra set of restrictions for the content in an <iframe>
scope	<th>	Specifies whether a header cell is a header for a column, row, or group of columns or rows
selected	<option>	Specifies that an option should be pre-selected when the page loads
shape	<area>	Specifies the shape of the area
size	<input>, <select>	Specifies the width, in characters (for <input>) or specifies the number of visible options (for <select>)

attribute name	tags	descriptions
sizes	<img>, <link>, <source>	Specifies the size of the linked resource
span	<col>, <colgroup>	Specifies the number of columns to span
spellcheck	Global Attributes	Specifies whether the element is to have its spelling and grammar checked or not
src	<audio>, <embed>, <iframe>, <img>, <input>, <script>, <source>, <track>, <video>	Specifies the URL of the media file
srcdoc	<iframe>	Specifies the HTML content of the page to show in the <iframe>
srclang	<track>	Specifies the language of the track text data (required if kind="subtitles")
srcset	<img>, <source>	Specifies the URL of the image to use in different situations
start	<ol>	Specifies the start value of an ordered list
step	<input>	Specifies the legal number intervals for an input field
style	Global Attributes	Specifies an inline CSS style for an element
tabindex	Global Attributes	Specifies the tabbing order of an element
target	<a>, <area>, <base>, <form>	Specifies the target for where to open the linked document or where to submit the form
title	Global Attributes	Specifies extra information about an element
translate	Global Attributes	Specifies whether the content of an element should be translated or not
type	<a>, <button>, <embed>, <input>, <link>, <menu>, <oject>, <script>, <source>, <style>	Specifies the type of element
usemap	<img>, <object>	Specifies an image as a client-side image-map
value	<button>, <iput>, <li>, <option>, <meter>, <progress>, <param>	Specifies the value of the element

attribute name	tags	descriptions
width	<canvas>, <embed>, <iframe>, <img>, <input>, <object>, <video>	Specifies the width of the element
wrap	<textarea>	Specifies how the text in a text area is to be wrapped when submitted in a form

CSS Selectors [55]

selector name	example	descriptions
.class	.intro	Selects all elements with class="intro"
#id	#firstname	Selects the element with id="firstname"
*	*	Selects all elements
element	p	Selects all <p> elements
element,element	div, p	Selects all <div> elements and all <p> elements
element element	div p	Selects all <p> elements inside <div> elements
element>element	div > p	Selects all <p> elements where the parent is a <div> element
element+element	div + p	Selects all <p> elements that are placed immediately after <div> elements
element1~element2	p ~ ul	Selects every <ul> element that are preceded by a <p> element
[attribute]	[target]	Selects all elements with a target attribute
[attribute=value]	[target=_blank]	Selects all elements with target="_blank"
[attribute~=value]	[title~=flower]	Selects all elements with a title attribute containing the word "flower"
[attribute|=value]	[lang|=en]	Selects all elements with a lang attribute value starting with "en"
[attribute^=value]	a[href^=”https”]	Selects every <a> element whose href attribute value begins with "https"
[attribute$=value]	a[href$=”.pdf”]	Selects every <a> element whose href attribute value ends with ".pdf"
[attribute*=value]	a[href*=”w3schools”]	Selects every <a> element whose href attribute value contains the substring "w3schools"
:active	a:active	Selects the active link
::after	p::after	Insert something after the content of each <p> element
::before	p::before	Insert something before the content of each <p> element
:checked	input:checked	Selects every checked <input> element
:default	input:default	Selects the default <input> element
:disabled	input:disabled	Selects every disabled <input> element
:empty	p:empty	Selects every <p> element that has no children (including text nodes)

selector name	example	descriptions
:enabled	input:enabled	Selects every enabled <input> element
:first-child	p:first-child	Selects every <p> element that is the first child of its parent
::first-letter	p::first-letter	Selects the first letter of every <p> element
::first-line	p::first-line	Selects the first line of every <p> element
:first-of-type	p:first-of-type	Selects every <p> element that is the first <p> element of its parent
:focus	input:focus	Selects the input element which has focus
:hover	a:hover	Selects links on mouse over
:in-range	input:in-range	Selects input elements with a value within a specified range
:indeterminate	input:indeterminate	Selects input elements that are in an indeterminate state
:invalid	input:invalid	Selects all input elements with an invalid value
:lang(language)	p:lang(it)	Selects every <p> element with a lang attribute equal to "it" (Italian)
:last-child	p:last-child	Selects every <p> element that is the last child of its parent
:last-of-type	p:last-of-type	Selects every <p> element that is the last <p> element of its parent
:link	a:link	Selects all unvisited links
:not(selector)	:not(p)	Selects every element that is not a <p> element
:nth-child(n)	p:nth-child(2)	Selects every <p> element that is the second child of its parent
:nth-last-child(n)	p:nth-last-child(2)	Selects every <p> element that is the second child of its parent, counting from the last child
:nth-last-of-type(n)	p:nth-last-of-type(2)	Selects every <p> element that is the second <p> element of its parent, counting from the last child
:nth-of-type(n)	p:nth-of-type(2)	Selects every <p> element that is the second <p> element of its parent
:only-of-type	p:only-of-type	Selects every <p> element that is the only <p> element of its parent
:only-child	p:only-child	Selects every <p> element that is the only child of its parent

selector name	example	descriptions
:optional	input:optional	Selects input elements with no "required" attribute
:out-of-range	input:out-of-range	Selects input elements with a value outside a specified range
::placeholder	input::placeholder	Selects input elements with placeholder text
:read-only	input:read-only	Selects input elements with the "readonly" attribute specified
:read-write	input:read-write	Selects input elements with the "readonly" attribute NOT specified
:required	input:required	Selects input elements with the "required" attribute specified
:root	:root	Selects the document's root element
::selection	::selection	Selects the portion of an element that is selected by a user
:target	#news:target	Selects the current active #news element (clicked on a URL containing that anchor name)
:valid	input:valid	Selects all input elements with a valid value
:visited	a:visited	Selects all visited links

Mostly used CSS Properties [228]

property name	descriptions
align-content	Specifies the alignment between the lines inside a flexible container when the items do not use all available space
align-items	Specifies the alignment for items inside a flexible container
align-self	Specifies the alignment for selected items inside a flexible container
all	Resets all properties (except unicode-bidi and direction)
animation	A shorthand property for all the animation-* properties
animation-delay	Specifies a delay for the start of an animation
animation-direction	Specifies whether an animation should be played forwards, backwards or in alternate cycles
animation-duration	Specifies how long an animation should take to complete one cycle
animation-fill-mode	Specifies a style for the element when the animation is not playing (before it starts, after it ends, or both)
animation-iteration-count	Specifies the number of times an animation should be played
animation-name	Specifies a name for the @keyframes animation
animation-play-state	Specifies whether the animation is running or paused
animation-timing-function	Specifies the speed curve of an animation
backface-visibility	Defines whether or not the back face of an element should be visible when facing the user
background	A shorthand property for all the background-* properties
background-attachment	Sets whether a background image scrolls with the rest of the page, or is fixed
background-blend-mode	Specifies the blending mode of each background layer (color/image)
background-clip	Defines how far the background (color or image) should extend within an element
background-color	Specifies the background color of an element
background-image	Specifies one or more background images for an element
background-origin	Specifies the origin position of a background image
background-position	Specifies the position of a background image
background-repeat	Sets if/how a background image will be repeated
background-size	Specifies the size of the background images
border	A shorthand property for border-width, border-style and border-color

property name	descriptions
border-bottom	A shorthand property for border-bottom-width, border-bottom-style and border-bottom-color
border-bottom-color	Sets the color of the bottom border
border-bottom-left-radius	Defines the radius of the border of the bottom-left corner
border-bottom-right-radius	Defines the radius of the border of the bottom-right corner
border-bottom-style	Sets the style of the bottom border
border-bottom-width	Sets the width of the bottom border
border-collapse	Sets whether table borders should collapse into a single border or be separated
border-color	Sets the color of the four borders
border-image	A shorthand property for all the border-image-* properties
border-image-outset	Specifies the amount by which the border image area extends beyond the border box
border-image-repeat	Specifies whether the border image should be repeated, rounded or stretched
border-image-slice	Specifies how to slice the border image
border-image-source	Specifies the path to the image to be used as a border
border-image-width	Specifies the width of the border image
border-left	A shorthand property for all the border-left-* properties
border-left-color	Sets the color of the left border
border-left-style	Sets the style of the left border
border-left-width	Sets the width of the left border
border-radius	A shorthand property for the four border-*-radius properties
border-right	A shorthand property for all the border-right-* properties
border-right-color	Sets the color of the right border
border-right-style	Sets the style of the right border
border-right-width	Sets the width of the right border
border-spacing	Sets the distance between the borders of adjacent cells
border-style	Sets the style of the four borders
border-top	A shorthand property for border-top-width, border-top-style and border-top-color
border-top-color	Sets the color of the top border
border-top-left-radius	Defines the radius of the border of the top-left corner
border-top-right-radius	Defines the radius of the border of the top-right corner
border-top-style	Sets the style of the top border
border-top-width	Sets the width of the top border
border-width	Sets the width of the four borders

property name	descriptions
bottom	Sets the elements position, from the bottom of its parent element
box-decoration-break	Sets the behavior of the background and border of an element at the page-break, or, for in-line elements, at line-break.
box-shadow	Attaches one or more shadows to an element
box-sizing	Defines how the width and height of an element are calculated: should they include padding and borders, or not
break-after	Specifies the page-, column-, or region-break behavior after the generated box
break-before	Specifies the page-, column-, or region-break behavior before the generated box
break-inside	Specifies the page-, column-, or region-break behavior inside the generated box
caption-side	Specifies the placement of a table caption
caret-color	Specifies the color of the cursor (caret) in inputs, textareas, or any element that is editable
@charset	Specifies the character encoding used in the style sheet
clear	Specifies on which sides of an element floating elements are not allowed to float
clip	Clips an absolutely positioned element
color	Sets the color of the text
column-count	Specifies the number of columns an element should be divided into
column-fill	Specifies how to fill columns, balanced or not
column-gap	Specifies the gap between the columns
column-rule	A shorthand property for all the column-rule-* properties
column-rule-color	Specifies the color of the rule between columns
column-rule-style	Specifies the style of the rule between columns
column-rule-width	Specifies the width of the rule between columns
column-span	Specifies how many columns an element should span across
column-width	Specifies the column width
columns	A shorthand property for column-width and column-count
content	Used with :before and :after pseudo-elements, to insert generated content
counter-increment	Increases or decreases the value of one or more CSS counters
counter-reset	Creates or resets one or more CSS counters
cursor	Specifies the mouse cursor to be displayed when pointing over an element
direction	Specifies the text direction/writing direction

property name	descriptions
`display`	Specifies how a certain HTML element should be displayed
`empty-cells`	Specifies whether or not to display borders and background on empty cells in a table
`filter`	Defines effects (e.g. blurring or color shifting) on an element before the element is displayed
`flex`	A shorthand property for the flex-grow, flex-shrink, and the flex-basis properties
`flex-basis`	Specifies the initial length of a flexible item
`flex-direction`	Specifies the direction of the flexible items
`flex-flow`	A shorthand property for the flex-direction and the flex-wrap properties
`flex-grow`	Specifies how much the item will grow relative to the rest
`flex-shrink`	Specifies how the item will shrink relative to the rest
`flex-wrap`	Specifies whether the flexible items should wrap or not
`float`	Specifies whether or not a box should float
`font`	A shorthand property for the font-style, font-variant, font-weight, font-size/line-height, and the font-family properties
`@font-face`	A rule that allows websites to download and use fonts other than the "web-safe" fonts
`font-family`	Specifies the font family for text
`font-feature-settings`	Allows control over advanced typographic features in OpenType fonts
`@font-feature-values`	Allows authors to use a common name in font-variant-alternate for feature activated differently in OpenType
`font-kerning`	Controls the usage of the kerning information (how letters are spaced)
`font-language-override`	Controls the usage of language-specific glyphs in a typeface
`font-size`	Specifies the font size of text
`font-size-adjust`	Preserves the readability of text when font fallback occurs
`font-stretch`	Selects a normal, condensed, or expanded face from a font family
`font-style`	Specifies the font style for text
`font-synthesis`	Controls which missing typefaces (bold or italic) may be synthesized by the browser
`font-variant`	Specifies whether or not a text should be displayed in a small-caps font
`font-variant-alternates`	Controls the usage of alternate glyphs associated with alternative names defined in @font-feature-values
`font-variant-caps`	Controls the usage of alternate glyphs for capital letters

property name	descriptions
`font-variant-east-asian`	Controls the usage of alternate glyphs for East Asian scripts (e.g. Korean and Chinese)
`font-variant-ligatures`	Controls which ligatures and contextual forms are used in the textual content of the elements it applies to
`font-variant-numeric`	Controls the usage of alternate glyphs for numbers, fractions, and ordinal markers
`font-variant-position`	Controls the usage of alternate glyphs of smaller size positioned as superscript or subscript regarding the baseline of the font
`font-weight`	Specifies the weight of a font
`grid`	A shorthand property for the grid-template-rows, grid-template-columns, grid-template-areas, grid-auto-rows, grid-auto-columns, and the grid-auto-flow properties
`grid-area`	Either specify a name for the grid item, or this property is a shorthand property for the grid-row-start, grid-column-start, grid-row-end, and grid-column-end properties
`grid-auto-columns`	Specifies a default column size
`grid-auto-flow`	Specifies how auto-placed items are inserted in the grid
`grid-auto-rows`	Specifies a default row size
`grid-column`	A shorthand property for the grid-column-start and the grid-column-end properties
`grid-column-end`	Specifies where to end the grid item
`grid-column-gap`	Specifies the size of the gap between columns
`grid-column-start`	Specifies where to start the grid item
`grid-gap`	A shorthand property for the grid-row-gap and grid-column-gap properties
`grid-row`	A shorthand property for the grid-row-start and the grid-row-end properties
`grid-row-end`	Specifies where to end the grid item
`grid-row-gap`	Specifies the size of the gap between rows
`grid-row-start`	Specifies where to start the grid item
`grid-template`	A shorthand property for the grid-template-rows, grid-template-columns and grid-areas properties
`grid-template-areas`	Specifies how to display columns and rows, using named grid items
`grid-template-columns`	Specifies the size of the columns, and how many columns in a grid layout
`grid-template-rows`	Specifies the size of the rows in a grid layout
`hanging-punctuation`	Specifies whether a punctuation character may be placed outside the line box

property name	descriptions
`height`	Sets the height of an element
`hyphens`	Sets how to split words to improve the layout of paragraphs
`image-rendering`	Gives a hint to the browser about what aspects of an image are most important to preserve when the image is scaled
`@import`	Allows you to import a style sheet into another style sheet
`isolation`	Defines whether an element must create a new stacking content
`justify-content`	Specifies the alignment between the items inside a flexible container when the items do not use all available space
`@keyframes`	Specifies the animation code
`left`	Specifies the left position of a positioned element
`letter-spacing`	Increases or decreases the space between characters in a text
`line-break`	Specifies how/if to break lines
`line-height`	Sets the line height
`list-style`	Sets all the properties for a list in one declaration
`list-style-image`	Specifies an image as the list-item marker
`list-style-position`	Specifies the position of the list-item markers (bullet points)
`list-style-type`	Specifies the type of list-item marker
`margin`	Sets all the margin properties in one declaration
`margin-bottom`	Sets the bottom margin of an element
`margin-left`	Sets the left margin of an element
`margin-right`	Sets the right margin of an element
`margin-top`	Sets the top margin of an element
`max-height`	Sets the maximum height of an element
`max-width`	Sets the maximum width of an element
`@media`	Sets the style rules for different media types/devices/sizes
`min-height`	Sets the minimum height of an element
`min-width`	Sets the minimum width of an element
`mix-blend-mode`	Specifies how an element's content should blend with its direct parent background
`object-fit`	Specifies how the contents of a replaced element should be fitted to the box established by its used height and width
`object-position`	Specifies the alignment of the replaced element inside its box
`opacity`	Sets the opacity level for an element
`order`	Sets the order of the flexible item, relative to the rest
`orphans`	Sets the minimum number of lines that must be left at the bottom of a page when a page break occurs inside an element

property name	descriptions
outline	A shorthand property for the outline-width, outline-style, and the outline-color properties
outline-color	Sets the color of an outline
outline-offset	Offsets an outline, and draws it beyond the border edge
outline-style	Sets the style of an outline
outline-width	Sets the width of an outline
overflow	Specifies what happens if content overflows an element's box
overflow-wrap	Specifies whether or not the browser may break lines within words in order to prevent overflow (when a string is too long to fit its containing box)
overflow-x	Specifies whether or not to clip the left/right edges of the content, if it overflows the element's content area
overflow-y	Specifies whether or not to clip the top/bottom edges of the content, if it overflows the element's content area
padding	A shorthand property for all the padding-* properties
padding-bottom	Sets the bottom padding of an element
padding-left	Sets the left padding of an element
padding-right	Sets the right padding of an element
padding-top	Sets the top padding of an element
page-break-after	Sets the page-break behavior after an element
page-break-before	Sets the page-break behavior before an element
page-break-inside	Sets the page-break behavior inside an element
perspective	Gives a 3D-positioned element some perspective
perspective-origin	Defines at which position the user is looking at the 3D-positioned element
pointer-events	Defines whether or not an element reacts to pointer events
position	Specifies the type of positioning method used for an element (static, relative, absolute or fixed)
quotes	Sets the type of quotation marks for embedded quotations
resize	Defines if (and how) an element is resizable by the user
right	Specifies the right position of a positioned element
scroll-behavior	Specifies whether to smoothly animate the scroll position in a scrollable box, instead of a straight jump
tab-size	Specifies the width of a tab character
table-layout	Defines the algorithm used to lay out table cells, rows, and columns
text-align	Specifies the horizontal alignment of text

property name	descriptions
`text-align-last`	Describes how the last line of a block or a line right before a forced line break is aligned when text-align is "justify"
`text-combine-upright`	Specifies the combination of multiple characters into the space of a single character
`text-decoration`	Specifies the decoration added to text
`text-decoration-color`	Specifies the color of the text-decoration
`text-decoration-line`	Specifies the type of line in a text-decoration
`text-decoration-style`	Specifies the style of the line in a text decoration
`text-indent`	Specifies the indentation of the first line in a text-block
`text-justify`	Specifies the justification method used when text-align is "justify"
`text-orientation`	Defines the orientation of the text in a line
`text-overflow`	Specifies what should happen when text overflows the containing element
`text-shadow`	Adds shadow to the text
`text-transform`	Controls the capitalization of text
`text-underline-position`	Specifies the position of the underline which is set using the text-decoration property
`top`	Specifies the top position of a positioned element
`transform`	Applies a 2D or 3D transformation to an element
`transform-origin`	Allows you to change the position on transformed elements
`transform-style`	Specifies how nested elements are rendered in 3D space
`transition`	A shorthand property for all the transition-* properties
`transition-delay`	Specifies when the transition effect will start
`transition-duration`	Specifies how many seconds or milliseconds a transition effect takes to complete
`transition-property`	Specifies the name of the CSS property the transition effect is for
`transition-timing-function`	Specifies the speed curve of the transition effect
`unicode-bidi`	Used together with the direction property to set or return whether the text should be overridden to support multiple languages in the same document
`user-select`	Specifies whether the text of an element can be selected
`vertical-align`	Sets the vertical alignment of an element
`visibility`	Specifies whether or not an element is visible
`white-space`	Specifies how white-space inside an element is handled
`widows`	Sets the minimum number of lines that must be left at the top of a page when a page break occurs inside an element
`width`	Sets the width of an element

property name	descriptions
word-break	Specifies how words should break when reaching the end of a line
word-spacing	Increases or decreases the space between words in a text
word-wrap	Allows long, unbreakable words to be broken and wrap to the next line
writing-mode	Specifies whether lines of text are laid out horizontally or vertically
z-index	Sets the stack order of a positioned element

JavaScript Events [70]

events	descriptions
`offline`	Triggers when the document goes offline
`onabort`	Triggers on an abort event
`onafterprint`	Triggers after the document are printed
`onbeforeonload`	Triggers before the document loads
`onbeforeprint`	Triggers before the document are printed
`onblur`	Triggers when the window loses focus
`oncanplay`	Triggers when media can start play, but might have to stop for buffering
`oncanplaythrough`	Triggers when media can be played to the end, without stopping for buffering
`onchange`	Triggers when an element changes
`onclick`	Triggers on a mouse click
`oncontextmenu`	Triggers when a context menu is triggered
`ondblclick`	Triggers on a mouse double-click
`ondrag`	Triggers when an element is dragged
`ondragend`	Triggers at the end of a drag operation
`ondragenter`	Triggers when an element has been dragged to a valid drop target
`ondragleave`	Triggers when an element is being dragged over a valid drop target
`ondragover`	Triggers at the start of a drag operation
`ondragstart`	Triggers at the start of a drag operation
`ondrop`	Triggers when the dragged element is being dropped
`ondurationchange`	Triggers when the length of the media is changed
`onemptied`	Triggers when a media resource element suddenly becomes empty.
`onended`	Triggers when media has reached the end
`onerror`	Triggers when an error occur
`onfocus`	Triggers when the window gets focus
`onformchange`	Triggers when a form changes
`onforminput`	Triggers when a form gets user input
`onhaschange`	Triggers when the document has change
`oninput`	Triggers when an element gets user input
`oninvalid`	Triggers when an element is invalid
`onkeydown`	Triggers when a key is pressed
`onkeypress`	Triggers when a key is pressed and released
`onkeyup`	Triggers when a key is released
`onload`	Triggers when the document loads

events	descriptions
`onloadeddata`	Triggers when media data is loaded
`onloadedmetadata`	Triggers when the duration and other media data of a media element is loaded
`onloadstart`	Triggers when the browser starts to load the media data
`onmessage`	Triggers when the message is triggered
`onmousedown`	Triggers when a mouse button is pressed
`onmousemove`	Triggers when the mouse pointer moves
`onmouseout`	Triggers when the mouse pointer moves out of an element
`onmouseover`	Triggers when the mouse pointer moves over an element
`onmouseup`	Triggers when a mouse button is released
`onmousewheel`	Triggers when the mouse wheel is being rotated
`onoffline`	Triggers when the document goes offline
`ononline`	Triggers when the document comes online
`onpagehide`	Triggers when the window is hidden
`onpageshow`	Triggers when the window becomes visible
`onpause`	Triggers when media data is paused
`onplay`	Triggers when media data is going to start playing
`onplaying`	Triggers when media data has started playing
`onpopstate`	Triggers when the window's history changes
`onprogress`	Triggers when the browser is fetching the media data
`onratechange`	Triggers when the media data's playing rate has changed
`onreadystatechange`	Triggers when the ready-state changes
`onredo`	Triggers when the document performs a redo
`onresize`	Triggers when the window is resized
`onscroll`	Triggers when an element's scrollbar is being scrolled
`onseeked`	Triggers when a media element seeking attribute is no longer true, and the seeking has ended
`onseeking`	Triggers when a media element seeking attribute is true, and the seeking has begun
`onselect`	Triggers when an element is selected
`onstalled`	Triggers when there is an error in fetching media data
`onstorage`	Triggers when a document loads
`onsubmit`	Triggers when a form is submitted
`onsuspend`	Triggers when the browser has been fetching media data, but stopped before the entire media file was fetched
`ontimeupdate`	Triggers when the media changes its playing position
`onundo`	Triggers when the document performs an undo

events	descriptions
`onunload`	Triggers when the user leaves the document
`onvolumechange`	Triggers when the media changes the volume, also when the volume is set to "mute"
`onwaiting`	Triggers when media has stopped playing, but is expected to resume